The Power of Images in the Age of Augustus

By his will, Mr. Thomas Spencer Jerome endowed the lectureship that bears his name. It is jointly administered by the University of Michigan and the American Academy in Rome, and the lectures for which it provides are delivered at both institutions. They deal with phases of the history or culture of the Romans or of peoples included in the Roman Empire.

F. E. Adcock, *Roman Political Ideas and Practice*

G. W. Bowersock, *Hellenism in Late Antiquity*

Frank E. Brown, *Cosa: The Making of a Roman Town*

Jacqueline de Romilly, *The Rise and Fall of States According to Greek Authors*

Anthony Grafton, *Commerce with the Classics: Ancient Books and Renaissance Readers*

Fergus Millar, *The Crowd in Rome in the Late Republic*

Claude Nicolet, *Space, Geography, and Politics in the Early Roman Empire*

Massimo Pallottino, *A History of Earliest Italy*

Jaroslav Pelikan, *What Has Athens to Do with Jerusalem?* Timaeus *and* Genesis *in Counterpart*

Brunilde S. Ridgway, *Roman Copies of Greek Sculpture: The Problem of the Originals*

Lily Ross Taylor, *Roman Voting Assemblies: From the Hannibalic War to the Dictatorship of Caesar*

Mario Torelli, *Typology and Structure of Roman Historical Reliefs*

Paul Zanker, *The Power of Images in the Age of Augustus*

JEROME LECTURES   SIXTEENTH SERIES

The Power of Images in the Age of Augustus

Paul Zanker

Translated by Alan Shapiro

Ann Arbor

THE UNIVERSITY OF MICHIGAN PRESS

Library of Congress Cataloging-in-Publication Data

Zanker, Paul.
    The power of images in the Age of Augustus.

    (Jerome lectures ; 16th ser.)
    Bibliography: p.
    Includes index.
    1. Art, Roman—Themes, motives.   2. Augustus,
Emperor of Rome, 63 B.C.–14 A.D.   3. Rome—History—
Augustus, 30 B.C.–14 A.D.   I. Title.   II. Series.
N5760.Z36   1988   709'.37   88-17279
    ISBN 0-472-10101-3 (alk. paper)
    ISBN 0-472-08124-1 (pbk. : alk. paper)

Excerpts from *The Complete Works of Horace* translated by
Charles E. Passage. Copyright © 1983 by the Frederick Ungar
Company. Reprinted by permission of the publisher.

Preface

Art and architecture are mirrors of a society. They reflect the state of its values, especially in times of crisis or transition. Yet it is notoriously difficult to analyze any particular work of art as an historical document in and of itself. This book tries to illustrate how a fundamental change in the political system led to the creation of a new visual language that both reflects an altered mentality and contributed significantly to the process of change. Bringing modern experience to bear on these issues, I have sought to emphasize questions such as the societal forces that fueled the change as well as the effect of psychological factors. Thus the form of a work of art is of no less importance than its message. Indeed, "style" itself is treated as a complex historical phenomenon.

Rarely has art been pressed into the service of political power so directly as in the Age of Augustus. Poetry and art are filled with the imagery of a blessed world, an empire at peace under the sway of a great ruler. The suggestive power of this imagery lives on to our own day, as its frequent use in contemporary advertising attests.

This ennobled image of Augustan art became clearly established first in the 1930s. During the building of Fascist Rome, major monuments of antiquity either came to light for the first time or, through excavation and reconstruction, were deeply impressed on modern consciousness: the Forum of Augustus, his Mausoleum, the Theater of Marcellus, the Ara Pacis. In 1937, as the two thousandth year from the birth of Augustus was commemorated, those in power in Italy and their supporters were drawn, consciously or not, to exploit Roman art in general and the Augustan Age in particular as an aesthetic justification for the folly of their mad ambition. The image of the Augustan period created then is, in one form or another, still with us today.

Yet the figure of Augustus himself had since antiquity been subject to critical appraisal, and not only from "Republicans" like Tacitus, Voltaire, and Theodor Mommsen. Even in the 1930s the craze for Augustus did not go unchallenged. Significantly, Sir Ronald Syme's celebrated book *The Roman Revolution* appeared in England in 1939. Unfortunately, his fascinating chapter on "The Organization of Opinion" takes no account of the role of art and architecture. Even today some historians regard the visual arts as purely aesthetic objects, handy for illustrating their books but otherwise unable to tell us anything not already well known from the literary sources. Admittedly, art historians and archaeologists have often done their part to encourage this view, with their self-referential interpretation of the work of art and lack of interest in its historical context.

After the Second World War, Augustan studies, when not carrying on the encomiastic tradition, concentrated to a considerable degree on formal problems. Particularly among German archaeologists, with their powerful orientation toward Greek art, the art of the Augustan Age was judged strictly according to its classicism and its technical qualities. The revival and transmission of Greek forms assured Augustan artists, so it was believed, a status of timeless importance—no less than a Vergil or Horace—in spite of the political function to which their work was put. At the same time, the influential Italian Marxist archaeologist Ranuccio Bianchi Bandinelli challenged the historical significance of Augustan art precisely *because* of its classicism, which he considered the expression of a reactionary political system. Since the late 1960s, studies of Augustan art as political propaganda, building on the work of Ronald Syme and Andreas Alföldi, have dominated the field. Evidence for the workings of a secret propaganda machine began to be uncovered everywhere, though no one could actually put his finger on the source.

In recent years, interest in Augustus and his age has grown remarkably by leaps and bounds. Lectures and colloquia are continually being held, especially in England, America, and Germany, and in addition to the flood of scholarly literature, lavishly illustrated books appeal to a broader public. As I write this, a major exhibition devoted to Augustus is being mounted in Berlin. Is all this simply part of the general trend of "postmodernism," which has stimulated interest in every "classical" epoch and personality? Or is it perhaps the fascination of a peaceful, well-ordered society, the ruler with the human touch, who brought security and prosperity, a patron of poetry and great building projects who, with all this, inspired his people to moral purity as well?

This book is based upon lectures delivered in Ann Arbor and at the American Academy in Rome in 1983 and 1984 as the Thomas Spencer Jerome Series. Without the stimulating experience of giving these lectures and the response to them, I would not have felt encouraged to publish a synthetic study of this kind. The reworking of the text into its present form was made possible by invitations to the Institute for Advanced Study, Princeton, in 1982 and to Wolfson College, Oxford, in 1985. My thanks are due most of all to these institutions and to the following colleagues: Peter H. von Blanckenhagen, John D'Arms, Glen Bowersock, Jasper Griffin, Christian Habicht, R. T. Scott, and Zvi Yavetz. In Oxford, Fergus Millar organized a joint seminar with other colleagues from which I learned a great deal.

During the many years that this topic has occupied my interest, I have enjoyed the help, good advice, and encouragement of so many that it is impossible to thank them here individually. I feel, however, a particular debt to my Munich friends, colleagues, and students for their stimulating help, and most especially to Christian Meier, Henner von Hesberg, and Michael Pfanner, as well as to my students Olof Dräger, Doris Lauenstein, and Reinhard Senff. Finally, my warmest thanks to Alan Shapiro for his careful and perceptive translation, as well as for many improvements along the way.

Contents

Introduction

After the death of Augustus Caesar, when the Senate met to discuss plans to bury and to honor him, one senator introduced a resolution to designate Augustus's entire lifetime the *Saeculum Augustum* and enter it into the official calendar under this name (Suetonius *Augustus* 100). Whatever opportunism may have inspired the resolution, the feeling was nonetheless widespread that this was the end of an era. Following the long dark years of civil war the Romans had enjoyed forty-five years of peace and security. Monarchy had at last brought orderly government to the vast empire, discipline to the army, bread and circuses to the Roman plebs, and a tremendous boost to the economy. The Romans looked out at their empire filled with a powerful sense of mission. Yet when Augustus had first consolidated his power (31 B.C.), an atmosphere of pessimism pervaded the Roman state, and there were many who, in their own moral decadence, considered Rome on the edge of destruction. How did this change in outlook come about? What caused the optimism and confidence which, as it was given expression by Augustan poets, left for posterity the concept of the *Saeculum Augustum?*

Roman society had been transformed by a dramatic process of acculturation that began in the second century B.C. With the Roman conquest of the Greek East, Hellenistic culture overwhelmed the still primitive society of the Roman city-state. In a reversal of the normal process, the superior military and economic power was the more strongly affected.

> Graecia capta ferum victorem cepit et artis
> intulit agresti Latio . . .
> [Captive Greece captured the victor and
> brought the arts to rustic Latium]
> > Horace *Epodes* 2.1.156

The effects on the Roman way of life, religion, and character were unmistakable. The contrast between the old *mores maiorum* and what would soon be condemned as *luxuria* in Rome could scarcely have been more striking. On the one hand, the Hellenistic Greek cities enjoyed a refined high culture, the brilliant pomp of kingship, the traditions of Classical Athens, especially the philosophical schools and rational thought, yet at the same time mystery cults promising individual salvation. In Italy, on the other hand, traditional religion was keyed to the lives of farmers and closely tied to the state; patriarchal family units were closely knit, the simple patterns of life had remained unchanged for generations, and cultural life was barren, with no literature or art. No wonder conflicts and instability arose from the collision of two such opposite worlds.

The effects of Hellenization were particularly marked because Roman society was at this time undergoing rapid internal changes, and the city-state, overburdened by the administration of a huge empire, would eventually collapse. The spoils of war, together with economic expansion, had led to a concentration of wealth and property in the hands of a few, while the masses of the poor fled the country for Rome. Large private armies gave rise to factions that in turn made the victorious generals into political powers rivaling the state itself. The radical redistribution of wealth loosened previously rigid class distinctions. Ambitious social climbers, especially leading men from the cities of Italy and wealthy freedmen, pressed for social recognition and political power. In the new, pervasive competitive spirit, no longer was it only the nobility who competed for the benefit of the Republic, but many others for personal advancement and material gain.

Hellenistic art, quickly adapted by the Romans, played an important part in these developments. It provided military victors with an impressive medium in which to express their assertions of power. The majority of their contemporaries, however, reacted to these new images with distaste, for their message was in many ways in startling opposition to their own traditions. Inherited Roman values were becoming no more than a meaningless ideology, even as men's behavior increasingly undermined them. Chapter 1 will illustrate how these borrowed images not only reflect this process of the dissolution of values but actually contributed to it. Without this background we cannot understand the new imagery of the Augustan Age.

As the Roman Republic finally collapsed in civil war, first between Julius Caesar and Pompey, then between Octavian and Marc Antony, people sought an explanation for the widespread sense of dislocation and believed they found it in a rejection of the gods and values of their ancestors. They could hardly have been aware of the fundamental structural weaknesses of the Republic. Patricians in lavish villas imagined the simplicity and piety of their forefathers, selfless leaders and self-sacrificing peasants. In light of the realities of Roman society at this time, such visions were reduced to empty rhetoric. In the turbulent upheaval of several generations not only was the Republic lost, but to a great extent Rome's cultural identity.

After Augustus had attained sole power in Rome (31 B.C.), he systematically sought to redress the situation. The goal of his "cultural program," pursued with far-reaching and concentrated effort over the next twenty years, was nothing less than a complete moral revival. And it did in fact achieve a turnaround in public thinking. The self-aggrandizement of rival generals was replaced by veneration of a ruler chosen by the gods, invidious private ostentation by a program of *publica magnificentia* (splendid public festivals and games), and immorality and neglect of the gods by a religious and spiritual renewal.

Such a program required a new visual language. The goal of this book is to examine the complex interrelationship of the establishment of monarchy, the transformation of society, and the creation of a whole new method of visual communication. Recent experience has tempted us to see in this a propaganda machine at work, but in Rome there was no such thing. What appears in retrospect as a subtle program resulted in fact from the interplay of the image that the emperor himself projected and the honors bestowed on him more or less spontaneously, a process that evolved naturally over long periods of time. I hope to show how those who were involved in the creation of the new imagery worked together and what interests and social constraints determined its spread. In what follows I refer often to "visual language" and "visual imagery," to suggest that I am not primarily concerned with the interpretation of individual monuments. This has been done often enough, and too often otiose descriptions and commentaries take on the lyrical tone of Augustan poets. My interest is instead in the totality of images that a contemporary would have experienced. This includes not only "works of art," buildings, and poetic imagery, but also religious ritual, clothing, state ceremony, the emperor's conduct and forms of social intercourse, insofar as these created a visual impression. I am concerned with the contexts of these images and with the effect of this tapestry of images on the viewer.

"Visual imagery," understood in this sense, reflects a society's inner life and gives insight into people's values and imagination that often cannot be apprehended in literary sources.

The power of images is realized in varying ways. Even those in power are affected by the image they project. Their image of themselves and of the role they play in public life are strongly influenced by their own slogans, and of course also by their opponents' slogans.

In the time of Augustus, the significance of imagery was not so much as advertisement of the new monarchy. For most of the population this would have been largely unnecessary and for disaffected aristocrats totally ineffectual. Augustus's imagery would have been useless without his legions and enormous resources. But in the long run its effect on the Roman temperament was not inconsiderable. Certain values, such as the religious revival, were first implemented in the steady stream of images created to embody them. Most importantly, through visual imagery a new mythology of Rome and, for the emperor, a new ritual of power were created. Built on relatively simple foundations, the myth perpetuated itself and transcended the realities of everyday life to project onto future generations the impression that they lived in the best of all possible worlds in the best of all times.

Fig. 1. Honorific Statue of a Roman general, ca. 180–150 B.C. The Roman is depicted like a Hellenistic king, the pose and nudity likening him to images of gods and heroes.

Chapter 1

Conflict and Contradiction in the Imagery of the Dying Republic

The Problem of Nude Honorific Statuary

When the splendid bronze statue (fig. 1) honoring a great general was displayed in Rome, some time before the middle of the second century B.C., the total nudity of the figure must have been extremely disturbing to most Romans. The statue is a typically Hellenistic work, especially in its powerful physical presence. The pose probably derives from Lysippus's famous "Alexander with the Spear," for the style of hair and beard and the emotional expression are all reminiscent of Macedonian royal portraits (figs. 2, 3). The entire statue is just like a Hellenistic ruler portrait and was probably made in a Greek workshop. Yet the fact that he has no royal diadem shows clearly that he is a Roman, perhaps even one of the victors over the kings of Macedon.

In the Hellenistic world such statues celebrated the ruler's superhuman strength and power. The pose and nudity are borrowed from statues of gods and heroes, to whom the subject is thus implicitly likened. Such ruler portraits must be understood in relation to the ruler cults that were established in many cities of the East on the model of divine cults, in order to commemorate the power and prestige of individual Hellenistic kings. All this was, however, quite foreign to Roman traditions. The standard type of public honorary statue during the Republic had always been the togate statue (fig. 4). In such a figure the honorand himself and his toga were characterized by particular attributes according to his political or religious office: consul, praetor, augur, etc. The sober and egalitarian style of togate statues thus reflected a strictly ordered power structure with officials rotating every year. Rival aristocrats held each other's ambitions in check and would not tolerate undue honors, let alone superhuman attributes, being accorded the accomplishments of one individual. A victorious general also received a togate statue, and even when he had celebrated a triumph was depicted not armed, but in a triumphal toga. This reflected the strict separation of the two realms *domi* and *militiae*. The Senate feared leaders who might make political capital out of military glory. For this reason, so long as the Senate could exercise its own will, it never authorized the splendid armed or equestrian statues that were commonly accorded Hellenistic kings and generals.

Fig. 3. Tetradrachm with portrait of the last Macedonian king, Perseus V (179–168 B.C.).

Fig. 2. Head of the statue in figure 1. Hairstyle, beard, and facial features show the same iconographical elements as Hellenistic ruler portraits (cf. fig. 3).

Significantly, it was Sulla, who broke so many other traditions, to whom the Senate first erected an official equestrian monument in the Forum (cf. fig. 30*b*). The Senate could not, however, prevent private individuals from setting up statues in the Hellenistic manner, for example as votive dedications in sanctuaries. Thus as early as 209 B.C. Fabius Maximus Cunctator had dedicated an equestrian statue of himself on the Capitol, next to the colossal Heracles he brought from Tarentum.

Early on, then, a contradiction arose in this central area of visual language. On the one hand, the Romans could somehow accept cuirassed and equestrian statues, however ostentatious, as incorporating traditional expressions of "honor for military achievement." But a nude portrait statue, on the other hand, at least at the beginning of the period of Hellenization, must have seemed incomprehensible, even shocking.

For those Senators who understood the Greek concept of the divinization of the ruler, such statues, with their self-conscious display of the body, made intolerable demands. But the majority of Romans, not yet Hellenized, can only have seen in them an immoral affrontery, for in 150 B.C. nudity was for most people simply an expression of shamelessness. Cato the elder was said to have refused to bathe with his own son and son-in-law, in accordance with ancient custom, "because he was ashamed to stand before them naked." The poet Ennius (d. 169 B.C.) wrote that "disrobing before one's fellow citizens is the beginning of perversion" (referring to Greek homosexuality).

It is possible that the first of these nude statues were set up in Rome in all innocence by Greeks, to honor their new rulers in the way they were accustomed to honoring their own kings. But even this presupposes that the men so honored had given their assent. Soon numerous monuments in Rome and Italy attest to the rapid spread of this new conception of the heroic and charismatic general. A few of these noble Romans had early on been Hellenized in the course of conquests in the East. Those who had been honored

Fig. 4. So-called Arringatore. Honorific statue of one of the leading men of Perusina (Perugia), ca. 80 B.C. He wears the *toga exigua,* and the broad borders (*clavi*) on the toga and *tunica,* as well as his footwear, characterize him as a member of the local aristocracy.

and revered there as kings could not remain immune to the new imagery of power once back in Rome. And Rome itself during the last two centuries B.C. increasingly became home to men from the East, especially freed slaves. At any rate, most of those in Rome who in 44 B.C. proclaimed the slain Julius Caesar a god and offered him sacrifice were far removed from the peasant farmers of the second century, now displaced by military service and the confiscation of their land.

Just how radically the outlook of leading Romans was altered by the experience of power and conquest can be seen in the following story about Gaius Marius, who was by birth a modest and upstanding *novus homo*.

> After his victory over Jugurtha and the Cimbri he would drink only from a kantharos, because Dionysos was supposed to have used this vessel on his triumphal procession through Asia. He wanted in this way to liken his own conquests to those of the god with each draught of wine. (Valerius Maximus 3.6.6)

And just how enthusiastically most Romans embraced this new self-image is illustrated by the honors accorded Q. Caecilius Metellus Pius in ca. 70 B.C., after his modest success against Sertorius in Spain.

> Cities welcomed him with altars and sacrifices. He had himself wreathed, took part in extravagant banquets, at which he gave toasts in his *toga triumphalis*, while cleverly contrived Victories hovered above and extended golden trophies and wreaths to him. In addition choirs of women and youths sang hymns of victory. (Plutarch *Sertorius* 22)

The new image of the Roman general was curious indeed. These anecdotes suggest that we must take into account not only received artistic forms but also the concomitant rituals and ceremonies. The whole lifestyle of phil-hellenic Romans became a challenge to traditionalists. Even when the Senate managed to limit the new extravagance to the city of Rome by means of sumptuary and other legislation, such laws could do nothing to stop the spread of Hellenization in the private sphere, especially in the villas of the Italian countryside.

Contradictions in Form and Intent

The imagery of the Late Republic was more varied and artistically far more attractive than during the Empire, when art was dictated by the rules of state ceremony. In the earlier period, the combination of wealthy Roman patrons, inspired by the need to rival one another and justify themselves, with Hellenistic artists practising a variety of styles, created remarkable results. Yet in spite of the considerable charm of artistic forms, their content was often full of contradictions, when one considers their function and setting. The new type of honorary statue is a good example.

The poses of Hellenistic ruler statues expressed clearly a superhuman, godlike quality, a royal power far beyond the imagination of the old *polis*. But in Rome even the greatest leaders were in constant competition and at the end of a year in office had to step down. City magistrates each felt like a king in his own little domain, and with the same naiveté they aspired to equal the highest foreign standards of dignity. In the time of Julius Caesar the marketplaces of provincial Italian cities housed nude or cuirassed statues of leading citizens, with muscles flexed and heads dramatically turned. But these men were also for the most part yearly officials. Eventually this borrowed symbolism lost its original meaning from overuse and became a generalized mark of distinction. More and more exaggerated means were required to convey the image of absolute power. The result was an inflation of the number of statues and attributes and of the cost of raw materials.

Under such circumstances the actual artistic form, or style, would have to lead to contradictions as well. At first the dramatic style of Hellenistic ruler portraits was unthinkingly taken over. A good example is the nude bronze portrait statue in Rome (cf. fig. 2). But because this type did not suit the traditional Roman aristocratic ideal of age, experience, and modesty, a more realistic portrait type gradually emerged. The Greek sculptors who portrayed Roman aristocrats were already skilled in the naturalistic rendering of the body. But thanks to the competitive nature of the Roman nobility a unique way of characterizing individual subjects through physiognomic traits was created.

At no other time in the ancient world did portraiture capture so much of the personality of the subject. One need only consider the irony and detachment in even a mediocre copy of the portrait of Caesar (fig. 5), the bonhommie of Pompey's countenance (fig. 6), or the energy and determination of the wealthy Crassus (fig. 7), and then compare these with standard honorific portraits of the late Augustan period (cf. figs. 83, 229). The immediacy of the individual's physical presence outweighed all considerations of aesthetic norms. Everyone was content to have himself represented just as he really looked, thin or fat, young or old, even toothless and bald, warts and all. Most of these portraits have a stern and serious look, but otherwise no ethical or aesthetic values are brought out in the image. There was not yet any standard model, as there would be after the founding of the Principate. Although this individualization reflects a freedom from an imposed system of values, the combination of simple physiognomies with heroic bodies points up the discrepancy between rhetoric and real accomplishment.

Even the portraits themselves often exhibit the same contradictions. The

Fig. 5. C. Julius Caesar (100–44 B.C.). Portrait of the *dictator* near the end of his life.

Fig. 6. Cn. Pompeius Magnus (106–48 B.C.). The original of this type was made about 55 B.C. The hair rising over the forehead is an allusion to Alexander the Great.

face is rendered with its individuality of shape and expression while, at the same time, a heroic passion is conveyed through the use of Hellenistic formulas. Thus, for example, the locks of hair rising from the middle of Pompey's forehead remind the viewer that by virtue of his own victories he considered himself a new Alexander. He probably had his own hair styled in the manner familiar from portraits of Alexander. The *anastole* thus helps transfer to Pompey's portrait the honorary title "The Great," also borrowed from Alexander. At age twenty-five Pompey went so far as to wear Alexander's chlamys in his triumphal procession, instead of the *toga picta,* and tried to enter Rome in a chariot drawn by elephants (unfortunately he had to switch to a horse-drawn carriage when the *porta triumphalis* was too narrow to accommodate an elephant). The clash of two opposite value systems is here expressed in concrete artistic terms. At the same time that the Romans admired the great charismatic rulers of the Hellenistic world, they clung to the enduring values of the Republic and insisted on keeping their own leaders in line. How curiously Alexander's flowing hair, like a lion's mane, descends over Pompey's simple peasant face, with its self-satisfied smile. This late portrait of Pompey has an ambiguous aesthetic effect, in contrast to an earlier type, more uniformly Hellenistic in its pathos and suppression of individual traits.

Fig. 7. M. Crassus *triumvir* (consul 70 and 55 B.C.). He was the richest man in Rome, but lost to the Parthians the battle standards later recovered by Augustus, and fell at the Battle of Carrhae (53 B.C.).

Fig. 8. Portrait of a man, perhaps a member of a leading family in Sardinia.

The Pompey portrait was surely not unique. A portrait in Cagliari, for example (fig. 8), of a toothless old man, combines a simple face and unheroically pursed lips with incongruously electric hair. The portrait of the young Octavian (cf. fig. 33) also falls into this category, with its nervous, intimidated features on the one hand and solemn bearing on the other.

Family Propaganda and the Collapse of the Aristocracy

Other forms of political imagery were also marked by these same characteristics: incongruities of style, overburdened symbolism, ambiguity, and obscurity. Tonio Hölscher has demonstrated this for the public art of the entire Late Republican period. Artistic style and imagery again prove to be faithful reflections of the political and social setting. By following coin types from the late second century on, we can observe how the particular interests of the individual mint official became more and more important. Earlier, the same imagery had been used on coins for generations, types that not only the Senators but all Roman citizens could identify: the Dioscuri, Roman Jupiter victorious, captured spoils of war. Young noblemen, who usually

held the office of mint master early in their careers, increasingly used the opportunity to celebrate the deeds of their ancestors or, later on, even their own (often undistinguished) achievements. So, for example, one C. Manilius Limetanus, mint master under the dictatorship of Sulla, put on both obverse and reverse of a coin allusions to his family's descent from no less than the god Hermes and his supposed son Odysseus (fig. 9). We find the same sort of thing on one of the biggest and most elaborate public monuments of the Late Republic, the so-called Ahenobarbus Base in Munich and Paris (fig. 10).

An aristocrat of the late second century had himself realistically represented on one of the four sides of a votive monument, performing a final sacrifice at the end of his term in office as censor. Only one element departs from the traditional Roman conception of their gods, the presence of the god Mars himself as recipient of the farewell sacrifice. This mixing of god and mortals is borrowed from the iconography of Greek votive reliefs. The other three sides of the base carried the Roman viewer far from the world of reality into that of Greek myth. In one relief he saw the wedding chariot

Fig. 9. Denarius of C. M. Limetanus. Rome, 82 B.C. The family of this mint official traced its ancestry back to Odysseus (reverse) and the god Hermes/Mercury (obverse).

a

Fig. 10*a*. Relief from the base of a monument erected by, or for, a Roman censor, ca. 100 B.C. or earlier. On the front, a scene of administrative duties attached to the office of censor, including, in the center, the official sacrifice at the end of his term in office. On the other three sides is depicted the wedding procession of Poseidon and Amphitrite (fig. 10*b*).

of Poseidon and Amphitrite, surrounded by a splendid gathering of sea centaurs and Nereids (fig. 10*b*). This scene has usually been interpreted as referring to a naval victory of the censor, but more likely the unarmed bridal couple was a reference to his descent from the sea god Poseidon. In any event, the mythological frieze is of much higher quality than the census scene and was probably made in Greece or Asia Minor and later reused on the Ahenobarbus Base.

The censor who dedicated the base belonged to two different worlds at once. His Greek ancestry and the seductive Nereids were as important to

b

Fig. 10*b*. Detail of the base in fig. 10*a*. Triton and Nereids. These mythological reliefs come from a workshop in the Greek East and were reused in Rome for the monument of the censor. Ca. 130 B.C.

him as his service to the Roman state. But even if he and his more educated contemporaries saw no contradiction in this, in the eyes of most Romans such imagery was hardly an advertisement for the venerable Republic and its spartan values. For Hellenized Roman families, however, such mythological genealogies were not simply a genteel game. They apparently had an important role in shaping the Hellenized Roman's image of himself. He could take his descent back to earliest Greek times and thus had no need to be ashamed of his ancestry. But naked Nereids and lascivious Tritons? Surely such images on a public monument, right beside the depiction of a religious ritual, must have had a disturbing effect.

Not every mint official could claim as ancestor such famous men of the past as Brutus or Marcellus, or commemorate on his coins a familiar building for which his family was responsible. As a result many coin types could only have impressed a small circle of rival families. Long inscriptions, full of abbreviations, could have been deciphered only by someone familiar with a particular family's history (fig. 11). Frequently these coins contained abstract symbols that referred to remote and little-known events of the past or to current political propaganda. Most of the specific messages on these intricately designed coins lay outside the realm of common experience.

We now only rarely find coin imagery that heralds the common defense of the state. An example will demonstrate to what extent public officials distanced themselves from political concerns. In 66 B.C. Q. Pomponius Musa issued a series of no fewer than ten coins with Apollo on the obverse and Hercules Musarum with the nine Muses on the reverse, all just to play on his own musical name. We need to keep such examples in mind when considering how every coin type issued under Augustus celebrated the new Republic and its leader.

a   *b*

Fig. 11. Denarius of Caldus. Rome, 51 B.C. *a*) Portrait of C. Coelius Caldus (consul 94 B.C.). The battle standard with HIS alludes to his victories in Spain, the standard with the boar to his successes in Gaul. *b*) Caldus as *VII vir epulo* (a major priesthood), preparing a feast for the gods. The victory tokens at left and right, however, refer once again to the Consul of 94 B.C. The *A* stands for augur, the *X* for *X vir sacris faciundis* (i.e., member of the priesthood of Apollo).

Fig. 12. Rome, Via Statilia. Tombs of Roman freedmen, ca. 100–80 B.C. The deceased had themselves portrayed with members of their families in framed reliefs, as if in a window.

It appears to be symptomatic of the disintegration of Roman society that individual rivalries and insecurity led to exaggerated forms of self-promotion, even among people who had nothing to gain by it. What began as a traditional agonistic spirit among the aristocracy degenerated into frantic displays of wealth and success. But the scope of opportunity for such display was often still rather limited.

A perfect example is offered by the ostentatious tomb monuments that during the last years of the Republic and in the early Augustan period increasingly crowded each other along the main thoroughfares leading out of Rome. Most wealthy freedmen were content mainly to advertise their citizenship and recently acquired freedom by having themselves depicted in a toga, surrounded by family members (fig. 12). But one such newly freed slave, the master baker Eurysaces, proclaimed his professional success as if it were a service to the state (fig. 13).

He chose a conspicuous site at a major intersection near the city. The architectural form of the monument he put up is utterly original. It is basically a tall cylinder whose shape recalls that of a baker's granary. The figured friezes celebrate the manufacture of bread by the latest technology. At this level of society, rivalry and self-promotion were mainly directed at fellow members of one's guild.

For the great families of the Senatorial aristocracy, however, the situation was rather different. They were often staggeringly rich, but had nonetheless no access to real power. Against a Pompey or Caesar, Antony or Octavian,

Fig. 13. Rome, before the Porta Maggiore. Tomb monument of the freedman M. Vergilius Eurysaces, proprietor of a large bakery. Ca. 40–30 B.C.

they did not have a chance. Significantly, one of the grandest tombs of the period around 30 B.C. was erected for a noble lady whose only claim to fame was that she was the daughter of a consul of noble family and wife of the richest man in Rome, the son of C. Crassus (fig. 14).

CAECILIAE Q. CRETICI F. METELLAE CRASSI reads the simple inscription, which confidently assumes that those named in it are known to everyone. The tomb was erected on a low rise at one of the most conspicuous spots on the Appian Way. It is made up of three sections: square socle, tall cylinder (which may recall a circular altar), and a tumulus which is no longer preserved. This last was meant to suggest archaic grave mounds and thus the antiquity of the family. The first two parts, socle and cylinder, served to elevate dramatically the actual burial tumulus. But the decoration includes a *tropaion* with Celtic weapons, which in fact probably commemorates a rather modest military victory of the deceased's husband when he was Caesar's quaestor in Gaul, a victory that no contemporary viewer would have recognized.

This monument illustrates just how extravagant and at the same time pointless the self-aggrandizement of the old aristocracy had become. They would commemorate some member of the family who had not distinguished himself at all and at best might call to mind other relatives or ancestors. There arises a bizarre disparity between the form of a monument and

Fig. 14. Rome, Via Appia. Tomb of Caecilia Metella. Ca. 30 B.C. In this period, consuls who fell in the service of the state received only a modest grave monument (cf. fig. 58).

its content. Only a few years before the erection of Caecilia Metella's tomb monument, the Senate had put up a tomb in honor of the consul Hirtius, who fell fighting for the Republic, only a fraction the size of hers (cf. fig. 58). Public monuments ceased to express any of the old political values, such as rank and service to the state. The architectural form itself of these monuments is revealing.

The compelling need to outdo the competition led to the use of every imaginable form of pretension or novelty of design. In addition to the usual forms of aedicula, altar, or temple, the archaic tumulus and even the pyramid were revived. Imitation triumphal monuments and palace facades were intended to overwhelm by their sheer size or by the multiplicity of architectonic symbols. In the tomb monument of the Julii at S. Remy, for example (fig. 15), no fewer than three architectural elements are piled on top of one another: a *quadrifons* (honorific arch) rises over a socle in the form of an altar, and above this stands a round tempietto with statues of the deceased. The passerby would have barely noticed them atop this curious hybrid monument. The monument's actual purpose is obscured by the combination of three such different architectural forms.

This eclectic vocabulary of forms was largely borrowed from Hellenistic architecture. But the grotesque exaggeration and especially the crowding of

Fig. 15. St. Remy (Glanum), Provence. Tomb monument of the Julii. The statues of the occupants of the tomb stood in round tempietto. Ca. 40 B.C.

tomb monuments along the roads leading out of Rome and other Italian cities are a unique phenomenon of the Late Republican period. We shall see how this helped shape the hybrid monumental architecture of the young Octavian until a new order—both architectural and political—grew up in its place.

The City of Rome as a Reflection of State and Society

Before the advent of Augustus, the physical appearance of Rome must have mirrored the peculiar state of Roman society. In our own daily lives we are aware of the symbolic value of public and private architecture, of streets and public squares, and we know that their effect on us cannot be overestimated. In any historical context the shape of a city presents a coherent system of visual communication that may affect its inhabitants even at the subconscious level by its constant presence. In Rome, at a time of civil war and struggles for power, proscriptions, and conspiracies, when public unrest and street fighting were rampant, the disquieting, even menacing aspect of the city was surely felt by people in a very immediate way. Still, one's reaction depends on one's perspective. Things looked different from a villa on the present-day Pincio than they did from one of the dank apartment blocks in the overcrowded inner city.

Since the days of Sulla's dictatorship the lifestyle of wealthy Romans had grown into one of unbounded luxury. The gap between rich and poor altered the face of the city as never before. Pretentious villas, in the manner of the famous Gardens of Lucullus, arose before the walls of the city (on the Pincio), commanding a view from their colonnades climbing up the hillsides hardly less magnificent than that from the vast terraced sanctuary at Praeneste. Those who lived in the "mean and narrow streets" (Cicero *De Lege Prov.* 2.35.96) darkened by overhanging balcony like structures, then every morning paid their respects to a Scaurus or a Vedius Pollio (p. 137) in his splendid mansion, its atria filled with hundreds of other *clientes* who daily paid court to their patron, experienced first hand the gulf separating rich and poor. The sudden population explosion in Rome had led to speculation in real estate and a housing shortage. Almost daily, buildings that were too narrow or too tall, built on inadequate foundations or of substandard materials, either collapsed or fell victim to fire (Plutarch *Crassus* 2), making whole sections of the old city dangerously unsafe. The great mansions stood like little walled cities in these warrens of narrow streets (cf. fig. 113).

Physically Rome bore no resemblance to the capital city of a vast empire. Back in 182 B.C. Rome's primitive and impoverished appearance was an object of ridicule at the court of Philip V of Macedon. Even 150 years later Rome was no match for the great cities of the Greek East. While the ancient cities of Campania and Latium, such as Capua, Tivoli, and Praeneste, had for years rivaled each other in building splendid sanctuaries, modern civic structures, streets, and squares, with the local aristocracy working together to beautify their city, Rome's condition had rather deteriorated. It had been decades since either the Senate or any of the nobility had paid attention to the overall plan of the city. In the second century the Senate had managed to keep the worst excesses of private luxury in check, and city magistrates still went about their job of governing a rapidly growing city with a certain sense of responsibility. Grain silos, aqueducts, streets, bridges, and basilicas all went up as Rome became an international economic center. Even the ancient temples had been fairly systematically restored. But ever since the first great internal crisis of the Gracchan period (132–121 B.C.) the needed repairs of temples and public buildings and especially the development of a reasonable infrastructure and city plan were completely neglected. When Caesar finally turned to the problem of Rome's appearance shortly before his death, it is revealing that his solution was a utopian one. He wanted to change the course of the Tiber, build a huge theater stretching from the slope of the Capitol to the Campus Martius, and create a new Hellenistic

Fig. 16. Rome. Theater of Pompey. Dedicated 57 B.C. Reconstruction of the interior, after Canina (1846).

city. Apparently he considered the old one beyond redemption (Suetonius *Divus Julius* 44; Cicero *Ad Att.* 13.33a. 1).

Rome's condition was the result of a process of rapid but haphazard building. Since the middle of the second century great generals had increasingly seized every opportunity to promote their own grandiose ambitions and curry favor with the people. But projects such as city planning, water supply, or sewage system were too slow and not flashy enough for their taste. Even the restoration of old temples did not provide a suitable means of self-aggrandizement, especially since such work was strictly regulated by religious law. The Senate considered the erection of buildings for public entertainment and recreation, such as theaters and bathing establishments, unacceptable for political and moral reasons. They wanted no political discussion or public demonstrations such as regularly took place in the theaters of Greek cities. For this reason the Senate permitted only temporary wooden structures to be put up at times of major festivals. Likewise the building of gymnasia or public baths was discouraged to prevent the importation of Greek-style culture and the creation of idle masses. Thus the building activity of the politically powerful was perforce limited to the *de jure* private sphere and manifested itself primarily in religious victory monuments that were dedicated to one of the gods but set up *in privato solo* (on private property). These offered the best opportunity, for one could indulge in self-promotion in the Hellenistic manner under the pretext of making a

Fig. 17. Two denarii of Petillius Capitolinus. Rome, 43 B.C. *a*) The new Temple of Jupiter Optimus Maximus. *b*) Head of the new cult statue, in Hellenistic style.

b

votive offering, and even an entire theater could be declared a gift to the god. Pompey dared to do just this in 57 B.C., when he built his enormous theater (fig. 16). Despite his tremendous prestige at the time he found it necessary to pretend that the huge auditorium was merely an accessory to the little temple to his patroness Venus Victrix that stood above it.

The Senate, though able to prevent the building of major recreational buildings for generations, was for its own part incapable of erecting large civic buildings or monuments with which all Romans could identify, much less of developing a coherent city plan. Rome itself never succeeded in implementing the most basic features that were taken for granted at the founding of each of her *coloniae*.

In 121 B.C., for example, the Senate had unexpectedly let the Temple of Concord in the Forum be restored by L. Opimius, the relentless foe of the Gracchi. For the supporters of the Gracchi the temple became a monument to their defeat. Shortly after 80 B.C. Sulla and Catulus made the strong foundations of the Tabularium into a symbol of the restored order and rebuilt at great expense, though after considerable delay, the Temple of Jupiter Optimus Maximus. But the new Tabularium glorified not the *res publica* as a whole, but rather the triumph of the optimates in a Senate whose weakness was every day more apparent. The new temple of the chief god of Rome, which was supposed to convey the *maiestas* of her people to foreign visitors, was embellished with the splendid columns brought back by Sulla as booty from the Olympieion in Athens. But even so the temple fell far short of contemporary aesthetic standards. This instance is again characteristic: the ground plan and podium could not be altered for religious reasons. This meant of course that the Hellenistic marble columns did not fit, and the pediment, crammed with decoration in the traditional manner (fig. 17*a*), was too steep and weighed heavily on the very tall, slender columns (Gellius 2.10).

The adaptation of an integrated Hellenistic temple plan to such a public monument was impossible because of religious constraints. In the attempt to be conservative and *au courant* at the same time, the Romans had to compromise at every turn. This led to results that were both aesthetically disturbing and problematical from the religious point of view. The commission for the new cult statue of Jupiter Optimus Maximus was given to an Attic sculptor, who produced a classicizing Zeus in the tradition of Phidias's gold and ivory cult statue at Olympia (cf. fig. 17*b*). That such an image took the place of an archaic terra-cotta statue surely must have impinged on religious sensibilities.

The confusion brought about by the "private" victory-sanctuaries in the Campus Martius was of a different sort. Victorious generals built modern Hellenistic marble temples to their patron deities, surrounded them with colonnades of the most expensive materials, and embellished these with the celebrated works of Greek art that they had looted while on campaign (fig. 18; cf. fig. 118). But the monumental statue of the victor might even have

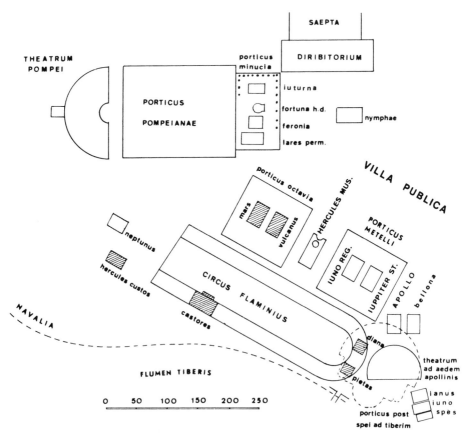

Fig. 18. Rome, Campus Martius at the time of the Late Republic, with votive sanctuaries and porticoes.

Fig. 19. Representation of a portico with over-life-size cuirassed statue in the garden and two altars in front. From Capua, first century B.C.

stood in the center of the sacred precinct, completely overshadowing the statues of divinities in the niches of the portico, as is seen on a relief from Capua (fig. 19). In 146 B.C. A. Caecilius Metellus Macedonius displayed in his portico the famous group of Alexander on horseback with his fallen comrades at the Battle of the Granicus, which had been made by Lysippus for the sanctuary of Zeus at Dion in Macedonia. His intention was not only a spectacular exhibition of the spoils of war, but also an homage to the greatest hero of the Hellenistic world. From the point of view of Republican traditions such an acknowledgment was clearly problematic.

While various aristocrats built splendid monuments for their favorite divinities, many of the oldest cult places in Rome were neglected and forgotten. Many may, like Cato, have questioned whether these nude marble statues of the gods by Greek sculptors would protect Rome the way the old terra-cotta ones had done. The sight of archaic temples and sanctuaries in ruins must have given pause before the shiny marble temples of the *triumphatores*.

The more glorious the fate of our Roman state becomes and the more her power grows—already we go over to Greece and Asia, tempted by all manner of excess, greedy for the treasures of kings—the more afraid

I become lest such things take control of us, instead of our taking control of them. Believe me, the art works brought into this city from Syracuse are a threat to us. For already I hear too many people admiring and singing the praises of embellishments from Athens or Corinth, while making fun of the clay pedimental figures of the Roman gods.

So spoke Cato as early as 195 B.C., according to Livy (34.4.3).

The "private" public monument entered a new phase with the Theater of Pompey and the Forum of Julius Caesar. The size and ostentation of these two monuments reflect the position of their patrons in the last years of the Republic. Pompey's theater represented the glorification of an individual on a scale that Rome had never before seen. It was covered with statues and pictures proclaiming the victories of this latter-day Alexander. But the theater was also a magnificent gift to the Roman people, and Caesar felt compelled to match this triumph of public relations. He tried to go Pompey one better by celebrating not only his own victories (an equestrian monument of Alexander, but with Caesar's likeness, stood before the temple in his forum) but also his divine ancestry. The temple that dominated the forum was dedicated to the goddess from whom his family claimed descent, Venus Genetrix. In using the temple and the square in front of it without hesitation to make public appearances, Caesar was the first Roman ruler openly to proclaim his superhuman status (Suetonius *Divus Iulius* 78.2). The Theater of Pompey, like the porticoes of the *triumphatores,* lay outside the *pomerium,* in the Campus Martius, but Caesar's new forum was in the heart of the city, right next to the old Forum Romanum. It was not without symbolic value that in its construction the recently renovated Curia was torn down and the Comitium, previously considered sacrosanct, together with its speaker's platform, was simply built over.

Octavian was no less adept at such self-aggrandizing display, as we shall see with the two major monuments he planned even before the Battle of Actium, the Temple of Apollo on the Palatine and the Mausoleum (cf. figs. 40, 59). Both were intended purely as propaganda for an ambitious general, with no regard for the traditions of the Republic.

Thus the city of Rome itself made it impossible for her people to identify with their country during these turbulent years and in fact sometimes became a source of new disturbances. In any event, the city offered no hope of stability or of constructive solutions for the suffering of her people that might instill faith in the future of the Republic. The shining inspiration of the good old way of life had dimmed to a flicker. Traditional symbols of duty and responsibility, which might have helped give people direction, were replaced by ever more obvious signs of the collapse of the state and the dissolution of society into personal rivalries and private interests. The great power struggle and its consequences were everywhere evident in the city.

The Villa and the Creation of Private Space

We have so far considered the complex imagery only of the city of Rome. In the old cities of Campania and Latium the effects of Hellenization were far less ambiguous. As early as the second century B.C., for example, Pompeii already had a stone theater, public baths, and probably a gymnasium as well. The sanctuary of Fortuna at Praeneste and the Temple of Hercules on the Tiber could rival anything in the East in their mighty foundations and impressive settings. With its streets and public squares Capua had the appearance of an up-to-date Hellenistic city (Cicero *de leg. agr.* 2.95 f.). The sophisticated local aristocracies, usually involved in commerce with the East, readily accepted new cultural influences without indulging in the rivalries and powerplays of Roman Senators. In these areas Roman ideology was irrelevant.

In the freer atmosphere of Campania wealthy philhellenes began building the first luxurious country houses by the middle of the second century, about the same time that anti-Greek sentiment first appeared in the Roman Senate. Perhaps I should have discussed this typical example of the process of acculturation at the very beginning of this chapter, since here the recently adopted Greek way of life could develop unhindered, then in turn pervade the public consciousness.

The phenomenon of the villa was originally a kind of social safety valve. They developed from seldom-used, small houses into aristocratic country estates. Far from Rome and its tradition-bound constraints, even a conservative aristocrat could indulge in the most frivolous distractions of Greek culture. "For in Rome that would be unacceptable," writes Cicero, quoting an edict of the orator M. Antonius, consul in 99 B.C. Under these conditions arose a dichotomy of the private and public spheres of life that would have profound consequences for later European culture. Tremendous personal and political tensions, brought on by the clash of *mores maiorum* with Greek culture now so eagerly sought, could thus be mitigated by a strict spatial and temporal separation. For the first time two key concepts arose, *otium* (relaxation, private life) and *negotium* (duty, political life in Rome), creating the powerful ideology of the Roman sense of duty.

Villas quickly became centers of Hellenistic-style luxury. One has the feeling that the restrictiveness of life in Rome created an almost pathological need for excesses of pleasure and exhibitionism. This private world of luxury grew with the collapse of the Senate's authority and reached its peak in

Fig. 20. J. Paul Getty Museum, Malibu (California). A reconstruction of the Late Republican "Villa dei Papiri" near Herculaneum (1985).

the time of Lucullus, Pompey, and Caesar. The original idea of rest and relaxation on one's own plot of land, in the company of congenial friends and good books, degenerated into a vulgar display of wealth and became, like everything else, a vehicle for self-glorification. It was during this same period in Rome that the last legal restrictions on private extravagance broke down.

The ambitious but naive Roman treated Greek culture as if it were some sort of package deal. He outfitted his villa with Greek colonnades, rooms for entertainment or relaxation, libraries and picture galleries, gardens and other areas nostalgically called by Greek names, such as gymnasium or palestra, or named for famous places in the Greek world. And of course he pursued here a Greek cultural life, in the company of real-life Greek artists and philosophers, turning his private world into a complete universe of things Greek. Most of the original works of Greek art stolen or extorted by "collectors" like the praetor Verres are now lost. But the marble and bronze copies found scattered over many villas give us a good impression of how such works were used in a variety of settings to recreate the appropriate Greek ambience. Statues and busts of the great poets, philosophers, and orators stood by the library, while in the colonnades known as the "gymnasium" were displayed statues of athletes, herms, or figures of Heracles and Athena. Dionysiac figures and erotic groups have been found lining paths through gardens. Elsewhere one might be transported into the world of Homeric myth, as at the large villa at Sperlonga, where an actual grotto

Fig. 21. Rome, Palatine. Casa dei Grifi. Ca. 100 B.C. The wall paintings imitate inlay of precious stones.

served as its setting. Most of these eclectic and schematically disposed groups of sculpture, divorced from their intended function and context, represented the Greek tradition as a purely didactic cultural standard. They invited one into a world of meditation, filled with books and beautiful things, far removed from political responsibilities.

Today one can best experience the total effect of such a villa not at the excavation sites in Italy, but in Malibu, California, where the oil magnate J. Paul Getty recreated the Villa dei Papiri at Herculaneum to scale, as a museum (fig. 20). Even some of the sculpture found in the eighteenth-century excavations of this villa are displayed in the gardens and colonnades in Malibu, in bronze casts. About eighty statues and herms were made for this villa in the years 30–20 B.C., and together they give a good impression of what a more or less complete ensemble would have looked like.

What is most interesting about this material for our purposes is the complete absence of Roman subject matter. As in virtually all other excavated villas, there are no depictions of Roman legends, no portraits of distinguished Romans of the heroic or historical past, nor of great Roman thinkers of the previous 150 years, no allegorical representations of Roman values and virtues. Instead of these there are portraits of Greek poets, philosophers, and orators, alongside those of Hellenistic rulers. The Senators took as their models Alexander and the great rulers of the successor kingdoms, not Roman consuls and generals. In this world of *otium* there was no place for the Romans' own national traditions. It was only with Augustus that political imagery penetrated the private sphere, and only under the Empire that portraits of Roman rulers, living and dead, appeared in every house.

Wall paintings in the so-called Architectural Style are equally instructive in explaining the mentality and aspirations of the Roman upper class. They decorated the living quarters of both large and small villas, as well as city dwellings in Roma and Pompeii. Their origins probably go back into the second century. They depict walls inlaid with the most expensive marbles, sometimes with colonnades in front of these precious walls and views into yet other colonnaded spaces (fig. 21). The imagined version of the walls took the place of richly decorated interiors or, when these were there too, it heightened their effect, surrounding the occupants with images of fabulous splendor. The idea was to create an environment combining every imaginable extravagance of raw material and architectural form. At its most extreme, when the walls of the smallest bedroom are broken up in a series of illusionistic renderings, which would have a disconcerting optical effect on anyone actually trying to sleep, the striving for the ultimate extravagance has become a neurotic obsession. Who would really want to sleep in a room like the cubiculum from Boscoreale or in the Villa of the Mysteries (fig. 22)?

As with sculpture, the subjects of these paintings have nothing to do with life in Rome. But neither do they reflect country life on the estates of their owners, as do, for example, the illusionistic paintings of Baroque villas in Italy. Instead the views are of impressive, richly outfitted sanctuaries that were associated with the palaces of Hellenistic kings and were perhaps actually built on some of the wealthiest Roman estates. Instead of a natural landscape we see intricately laid out parks, picture galleries decorated with herms, large-scale pictures of Hellenistic monarchs, a Greek philosopher looming large, landscapes in which mythological scenes are enacted, or a Dionysiac initiation ritual, in which the owners of the villa are portrayed alongside the mythological devotees of the god. It is dream world of luxury and refinement à la grecque. Like the sculpture, these images were intended to evoke learned associations and fond memories, to answer a longing for an imagined environment of magnificence, and to carry the viewer off into a new world of beauty.

The next style of wall painting, created around the time of the *ludi saeculares* (cf. fig. 224), shows clearly how in Augustan circles the old style was perceived as a mere show of extravagance and self-deception. The es-

Fig. 22. Even small bedrooms, here about 10 m², were painted with impressive architectural fantasies. Pompeii, Villa dei Misteri. Ca. 40 B.C.

cape into a Greek world of make-believe even included the wearing of appropriate costume. When cultivated Roman Senators reclined beside a portrait of Plato or Aristotle to philosophize or read poetry, they would often affect a Greek himation, Greek sandals, and a wreath in their hair (Cicero *Rab. Post.* 26). They imagined themselves artists and *literati*, Greeks in the company of Greeks. Finally, they created memorials to themselves in this style.

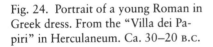

Fig. 23. Statue of the Greek comic playwright Poseidippos. The head has been reworked into the portrait of a Roman.

Fig. 24. Portrait of a young Roman in Greek dress. From the "Villa dei Papiri" in Herculaneum. Ca. 30–20 B.C.

A vivid illustration is the statue of the Greek comic poet Poseidippos (third century B.C.), whose hair and facial features have been transformed into the portrait of a Roman of the first century B.C. (fig. 23). The philhellene nevertheless insisted that his social status be made evident, by the addition of Senatorial shoes. This the sculptor was able to accomplish only by using bronze laces. And the statue of the "young Greek orator," between those of Aeschines and an old poet in the gymnasium of the Villa dei Papiri (fig. 24), commemorates a contemporary Roman, perhaps again the villa's owner. For his hairstyle is one most popular in the years around 30 B.C.

In their leisure time people thus tried to shed all that was Roman about them as they did their toga. The creation of an alternative way of life in the private sphere, that is, removed from the empire building of the Late Republic, clearly explains the collapse of the integral system of values among the Roman upper class. The two different cultures were imposed one on the other, rather than blending together. One simply became accustomed to living simultaneously in two different worlds, speaking two languages, and adopting a dual standard of ethics. The pleasures one enjoyed in private were then attacked in public speeches before the Roman people.

The world of *otium* became the perfect setting for personal growth and edification in the pursuit of Greek culture. It was a "neutral territory" where a spiritual existence quite apart from political life could be achieved. One could escape into this realm from the chaos of the civil war and the suffering of the Republic in its death throes, and in it one could seek new avenues to self-fulfillment. Here not only books, but also painting and sculpture took on a new importance. They became the markers with which one could delineate the world of the spirit, the stimuli toward intellectual growth and depth. Previously, it was only through service to the Republic that a Roman aristocrat could hope to achieve a rewarding life. Now, however, the world of *otium* offered the possibility of fulfillment outside the political arena. There is no doubt that the private life of luxury and aesthetic pleasures in country villas enabled an already enfeebled aristocracy to accept more easily the transition to one-man rule.

Chapter 2

Rival Images: Octavian, Antony, and the Struggle for Sole Power

After Caesar's death (44 B.C.) the struggle for sole power lasted another thirteen years, and art and architecture played a considerable role in this contest. Although indications of future changes first appeared at this time, the structure of the visual language remained essentially the same. The collapse of the old order reached its climax, and in the power struggle the disturbing images and symbols of the protagonists were carried to extremes. One has the impression that two Hellenistic kings are competing for control of Rome.

Divi Filius

When C. Octavius entered into the contest for his legacy in 44 B.C., at the age of eighteen, his only advantage was the name of his great-uncle and adoptive father, Caesar. From the beginning he called himself C. Caesar, omitting the customary cognomen Octavianus, although by modern convention we call him Octavian in spite of this. The "youth who owed everything to his name," as Marc Antony called him (Cicero *Phil.* 13.11.24) left no doubt as to his goal from the very start. "May I succeed in attaining the honors and position of my father to which I am entitled," he proclaimed at a popular assembly as early as the end of the year 44, as he pointed dramatically at the statue of the slain *dictator* (Cicero *ad Att.* 16.15.3). Such images made a deep impression. The nobility was disconcerted, and even the young Caesar's friends felt uneasy. Cicero remarked, "I would not wish to be saved by such a one."

Soon after attaining sole power in 31 B.C. Octavian altered his political style, and in 27 he "restored the Republic." As a savior of the state he received the honorific title Augustus. Henceforth he did everything possible to separate this period from that which had gone before, and with good reason. Much that had happened between 44 and 27 had to be forgotten; the image of himself that Octavian promoted before this turning point is fundamentally different from that which he later conveyed so successfully as Augustus. Before the change, symbols and images operated entirely within the framework of the ambivalent and contradictory pictorial vocabulary of the Late Republic. What was expressed, and how it was expressed,

a   *b*

Fig. 25. *a*) Denarius of L. Lentulus, Rome, 12 B.C. Augustus (with the *clipeus vir-tutis* of 27 B.C.) places the star on a statue of Julius Caesar: a reference to the appearance of the *sidus Iulium* in 44 B.C. *b*) Denarius of Octavian, 42 B.C.: Cae-sar's official seat with his golden wreath. On the *sella* stands CAESAR DIC (tator) PER (petuus).

was determined by the struggle for power. The competition between the protagonists was the decisive factor in the elaboration of specific imagery and even shaped its artistic form.

At first the primary concern was the evocation of Caesar's memory in the army veterans and the *plebs*. This was Octavian's most valuable political tool. How deliberately the party of the young Caesar used it is especially evident in the way they promoted the murdered *dictator's* deification and regularly used a comet, the *sidus Iulium,* as its symbol.

When Octavian in July of 44 staged the *Ludi Victoriae Caesaris,* over the objection of the responsible officials—games which Caesar had earlier vowed to Venus—a comet promptly appeared in the sky. Augustus later recorded in his autobiography that this comet had been visible all over the

Fig. 26. Aureus of Octavian (en-larged), 36 B.C. The Temple of the Divus Iulius (before it was built). In the temple, the cult statue with augur's staff (*lituus*), in the pedi-ment, the *sidus Iulium;* alongside, the memorial altar, commemorat-ing the spot where Caesar's corpse was burned.

a *b* *c*

Fig. 27. *a*) Denarius of Caesar, 46 B.C. Aeneas fleeing Troy, with his father Anchises, holding the Palladium. *b*) Denarius of L. L. Regulus, Rome, 42 B.C. Aeneas with Anchises, who looks back in terror. *c*) Denarius of Octavian, before 31 B.C. Venus Genetrix with the arms of Mars. Legend: CAESAR DIVI F(ilius).

world for seven days and had been generally understood as a sign of Caesar's apotheosis. For this reason he put a star on the head of the statue of Caesar dedicated soon after in the Forum—"but inwardly he rejoiced in the sign of the star, to which he would himself ascend" (Pliny N.H. 2.93–94).

Elsewhere we learn that it was none other than Octavian himself who inspired in people this belief in the star, that he set the *sidus Iulium* upon all Caesar's statues (fig. 25*a*), and that later the star shone on his own helmet. A *haruspex* named Vulcatius contributed by interpreting the comet as heralding a new age of happiness, then, scarcely having uttered this good news, conveniently died (Servius *in Verg. Buc.* 4.46–47.). Soon the star appeared as a symbol of hope on coins, finger rings, and seals. In 42 B.C. Octavian obtained the admission of the deified Julius Caesar into state cult and the worship of the new god in all Italian cities. From now on he could call himself *divi filius*, son of the deified Caesar. Altars were set up everywhere; a temple was begun on a prominent spot in the Forum and was shown on coins (fig. 26) years before its completion in 29 B.C.

This coin is a good example of the effective use of the new visual language by Octavian's supporters. The large *sidus Iulium* appears in the pediment, and below stands the strikingly oversized dedication "Divo Iulio." The cult statue of the new god is visible between the columns. Next to the temple is the memorial altar, which was later effectively incorporated into the building. This altar carried a particular emotional charge, since it stood on the spot where Caesar's body was buried.

Poets soon began to sing of the *Caesaris astrum* or *sidus Iulium* and make it shine on all important occasions. The star later appears repeatedly on coins, especially together with celebrations of the *saeculum aureum* and with the promotion of the princes Gaius and Lucius as successors of Augustus (cf. fig. 132*b*). The symbolic power of the star was based on a strong

a

b

c

Fig. 28*a*–*c*. Portrait of the Caesar Divi filius opposite that of the Divus Iulius. *a*–*b*) Sestercius of Octavian, ca. 40 B.C. DIVOS IULIUS, DIVI FILIVS. *c*) Denarius of Octavian, 38 B.C.

and widespread willingness to be influenced by celestial signs, an effective exploitation of this willingness, and a calculated association of public apparitions with eternal visual symbols.

Most of the images promoted by Octavian's supporters in the first few years are associated, directly or indirectly, with Caesar. For example, gold coins with *sella*, wreath, and the legend CAESAR DICTATOR recall Octavian's attempt publicly to display Caesar's golden throne and jewel-studded wreath to arouse emotions (fig. 25*b*). Caesar had already put Venus and Aeneas on his coins as a sign of the Julian *gens'* divine ancestry (fig. 27*a*). The younger Caesar, in borrowing this image, now also laid claim to the divine and heroic ancestors of the Julian house (fig. 27*b, c*). Marc Antony had nothing comparable with which to rival these. The likeness of son to father is evident on numerous coin portraits of the early years. Octavian's youth was exploited masterfully: sometimes he is strikingly boyish (fig. 28*b*), at others like a young hero (fig. 28*c*). Here too the model of the youthful Alexander is ever-present, lending an aura of the miraculous to the young Caesar.

Even out of tense and dark moments arose impressive symbols of the close association of father and son. Thus, the story was told that the head of Caesar's murderer Brutus had been sent to Rome, to be placed at the feet

Fig. 29. The equestrian monument voted Octavian in 43 B.C., proclaimed immediately thereafter on coins. *a*) Aureus, 42 B.C. *b*) Denarius, 43 B.C. *c*) Denarius, 41 B.C.

of Caesar's statue (Suetonius *Augustus* 13; Dio 47.49.2). And the grisly episode when, it was said, 300 men from Perugia were slaughtered was supposed to have taken place at an altar of the Divus Iulius, in memory of the *dies nefastus* on which Caesar was murdered.

The meaningful use and repetition of images and messages was a new phenomenon, particularly when one considers that the coin types of the previous decades had seldom aimed at such effects.

The Imposing Statues of the Young Caesar

Octavian's most urgent concern at first was public acknowledgment of his services to the state and of his abilities as a commander of the army. This

Fig. 30. *a*) Denarius of Octavian, before 31 B.C. The equestrian monument voted 43 B.C., in its final form. Octavian, with torso nude, on a galloping horse.
b) Aureus of A. Manlius, Rome, before 80 B.C. Equestrian monument of L. Sulla. In contrast to Octavian, Sulla is depicted in a *toga*.

would best be made manifest in honorific statues put up under official auspices. The first of such statues, voted him on 2 January 43, when he was still only nineteen, was in some ways also the most important: a gilded equestrian statue which was to stand on or beside the speaker's platform. The monument was voted him by the Senate and people, along with a series of other honors, and, standing as it did at the most conspicuous spot in Rome, testified to the fact that Julius Caesar's heir had in only a matter of months become a major political power in his own right. The Senate had not only declared his illegal conscription of an army an extraordinary service to the state, but had granted the "youth" a place of honor in the Senate and the right to stand for office ten years before he had reached the minimum age, in effect a legalized *imperium*. Now the young Caesar was acting officially as commander-in-chief in the service of the Republic. It is thus not surprising that this monument became the symbol of his political coming of age. Even before the statue could be completed and unveiled, the partisans of Octavian used it as a coin type.

On one of the earliest coins (fig. 29*a*), we see the monument as it would later look, decked out with two large tokens. The horse stands on a ledge, under which is a ship's prow (*rostrum*), symbolizing the monument's prominent location, at the speaker's platform. The augur's staff in the young Caesar's hand refers to his competence as commander of the army. The letters S(enatus) C(onsultum) emphasize that the honor accorded Octavian was in the form of an official resolution of the Senate. The insistence on trying to legitimize his rule is clear.

The statue was a rather extravagant honor for a young man who had never held public office, let alone led an army. Not only that, it was intended to rival the equestrian monuments of Sulla, Pompey, and Julius Caesar. The Senate could scarcely have made more evident how little regard it had for its own traditions.

Coins dating from 43 B.C. show that the statue was at first conceived like Sulla's monument, with the horse standing still (fig. 29*b*). Later this was changed to a galloping pose, as is shown on coins of 41 B.C. (fig. 29*c*). Now, however, the legend POPULI IUSSU is also added, as a bit of demagogic sloganeering. The people had granted this honor, not the Senate, whose support Octavian had in the meantime completely lost. But only a few years later do the coins give us a detailed picture of the statue (fig. 30*a*). They show Octavian as *divi filius*, dressed not as a general, but with bare chest and only a garment fluttering about his hips. The new monument, with its dramatic appearance, thus outshone Sulla's statue (fig. 30*b*). Even the outstretched hand took on a broader significance in this context, as a sign of all-encompassing power. The son of the deified Caesar appears here like the

Dioscuri on earlier coins of the Republic. This is no ordinary Roman general, but a superhuman savior in time of need.

The image matches Cicero's obsequious flattery of Octavian before the Senate, explicitly setting the achievements of the *divinus adulescens* above those of Sulla and Pompey (*Phil.* 5.15.42). It is true that Sulla had gone so far as to have the inscription IMPERATOR FELIX placed beneath his statue. But the costume and sword, as well as the pose of the tame horse, make the monument a specific image of military valor. Since the two statues stood next to each other, the contrast must have struck every viewer. The dedicatory inscription, with its insistence on giving Octavian's age (nineteen; cf. Velleius Paterculus 2.61.3) illustrates how thoroughly the Senate had abandoned its traditional prerogatives. Besides, Cicero, the leading spokesman for the *res publica,* had already tried to justify the extraordinary honors for Octavian by comparing him with Alexander the Great (*Phil.* 5.17.48).

An equally important statue is also known only from coins (fig. 31*a*). Since this one appears in the series of coins minted after the sea battle at Naulochoi (36 B.C.), together with other monuments put up in Rome, it must also have been a famous work celebrating the victory over Sextus Pompey.

Octavian is again represented nude, this time in a pose familiar from late Classical Greek art. The model may well have been a famous statue of Poseidon by Lysippus. The victor in a sea battle, he holds in his right hand the stern (*aphlaston*) of an enemy ship as a trophy, while the lance in his left hand marks him as a general. He rests his right foot on a *sphaira,* symbol of all-embracing rule over land and sea.

This highly expressive pose had already been used for statues of Hellenistic rulers, to bring out the idea of god-like strength. By the time of Octavian's statue, however, even this type suffered from overuse (for Cartilius Publicola, for example, a leading citizen of Ostia about 30 B.C.) and as a result had lost its effectiveness. Nevertheless, by virtue of its context and setting, and Octavian's own position at this time, it took on a special significance.

Sextus Pompey, son of the great Cn. Pompeius Magnus, had emerged in the years after Caesar's death, alongside the Second Triumvirate (Octavian, Antony, and Lepidus), as head of a sort of naval empire, with his power base in Sicily. After early victories over the young Caesar and his generals, he claimed that, like his father before him, he was the special protégé of Neptune and had in fact been adopted by the god as a son. Octavian was clearly not the only one who had to have divine ancestry. Sextus wore a sea-blue chlamys instead of the general's cloak, sacrificed bulls with gilded horns to his "father" Neptune, and even made offerings of horses lowered into the sea (Dio 45.48.5). He became extremely popular with the Roman *plebs*. When a statue of the sea god was brought into the Circus during a *pompa* in 40 B.C., the crowd went wild, showing its support for the son of Neptune against the *divi filius*. When Octavian then had the statue removed from the *pompa* and boasted that he would triumph even "over the will of Neptune," there were riots in which not only his own, but statues of the other triumvirs were overturned.

All marine imagery and symbols of the sea god were naturally associated with Sextus Pompey in this period, at least those which appeared in a political context. As early as 42 B.C. he had celebrated his naval victories by minting coins with appropriate mythological scenes. Along with various tokens of victory and likenesses of his own father and son, he put on his coins Neptune and his helper Scylla. Thus Scylla, who appears often on coins at this time, also carries a political connotation.

Most interestingly, one of the coins in this series shows a statue in the same pose as the later statues of Octavian (fig. 31*b*). As in that instance, this is not a statue of a god, but a victory monument to Sextus (or his father Cn. Pompeius). The victor holds an *aplustre*, just like the statue of Octavian, but here the foot rests on the beak of a ship. On either side of this towering monument were the brothers from Catania rescuing their parents. This story was already well known to the Romans from coins as an *exemplum pietatis* toward one's parents. Sextus used it to allude to the epithet *pius*, which he had added to his own name to emphasize his close relationship with his father. It was also of course a jab at the young Caesar, who had made so much of his own *pietas* toward his adoptive father ever since the Battle of Philippi. The victory of Pompey's son over Caesar's heir is celebrated on the coin as belated revenge for Pompey's defeat at the hands of Caesar at Pharsalus.

Against this background the victory monument erected by or for Octavian (fig. 31*a*) takes on the character of a polemic in answer to Sextus's earlier propaganda. Years later, as an old man, Augustus, in the *Res Gestae*, refers contemptuously to Sextus Pompey as *piratus*.

But the monument only assumes its full meaning when considered together with another of the same type that had been dedicated to Julius Caesar a decade earlier. This was a bronze statue, the foot propped up on a sphere explicitly meant to symbolize the *oikoumene* (Dio 43.14.6), with the inscription underneath "because he is a demigod." Caesar himself later had this phrase removed, most likely because it made the statue into too blatant a statement of apotheosis.

Sextus's statue was connected with a specific victory, alluded to in the

a   b

Fig. 31. *a*) Denarius of Octavian, before 31 B.C. Honorific statue of Octavian commemorating the victory over Sextus Pompey, 36 B.C. The globe is a symbol for his claim to sole power. *b*) Denarius of Sextus Pompey, Sicily, 42–40 B.C. Statue of Sextus Pompey, or of his father. The foot rests on a *rostrum*, a token of victory over Octavian's fleet.

ship's beak under the victor's foot. In Octavian's, as in Caesar's statue, by contrast, its place is taken by the globe. This proclaimed quite openly, years before the decisive victory at Actium, the all-encompassing power of the *divi filius,* inherited from his father.

The extravagant honors with which the Senate celebrated Octavian's victory over Sextus Pompey include a third monument (fig. 32*b*).

> Of the honors voted him he accepted an *ovatio* (a solemn procession into the city, or so-called lesser triumph), an annual victory celebration, and a gilded statue. He would be represented in those garments which he had worn at his entry into the city, and the statue would stand atop a column decorated with the beaks of vanquished ships. But the inscription would say that he has restored the peace on land and sea which had for so long been rent with discord. (Appian 5.130)

Dio reports other honors, including the right to wear a laurel wreath at all times. Indeed, the portrait of Octavian on the obverse of the coin with the *columna rostrata* does have the laurel wreath, unlike other portraits in this series (fig. 32*a*). In this instance again the monument took on added significance because of its location and its association with a recent event. The form copied the Column of Duilius, commemorating a naval victory over the Carthaginians (260 B.C.). The partisans of Octavian felt no compunctions in likening a victory in a civil war with one over a foreign enemy, by setting up the new column next to the old, at the speaker's platform. In

a   b

Fig. 32. Denarius of Octavian, before 31 B.C. *a)* Octavian with laurel wreath.
b) Columna rostrata with nude statue of Octavian.

addition, the mantle gloriously fluttering behind recalls the victor's entry
into the city. Octavian thus seems to follow the model of Pompey the Great
and Sextus Pompey by wearing not a toga, but the Greek chlamys with all
its heroic and regal connotations.

We can gain some idea of the heads of these statues of Octavian from his
earliest portrait type on coins, which first occurs about 40 B.C. (fig. 33). The
prototype was probably created for a major honorary statue, perhaps the
equestrian statue at the *rostra*. By the Late Republic it was already common
practice to circulate the portrait of a political leader in the form of casts,
from which copies, either life-size or reduced, could be made for other statues, coins, and gems. The young Caesar is portrayed with bony face, small
eyes, and nervous expression. Unlike later portraits of Augustus, this one
seems truly to capture something of the ambitious and power-hungry young
man. Artistically, the portrait betrays the same contradictory qualities of
other Roman portraits of this period.

The types of these three statues set up in the heart of Rome and spread
further afield through coins are entirely consistent with Hellenistic ruler
portraits and thus in every way opposed to the traditions of the Republic.
The same man who, in 36 B.C., in a speech to the Senate, promised the
restoration of the state, had himself commemorated in these statues like one
of the "saviors" of the Greek East. These statues were polemical and deliberately inflammatory; they celebrated the superhuman triumph of the *divi
filius* and announced his claim to sole power more clearly and directly than
anything said in the Senate. The language was loud and clear, perhaps to
appeal to the masses, but against the background of Republican traditions,
the message was problematical to say the least. For the young Caesar was
certainly no Hellenistic king. Rather, since 42 B.C. he was officially "triumvir for the restoration of the state," and had to act in a political arena de-

Fig. 33. Portrait of Octavian, ca. 30 B.C. The original of this marble copy belongs to the earliest years of his political career.

fined by totally different rules and traditions. The new imagery was fine for
making a big splash, but it was not a language in which one could formulate
a new program for Rome. This was imagery which spoke only of the ruler
and his personal ambition, but said nothing of the old *res publica* and its
future. Yet the principals in this power struggle were as yet dependent on
this type of Hellenistic visual imagery, so long as there was no alternative.

Man and God: Role-Playing and Self-Image

It was always an old tradition among the Roman aristocracy to trace one's family back to Greek gods or heroes (cf. figs. 9, 10). In this way they imitated the great Hellenistic royal families and, especially thanks to their supposed descent from the Trojans, were able to claim a place in the Greek world from time immemorial. Ideas of divine patronage and protection and of identification with mythological figures, originally a kind of genteel game, began more and more to inform the noble Roman's view of himself in the Late Republic. For Pompey, the comparison with Dionysus or Heracles was still understood as a metaphor for the splendors of his military victories in the East. But Julius Caesar was perfectly open in proclaiming himself a demigod. Not only did he build the great temple to his ancestress Venus Genetrix in his Forum Iulium, but he sat in the entrance to this temple to receive Senators (Suetonius *Caesar* 78).

Sextus Pompey, the *dux Neptunius* (Horace *Epode* 9.7), illustrates how after Caesar's death even second-rate figures automatically proclaimed themselves under divine protection and favor. During the struggle for power that followed Caesar's murder, the contestants tried to outdo one another in such identification with gods and heroes.

But mythology served not only as a tool for propaganda. In the struggle between Marc Antony and Octavian we can observe how mythological figures and imagery gradually shaped the protagonists' own view of themselves and began to affect their behavior. In particular the gods Dionysus and Apollo seem to have served in certain situations as models for Antony and Octavian, respectively, helping to determine the way they behaved and thus how they responded to the hopes for salvation attached to each god.

The uncertainties of the present and the capriciousness of politics in Rome, along with the absence of any concrete or realistic expectations of what the future might bring, provided fertile soil for seers and soothsayers, irrational longing for a savior, and predictions of a new and blessed age. The mood which inspired Vergil's famous Fourth Eclogue shows that even his educated contemporaries harbored such fervent hopes. In times like these the old rallying cries and slogans of the Republic, as in Cicero for example, no longer had any impact. Any serious contender for power had somehow to deal with these expectations of salvation and proclaim himself the savior.

The only language available in which to express such ideas was that of Greek myth. This imagery was indeed effective in Rome, but could sometimes backfire when it came into conflict with old Roman traditions. Marc Antony's attempt to identify himself with Dionysus, which ultimately had disastrous consequences, is the best example.

Fig. 34. Aureus of L. Livineius Regulus, Rome, 42 B.C. *a*) M. Antonius. *b*) Anton, son of Heracles, ancestor of the Antonii.

Antony's family traced its origin to an otherwise unknown son of Heracles named Anton. Antony himself had coins minted with an image of this ancestor (fig. 34*a*, *b*) and made a rather infelicitous comparison with the great figure of Aeneas, the son of Venus. Antony was pleased and flattered to be compared with Heracles: "The finely formed beard, broad brow, and aquiline nose lent him a powerful, masculine look which reminded people of paintings and statues of Heracles, whom he was thought to resemble" (Plutarch *Antony* 4).

He used the identification with Heracles to best effect as the macho soldier fraternizing with his men. An engraved stone from a ring, found at Pompeii (fig. 35), shows that there were statues of him of this type and that

Fig. 35. Carved stone from a ring.
Hercules with the features of
M. Antonius.

his followers gladly carried such an image of their hero on a ring and used it as a seal. Such testimonia of political or intellectual affinity are especially popular in the Late Republic and Early Empire. We shall encounter many more.

When Marc Antony came to Athens and Asia Minor, however, after the partition of the empire among the triumvirs (42 B.C.), he found the figure of Dionysus a much more attractive and effective model, in the manner of Alexander the Great. It was a role to which he was ideally suited, given his passionate nature, generosity, and naiveté, his love of wine, elegant parties, worldly women, and flashy affairs.

When this new Dionysus arrived at Ephesus, drunk and accompanied by his followers dressed up as a thiasos, the Greeks there were reminded of the days of King Mithridates Eupator:

> As Antony entered Ephesus, women garbed as maenads, men and youths as satyrs and Pans all sported before him. The city was filled with ivy and thyrsoi, with the music of the flute, syrinx, and lyre. All welcomed him as Dionysus bringer of joy, gentle and kind. (Plutarch *Antony* 24)

And when this most unlikely Roman general then came to Tarsus as Dionysus-Osiris, to meet the Queen of Egypt, herself in the guise of Aphrodite-Isis, then it seemed to many that Rome was transformed and a new age of glory was upon them.

> Cleopatra came in a bark with golden prow and purple sails. The silver oars moved in time to the sound of flute, syrinx, and cithara. The queen herself lay beneath a gilded parasol, garbed and adorned as in pictures of Aphrodite. Youths made to resemble painted Erotes fanned her from either side. The most beautiful handmaidens stood dressed as Nereids and Graces on the rudder and rigging. And the most magnificent odor of incense spread over the banks and beyond. (Plutarch *Antony* 26)

It is no accident that these comparisons with Heracles and Dionysus are always made in terms of statues and paintings, for the use of costume made myth and art come alive. But the paintings and statues were but the inspiration for such epiphanies, and pale reflections at best. We cannot fully comprehend the powerful effect of such vivid images. Not only the spectators but the actors themselves fell under the spell. Dionysus and Aphrodite were not merely symbols of wine and love, but embodiments of human perfection. At a splendid feast all the participants could relive the experience of being liberated from ordinary existence. The life of intense pleasure and indulgence which Marc Antony unabashedly enjoyed in Athens and

Alexandria could be viewed as a means to freedom and salvation, to release from suffering, with the promise of a happy future, and this, as we shall see, not only in the Hellenistic East.

The Alexandrians understood the meaning of those statues that showed Antony as Dionysus, with full physique, sensuous eyes and lips, wearing a long, transparent garment, and holding a kantharos. When Antony entered Alexandria in the guise of Dionysus triumphant after his victory in Armenia, this was perceived as an appropriate form of celebration. The Roman commander had truly proved himself the *neos Dionysos,* through whom the god's irresistible power could overcome any foe. This Roman aristocrat, who previously only found it advantageous to play a mythological part, now fully entered into it in the palace of Cleopatra. Toward the end, his entire lifestyle was shaped by this role. He celebrated the outbreak of war with dazzling feasts, went out to face Octavian as Dionysus with his thiasos, and even when he knew his cause was lost remained in character, treating life as one great party.

> It seemed as if he took pleasure in abandoning all hope. Antony and Cleopatra disbanded their thiasos of "inimitable bon vivants" and created a new one, no less glamorous, profligate, and extravagant, which they called "friends unto death." (Plutarch *Antony* 71)

In the night before the capture of Alexandria, her people thought they heard a reveling thiasos leaving the city in the direction of Octavian's camp. "Many believed that the god now abandoned Antony, that god whom he most resembled and whose behavior he had always imitated" (Plutarch *Antony* 75). Antony himself probably perceived it in the same way, for he was by now completely trapped in this mythical world.

Meanwhile, Octavian had grown into a very different role in Italy. The *divi filius,* he had inherited both Caesar's charisma and his popular support. But even though this aided him at the outset with the army veterans and the *plebs,* the figure of Caesar was nevertheless clouded by memories of the *tyrannis* and the civil war. Besides, it was no help in creating a vision of the future or answering prayers for reconciliation. These hopes were naturally directed at the youthful savior Octavian and from the very start lent him an aura of divine grace.

At first the miraculous tales are of all different sorts. Already as a boy he had superhuman powers, and even frogs obeyed his command. Later, when he first took the auspices as a general, all the victims' livers were bent inward, and when he first entered the office of consul, twelve vultures appeared, as they had to Romulus. A number of dreams and omens associated the youth with the sun and the stars, in keeping with the popular expecta-

Fig. 36. Series of Cistophori, Pergamum, 27/26 B.C. *a*) Capricorn carrying a cornucopia and framed by Apollo's laurel wreath. *b*) The Sphinx proclaims a new age. *c*) Stalks of wheat promise peace and prosperity.

tion of a new age and a ruler sent by the gods. As a baby he was said to have climbed out of his crib and up a tall tower, where he was found turned toward the sun. It was not only his mother and father who had these dreams of a child of the sun and stars. Even so respected a figure as Cicero was supposed to have seen in a dream a youth lowered from the heavens on a golden chain and receiving a whip from Jupiter Capitolinus. Some of these stories were apparently already circulating in his early years, so that even at his first entry into Rome the crowds believed they saw a halo of light around the sun.

The boy wonder himself could not help but be deeply affected by all these miraculous images. One time, when Caesar was still alive and the young C. Octavius was a student in Apollonia, the astrologer Theogenes fell on his knees before him after seeing the configuration of the heavens at his birth.

> From this moment he had such great faith in his own destiny that he made public his horoscope and later minted a silver coin with the Zodiac sign Capricorn, under which he was born. (Suetonius *Augustus* 94)

Capricorn does in fact appear quite early on coins and glass beads, which his followers would have worn in rings as cheap substitutes for precious stones. Later on, the birth sign will be placed on coins, both on the occasion of military victories as well as within the programmatic imagery of peace, as a reminder that Augustus's role as savior of the state was "in his stars" (fig. 36). Starting in 30 B.C. his birthday was officially celebrated as a day of good omen.

But this abundance of signs and portents surrounding Octavian had to be fitted into some kind of mythological framework. We can trace in the literary and archaeological sources, despite the fragmented state of our evidence, how he gradually took on the role of protégé of Apollo. This process

a   *b*

Fig. 37. Aurei of C. Cassius, 43/42 B.C. *a*) Head of Libertas. *b*) Tripod decorated with fillets and laurel branches.

was carried further in Octavian's struggle with his opponent, the alter ego of Dionysus, and eventually developed into the mythological foundation of his later role as Augustus.

Significantly, "Apollo" was the battle cry that issued from both sides, the murderers and the avengers of Caesar, at the Battle of Philippi (42 B.C.). From the time of Sulla, Apollo and his symbols—tripod, sibyl, cithara—appear on coins, alluding to the promise of a bright future. Combined with the head of Libertas and a dagger on coins of Brutus and Cassius, the tripod carries this message: liberation from tyranny and the restoration of the Republic are the prerequisites for a new and better age (fig. 37). But who would put faith in a Republic with the Senate restored to power? The outcome of Philippi showed clearly that Apollo was on the side of Caesar's heir. Besides, it was a member of the Julian family who had built the first Temple of Apollo in Rome, and Caesar had lent the *ludi Apollinares* a new splendor. Thus when Antony left for the East as the new Dionysus, it was time for Octavian to put all his faith in Apollo. Soon rumors circulated of a notorious "feast of the twelve gods," staged by Octavian and his friends, at which he appeared dressed as Apollo. The Roman *plebs*, suffering from a grain shortage due to Sextus Pompey's embargo, reacted to stories of this feast with anger and ridicule. But such costume parties were hardly unusual, as the events in Alexandria at about the same time confirm. There at a costume party hosted by Cleopatra and Antony, no less a figure than Munatius Plancus, consul in 42 B.C., came dressed as the sea god Glaucus, his nude body painted blue, and, with a fish-tail swaying behind him, danced on all fours. Dionysiac masques also took place in private homes, as shown by the painted scene in the Villa of the Mysteries.

At about this time Caesar's heir also began to use as his seal the sphinx, symbol of the *regnum Apollinis* prophesied by the sybil (Pliny N.H. 37.1.10; Suetonius *Augustus* 50), and soon this oracular creature became a frequent element in Augustan art (fig. 38). Octavian began to wear Apollo's laurel wreath more and more often on public occasions, and in these years several new miraculous happenings reinforced the direct identification with Apollo.

It was a divine palm tree which was said to have prompted Caesar's adoption of the boy. Then, soon after Octavian's marriage to Livia, an eagle dropped in her lap a hen carrying a laurel branch in its beak. From this branch grew a mighty tree at Livia's villa, and from the tree future Caesars would cut their victory wreaths (Pliny N.H. 15.136). A story was spread as early as the 30s B.C. that Octavian's mother Atia had conceived the boy not by his putative father, but by the god in the form of a snake. The same had been said of Olympias, mother of Alexander the Great. Apparently the story of the snake was widely repeated, and a small glass cameo provides evidence that Octavian's partisans made use of it in their artistic propaganda (fig. 39).

Given this affinity with Apollo, it is no surprise that Octavian ascribed his final victory over Sextus Pompey primarily to the help of Apollo and his sister Diana. There was at least one sanctuary of Diana conveniently located near Naulochoi, where the decisive victory over Sextus took place. And it was during this battle that Octavian was said to have vowed the great temple of Apollo on the Palatine. It is fascinating to observe how deliberately Octavian pursued this relationship to Apollo over the next twenty years or, to put it another way, how his sense of mission and his entire program for healing Rome's wounds bore the stamp of Apollo. He built the new temple of Apollo right next to his own house and considered that the decisive Battle of Actium had been won through the direct intervention of the god. His new portrait type, created soon afterwards (cf. fig. 83), has a kind of ageless beauty which would have reminded his contemporaries of Apollo's own features. The god was also held to be responsible for the victory over the Parthians and for the social legislation of 18 B.C. When finally

Fig. 38. Sphinx on a seal impression. Augustan.

Fig. 39. Glass cameo. The Apollonian snake winds around the tripod, behind its head a nimbus of sunlight. Tripod, feeding chickens, augur's staff, and ladle (*simpuvium*) allude to the three priesthoods to which Octavian then belonged, thus linking the snake of Apollo directly to him.

the time had come to herald the *saeculum aureum,* Augustus again invoked the protection of Apollo and Diana, had the Sybilline Books purged of any inappropriate prophecies, and placed these in a golden vessel at the feet of their cult statues, as a guarantee that the new Golden Age would last forever.

But it was surely the striking proximity of Octavian's residence to Apollo's temple on the Palatine that attested most dramatically to the close relationship of the two (fig. 40). Recent excavations have shown that a ramp connected the house directly to the forecourt of the temple. The bond between the god and his protégé could not have been more explicitly conveyed. The house itself was relatively modest, but the temple area, because of its close proximity, became like a part of the whole complex. In this Octavian took his cue from the Hellenistic kings. In Pergamum and Alexandria, for example, a sanctuary adjacent to the palace served as a kind of showplace. This idea of living next to the god originated in the period just after the Battle at Naulochoi. A thunderbolt had conveyed the god's will and designated the spot where he wished his temple to be built, right next to Octavian's house. It was in addition an impressive site, high above the Circus Maximus and in an area rich in reminders of Romulus and the founding of Rome (cf. fig. 52).

The relationship with Apollo would prove to be ideally suited to Octa-

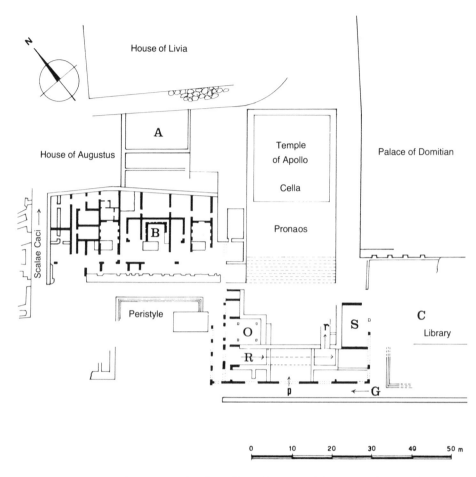

Fig. 40. Rome, Palatine. Temple of Apollo and House of Augustus. A ramp (R) connects the lower residential quarters and the peristyle directly with the temple terrace.

vian himself and to furthering his political image. All his goals and objectives, both during the struggle with Antony and then later in the building of the new order, could be associated with the god. Apollo stood first of all for discipline and morality. After Octavian and Antony signed the treaty of Brundisium in 40 B.C., dividing the empire between them into East and West and letting the third triumvir, Lepidus, make do with Africa, they invited each other to dinner. Octavian was said to have displayed a "soldierly" and "Roman" demeanor, while Antony behaved rather like an Oriental or Egyptian (Dio 48.301). Apollo also stood for purification and for punishment of any form of excess. As such he could well represent Italy's position during the civil war with Antony, with the motto "Italy versus the Orient with its *luxuria,* against Egypt with its animal-headed gods and its decadence." But after the victory was won, then Apollo took on his role as singer, lyre player, and god of peace and reconciliation. And as the prophetic god, with sibyl and sphinx, it was he who proclaimed the long-awaited new age.

The Programmatic Silver Coinage of Octavian

Apollo offered a much greater range of possibilities than Dionysus, who dictated a rather narrow and one-sided persona for Antony, especially in the cultural climate of Alexandria. And there was room for other gods' help beside that of Apollo and Diana. Neptune had obviously abandoned Sextus Pompey at Naulochoi and gone over to Octavian's side, and his ancestress Venus, Mars the avenger, Mercury, and Jupiter himself were all arrayed behind the *dux Italiae* when it came down to the final confrontation. At least this was the message of the handsome silver denarii that Octavian began to mint even before Actium and used to pay his troops.

These coins, on which are represented the three statues considered earlier, were issued in series of two or three related types, like stamps nowadays, in which the depiction of the CAESAR DIVI FILIUS or IMPERATOR CAESAR, as he is called in the legends, is associated as closely as possible with a divine image. It is possible here to consider only a few of the most important implications of these programmatic statements.

In a set of six coins, conceived as three pairs (figs. 41, 42), one coin has the head of a divinity on the obverse and a full-length figure of Octavian on the reverse. On the companion, a portrait head of Octavian is on the obverse and a full-length image of the same divinity on the reverse. If we set the three coins with goddesses alongside their companion pieces, we can read them as an intentional progression: before the battle Octavian addresses his troops and followers in the pose of *adlocutio.* Peace, the goal of every battle, is depicted as a goddess with laurel and cornucopia. On the second coin, Octavian leads his army's charge into battle. His protectress is Venus Genetrix, who on one coin wears a fine necklace and on the other regards the arms of Mars, with the *sidus Iulium* blazing on the shield. The third coin, however, celebrates the victor. Victoria races toward him on the globe, as he stands in the pose of Neptune, as in the statue discussed above. In the situation which obtained just before Actium, the sequence was programmatic, matching each of the *topoi* in Octavian's speech before the battle, as it is recorded for us in Dio Cassius (50, 24ff.): allusions to previous accomplishments, divine protection, and the blessings of peace won through victory in battle.

Fig. 41. Denarii of Octavian, before 31 B.C. Series of three, A: on the obverse of each, portrait of Octavian; on the reverses, the goddesses Pax, Venus, and Victoria.

Other coins belonging to the same series of silver denarii can be ordered and interpreted in similar ways. For example, in one set two monuments commemorating the victory over Sextus Pompey, *tropaion* and arch, are associated with the Curia recently built by Octavian (fig. 43c). In this context, the Curia symbolizes Octavian's promise, made as early as 36 B.C., to restore the Republic. On another coin, the *columna rostrata* alluding to the same victory was paired with Mercury, who represented peace and prosperity.

Never before had coins of such beauty been minted in Rome. But it was a case of aesthetics in the service of political ends. In comparison with the crowded and barely legible coins of the Late Republican period (cf. fig. 11) these were models of clarity and simplicity. The legend could be dispensed with, save for the name of the individual being commemorated. The images needed no explanatory words and were in fact more effective against a plain background. The minting of related series of coins may have inspired people to form collections and that would also have drawn attention to their message.

One pair of coins in this series is particularly interesting for the question of the equating of man and god (fig. 44). One of these had a herm and thunderbolt, the other, the head of the same herm, again with thunderbolt. But on the latter the god clearly has the features of Octavian. This must

Fig. 42. Denarii of Octavian, before 31 B.C. Series of three, B: on the obverse, heads of divinities as in figure 41; on the reverse, Octavian: addressing the army, giving the signal to attack, and triumphal statue of Octavian.

Fig. 43. Denarii of Octavian. Series of three with victory monuments: *a–b*) monuments to the victory over Sextus Pompey; *c*) Curia Iulia.

surely represent some public monument in Rome and suggests that Octavian had now reached the stage of blending his own image with that of a god. That is, he employs exactly the same kind of imagery in Italy that Antony and the kings of the Greek East used, only likening himself to different divinities.

Earlier, Sextus Pompey had put the god Janus on his coins with the por-

Fig. 44. Two denarii of Octavian, before 31 B.C. *a–b*) Octavian, Jupiter-Herm. *c*) Herm head with the features of Octavian. *d*) Octavian on the *sella curulis*, with Victoria on his hand.

trait features of his father, symbolizing the promise of peace. This may have been the inspiration for Octavian's coin, which has so far proved difficult to understand. Perhaps the god is meant to be Jupiter Feretrius, whose ruined temple on the Capitol Octavian had rebuilt just before the Battle of Actium, at the suggestion of P. Atticus (Nepos *Att.* 20.3). The temple was said to have been built by Romulus, who dedicated in it the arms of an enemy defeated by his own hand (*opima spolia*). This would have provided a most favorable omen on the eve of the battle. Perhaps the herm which appears on coins at this very time is a replacement for the ancient aniconic image of the god. In any case, the thunderbolt proves that a specific identification with Jupiter is intended. He too is brought into direct association with Octavian's victory, for on the reverse of the companion coin the victor sits on the *sella curulis*, wearing a toga, with Victoria perched on his hand: magistrate and ruler in one.

The message of this coin is again divine patronage, victory, and a return to order and stability. Those of the famous silver denarii discussed here are indeed an accurate reflection of the situation before the Battle of Actium.

These coins undoubtedly attracted widespread attention. Compared with the flood of visual stimuli with which we are nowadays bombarded, new images were relatively rare at this time. Here was a whole new repertoire of beautiful images impressed on precious metal. The issues were unusually large, and the findspots show that they circulated all over the western half of the Empire on the eve of the final showdown with Antony.

Antony Betrayed by His Own Image

Marc Antony made it easy for his enemies to attack him. He did not care what kind of impact the images and symbols he made use of would have in Rome and Italy. For his own part, in the mutual defamation campaign waged in letters, speeches, and pamphlets, he employed the usual *topoi*, accusing Octavian of cowardice in battle and of breaking his word, and, as a member of an old aristocratic origin, slighting Octavian's "obscure" origins. The supporters of Octavian, meanwhile, exploited mercilessly the opportunities offered by Antony's identification with Dionysus. Slogans previously used to attack adherents of the Dionysiac mysteries were a ready-made supply of ammunition with which to denounce Antony's Dionysiac revels as foreign decadence and *luxuria*. What Antony and Cleopatra and their followers were doing out in the East was simply an extension of the same weakness and debauchery that had in a few generations brought Rome to the brink of the abyss. In addition, old-timers still remembered how King Mithridates VI, like a new Dionysus, had mobilized the forces of the East to challenge Rome's power. Apollo's protégé, by contrast, had a splendid opportunity to present himself as a man of order and exemplary morals. Besides, this was not the first time that Apollo had come to Rome's rescue at a critical time.

After the final break with Antony the accusations sank to new depths: Antony had become totally corrupt, godless, and soft, and was bewitched by Cleopatra. What else could explain why a Roman general would award conquered territory to the children of an Egyptian queen and even put in his will that he wanted to be buried in Alexandria beside Cleopatra (a notion that is crucial, as we shall see, for our understanding of Augustus's Mausoleum)? Antony was no longer a Roman, thus this would be no civil war.

He referred to his army headquarters as the royal palace, wore an oriental dagger in his belt, and dressed in a totally unroman fashion. He appeared in public either on a *kline*, as Dionysus, or on a golden throne, like a king. He commissioned paintings and statues of himself with Cleo-

a

Fig. 45. Mold for Arretine clay bowl, ca. 30 B.C. Heracles and Omphale in a chariot drawn by centaurs, an allusion to Antony and Cleopatra. *a*) Omphale/Cleopatra. *b*) Herakles/Antony looks longingly back to Omphale/Cleopatra.

patra, he as Osiris or Dionysus, she as Selene or Isis. More than anything else this created the impression that she had cast some kind of spell over him. (Cassius Dio 50.5)

The mud-slinging campaign, which was so crucial for the mobilization of Italy and preparation for the civil war, was of course primarily expressed in public speeches. But there is also preserved some visual evidence that shows how word and image were closely intertwined in such a way that the speeches drew upon the images for their effectiveness.

The statues that showed Antony in the guise of Dionysus were to be seen only in the East, but the partisans of Octavian did all they could to play up their scandalous nature. This was not hard, since there were figures of Dionysus all over Rome, and one could conjure up the image of Antony's features on these effeminate bodies. For a more discriminating audience M. Valerius Messala Corvinus may have concocted a subtler form of argumentation. His two lost polemics, "de Antoniis statuis" and "contra Antonii litteras," were probably composed for this purpose. In these, the Dionysiac statues and Antony's florid Asiatic style of oratory were probably condemned as manifestations of the same spiritual weakness.

b

A fine example of the use of mythological models to attack Antony is one that had once been used against Pericles, Heracles enslaved to Omphale.

Just as in the paintings of Omphale taking Heracles' club and donning his lion skin, so did Cleopatra disarm Anthony and make sport of him. Then he would miss important appointments and forego military exercises, just to cavort with her on the banks of the Canopus and Taphosiris and take his pleasure with her. (Plutarch *Antony and Demetrius* 3.3)

A scene reminiscent of this was depicted on a finely worked silver bowl of early Augustan date, a mold of which was then made available to the pottery of Perennius in Arezzo. The silver bowl itself is lost, but several clay impressions and bowl fragments from Perennius's workshop are preserved (fig. 45*a*, *b*). These attest to the relatively wide distribution of bowls with this scene. Heracles/Antony sits in a chariot drawn by centaurs, dressed in soft, transparent women's clothing. With a lascivious expression he looks round at Omphale, who follows in a second chariot. Two servant girls follow alongside Heracles' chariot with fan and parasol: the emasculated hero's skin is delicate (cf. Horace *Epode* 9.15f.). Driving behind him, Cleopatra/Omphale proudly wears the hero's lion skin like a helmet and wields the hero's club. A slave girl extends toward her an enormous drinking cup. This touch is aimed directly at Cleopatra, who was ridiculed by Octavian

Fig. 46. Old man with ivy wreath and kantharos at a Dionysiac feast. Through the portrait features the image takes on the character of personal devotion to Dionysus. Ca. 50 B.C.

and his circle for her bibulousness (cf. Horace and Propertius). On most examples of the bowl (but not the one illustrated here), the boldly marching pair of men behind the chariot carry spears. These are Cleopatra's guard of *doryphoroi*. To whip up emotions Octavian claimed that they were Roman soldiers reduced to serving the queen. Both men heft large objects on their shoulders, possibly intended as huge drinking horns.

Marc Antony defended himself against the charge of drunkenness in a work now unfortunately lost, but still extant in the early Imperial period, with the rather confident title *de ebrietate sua* (on his own drunkenness). In it he may not only have denied unwarranted accusations, but also sung the praises of his god, the great liberator who frees us from all our burdens. The work was directed at people who not only could read, but understood such aspects of Hellenistic culture as lavish banquets and Dionysiac symposia. There were many such men in Rome, and some idea of how much they valued the Dionysiac symposium is offered by the image of a reveler who had himself immortalized holding a kantharos (fig. 46).

In spite of all attempts to destroy his character, Antony still had a constituency in Rome. There were still people there who, as Plutarch comments, "accepted his luxurious life-style and decadence (*truphai*), his excesses and egocentrism, as gaiety and good fellowship and even commended it as a dazzling display of power and good fortune" (*Moralia* 156E).

Antony was apparently a special favorite among the *jeunesse dorée*, who loved the sybaritic pleasures of the East and in private life devoted themselves to art and Hellenistic culture. We gain some idea of this world from the neoteric poets, especially in the love elegies of Propertius and Tibullus. In two fascinating studies Jasper Griffin has shown how inextricably linked were poetry and reality in these circles, and how for Propertius, Antony was the model of a heroic life in love. The poet portrays the great general as chief exponent of a hedonistic ideal, set up in conscious opposition to traditional Roman *virtus*. In the years after Actium, when Octavian was already securely in power, Propertius sang of a night with his beloved:

In such a night could any of us become a god. If only we all wished to lead such a life and to stretch out our limbs heavy with wine and recline. Then there would be no dread sword, no ships of war, and the sea at Actium would not roll over the bones of our comrades. And Rome would not have to loosen her hair in perpetual mourning for the triumphs won at her own expense. (Propertius 2.15.39–47)

This was daring stuff. Not only does the poet criticize the civil war; he openly advocates an alternative way of life. Marc Antony was filled with this same feeling and allowed it unthinkingly to shape his political image, as we can see on an unusual coin from the period just after the treaty of Brundisium, when Antony was married to Octavian's sister Octavia. The happy couple rides over the sea like Poseidon and Amphitrite (fig. 47). The Roman triumvir, blessed by love, stands in a car drawn by hippocamps and embraces his wife: a symbol of the renewed alliance with the young Caesar, but expressed in an image drawn from erotic poetry. But Antony was a public figure, not like the poets who could happily proclaim their disdain for whatever reeked of politics, business, or war. Admirers of romantic poetry in Rome were thrilled when they saw how their hero had the courage to put first his wife Octavia, later even his lover Cleopatra on coins (fig. 48).

Fig. 47. Sestercius from the "Fleet-Coinage" of M. Antonius. Corinth (?), ca. 36/35 B.C. *a*) Antonius and Octavia. *b*) The same pair as Poseidon and Amphitrite in a chariot drawn by hippocamps.

a   *b*

a   *b*

Fig. 48. Denarius of Antonius, 32 B.C. *a*) Antonius; behind the portrait the Armenian tiara as an allusion to his conquests in the East. *b*) Cleopatra with diadem, in front of the bust a ship's bow as an allusion to her war fleet.

At the same time, such sentiments and images all went to fuel the propaganda of Octavian and his partisans. Antony's tragedy was a result of the unbridgeable gulf between the traditional Roman character and the Hellenistic sense of joie de vivre.

Mythological symbols and parallels also offered contemporary Romans the chance to express their affinity with one side and its lifestyle or the other. It is becoming increasingly clear that the political affiliations that can be detected in poetry are intimately related to those expressed in the visual arts, even in the private sphere, as in the decorative scheme of a room or in such diverse objects as tableware and seal rings. In looking at wall painting of the Second Style, for example, we can observe the increasing use of attributes and symbols which allude to Apollo and Diana, mirroring Octavian's programmatic use of these divinities (cf. fig. 209). Two relief plaques are especially interesting in this connection. They belong to a Hellenistic/Early Imperial type of monument that was set into the wall of a room as decoration. Quite a few replicas of each of the two types are preserved, and stylistically they should belong to the decades just after the death of Julius Caesar.

Although the background landscape and the principles of composition are very similar on both, the figure styles are quite different. On one relief, Dionysus and his rowdy thiasos enter the house of a devotée to the music of the flute (fig. 49). We are reminded immediately of Antony's entry into Ephesus. The drunken god supports himself on a little satyr, while another hurries to take off his shoes. Next to the worshipper, who warmly greets the god, reclines a woman on a *kline,* admiring the miraculous epiphany. Masks lying at the foot of the couch allude to the world of the theater. A small votive relief on a tall pillar stands behind Dionysus, emphasized by its prominent position. One of the replicas preserves the scene on this relief:

Fig. 49. The drunken Dionysus with his retinue visits the house of a devoté, who recognizes him as an epiphany. Ca. 40–30 B.C.

Victoria in a galloping chariot, hardly an appropriate image for this setting of domestic bliss.

On the other relief Victoria is a much more important figure. Within a sacred precinct the Apolline Triad solemnly approaches an altar (fig. 50). Victoria pours wine into Apollo's *phiale* for a libation, and more Victories are visible in the background, as oversized akroteria figures on a temple. The divinities are flanked by two pillars, one carrying a tripod, the other an archaizing statue of Apollo.

Even if some of the individual motifs originated in an earlier period, the significance of these two reliefs, the one Apollonian, the other Dionysian, could not have been unaffected by the growing political and ethical polarization of Rome. The connotations of each scene are apparent, whether those who designed or commissioned the reliefs intended it or not. A contemporary who had witnessed the spectacular reconstruction of Apollo's temple in Rome could scarcely fail to make the association with the temple depicted behind the Apolline Triad or the figure of Victoria.

The figures on the Apollo relief are depicted in a hieratic, archaizing style, quite unlike the Hellenistic baroque vocabulary in which the Dionysiac procession is expressed. The former style would soon become a hallmark of the new regime, as the medium of its program of religious revival.

Fig. 50. Apollo with his sister, Diana, and mother, Latona, at a sacrifice, with Victoria. The divinities are depicted in archaistic style. The temple in the background perhaps refers to Octavian's temple to Apollo on the Palatine; at left a tripod on a tall pillar. Relief, ca. 30 B.C.

Indeed, the difference in style between the two reliefs seems to reflect the opposing images of the two rival camps. Antony's rhetorical style was derived from the ornate and expressive "Asiatic" style popular in the Greek East (Suetonius *Augustus* 86.2). The "Atticizing" school, to which Octavian belonged, held this style to be not only wholly lacking in aesthetics, but also an expression of moral decay. *Talis hominibus fuit oratio qualis vita* (As a man's speech, so his way of life), wrote Seneca (*Epistles* 114.1).

The pros and cons of the two rhetorical styles had long been a topic of debate in the Hellenistic world. Now the debate took on a political character, as the aesthetic issue turned into a moral and ethical one. Similarly, the style of visual imagery became politicized, not just its content. We shall see eventually how Octavian's adoption of the Atticizing style of rhetoric to a great extent determined the style of Augustan art. After the final triumph of Octavian, Hellenistic art, with its emphasis on emotion, was passé. The dramatic immediacy of Hellenistic art, in its depictions of powerful rulers, large crowds, and the tumult of battle, is entirely absent from Augustan state monuments. This had been the visual language of Asiatic rhetoric, which now epitomized the decadence and debauchery of the East, to which Antony had fallen victim.

We may speculate at this point on whether Roman culture would have developed much differently, had Antony won out. Probably not, as far as the creation of a monarchy is concerned, or at the level of popular culture. But in some respects the overall picture would indeed have been different. As monarch, Antony would surely have patterned himself more closely after Hellenistic kings, as Nero later tried to do. This would in turn have created a more emotional relationship between ruler and ruled. Would there have been a Principate at all? Perhaps the longing for a religion of salvation would have been directed towards the indispensable ruler cult. It is significant that Dionysus is not among the many divinities with whom Roman emperors would later identify themselves, although he was the favorite of Hellenistic rulers. The association was ruled out by the role it had played in the struggle with Marc Antony. But this is idle speculation. As far as art is concerned, it is clear that if the outcome of the civil war had been other than it was, classicism would not have become the dominant style that it did, and instead Roman art would have remained essentially Hellenistic.

Architecture: Competition and Innovation

The decade of the Second Triumvirate (42–32 B.C.) did not witness the construction of any great monuments comparable to those of Pompey and Julius Caesar. Nevertheless, architects in Rome were kept extremely busy. Many new buildings were planned and begun, but most could only be completed after the Battle of Actium. This explains why in some cases buildings commissioned by followers of Antony in their decorative program glorify Augustus and his victory.

During the 30s Octavian was the most important patron of new building in Rome, but there were about ten others who put up temples and other public buildings. The result of this mutual rivalry was architectural novelties and hybrid forms. But in sheer size and expense Octavian's sanctuary of Apollo and his enormous Mausoleum overshadowed all other projects.

Rome had never before celebrated so many triumphs in so short a span of time and with such trivial pretexts. But as a rule the victors were not independent agents. Rather, their monuments, financed by the spoils of war, were intended primarily to give added visibility to one or the other rival faction in Rome. Yet at the same time, the partisans of Octavian, who were already dominant in Rome by virtue of their very presence there, probably had more choice in determining what sort of monuments they wanted to build than they would have later on. Thus the construction planned during this decade gives us not only an impression of the kind of programmatic thinking that was then in the air, but also some notion of the spectrum of styles and taste that existed before an officially mandated classicism and archaism took over after Actium.

Ever since Caesar had begun to renovate the temple of Quirinus, the building of temples had become more and more fashionable. Varro's appeal for the rescue of the temples fallen in ruins apparently found a willing response, particularly in a time of crisis. Munatius Plancus, after his triumph *ex Gallia* (42 B.C.), went to work on the hallowed temple of Saturn in the Forum. Another of Marc Antony's men, C. Sosius, after his triumph *ex Judaea* in 34 B.C., planned to rebuild the old temple of Apollo *in Circo*. On Octavian's side, C. Domitius Calvinus, the victor in Spain in 36 B.C., rebuilt the Regia in the Forum which had recently burnt down. L. Cornificius, a man of undistinguished family, who had held off Sextus Pompey and celebrated a triumph *ex Africa* in 33 B.C., agreed to rebuild the old temple of Diana of the *plebs* on the Aventine. This was not among the more prestigious temples in Rome; in fact its dedication was celebrated on August 13, the great feast day for slaves. Perhaps this is why Octavian entrusted to a *novus homo* an otherwise important temple to his patron goddess.

The ground plan of this temple of Diana Cornificia, preserved on a frag-

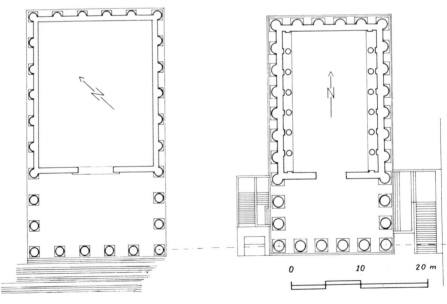

Fig. 51. Ground plans of the temples to Apollo built by Octavian and by C. Sosius (to scale). The later design (right) is more lavishly conceived.

Fig. 52. View of the Temple of Apollo and the House of Augustus on the Palatine. Model.

ment of the Forma Urbis, clearly shows that Cornificius's project surpassed Octavian's temple of Apollo, at least in expenditures for the building itself. Cornificius's temple was dipteral, in the East Greek tradition, having a double row of columns along the long sides and eight columns across the front, while Octavian's was only pseudodipteral, with six across the front and half-columns in the cella (fig. 51a). The Diana temple betrays an unmistakable desire to outdo the competition, especially as it was planned only three years after the temple of Apollo. The new temple of Apollo built by C. Sosius *in Circo* also tried to overshadow the temple on the Palatine, with its more densely packed columns and lavish interior architecture (fig. 51b).

Nevertheless, the sanctuary of Apollo still managed to surpass the competition, thanks to its setting and the association with Octavian's residence. It was set on a tall substructure, impressively high above the Late Republican Circus Maximus (fig. 52), in this respect comparable to the great sanc-

a

Fig. 53. Rome, entablatures of: *a*) the Temple of Saturn; *b*) the Temple of Apollo *in circo*. Patrons vied with each other in the wealth of decoration.

tuaries at Palestrina and Tivoli. The complex arrangement on various levels of interconnected buildings, courtyards, and gardens, comprising the stairways, temple precinct, sacred grove, libraries, the house of Augustus, and the portico of the Danaids, was unparalleled in Rome. Perhaps this accumulation of elements was an afterthought, inspired by the spirit of competition. In any event, the view from the temple out over the Circus Maximus and across to the Aventine, where the construction of Cornificius's temple would have been visible, must have been most impressive.

The sudden increase in the wealth and variety of architectural decoration must have arisen from the need to surpass one's rivals and draw as much attention as possible to one's own project. In the development of the console cornice, for example, we can follow how this element of temple architecture was elaborated into a kind of showpiece in the course of only a few years. The richly ornamented cornice of Sosius's Apollo temple (fig. 53*b*) is in striking contrast to the earlier, much simpler type on the temple of Saturn (fig. 53*a*) and the Regia. The same is true of column bases, capitals, and friezes, as well as cornices (figs. 54, 55, 72). C. Sosius (32 B.C.) had fought on Antony's side at Actium, then went over to Octavian and was pardoned. The extraordinary lavishness of his temple was thus a special

Fig. 54. *a*) Capital from the Temple of Apollo on the Palatine, after 36 B.C.
b) Capital from the Apollo Temple of C. Sosius, ca. 25 B.C.

way of expressing his loyalty to Apollo and the god's protégé. Even the triumphal procession depicted on the frieze is not that of the patron, but rather of Octavian (fig. 55). His loyalty did not go unrewarded: at the Secular Games this one-time follower of Marc Antony could be seen among the procession of priests, the *XV viri sacris faciundis*.

Thus in the 30s and early 20s B.C., even before Augustan ideology made the use of rich architectural decoration into state policy with the motto "only the best for the gods," this tendency had grown dramatically as a means for wealthy patrons to call attention to themselves. The varieties of ground plans and the mixing of Ionic, Corinthian, and Doric-Tuscan orders also reflected the diversity of Late Hellenistic architecture. The 30s were still far removed from the Early Empire, with its uniformity of temple architecture. As we shall see, the Augustan temple was thus not the result of a gradual development, but rather the product of a set ideology, in accordance with which Augustus's architects created an appropriate style.

The earlier variety of architectural styles is matched by a similar variety of tastes in rhetoric, literature, and the visual arts of the same period. A good example of the latter is the monument of Asinius Pollio.

Asinius Pollio, consul in 40 B.C., had been a Caesarian, who later won a victory over the Parthians in Dalmatia (39 B.C.). He then, however, gave up politics to write a history of the age that was rather critical of Augustus. A distinguished man of letters, he used the booty he had won to rebuild the *Atrium Libertatis* at the foot of the Capitol. In the political climate of the time, the choice of this project was no statement of loyalty to the Triumvirate. In accordance with an express wish of the slain Julius Caesar, Asinius Pollio included in his *monumenta* the first public library of Greek and Latin authors in Rome. Here he displayed busts of famous writers, among whom

Fig. 55. Rome, Apollo Temple *in circo*. Frieze block. C. Sosius celebrated Octavian's triple triumph, not his own. The northern barbarians (Illyrians?) wear trousers.

the only one still alive was the polymath Terentius Varro, of whom we shall have more to say presently. When Octavian not long after began work on his own Greek and Latin library, it must have seemed a rival to Pollio's, and the decoration of it must also be understood in this light. Both libraries express a radically changed public attitude toward Greek culture in Rome.

Pollio's library was attached to a magnificent art collection. From the Elder Pliny's description we gain some impression of the collector's taste. Asinius Pollio loved Hellenistic art at its most imaginative, even including the rather extravagant group known as the "Farnese Bull." Dionysus with satyrs and maenads, centaurs and water nymphs must have lent the collection an amusing ambience, probably displayed in a garden setting. For the contemporary viewer it must have offered a startling and rather pleasant contrast to Octavian's heavy-handed homage to Archaic and Classical Greek art, which would soon be visible in the sanctuary of Apollo. Like the library, Pollio's art gallery was open to the public: *spectari monumenta sua voluit* (Pliny N.H. 36.33). At least in this respect it accorded better with the future emperor's policies than did the collector's taste in art. But even this emphatically unpolitical monument, given the hypersensitive situation before the outbreak of a new civil war, became a form of special pleading. The elegiac poets would have felt at home in Pollio's sculpture garden. Among the great patrons of architecture he was the only one who remained "neutral," and the only one who did not take part in the Battle of Actium.

As the political crisis came to a head, the commissions of Octavian's partisans became ever more provocative. Statilius Taurus celebrated a triumph *ex Africa* in 34 B.C., then began work on a small but apparently the first public stone amphitheater in Rome (dedicated in 29 B.C.). It was located in the Campus Martius, near the Circus Flaminius, and was intended principally for gladiatorial contests and animal games (Dio 51.23.1). Statilius Taurus was an example of a *novus homo* who, by virtue of his service as one of Octavian's generals, was able to amass a huge fortune and become the founder of a noble house.

Another example, indeed the most important, is Marcus Vipsanius Agrippa, who up to the time of his death in 12 B.C. was the number two man in Rome. In the same year that Statilius began the construction of his amphitheater, Agrippa, who had already been consul, rather conspicuously assumed the lower office of aedile and began energetically, as it was even then conceived (Fronto *Aqu.* 98), to rebuild the much neglected infrastructure of Rome.

> Without even touching the state treasury he repaired all the streets and public buildings, cleaned out the sewers and even rode in a boat through the *Cloaca Maxima* to the Tiber. (Dio 49.31)

What an impressive image: generations' worth of garbage was finally gotten rid of. But Agrippa's greatest and longest-lasting achievement was in assuring Rome a steady supply of water. First he repaired all the old aqueducts, then later built several new ones. It was a long-term project, but at least a beginning had been made. People would realize that life would indeed get better thanks to the young Caesar and his associates. While Antony squandered all his wealth in Alexandria, Octavian was at least trying to do something for the people of Rome, even in these difficult times.

But Agrippa did not hesitate either to play the demagogue. He extended the *ludi publici* to fifty-nine days and virtually turned Rome into the Promised Land. Oil and salt were distributed to all, and there was free admission to the baths all year round for both men and women. In the theater tokens were tossed into the crowd which could be exchanged for money or clothing. The best shows were put on in the Circus and everyone was invited. One could even get a shave and charge it to the aedile—Agrippa knew just how to appeal to the people.

In the Circus Maximus he installed a new mechanism on top of tall columns for counting laps in the horse race. It was in the form of shining silver dolphins, a good choice for the victor in the sea battle at Naulochoi. Ceramic workshops immediately responded to the public enthusiasm by producing even humble lamps with an image of the counter and silver dolphin (fig. 56). All this was meant to show people that in spite of all Octavian's harping on *virtus*, life would go on. The plan was a great success: *plausos quos fert Agrippa* (Horace *Satire* 2.2.185).

Fig. 56. Early Imperial clay lamp with representation of Agrippa's "dolphins" in the Circus Maximus.

The Mausoleum of Augustus

Octavian had inherited from Julius Caesar a whole series of building projects either incomplete or not even begun: the Basilica Iulia, the new Curia, a theater, etc. The temple of the Divus Iulius in the Forum was still unfinished, and Octavian himself had vowed a great temple to Mars the Avenger at the Battle of Philippi (42 B.C.). But he took his time with all these and instead concentrated all his energy on the two buildings which were to be the clearest statements of self-glorification, the Temple of Apollo and the Mausoleum (fig. 57).

Why would the thirty-year-old Octavian put up an enormous tomb monument for himself, before he had even won sole power? K. Kraft has explained his decision with reference to Marc Antony's will, which Octavian had illegally made public. In this document, alongside other problematical clauses, Antony expressed the wish to be buried beside Cleopatra in Alexandria, a desire which was fatal to his reputation in Rome. Octavian's followers cited this in their propaganda as proof that Antony had intended to move the capital from Rome to Alexandria and there create a Hellenistic kingdom. "Even his one-time supporters made this accusation against him" (Dio 50.4.2). After the capture of Alexandria, Octavian of course insisted

Fig. 57. Rome, Mausoleum of Augustus. The ruins in their present state, framed by Fascist buildings in the background.

that Cleopatra arrange for the burial of Antony's body. While his rival lay beside the Ptolemaic kings and queens, there rose in Rome the gigantic tomb of the victor.

This interpretation of the Mausoleum as an instance of Octavian's demagoguery is very attractive. The date of the actual start of construction is not really as important as when it was first planned and publicized. Such a monstrosity is best understood in the context of the crisis atmosphere just before Actium and the elation of victory just after. By 28 B.C. the work had progressed to the point where the large adjacent park (*silvae et ambulationes:* Suetonius *Augustus* 100) could be opened to the public. Was the monument then simply an expression of Octavian's loyalty to Rome and Italy? This might indeed explain its original purpose, but the connotations which contemporaries must have seen in the completed structure went much further.

The monument was first of all a demonstration of its patron's great power. The name Mausoleum, which it bore from the beginning, was thus totally justified. The term embodies a sense of marvel at its sheer size, which far overshadowed all earlier such structures in Rome and could only be likened to the tomb of the Carian dynast Mausolus, one of the Seven Wonders of the world. It was bigger even than the tombs of the kings of Numi-

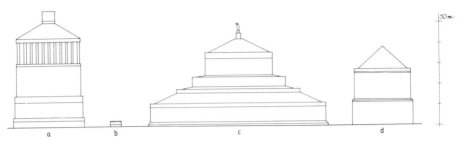

Fig. 58. Schematic comparison by size. *a*) Mausoleum of the Carian dynast Mausolos, Halicarnassus, fourth century B.C. *b*) Public tomb of the consul A. Hirtius (died 43 B.C.). *c*) Mausoleum of Augustus. *d*) Mausoleum of C. Metella (after J. Ganzert).

dia. A comparison with the dimensions of the tomb of Caecilia Metella, let alone the honorary tomb monuments of the consuls Hirtius and Pansa in the Campus Martius (43 B.C.) clearly makes the point (fig. 58). The Mausoleum dominated the natural landscape between the Tiber and the Via Flaminia, in the Hellenistic manner. Its massive dimensions were made even more imposing by the setting in an extensive park, isolated from neighboring construction. Even in its present ruined state, lying well below the modern street level, the nine-meter-high walls of the exterior cylinder make a

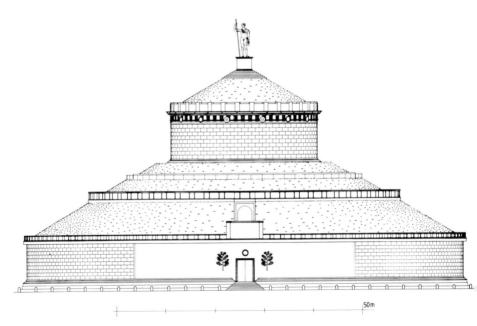

Fig. 59. Rome, Mausoleum of Augustus. Reconstruction by H. von Hesberg.

Fig. 60. Head of a co-
lossal statue of Octa-
vian, with Baroque ad-
ditions to the hair (H:
ca. 1.20 m).

powerful impression (fig. 59). The original structure was eighty-seven meters wide and nearly forty meters high. It consisted of two concentric cylinders, each sheathed in marble or travertine, between which trees were
planted on the sloping terrain. This is Strabo's description, written soon
after its completion:

> Most worth seeing is the so-called Mausoleion, a large mound set upon
> a tall socle by the river. It is planted with evergreen trees up to the top.
> Above stands the bronze statue of the Emperor Augustus. Within the
> mound are the graves intended for him, his relatives, and friends. Behind
> there is a large grove with splendid walks, in the midst of which is
> an elevated place (the *ustrinum*), where Augustus's corpse was burnt.
> (Strabo 5.3.9)

Because of the vegetation, Strabo connected the Mausoleum with the
type of grave mound that his contemporaries would probably associate
with ancient graves of heroes, such as were still visible in the necropoleis of
Etruria. This form was occasionally reproduced by those wanting a tomb
monument in archaizing style. But in such instances, as in the monument of
Caecilia Metella, the tumulus at the top was only one element (cf. fig. 14).
One could also view the two shining white cylinders as simply a monumen-

tal base for the statue of Augustus, whose proportions must have been colossal, to match those of the Mausoleum.

That such colossal statues of Octavian did in fact exist in Rome at this
time is attested by a head about 1.3 meters high, in the Cortile della Pigna
of the Vatican (fig. 60). In spite of the baroque restoration of many locks of
hair, it is clear that the head belongs to Augustus's earliest portrait type (cf.
fig. 33), and the sharp and bony features of the youthful portraits are unmistakable. Since the head must have belonged to another statue, not the
one on the Mausoleum, it is further evidence for the unprecedented claims
Octavian was making for himself at this time.

When the Mausoleum was completed, after the defeat of Antony, it no
doubt gave the impression of a triumphal monument, one erected by the
victor himself. In fact its form does recall that of later *tropaia*, such as the
one at S. Tropez. This aspect was further underscored by the small obelisks
on either side of the entrance, which were probably placed there soon after
the conquest of Egypt. The combination of different messages was not an
uncommon phenomenon in Late Republican tombs, as we have seen in the
case of the Monument of the Julii at Glanum (cf. fig. 15).

The Mausoleum is overwhelming in its sheer size, but the architect did
not succeed in giving it a unified appearance. In the chaotic years before
Actium, when the need to display power was all, no innovative architectural
forms arose to express such claims. The eclectic mixture of elements and
the use of small-scale ornament were not sufficient to articulate the enormous mass in a meaningful way. The mausoleum of Hadrian, by contrast,
using only a few large forms, speaks a clearer architectural language. The
ambiguity of the architectural vocabulary, like that of Augustan portraits,
betrays the absence of a coherent message.

In addition to the popular name Mausoleum, which also occurs in inscriptions, a more official designation was used later on, *tumulus Iuliorum*.
This had an old-fashioned ring, but also, in light of the size of the monument, clearly heralded the dynastic pretensions of the new ruling family.
And every official funeral, starting with that of Marcellus in 23 B.C., repeated that claim. Yet Octavian did not want to come across as a dynast,
especially after his "restoration of the Republic." He simply wanted to
claim that his power was greatest and that he was the only one capable of
returning order to the state. But the pressure of rivalry and the availability
of only foreign and misunderstood architectural forms led here too to
meaningless excess. The adoption of an architecture created for the self-
glorification of kings in the Greek East, just like the borrowing of the nude
honorific statue and the baroque portrait style, was not fully compatible
with what Octavian was trying to express.

But the future Augustus did not suffer from any negative associations.

On the contrary, for the great majority of the by now largely Hellenized populace, who were ready for monarchy (unlike the old aristocracy), it was a most congenial style, even with all its contradictions and formal ambiguities. In any case, between the Mausoleum and the "house" which the young Caesar put up beside the temple of Apollo in the heart of the ancient city of Romulus, he left no doubt as to who would determine Rome's fate from now on. The presence of the Mausoleum, which remained standing long after 27 B.C., should not be forgotten when we try to assess the "Republican style," personal modesty, and *pietas* of the future princeps.

Chapter 3

The Great Turning Point:
Intimations of a New Imperial Style

After the Battle of Actium (31 B.C.) and the capture of Alexandria in the following year, extraordinary honors awaited the victor in both East and West. The days of uncertainty were over, and for the first time all the power in Rome was concentrated in a single individual. There could be no doubt who pulled the strings, to whom one must turn for help, and to whom one had to give thanks.

Glorification and self-glorification proceeded hand in hand. In Rome Octavian's "Diadoch Style" reached its peak. He used the image of Alexander as his seal, and Agrippa planned a Pantheon to house the ruler cult, in which a statue of the *divi filius* would stand beside those of his deified father and his patron gods (Dio 53.27). Senate and people included Octavian in their prayers, immortalized his name in song, and instituted libations to him at all public and private banquets. The huge Mausoleum and the temple of Apollo, the bringer of victory, approached completion.

The Forum as Showplace of the *Gens Iulia*

The transformation of the Forum Romanum is a remarkable example of the way Octavian after his victory automatically took possession of the entire city (fig. 61). In August of 29 B.C. he celebrated a magnificent triple triumph (Illyrium, Egypt, and the Battle of Actium). As part of this triumph he dedicated the Temple of Divus Iulius in the Forum, which had been planned as early as 42 B.C., as well as the new Curia, which had also been long under construction and would henceforth bear the name Iulia. Both buildings were outfitted with "Egyptian" trophies, like victory monuments.

The facade of the Curia is represented on a coin of a well-known series of denarii (fig. 62a). On the apex of the roof is the figure of Victoria, proclaimed even before the battle, carrying a wreath in her right hand and racing over the globe (fig. 62b). The side acroteria seem to have been statues of other divine helpers on the battlefield. On the clearest specimens it is possible to make out an anchor and rudder in their hands. Inside the Curia, however, Octavian set up the original statue of Victory, an Early Hellenistic work which came from Tarentum, and she was regarded as his personal patron goddess. Probably Octavian at first had it mounted on a globe, the symbol of his claim to sole power, but now the goddess was given Egyptian booty (in the form of captured weapons) in her hand and was set atop a pillar at the most conspicuous spot in the council chamber, behind the seats of the consuls. From now on she would be present at every meeting of the Senate.

Captured booty also decorated the Temple of Caesar and the newly erected speaker's platform. In the cella of the temple, the spoils stood beside a famous painting by Apelles, the Venus Anadyomene, a reference to the ancestry of the Julian house. The prows of captured Egyptian ships (*rostra*) were mounted on the facade of the speaker's platform, in front of the

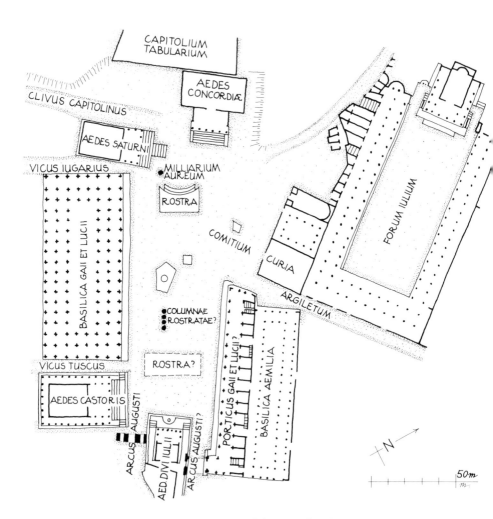

Fig. 61. Forum Romanum, ca. 10 B.C. Schematic drawing.

a   *b*

Fig. 62. Denarii of Octavian. *a*) Curia Iulia. *b*) Victoria flying over the globe, with standards and victory wreath.

temple. The new platform was located exactly opposite the old one, which Caesar had moved to the middle of the west side of the Forum (fig. 61). Thus the prows from the Battle of Actium were unmistakably linked with those from a much earlier victory over the Antiates in 338 B.C. and consciously set up a comparison between a victory in civil war and a historic naval victory of the old Republic. Meanwhile the Senate tried to flatter Octavian by placing the triumphal arch for his victory at Actium (or was it for the earlier Battle of Naulochoi?) right next to the Temple of Caesar, thus underscoring the close association between the victor and the latest addition to the Roman pantheon.

Octavian's equestrian monument of 43 B.C. (cf. fig. 30*a*) and the *columna rostrata* commemorating the victory at Naulochoi already stood near the speaker's platform (cf. fig. 32*b*). Now Octavian set up nearby four bronze columns with ships' prows, cast from the bronze of Egyptian ships' *rostra*. Their original location, in the middle of the Forum, can be inferred from the later removal of the columns to the Capitol by Domitian. They were apparently removed to make way for the colossal equestrian monument of Domitian (Servius *ad Georg.* 3.29).

These monuments set up by or for Octavian transformed the appearance of the Forum. Wherever one looked, there were symbols of victory. In the pediment of the recently completed Temple of Saturn, for example, instead of an image of the ancient god of the sowing season, there were Tritons gaily blowing on trumpets. Triton was widely recognized as one of those marine creatures who had assisted in the victory at Actium, and the temple's patron, Munatius Plancus, thus joined in the universal praise of Octavian.

Later, yet another arch celebrated Augustus's victory over the Parthians; Tiberius had the Temples of Concordia and the Dioscuri rebuilt in marble at great expense; and Augustus himself enlarged the Basilica Iulia, erected

Fig. 63. Marble ship's beak, Triton with conch.

an ornate portico before the Basilica Aemilia, and named both of these after the lately deceased princes Gaius and Lucius. In the end, what had once been the political center of the old Republic became the showplace of the Julii, where the presence of Republican monuments was only incidental. They were, to be sure, reminders of a glorious past, but one now overshadowed by the dazzling splendor of the present.

Allusions to the Victory at Actium

Looking at the wealth of monuments commemorating Actium, one easily forgets how tricky it must have been to celebrate a victory without being allowed ever to refer to the defeated enemy. Antony had been a great figure, he had children who were nephews of the victor and lived in his house, and many of the fallen "enemy" were Roman citizens. Since the image of the enemy himself could not be represented, nor could the victory in Egypt alone suffice to convey Octavian's succession to sole power, artists had to employ more nonspecific and abstract symbols of victory. In this Octavian himself probably led the way, as in the decoration of the Temple of Caesar and the Curia. There was only a small repertoire of simple tokens: ships or parts of ships (*rostra*), marine creatures, dolphins, and the figure of Victoria on the globe, which we have already seen. The advantage of such imagery

Fig. 64. Antefix. Victoria with trophies above the globe, with Capricorns.

Fig. 65. Antefix. Dolphins flanking a trophy, over ship's beak.

was that it could be easily reproduced and could with no difficulty be employed in a variety of settings in conjunction with various other symbols.

Up to this time public monuments in Rome were essentially for local consumption; their political imagery was directed at residents of the capital and had little meaning outside its borders. In principle this changed little under Augustus, but since the whole Empire was now focused on Rome, this simple and easily grasped symbolism could be spread abroad as well. Thus, for example, the bronze ships' prows on Roman victory monuments were copied in marble in other cities, where they could be outfitted with their own individual decoration.

We gain some idea of how this worked from a marble battering ram in Leipzig (fig. 63) which, like many other such monuments, comes from one of the Italian cities outside Rome. Both sides are carved in relief, one with the familiar jolly Triton, the other possibly with Agrippa as admiral, crowned by Victoria. It is unclear whether this was part of a public monument or perhaps an extravagant tomb. In Ostia, for example, *rostra* have been found decorating grave monuments. These could of course attest to the participation of the deceased in the decisive battle, but there is reason to doubt that every grave so decorated contained one of Octavian's veterans.

The spread of the new imagery was by no means confined to political monuments. Tritons and hippocamps, as well as Victoria herself, sometimes

Fig. 66. Ring stone with ship, Capricorn, and *sidus Iulium*.

Fig. 67. Glass paste with portrait of Octavian, rostrum, and dolphin.

turn up as decorative elements in private homes. Even on simple roof tiles, for example, Victoria is linked with Capricorn or with dolphins and *rostra* as symbols of victory (figs. 64, 65). Apparently many private individuals used the new symbols on their seals, judging from the dolphins, ships, and prows that occur, together with the victor's likeness, on stones and glass paste from seal rings (figs. 66, 67).

Over the years the Battle of Actium came to be regarded as a kind of secular miracle, out of which the new rule of Augustus was born. The memory of those dark times that led up to it began to fade. But even right after the event some did not hesitate to compare the victory with that of the Athenians over the Amazons or the Persians. C. Sosius put an Amazonomachy in the pediment of his Temple of Apollo, an original work of the Classical period, and later, in 2 B.C., at the dedication of the Forum of Augustus, the Emperor had the Battle of Salamis re-enacted in an artificially constructed lake (*naumachia,* Cassius Dio 55.10.7). Just as in the heroic victories of Athens, Actium was Augustus's triumph over the so-called eastern barbarian. Poets and artists, whenever they wanted to celebrate subsequent victories or other great events, could always hark back to the victory that created the Principate. In A.D. 26–27, for example, the city Arausio (Orange, in Southern France) put up an unusually elaborate triumphal arch for the Emperor Tiberius, after he had put down a revolt of Gallic tribes. Alongside the *tropaia* with captured Gallic arms and armor the city fathers placed all kinds of ships' parts in large relief panels and Tritons carrying rudders in the pendentives.

These basic symbols for the Battle of Actium are the beginning of a new imperial imagery, whose development and elaboration we shall follow in the next few sections. A particular feature of this symbolism was its simplicity and clarity, especially when we recall the indecipherable imagery of Late Republican coinage. Now all the symbolism pertains to one individual, the Emperor.

A Change of Focus: Self-Glorification
Gives Way to Religious Devotion

After the Battle of Actium was won with the help of Apollo, Octavian might easily have outfitted the sanctuary on the Palatine like a victory monument. Instead, when the official dedication took place on 9 October 28 B.C., the rich decoration of rooms and courtyards was of a very different order. To be sure, the great votive to the Apollo of Actium stood before the temple on a high podium, again decked out with ships' prows (fig. 68), and the carved scenes on the doors of the temple, the slaying of the children of Niobe and the Gauls driven out of Delphi (Propertius 2.31.12–14), portrayed Apollo as the god of vengeance and, in this context, must have been understood as veiled metaphors for the defeat of Antony. But the victor himself was nowhere to be seen. Instead of the powerful and dramatic imagery of Hellenistic kings, symbols of peace and religious devotion filled the sanctuary. Instead of his own triumphal chariot Octavian displayed a marble quadriga with Apollo and Diana, the work of the Classical sculptor Lysias, and in the two great statues of the god, the Apollo of Actium and the cult statue (cf. fig. 186), the god was celebrated not as the avenging archer, but as singer and bringer of peace (Propertius 4.6.69). The Apollo of Actium also held a libation bowl and stood before an altar. This prompted thoughts of guilt

Fig. 68. Denarius of C. Antistius Vetus, Rome, 16 B.C. The statue of Apollo Actius on a tall base decorated with *rostra*.

Fig. 69. Modern impression from a mold for Arretine bowl, ca. 25 B.C. Two winged genii pay homage to a tripod with music; on either side, large candelabra.

and expiation, just as did the Danaid monument, with its many figures, described by Propertius. The misdeeds of the civil wars were to be redeemed through sacrifice and religious piety and Apollo won over as guarantor of the new spirit of peace. Octavian himself, whose proud victory monuments dominated the Forum, would set the example:

> The statues of myself in the city, whether standing or on horseback or in a quadriga, numbering eighty in all and all of silver, I had removed, and from this money I dedicated golden offerings in the Temple of Apollo, in my own name and in the names of those who had honored me with these statues. (*Res Gestae* 24)

From Suetonius we learn that the golden offerings were in the form of tripods (*Augustus* 52). These must have been very large and ornate, an impressive visual testimony to the piety of the dedicator. The spectacular gesture of melting down so much sculpture was, incidentally, a convenient opportunity for Octavian to get rid of some statues of himself spouting self-assured gestures which did not fit in with his gradually evolving new style and image. Reflections of the golden tripods on the Palatine can be found in wall painting (cf. fig. 209), architectural terra-cottas (cf. fig. 193), and on Arretine bowls of this period (fig. 69).

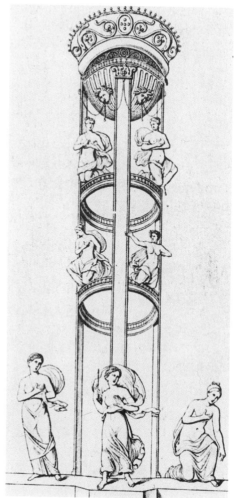

Fig. 70. Photograph (left) and drawing (right) of a Pompeiian wall painting. The picture gives some idea of the monumental golden tripods dedicated by Octavian in the Temple of Apollo. The slaughter of the sons and daughters of Niobe is rendered as a paradigm of Apollo's punishment of man's hybris.

On a fragment of contemporary wall painting we see two tripods, on whose handles the dying Niobids are depicted (fig. 70). Reliefs show the blinding of Polyphemus between the legs of another tripod. Such mythological scenes, like those on the temple doors, can be read as similes for Octavian's defeated enemies. But elsewhere, figures of Victory and other imagery, especially the vegetal ornament, suggest that this major dedication was interwoven with other iconographic symbols of thanksgiving and hope.

The best example of this is the representation of tripods on the marble door frames of the Temple of Apollo, an actual fragment of which has been found in excavation. To the left and right of the door, a seemingly endless spiral of vines grows out of each tripod, which were in turn flanked by Apollo's griffin and the avenging goddess Nemesis, and they meet over the center of the door. The significance of the vine is clearly brought out by its shape, the setting, and the association with the tripods. A conventional decorative element had been turned into a symbol of happiness and the bless-

Fig. 71. Aureus. Candelabra surrounded by offering bowls and bucrania, 17 B.C., minted on the occasion of the Secular Games.

Fig. 72. Rome, Temple of Apollo *in circo*, 30–25 B.C. On the frieze, candelabra, laurel branches, and bucrania.

ings of peace. We shall have more to say of this imagery in connection with the spread of the Golden Age motif.

In the meantime, the design of this door frame clearly illustrates how the tripod had become a wide-ranging symbol, not only for the worship of Apollo, but for piety in general and for the hope that a new era had begun. The prominence and place of honor given this motif on early Augustan Arretine pottery attests to its rapid spread and enthusiastic reception.

The tripod was not the only symbol whose popularity was inspired, or at least encouraged, by the decorative program of the sanctuary of Apollo. The bronze candelabra, which could be used as incense burners, appear on coins (fig. 71), and soon hundreds of copies were produced in marble, sometimes embellished with Apollonian or other newly popular themes. In the decoration of C. Sosius's Temple of Apollo, the candelabrum was combined with laurel as symbols of the god's worship (fig. 72). Eventually it too became a generalized symbol of *pietas,* which one might even, for example, have placed on an ash urn, as a sign that one had led a god-fearing life.

Another symbol of Apollo is the so-called baitylos, an archaic cult object. On a fine architectural terra-cotta found in the sanctuary of Apollo it is decorated with highly stylized temple maidens holding fillets and other attributes of Apollo (fig. 73). It is probable that large-scale versions of such an object also stood in the sanctuary itself; one such, in marble and several meters tall, may even be the so-called Meta now in the Villa Albani.

The decoration of the new Temple of Apollo would, however, have attracted most attention, from the more educated visitor at least (Propertius 2.31), on account of the wealth of famous works of Archaic and Classical Greek art on display there, proclaiming a new cultural agenda and new standards in art. The tokens of piety and optimism were linked to the acknowledged moral superiority of Greek art of the Archaic and Classical periods. The style of Greek art of the best period was meant to heighten the sacred aura of the neighboring images. The combination of Classical style and thoroughly Greek subject matter made the entire decorative program into an homage to Greek culture. Soon it would become apparent that it was a part of the new emperor's cultural program not only to imitate the best the Greeks had to offer, but to create something that would be the equal of Classical culture.

Res Publica Restituta

Once the brilliant triumphal celebrations of 29 B.C. were over, Octavian was confronted with a completely changed situation. He had all the power,

Fig. 73. Terra-cotta relief plaque. Cult image decorated with Apollo's lyre and Diana's quiver and adorned by priestesses with fillets. From the sanctuary of Apollo on the Palatine.

and everyone looked to him expectantly to see what would happen next. On the arch put up by the Senate for the victor in the civil war stood the legend "res publica restituta." Octavian had saved the Republic from destruction, but now it was up to him to "restore" it. No one sizing up the situation could realistically have expected the victor to return all the power to the Senate, but he would at least have to find ways to make monarchy acceptable to old noble families.

It was an unstable peace, based at first not on general consensus, but on brute force. Of the enemy sympathizers, those members of the old ruling class mostly remained skeptical and bided their time, while even Octavian's friends were hardly optimistic. For years he would be faced with the danger of revolution. On some occasions he would wear armor in the Senate house, beneath his toga; the specter of Caesar's death was always before him. The populace sensed this insecurity, that peace did indeed depend on Octavian's staying alive. For this very reason they tried to force him into taking on the role of monarch. But his new style of leadership was directed rather at the old aristocracy, whose cooperation he most needed. He had to show them that things would be different, that he could bring a true peace. The melting down of those overbearing statues was the first indication of a change in his view of himself. Now it remained to be seen whether he would live up to the promises repeatedly made before Actium and return the Republic to its traditional legal foundation after fourteen years of anarchy. In 28 b.c. Octavian canceled all the illegal measures of the past several years, though this probably had little real effect, and at that famous meeting of the Senate in the following year he did officially return control of the state to the Senate and people.

> Since that time, while I have exceeded all others in respect and influence (*auctoritas*), I have possessed no more power (*potestas*) than any of those who were my colleagues in any office. (*Res Gestae* 34)

We know well, of course, that this sentence, drawn from the political autobiography of the aged ruler, is really a half truth. In fact, by means of a complicated system of prolonged extraordinary powers, special privileges, and long-term offices, and especially thanks to his huge personal fortune, the savior and restorer of the Republic was able to keep firm control of the army and thus of all the power. A coin minted more than ten years later makes quite explicit the relationship of savior and Republic (fig. 74): the *res publica*, represented in the scheme usual for a conquered province, kneels

Fig. 74. Aureus of C. Lentulus, Rome 12 b.c. Augustus helps the fallen *res publica* to her feet.

before Augustus, and he helps her to her feet. The savior stands beside the restored Republic, which is in need of his leadership. Most people will have felt the same way back in 27 B.C., but the act of relinquishing power was a great gesture which allowed the aristocracy to save face and in future to be partners in the new state.

> For this service [the "restoration"] I was named *Augustus* by resolution of the Senate. The doorposts of my house were officially decked out with young laurel trees, the *corona civica* (an oak wreath) was placed over the door, and in the Curia Iulia was displayed the golden shield (*clipeus virtutis*), which the Senate and the people granted me on account of my bravery, clemency, justice, and piety (*virtus, clementia, iustitia, pietas*), as is inscribed on the shield itself. (*Res Gestae* 34)

The laurel trees, the *corona civica*, and the *clipeus virtutis* were modest and simple honors in the old Roman tradition. They suited the new image of the honorand, who was now quite restrained and conceived his relationship with the Senate as that of princeps ("first among equals"), and behaved accordingly. But a major difference in the new "Principate Style" was that after 27 B.C. the impetus for honoring the ruler always came from others— the Senate, the cities, local societies, or private individuals. The princeps himself had suddenly become quite modest and eschewed such self-promotion as the Mausoleum embodied. The honors voted by the Senate were particularly well-chosen—no doubt in consultation with the honorand himself. For those familiar with Roman tradition, such honors suggested many associations with the spirit of the old Republic, while their lack of specificity also admitted a very different interpretation.

Laurel wreaths and branches had always crowned victors and were the

Fig. 75. *a*) Aureus of Caninius Gallus, Rome, 12 B.C. Young laurel trees beside the House of Augustus; above, the *corona civica*. *b–c*) Aurei, Spain and Gaul, both 19/18 B.C. The *clipeus virtutis* between laurel trees.

Fig. 76. Aurei. *a*) Spain, 19/18 B.C. *b*) Ephesus, 27 B.C. Jupiter's eagle with the *corona civica*; behind, small laurel trees. *c*) Rome, 19/18 B.C. Augustus wearing the oak wreath, awarded him *ob cives servatos*.

attribute of Victory herself, but the laurel is also Apollo's tree. The positioning of the two laurel trees on either side of the entrance to Augustus's house will have had a special association for the contemporary viewer (fig. 75*a*). Since Archaic times such pairs of trees had flanked the headquarters of the oldest priesthoods, at the Regia, the Temple of Vesta, and the seat of the *flamines* and *pontifices*. Thus the laurel trees conferred on the entry to Augustus's house a sacred aura and invoked the powers of primordial religion.

The *corona civica* was rooted rather in the military sphere. The oak wreath had traditionally been awarded for rescuing a comrade in battle. The restorer of the Republic was now awarded it "ob cives servatos," i.e., for rescuing all his fellow citizens (fig. 76*a*). But the oak wreath has other associations too, since it comes from the tree sacred to Jupiter. In fact, in this same year coins were minted in Asia Minor in honor of the new Augustus, with Jupiter's eagle holding the *corona civica* in its claws (fig 76*b*). This impressive image had of course been created in Rome, where it first appears on a magnificent cameo (fig. 77). This kind of elaboration of a symbol which was originally intended as a modest honor in the spirit of early Rome soon transformed its connotations. The simple honors granted Augustus in 27 B.C. were thus turned into tokens of monarchical rule through their use in combination with other symbols, in particular in the decoration of temples for the ruler cult. The tendency to treat Augustus as a monarch came naturally, and everyone was well prepared. Only ten years later mint officials, who had a pretty free hand in choosing coin types, were depicting the likeness of Augustus crowned with the *corona civica*, like the royal diadems of Hellenistic kings (fig. 76*c*). By the addition of gems and fillets the simple wreath was turned into a kind of crown. As early as 13 B.C. a coin portrait places the *corona civica* above the head of Augustus's daughter Julia, as a token of dynastic succession (cf. fig. 167*b*). For Augustus's suc-

Fig. 77. Eagle cameo, after 27 B.C. The Eagle of Jupiter carries the palm of victory and the *corona civica*.

cessors the oak wreath became an insigne of power, completely removed from its original meaning.

Again, laurel tree and oak wreath were honors voted Augustus, not symbols which he promoted to glorify himself. And it was as tokens of honor and devotion that they were soon employed in every imaginable place, in the most varied forms, including simple leaf patterns instead of tree or wreath. These pointy, sharp-edged leaves, so ideally suited to ornamental fantasies, sprouted all over the place—from coins and architectural decoration to small painted panels with bucolic scenes. The artists and their patrons always managed to allude to the special meaning of these leaf patterns, either by enlarging them or placing them prominently. So, for example, an altar of the Lares from Rome has an ornamental band composed of acorns (fig. 78), and on the frieze of Sosius's Temple of Apollo the laurel stands out, spreading between candelabra and bucrania (cf. fig. 72). Thus laurel and oak leaves became widely understood as synonymns for "Augustus" and gradually lost their original meaning.

Fig. 78. Frieze with conspicuously prominent acorns. Detail from an altar of the Lares.

The *clipeus virtutis* (honorific shield) was also exploited by devotees of Augustus and became something of a mystic symbol. This type of shield, with noble qualities and achievements recorded on it, had been a popular form of honor in the Hellenistic world. But since the honorand was now in fact also the ruler, those qualities singled out for praise came to define what the Senate expected in a virtuous ruler and how that ruler defined himself.

A marble copy found in Arles (fig. 79)—there must have been copies like this one displayed in many cities—preserves the text: (*clupeus*) *virtutis L. clementiae, iustitiae pietatisque erga deos patriamque.* Military excellence (*virtus*) and justice (*iustitia*) are of course attributes of the noble ruler. *Cle-*

Fig. 79. Marble copy of the bronze *clipeus virtutis* from Arles. 26 B.C. (one year after the official conferral). Similar copies were probably set up in most Roman cities in honor of Augustus.

Fig. 80. Denarius and aurei with representations of the *clipeus virtutis*. Spain, 19/
18 B.C. *a*) CL(ipeus) V(irtutis). *b*) Held by Victoria, the column recalls the display
in the Curia. *c*) Between the standards recaptured from the Parthians: *signis re-
ceptis.*

mentia, i.e., sparing the defeated enemy, had already been Julius Caesar's
great motto. In the circumstances after Actium it naturally became a very
real issue, especially since the memory of Octavian's ruthless treatment of
his earlier enemies still lingered. But it was *pietas,* as we shall see, that
became the focal point of the new emperor's cultural and political program.
In the phrase "toward gods and fatherland," the Senate also intended a
reference, of course, to the respect that it sought for the traditions of the old
Republic.

Fig. 81. Sardonyx. Augustus in a
chariot drawn by Tritons. The
sea creatures hold rudders; Victoria with oak wreath and *clipeus
virtutis* with Capricorns and
globe.

Fig. 82. Agate intaglio. Octavian in a chariot drawn by hippocamps. In the waves, the head of an enemy, either Sextus Pompey or Antony.

The original golden *clipeus virtutis* was displayed in the Curia, thus associated quite intentionally with the Victoria of the hero of Actium. The result was that in the future the shield was almost always combined with the goddess of victory and became a symbol of perpetual and god-given right to rule (fig. 80*b, c*). On an Augustan monument now known only in later derivatives, Venus herself, the ancestress of Augustus, records on the shield his virtues.

Such combinations of symbols indeed prove to be a fundamental characteristic of the new pictorial language. The honorary tokens voted Augustus in 27 B.C. are combined in every imaginable way, not only with one another but with earlier or more recent symbols of victory or salvation. In the process, the actual sequence of historical events becomes incidental, compared with the vision of a necessary and predestined result. A small cameo in Vienna, for example, unites all three of the honorary tokens with the imagery of Actium (fig. 81). The victor rides majestically over the waves in a car drawn by sea centaurs, his helpers in the naval battle. But these jolly creatures hold aloft, like trophies, the tokens associated with the restoration of the Republic. They are mounted on globes, like imperial insignia: Victoria with the *corona civica* on one side, the *clipeus virtutis* framed by oak wreaths and born by Capricorns on the other. The direct association is clear: without Actium there could be no restoration.

Only a few years earlier the victor of Actium had been very differently portrayed, on a cameo now in Boston (fig. 82). Nude and carrying a trident, he is likened to Neptune as he charges past an enemy sinking beneath the waves. On the later cameo, the pathos of dramatic movement has been replaced by a virtually heraldic composition, the victor seen *en face*. He is presented not as a god, but as a Roman *triumphator*, wearing a toga and holding out a laurel wreath, his virtues and service to the state displayed by means of the symbolic tokens. Augustus's new image required a new pictorial style. But there was no attempt to disguise the monarchy; rather, the hieratic style reflects the new imperial mold.

The Title "Augustus": A New Image

While the full potential and manifold nuances of these tokens of honor were only gradually revealed, the real significance of Augustus's greatest honor, the conferral of his new title, was clear from the start. The young Octavian had once thought of having himself called Romulus, but by 27 B.C. this would not have suited his new image, since it smacked of kingship. *Augustus* was an adjective with a broad range of meanings, including "stately," "dignified," and "holy." It could also be connected with the verb *augere* ("increase"). After all, had he not made the Empire grow? Alternatively, it could recall the *augur*, the priest who interprets omens. The first time he had taken the auspices as general, he had evoked comparisons with Romulus, an occasion later alluded to in the pediment of the Temple of Mars Ultor (cf. fig. 150). As an honorific title, Augustus was a brilliant choice, for, even as he officially relinquished power, it surrounded him with a special aura, "as if the name alone had already conferred divinity upon him" (Florus 2.34.66). The Senate also wanted to rename the month Sextilis and call it "Augustus," an honor which he did eventually accept. His title was thus immortalized in the Roman calendar.

A new portrait of Caesar Augustus (as he was now commonly known) must have been created at about this time (fig. 83), to take the place of the emotional youthful portrait type (cf. fig. 33). The new likeness was unlike anything to be found in Late Republican portraiture. It expresses Augustus's new image of himself, how he imagined himself as "Augustus," and how he identified himself with the new title. Whoever commissioned the individual honorary statues employing this portrait type, the original must have been designed with Augustus's approval, or even at his own instance. It is equally obvious that the chosen sculptor, like a kind of court artist, was working from a set of prerequisites dictating style and overall conception.

In place of the bony and irregular features of Octavian's portraiture, the new type is marked by a harmony of proportions, inspired by the Classical canon. The animated and severe qualities of the earlier type, and its arrogance, are completely done away with. The face is now characterized by a calm, elevated expression, and the spontaneous turn of the head in the youthful portrait has given way to a timeless and remote dignity. Instead of the tousled hair over the forehead, each lock has been carefully arranged

Fig. 83. Augustus. After an original of the year 27 B.C. Head of the cuirassed statue, figure 148a.

Fig. 84. Partial copy after the Doryphorus of Polyclitus. Bronze herm from the Villa dei Papiri.

according to Classical principles of symmetry, as in the work of Polyclitus (fig. 84). The new portrait is a completely intellectual and artificial work of art, composed of Classical forms subtly mixed with just a few authentic physiognomic traits. The youthfulness of Octavian is transformed into an ageless "classical" beauty.

The portrait enjoyed enormous success. It was reproduced in every part of the Empire and fixed the visual image of Augustus for all time, although it had little to do with his actual appearance. Seen as a reflection of the man's own self-image, it suggests a rather lofty claim. For in this period the Classical forms, especially in Polyclitan sculpture, represented the highest achievement in the rendering of the human figure, the embodiment of perfection and nobility (cf. p. 248). Quintilian calls Polyclitus's Doryphorus *gravis et sanctus*, full of dignity and holiness. This accorded perfectly with the connotations of Augustus's new title. The new portrait type is indeed the visual equivalent of the title "Augustus" and exploits all the best possible associations of the name. Augustus's extraordinary position in the Roman state is here defined in art. The image is far more candid than what

Augustus says in the *Res Gestae* and gives a clear idea of what he meant by the simple and old-fashioned term *auctoritas*. We are dealing here with a ruler portrait, but of a novel type, whose language only the more cultivated would have grasped. But even the ordinary citizen would have inferred such concepts as beautiful, ageless, thoughtful, and remote.

The tokens of honor from 27 B.C. and the new portrait type illustrate how a new set of imagery arose to meet the needs of changed circumstances after Augustus had won sole power and "restored the Republic." A subtle web of associations replaced the mindless self-glorification of the earlier rivals for power. The princeps of course determined the themes and general tenor of this imagery, and in fact his political style was in some respects no less important than what he actually did. The "rescued" citizenry responded to him with all manner of honors, whether as individuals or through their various organizations and chosen representatives. These honors might be either simple traditional tokens, in accord with the changed political situation, or ones uniquely suited to the princeps, such as the title Augustus. The honorand himself was utterly restrained, but of course did not do anything to prevent this general outpouring of honors. He was able to identify fully with the imagery created by others to glorify him, including the new portrait, and let others propagate the image. The "restoration of the Republic" was not simply a sham intended to fool the Roman public, as is often maintained. Even before 27 B.C. it was clear that Augustus's new political style did not represent a departure from the sense of mission that had always motivated him. It was simply that as sole ruler he conceived of his role somewhat differently from before.

But we have gotten a little ahead of ourselves. The enthusiastic reception given the new symbols of victory, of the worship of Apollo, and of the restoration of the state were rooted in a general feeling of approval for the new regime. This was, however, not something that could be taken for granted after the defeat of Antony, at least not in Rome. It had to be earned.

Chapter 4

The Augustan Program of Cultural Renewal

The mood in Rome, even in the first years after Actium, remained pessimistic, especially among the upper class. They were not hopeful for the future, primarily because they saw the civil war and all the other calamities as a consequence of a complete moral collapse. Apparently they had internalized all the political sloganeering to this effect that they had been hearing for years. Even Livy, who was so enthusiastic about the new regime, takes a rather dim view of the present at the start of his history: "... up to our own time, when we can no longer tolerate either our own ills or the cure for them [. . . *donec ad haec tempora, quibus nec vitia nostra nec remedia pati possumus, perventum est*]."

But at the same time there were also hopes of a utopian sort. Sibyls, prophets, and politicians had all promised a new age of peace and prosperity. As often in times of transition, grave doubts and wild optimism existed side by side. The new princeps was confronted simultaneously with deep mistrust and high expectations. He had to demonstrate that he was concerned not simply with securing his own power, but with actually rebuilding the state and Roman society. He needed to create the impression that he was in a position to address the real causes of the ills that plagued Rome. Then he had to show proof.

At the same time as his "restoration of the Republic" and the creation of his new political style, Augustus also set in motion a program to "heal" Roman society. The principal themes were renewal of religion and custom, *virtus*, and the honor of the Roman people. Never before had a new ruler implemented such a far-reaching cultural program, so effectively embodied in visual imagery; and it has seldom happened since. A completely new pictorial vocabulary was created in the course of the next twenty years. This meant a change not only in political imagery in the narrow sense, but in the whole outward appearance of the city of Rome, in interior decoration and furniture, even in clothing. It is astonishing how every kind of visual communication came to reflect the new order, how every theme and slogan became interwoven. Again, however, there was no master plan outlining some sort of a propaganda campaign for the revival of Rome. As in the development of imagery after Actium, much happened as if of its own accord, once the princeps had shown the way and taken the first steps.

Augustus did not need to formulate a new program himself; it had already been done for him. For generations the ills of state and society had been proclaimed, described, and lamented as incurable evils. The surprising thing, for many people virtually a miracle, was that the new ruler actually took the lament seriously and decided to do something about it. He was utterly irrepressible as he set about addressing, in terms of concrete policies, all the problems that he had himself decried back in the 30s B.C., immediately creating the foundation on which he would build his programs. In the next sections we shall observe the remarkable confidence—one might almost say naiveté—with which he went about building on that framework, step by step, going through the whole catalog of ills left over from the Late Republic, until in 17 B.C. he could sail the rebuilt ship of state into a safe harbor called the Golden Age.

It started with the program of religious revival in 29 B.C. There followed efforts toward *publica magnificentia* and the restoration of Roman *virtus* in the Parthian campaign of 20 B.C. Two years later, in 18, with the Romans' confidence in their ability to rule an empire now bolstered, a legally imposed moral renewal was required. This completed the internal overhaul of Rome, and nothing now stood in the way of the new Golden Age. Nothing could be simpler!

At first, of course, each of these points in the Augustan program amounted to little more than one of the old slogans. They were statements of intention, which then had to be realized in action and in architecture and the visual arts. The princeps would need the help and cooperation of many. Since no written source gives us a picture of how the complex machinery of this cultural program actually worked, we must try to infer from the results themselves an idea of the collaboration and the mutual influence on one another of princeps, political cronies, creative poets, architects, and artistic ateliers.

PIETAS

Pietas was more than just one of the virtues of the princeps recorded on the honorary shield. It was to become one of the most important leitmotifs of the Augustan era. Ever since Cato the Elder, the dissolution of tradition and of the state, the self-destructiveness that threatened to destroy Rome, had all been ascribed to a neglect of the gods. "You will remain sullied with the guilt of your fathers, Roman, until you have rebuilt the temples and restored all the ruined sanctuaries with their dark images of the gods, befouled with smoke" (Horace *Carmen* 3.6).

In this regard the "savior" had to lead the way, and he acted swiftly and decisively. As early as 29 B.C. a program of religious rebuilding was proclaimed. Octavian had himself commissioned by the Senate to bring the old priesthoods up to their full complement. Cults, many of which existed in name only, were newly constituted, with statues, rituals, priestly garb, and chants all revived or, if need be, recreated in archaic style. From now on all religious texts would be followed to the letter. A year later came the dedication of the Temple of Apollo and, with it, the beginning of the great program to rebuild the ruined temples. "During my sixth consulate, by order of the Senate I restored 82 temples of the gods in Rome and did not omit a single one which was at that time in need of renewal" (*Res Gestae* 20).

The necessity for such measures had long been recognized. The identity crisis of the Late Republic is nowhere so clearly expressed as in its interest in traditional religion. The best example is the polymath and writer M. Terentius Varro (116–27 B.C.; praetor in 68 B.C.), who composed a sixteen-volume work, *Antiquitates rerum divinarum,* in which he gathered all that was then still known of the ancient cults and tried to reconstruct what had already been utterly forgotten. Augustus's program of restoration could not have been carried out so extensively without Varro's work. He undertook his research with patriotic zeal and great enthusiasm. In a fragment quoted by Augustine in the *City of God,* Varro says he

feared that the gods would be driven out, not by enemy attack but by the indifference of the Roman people. He would save them from destruction with his books and preserve them in the memory of good men. This he considered more worthy than Metellus's rescuing of the *sanctissima* from the Temple of Vesta or Aeneas's saving the Penates in the sack of Troy.

These were images of great emotional power, which had a profound impact on Augustus. Varro had dedicated his work to Julius Caesar, in the hope that it would spur him on to action. But no matter how vigorously the idea of religious revival may have been discussed in those years—one thinks of all the temples planned in the 30s B.C.—a systematic program was only possible in the changed circumstances after Actium.

In 32 B.C. the impulse for temple building still had to come from outside. In that year Atticus, the cultivated and wealthy friend of Cicero and father-in-law of Agrippa, had inspired Octavian to rebuild the Temple of Jupiter Feretrius, arguing that then the *dux Italiae* could liken himself to the heroic founder of Rome. Clearly Octavian liked this sort of display. For his declaration of war on Antony and Cleopatra he went to the Circus Flaminius, dressed in the traditional garb of the *fetialis,* to cast the ritual wooden lance into the symbolic enemy territory and utter a magic formula. This kind of performance was at first probably off-putting or was interpreted by the more educated as an affected archaism. But soon such gestures multiplied: in 29 B.C., as a symbol of peace, the doors of the Temple of Janus were solemnly closed, an archaic ritual which no one in Rome had ever seen before; the old *augurium salutatis* was restored and consecrated to the healing of the state; and in the next year the actual restoration of "all" the old temples was ostentatiously begun. By now no one could doubt that Augustus was serious about this return to the old gods. He was evidently determined that, with himself as "founder and restorer of all sanctuaries" (Livy 4.20.7), "the temples would no longer show signs of age" (Ovid *Fasti* 2.61).

Aurea Templa

Such an extensive program demanded careful planning and organization. This began with the apportioning of the various building activities, which would in the future be more strictly separated into sacred and secular. Even the residence of the ruler did not take precedence over the building of sanctuaries, which Augustus considered his most important mission. Among Agrippa's many building projects, by contrast, there are no temples, apart from one special case, the Pantheon, intended for the ruler cult. Tiberius,

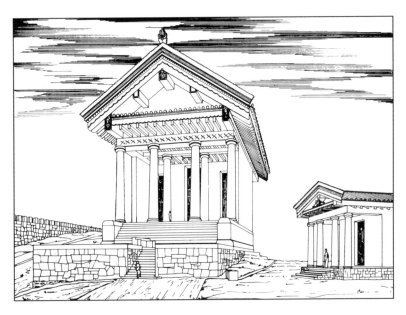

Fig. 85. Cosa, Capitolium, third to second century B.C. The old-fashioned temples, with their wooden roofs and terra-cotta sculpture were in striking contrast to the new marble temples.

Fig. 86. Sacrificial scene in front of the Temple of Mars Ultor. Relief from an altar of Claudian date similar to the Ara Pacis (cf. fig. 126).

however, as designated successor of Augustus, could rebuild in marble two hallowed old temples in the Forum, those of the Dioscuri and Concordia, and officially dedicate them in A.D. 6 and 10, respectively (cf. fig. 62).

"Nothing is too good for the gods" was now the slogan. The gleaming white temple facades, built of marble from the new quarries near Luni (Carrara), with their dazzling ornament, sometimes of real gold, became hallmarks of the new age. The best architects and artists of the East flocked to Rome, drawn by the prospect of large and lucrative commissions.

The chief among these will no doubt have received explicit directives concerning the purpose of these projects and the basic concept of the program for religious renewal. There would be no more temples built in the old style, out of tufa, with heavy wooden roofs and terra-cotta decoration (fig. 85). Instead, the idea was to imitate the finest and most impressive elements of Greek temples, even to surpass them, but also to combine them with certain traditional elements of the Italic/Roman temple: the high podium, deep pronaos, and the steeply sloping, exuberantly decorated pediment.

The temple facades depicted on the reliefs of the so-called Ara Pietatis (fig. 86) give us a better idea than the actual remains of the original effect of

Fig. 87. Rome, Temple of Mars Ultor. Marble steps with built-in altar (only the core preserved).

these marble temples, which were designed specifically to set off the impressive facade. A steep, free-standing staircase, often with the altar incorporated in it, was placed in front of the podium (fig. 87). The altar thus seemed to form part of the facade, and the facade itself could serve as a backdrop for rituals at the altar. Behind rises a dense row of extremely tall columns, almost always in the Corinthian order. This type of capital (fig. 88) was no doubt chosen for its highly elaborate quality, and as a result, the other orders soon disappeared from religious architecture. Not only are the column capitals richly decorated, but also the bases, cornices, simas, and friezes. Then came the extravagant sculptural decoration, in the pediments, along the staircase, and for the acroteria. The tendency toward excessive ornamentation, which in the 30s had been the result of competition among patrons, was now simply a form of serving the gods, of living up to the motto "nothing is too good for the gods."

The skillful mixture of such varied architectural elements presupposes that it had all been well thought out in advance. In particular, the magnificent facades suggest that the religious revival, as the pious princeps conceived it, was nothing like that envisioned by the antiquarian Varro. These

Fig. 88. Rome, Forum of Augustus. Capitals with entablature. Before 2 B.C.

marble temples were not simply a stately setting for newly revived rituals, but were in themselves an expression of the new mood of self-confidence. The worship of the gods and *publica magnificentia* could go hand in hand.

All this had to be made clear to the leading artists of the day, so that their artistic talents could be properly channeled. There had to be on-going discussion, a continuous give-and-take of ideas from all sides. Perhaps the few top artists and architects had access to those elite circles, the sort we hear about from the poets, which would meet at the house of a Maecenas and sometimes even had direct access to the princeps. Certainly there was a commission to oversee each of the major projects and issue guidelines. Since the artistic and the poetic expressions which grew out of certain key events, like the victory over the Parthians or the Secular Games, share to a great extent the same themes and slogans, we must assume that leading artists very quickly got wind of the new imagery formulated by the poets. In this whole process, however, the role of the visual artist was somewhat different from that of the poet. While the latter was essentially free to express his praise for the ruler and his deeds in any way he liked—or not at all, as, for example, in the case of Tibullus's elegies—the architects, sculptors' workshops, and those in charge of staging festivals and religious rituals were all directly answerable to their patrons. It was their job to fulfill someone else's desires, not their own. In this sense, the concept of the artist making "art for art's sake" was unknown in antiquity.

In the case of the renewal and new construction of temples, the princeps himself set the guidelines by determining the location and the level of expenditure for raw materials and building costs. In principle all the old temples were to be restored, but in practice the expenditure allotted for the worship of each divinity varied considerably. The most lavish structures were not those in the oldest sanctuaries or for the principal gods of the old Republic, but rather for those most closely associated with Augustus: Apollo on the Palatine and Mars Ultor in the new Forum of Augustus. These new temples could even rival that of Jupiter Capitolinus, thanks to their surrounding porticoes and ancillary buildings, their rich decoration and votive offerings, and not least the rituals and state ceremonies for which they provided the setting. Despite the ostentatious dedications with which Augustus constantly honored Jupiter, the god was supposed to have complained that his worshippers were being diminished (Suetonius *Augustus* 91.2). And in fact under Augustus he was no longer the chief focal point of the state religion. He lost the Sybilline books to the Palatine Apollo (17 or 12 B.C.), and the ceremonies before and after a military campaign were transferred to Mars Ultor, whose temple became the center for the staging of activities relating to war and peace (p. 113). But the Temples of Venus, Apollo and Mars were not the only ones directly linked with the princeps. The cult of Jupiter on the Capitol, with its new temple, was also brought into close association with him.

In the campaign against the Cantabri, Augustus had been miraculously spared when a lightning bolt grazed him and struck the slave lighting the way for him. Was this not a sign that he was the chosen of Jupiter, on intimate terms with the thundering sky god? Immediately he built an exquisite small marble temple to Jupiter Tonans, right in the vicinity of the great Temple of Jupiter, and called attention to it by his frequent visits. On a series of coins issued after the "victory over the Parthians," the hexastyle temple appears, its cult statue a Zeus by the Late Classical sculptor Leochares (fig. 89*a*), significantly associated with Mars, the recaptured standards, and the honorary tokens of 27 B.C. (fig. 89*b*).

The rebuilding of temples for the old state gods, such as Castor and Pollux or Concordia, required no less an expenditure, but in these and other instances the location and sometimes even the plan were fixed by the dictates of *religio,* now so strictly observed. This meant severe restrictions in the overall plan, no matter how lavish the individual elements. Much further down the scale were the eighty-two temples and shrines of the old gods which had been restored in 28 B.C. They were for the most part only

a   *b*

Fig. 89. Denarii, Spain, 19/18 B.C. *a*) Temple of Jupiter Tonans on the Capitol. A statue of Zeus by the Classical sculptor Leochares served as the cult image. *b*) Small round temple of Mars Ultor on the Capitol. Mars holds the *signa* returned by the Parthians. Cf. fig. 148*b*.

spruced up, and the tufa columns got a new coating of stucco, but the old-fashioned wooden roofs and terra-cotta roof tiles were retained. This of course made painfully obvious their status vis-à-vis the new marble buildings for the gods of the imperial house.

The princeps had no use for the Oriental and Egyptian gods which were at this time extremely popular in Rome, especially Isis. She was not included in the official calendar of the state religion, and periodically her cult was even banned. For Augustus, as he proceeded to expand and reshape the traditional Roman religion and associate the venerable cults with himself and his house, the Oriental cults presented a problem. These ecstatic cults promising salvation appealed to people as private individuals, not as Roman citizens, and were thus incompatible with the principles of the Roman state religion. The new regime, just as had the Senate much earlier, saw in these cults a danger of alienation, the dissolution of society, and the creation of secret sects. An exception was made only for those foreign cults that had long been rooted in Rome and thanks to their services to the state had been accepted into the state religion. But here again the hierarchy was clear.

The Temple of Magna Mater (Cybele) on the Palatine, which had been erected in 205 B.C. in response to a command from the Sybilline Books, burned down in A.D. 3. Even though the poets emphasized Magna Mater's position as a state divinity, her link with the ancient Trojans, and her role as protectress of cities and city walls, Augustus did not rebuild the temple, which lay near his house, in marble, but only in tufa (peperino) and relegated the exotic cult, with its ecstatic dances and long-haired priests (*galli*), to freedmen. Apparently Augustus had not actually repaired all the old temples in 28 B.C., as he claims in the *Res Gestae*. Some projects were more pressing than others. Among the less pressing was, significantly, the popular

Temple of the Dionysiac Triad (Liber [Bacchus], Libera, and Ceres) on the Aventine, which was suddenly destroyed by fire in the year after the Battle of Actium. It was not rededicated until A.D. 17, under the Emperor Tiberius (Dio 50.10; Tacitus *Annals* 2.49).

The varying levels of expenditure in the building of so many temples created in the popular mind a vivid impression of the different status of each divinity. The dominant ones were clearly those to which Augustus felt closest.

The grandeur of each temple corresponded with that of the divinity (Ovid *Fasti* 5.553). But the multiplicity of small Archaic cults which now sprang up with renewed attention between the great sanctuaries were clear testimony that this religious revival was closely bound to the traditions of the old Republic. The new *pietas* was the equivalent of the primitive religiosity of early times, but of course on a much grander scale.

> "Simplicitas rudis ante fuit nunc aurea Roma est
> et domiti magnas possidet orbis opes"
> [There was a rude simplicity before, now Rome has turned to gold,
> For she possesses the great treasures of a conquered world.]
> Ovid *Ars Amatoria* 3.113f.

A New Kind of Imagery

The vast program of temple building, carried out over a period of forty years, created for the leading artists and architects problems of organization and execution on a scale which the Greco-Roman world had only rarely witnessed before, as for example in the great building program of the kings of Pergamum. The wealth of architectural decoration required by those who handed out the commissions, the sometimes great expanses that had to be decorated within a limited space of time, demanded not only a coherent overall plan, but the creation of carefully thought-out decorative schemes. How, for example, could the long porticoes of the sanctuaries of Apollo and Mars be filled with the kind of meaningful and didactic ornamentation that the princeps required, at least for the buildings he personally commissioned? How would the many temple facades be decorated, so as to bring out equally their ancient traditions and their relevance to the present? How should the temple cella and interior rooms and the cult statue be thematically linked with the rest of the decorative program? The occasion for the new temple, the relation of other divinities to the one worshiped there, and the association of all of them to the restored Republic and of course the princeps himself—all this had to be taken into consideration.

Fig. 90. Sestercius, Rome, A.D. 36.
Temple of Concordia in the Forum
Romanum. The new temples were
adorned with many programmati-
cally arranged sculptures.

The Temple of Concordia, as it appears on a coin (fig. 90), gives a good
idea of the web of imagery in the facade of a typical Augustan temple.
Above the central axis of the pediment stood three closely overlapping figures, probably Concordia with two divinities linked with her in meaning
and in cult, such as Pax and Salus or Securitas and Fortuna. The motif of
the three divinities embracing was of course a meaningful symbol. The side
acroteria, figures carrying armor and trophies, made the connection with
the patron and his triumph, which was the occasion for the new temple. In
addition there would have been the pedimental sculpture, not shown on the
coin but no doubt containing a carefully chosen grouping of divinities, as
illustrated by the pediment of the Temple of Mars Ultor (cf. fig. 150). Even
on the staircases there were two suggestive figures, Hercules and Mercury.
The former stood for the security, the latter for the prosperity that the new
regime, symbolized by Concordia, had brought.

But in this whole process the artists had very little freedom of choice. As
we shall see, relatively few mythological figures and stories fitted into the
new official mythology of the state. In addition, the princeps's modesty and
the simplified tokens of honor set further limits. Furthermore, an artistic
vocabulary was imposed on them that would be quiet and static, at the beginning at least restricted to Archaic and Classical styles (cf. p. 239). Many
areas of traditional ruler iconography were apparently off-limits, because
they were considered to be in the "Asiatic" style. Augustan art has virtually
no battle scenes or glorification of the ruler in the form of animated, heavily
populated narrative scenes. Compared with the extraordinary possibilities
open, for example, to the designer of the Pergamum Altar, Augustan artists
had extremely narrow scope within which they could create new imagery.
What they *could* do was to combine the various symbols or deliberately

Fig. 91. So-called Ara Grimani. Augustan decorative base with Dionysiac motifs. The extensive and carefully worked ornament is characteristic.

exaggerate them, invent noble personifications and outfit them with appropriate attributes, and design sacred memorials and divine statuary in archaistic or classicistic style. The only aspect of a public building in the design of which they had a free hand was the decorative ornament. The
richness of the ornament they evolved had never been seen before and was
not constrained by any traditional canon. This was true not only for the
ornamental borders of architectural members (cf. fig. 203), but for every
part of the figural decoration. For example, the bases of statues and votive
dedications overflow with virtual cascades of decorative bands (fig. 91).

In these new sanctuaries the viewer was confronted with something he
had never experienced. Never before had he encountered such an extensive,
fully integrated set of images. Through didactic arrangements and constant
repetition and combination of the limited number of new symbols, along
with the dramatic highlighting of facades, statues, and paintings, even the
uneducated viewer was indoctrinated in the new visual program. The key

messages were quite simple, and they were reiterated on every possible occasion, from festivals of the gods to the theater, in both words and pictures. Even the rich decorative program of the Forum of Augustus was built around very few images (fig. 92; cf. fig. 149).

Ovid's description provides a synopsis and selection of images which conveys some idea of the effect they would have had on the average visitor.

> Mighty is Mars and mighty his temple. He could not reside in the city of his son Romulus in any other way. The building itself would have been a worthy monument to the victory of the gods over the Giants. Mars [Gradivus] may unleash savage war from here, when an evil-doer in the East incites us or one in the West tries to bend us to his yoke [a reference to the state ceremonies that took place in the Forum at the *profectio* of a general]. Mars strong in armor looks upon the temple pediment and rejoices that unvanquished gods occupy the places of honor [cf. fig. 150]. At the entranceways he sees arms of all sorts from all the lands conquered by his soldier [Augustus]. On one side he sees Aeneas with his precious burden and about him the many ancestors of the Julian house; on the other, Romulus, son of Ilia, with the arms of the enemy chief he conquered with his own hand and statues of distinguished Romans with the names of their great deeds. He gazes upon the temple and reads the name Augustus. Then the monument seems to him even greater. (*Fasti* 5.533 ff.)

Fig. 92. Rome, Forum of Augustus. Reconstruction drawing (cf. fig. 166).

The text shows how intimately architecture and imagery were linked to corresponding ceremonies, while particular images were linked to widespread expectations and slogans. No matter how multifaceted and complex the individual symbols, or how elitist the archaizing or classicizing style of the images, the message was comprehensible to all. That the monumental devotion of the ruler was in the end seen as a sign of his own greatness is not just Ovid's panegyric of the princeps.

Festival and Ritual

This account of the Temple of Mars Ultor is equally applicable to all Augustan temples. These were no mute stones, but monuments that came alive in the festivals connected with them, especially on the *dies natales*. Increasingly, these festivals to celebrate an *ex-voto* or the foundation of a sanctuary were made to fall on commemorative days for the princeps or to coincide with important events in the life of his family. New sanctuaries were dedicated only on festival days of the imperial house and gradually many of the old foundation days were moved onto these as well. On the basis of marble calendar inscriptions found in various Italian cities and from the *Fasti* of Ovid we can ascertain a fairly full picture of the schedule of festivals in a typical year during the early Empire, both in Rome and in the western provinces. It was filled with memorial days and festivals of supplication and thanksgiving for the imperial house. The days of Augustus's personal celebrations were particularly crowded with feasts of the gods; on his birthday, for example, there were no fewer than seven. Several feast days clustered around a major one and were turned into holidays by the addition of theatrical and circus games. For the contemporary Roman each year unfolded in a continuously repeating pattern of religious/dynastic festivals filled with spectacle. On every feast day rituals took place, in which priests and sacrificial animals moved in procession to the appropriate temple.

Artistic depictions of such events had always emphasized the prescribed number, type, and appearance of the sacrificial animals (cf. fig. 10*a*). On one of the reliefs of the so-called Ara Pietatis, the splendid bull is being readied for sacrifice (cf. fig. 86). And on one of the silver bowls from Boscoreale we see an attendant (*popa*) delivering a mighty coup-de-grace (fig. 93). The new iconography conveys the dramatic experience of the ritual slaughter, which was able to unleash powerful emotional forces every time. Artists heightened the effect by representing the moment of the final blow and by pushing this scene into the foreground of an image. The imagined temple facade set immediately adjacent to the ritual scene thus takes on a deeper symbolic meaning and is spotlighted by the accomplishment of the

Fig. 93. Silver cup (scyphus), Late Augustan. Sacrificial scene at the departure of Tiberius (cf. fig. 181). From Boscoreale, near Pompeii.

sacrifice. The close association of ritual with its architectural setting created the indispensable prerequisite for the *aurea templa* to achieve their full effect.

This was also true of the interior rooms of temples, which were lavishly decorated in the most expensive materials (fig. 94). Because of the valuable dedications displayed here, these rooms were usually closed off. But on *dies natales* and on days of especially important sacrifices (*supplicationes*) the temple doors were wide open, sometimes even in every sanctuary in the city. The cult statue could then be glimpsed through the open doors (cf. fig. 90). Upon entering, the visitor was immediately surrounded by a plethora of images, not only the cult statue, but the precious votives and souvenirs filled with historical associations. The Temple of Concord, for example, housed a whole collection of sculpture which Tiberius had put together. The recovered battle standards once lost by Crassus to the Parthians were set up in the Temple of Mars, next to colossal statues of the gods in the apse. Because the temples were open so rarely, curiosity to see what was inside was naturally all the more intense.

In an earlier age, before the superabundance of new imagery, religious rituals were real experiences. Special occasions, such as the celebrations in connection with the initiation of the *saeculum aureum* in 17 B.C., when the princeps himself uttered magic formulas and carried out arcane rituals, were remembered and retold for years. Otherwise the mint masters would not have put such scenes on the coins they issued (cf. fig. 134). Since ritual and sacrifice played such a central role in everyday life, it is not surprising that this type of imagery gradually came to dominate the new pictorial vocabulary. There is hardly a single monument or building that does not include in its decorative scheme the skulls of sacrificial animals, offering bowls, priestly tokens, or garlands wound with fillets, even when the structure itself is purely secular. These images recalling sacrifice, which had in

Fig. 94. Rome, Apollo Temple of C. Sosius. Reconstruction of the lavish interior architecture.

Fig. 95. Metope with bucranium, from the Porticus Gai et Luci Caesaris (?) in the Forum Romanum. Symbols of *pietas* in suggestive arrangements were now ubiquitous.

the past served merely as conventional ornament, now became meaningful symbols. Artists were at pains to intensify their effect even further by expressing them in new ways.

This is particularly evident with bucrania. Previously the whole animal's head was usually depicted, while now artists show only the much more suggestive pale bones of the ox skull. So, for example, in the antechamber of the Basilica Iulia (perhaps known as the Porticus Gaii et Luci Caesaris) the bucrania are remarkable for their subtly layered arrangements of bones, clever ornamentation, and the dark hollows of the eye sockets. An oversized fillet emphasizes the religious character (fig. 95).

On the interior of the Ara Pacis, a sacred precinct is suggested by a construction of planks and scaffold (fig. 96). But the illusion of reality is then transformed into fantasy, to the point where the symbolic bucrania seem to hover in midair, although they carry heavy garlands. These bucrania are also associated with the idea of sacrifice through the addition of fillets and emblematic libation bowls. As elsewhere, the garlands here take on their own particular significance. The many different fruits express thanks to the god and at the same time convey the notion of blessings and abundance.

Fig. 96. Rome, Ara Pacis Augustae, 13–9 B.C. Interior side of the marble altar enclosure, with garlands, bucrania, fillets, and phialae (cf. fig. 126).

The particular trees and plants sacred to each of the gods were continually incorporated into this imagery, whether playfully or reverentially. An example are the branches of white poplar on a base of superb quality (possibly for a statue) from a small sanctuary of Heracles. Here too the bucranium appears significantly in the middle of the picture, like a divine epiphany (fig. 97).

The effectiveness of such symbols of piety derived from their infinite repetition and from the close association of image and ritual experience. What seems to us now merely ornamental or decorative was then something new and exciting in the emotional mood of the "new age."

The Chief Priesthoods

The priesthoods founded or reorganized by Augustus starting in 29 B.C. naturally played an important part in all festivals and sacrifices to the gods. Priests wore traditional garb, and each could be recognized by his special attribute: the leather cap with metal point (*apex*) and long-haired woolen cloak for the *flamines* (fig. 98), or the cloak with bared shoulder for the *XV viri sacris faciundis,* who were principally responsible for the cult of Apollo

Fig. 97. Marble statue base from a small sanctuary of Hercules on the Tiber, Augustan. Rome, Museum delle Terme. Foliage and animals' skulls evoke a sacrificial ritual.

(fig. 99). It seems, however, to judge from the few extant representations, that the dress of important priests was subject to only modest archaism in the religious revival, likewise the detailed regulations governing their behavior. These were sufficient to reflect the high antiquity of the priesthoods, without becoming too burdensome for the priest himself (cf. Tacitus *Annals* 4.16). Still, the old ritual dances had to be performed, the ancient songs, now largely incomprehensible, still sung.

We are most fully informed about the rites of the Arval Brethren. This priesthood, revived by Augustus and once restricted to patrician families, was originally concerned with the worship of the simple fertility goddess called Dea Dia. Now the Brethren reenacted primitive ceremonies a few times a year, by distributing fruit and grain at a public feast, uttering solemn formulas, and assembling in a sacred grove of the goddess far outside the city. But their primary activity consisted of prayers and sacrifices on behalf of the imperial family. At all gatherings a specific protocol was observed, which governed with strictest precision even the most routine aspects of the ritual. According to ancient belief, this insured the religious validity of the proceedings, while at the same time it showed that prayers on behalf of the emperor were bound up with the most ancient traditions. On certain

Fig. 98. Rome, Ara Pacis Augustae. Chief priesthood of *flamines*. Detail from the processional frieze on the south side (cf. fig. 100).

occasions the Arval Brethren apparently wore simple wreaths of grain, a reference to the fertility of the fields, for which these aristocrats prayed. But when Augustus himself was represented wearing this wreath, his contemporaries will have been reminded rather of his efforts to insure the grain supply in Rome. Thus it made sense that the prayers of the Arval Brethren were primarily for his benefit.

Membership in a given priesthood was alotted to a specific social class, in accordance with the ranking of each *collegium*. The highest priesthoods and fraternities were naturally reserved for the upper class, particularly for patricians. (The emperor could, however, elevate men of his choice to patrician status.) Since the total membership of the highest priesthoods was far smaller than the number of seats in the Senate, holding one or more priesthoods was a sign of extremely high status. Some felt driven to suicide when they were removed from one of these coveted priesthoods. The frequent public appearances of the priests and the special privileges attached to their office, such as places of honor in the theater, were constant reminders to the general public of their status in society.

We must bear all this in mind when studying the Ara Pacis Augustae, which was erected by the Senate from 13 to 9 B.C., in honor of Augustus's safe return from campaigns in Gaul and Spain. A solemn procession is depicted on two long relief panels on the exterior of the marble structure enclosing the altar (fig. 100*a, b*). Two-thirds of these scenes are occupied by members of the four principal colleges of priests (*pontifices, augures, XV viri sacris faciundis, VII viri epulonum*) and the four chief priests (*flamines*). At first glance these figures seem scarcely distinguished from the dense rows of others. But while most of the participants in the sacrificial procession are merely wreathed, the priests, like the two *togati* on the north side, have their togas pulled up over their heads, signifying that they will actually perform the sacrifice. On careful examination we notice that most of the lictors stand beside Augustus and that the procession is gathering about him, his companions forming a kind of circle around him. Is he starting the sacrifice?

It was typical of the innovations brought about by Augustan state religion that the annual sacrifice to the Pax Augusta at the Ara Pacis was entrusted not to a single college, but to officials of all the major priesthoods, including the Vestal Virgins (*Res Gestae* 12). Previously the individual priesthoods had performed only those functions specifically assigned to them, sometimes in so doing also enjoying considerable political influence (especially through the interpretation of omens and consultation of the Sibylline Books in critical situations). Under Augustus, however, the various colleges acted more often in conjunction, creating an impressive outward appearance but obscuring the fact that their common responsibilities now consisted only in prayers and otherwise allowed them hardly any influence. Bad omens were eliminated, the purified Sibylline Books remained well hidden beneath the cult statue of Palatine Apollo, and before military campaigns the princeps himself took the (always positive) auspices (fig. 101). In his hand was the augur's staff (*lituus*), which he may also have carried on the Ara Pacis, simply as a sign of priestly office, marking him as a kind of mediator between men and gods (cf. fig. 182).

The veiled heads of the officiating priests on the Ara Pacis show that the ceremonies have already begun. A woman in the foreground gives the command for silence. The dense rows of figures all similarly veiled in their togas give the impression of unity and uniformity. The sculptural style and composition, inspired by Classical reliefs, elevates the scene beyond the historical occasion into a timeless sphere. Not all the figures depicted were actually in Rome on the day of the dedication. The Senate, which commissioned the monument, was concerned not that every figure be recognizable, but with the correct grouping of each of the priesthoods. Significantly, only the most important men have portrait features, while the rest have idealized faces that conceal their individual identity. The figure embodies the office, not the man who happened to hold it at the time. Self-glorification and rivalry between office holders have given way to the common cause. In the service of

a

Fig. 99. Augustan tripod-base. *a*) *Quindecemvir sacris faciundis* at a sacrifice, framed by young laurel trees. In the narrow interstices, plantlike candelabra associated with the motif of drinking birds. *b*) Apolline tripod with raven and vines. *c*) Wreath of grain with eagle. On the base, sphinxes.

the newly revived *pietas* all problems of status and power disappear. The historical moment becomes emblematic of an eternal order.

On both sides of the altar enclosure the procession of priests is followed by the family of the princeps, also wreathed and carrying laurel branches. The safety of the state did indeed depend on them: "that the house which insures peace may last forever," was the priests' prayer (Ovid *Fasti* 1.719). The women wear simple garments, sometimes draped in the manner of Classical statues. In their midst appears Drusus, distinguished by his general's garb, then on campaign in the North. And of course children occupy the foreground, the promise of the future, clinging to their parents. The seemingly casual arrangement of figures actually conceals a significant ordering.

b   *c*

Children and parents belonging to the imperial family, as far as we can identify them, are disposed according to their proximity to the throne (cf. figs. 169, 170).

The sacrificial procession on the Ara Pacis is a carefully planned, idealized reflection of the renewed Republic, designed not by order of Augustus himself, it is important to remember, but of the Senate, to honor itself and the state. In essence we are seeing here the newly constituted leading aristocracy of Rome as it wished to be represented and as it wished, at least outwardly, to be closely identified with the new order. To what extent this spectacle suppresses certain things or passes over others in silence, to what extent the artificialities of the style betray a deeper deception; in short, how much of this ideal vision consists of wishful thinking—all this is another matter. But even if the image presented here seems to us to go far beyond political realities, to Augustus's contemporaries it would not have seemed so far removed from reality. For they had experienced many such ritual processions and over the years had come to realize that power and public office, the Senate, or even military conquest were not what mattered most, but the worship of the gods and the well-being of the imperial house.

The same notion lies behind a relief frieze with still-life that must come from a public building at or near the Porticus Octaviae (fig. 102a, b). In place of the members of the highest priesthoods, as on the Ara Pacis, here only their attributes and implements refer to them symbolically: the *lituus* (curved staff) of the augurs, the *apex* (headgear) of the *flamines,* the *acerra* (incense box) and libation jug with laurel branches of the *XV viri sacris faciundis,* the *simpuvium* (ladle) of the *pontifices,* the *patera* (offering

a

Priesthoods and Social Status

The princeps offered himself as the most impressive paradigm of piety. He was a member of the four most important colleges of priests and was *de facto* chief priest long before he was able officially to assume the office of *pontifex maximus*. Coins celebrate this role (fig. 103*a*), and Augustus himself described it thus: "I was *pontifex maximus, augur,* belonged to the

b

Fig. 102. *a*) Part of a frieze (?), probably from the Porticus Octaviae. Sacral objects between bucrania with fillets. *b*) Detail. Anchor, ship's bow with *rostra*, rudder. The mixture of sacrificial implements and arms alludes to the association of *religio* with victory.

colleges of the *XV viri sacris faciundis* and the *VII viri epulonum*, was an Arval Brother, *sodalis Titius*, and *fetialis*" (*Res Gestae* 67). Certainly from the time of the Secular Games in 17 B.C., and probably much earlier, in the 20s, the princeps must have made it known that henceforth he preferred that statues put up in his honor show him togate at sacrifice or prayer. His piety was put on display for every Roman to see, making it clear that he considered the performance of his religious duties his greatest responsibility and highest honor. It is astonishing how many portraits of Augustus made during his lifetime, both on coins (fig. 103*b, c*) and as honorific statues, show him veiled in a toga (fig. 104). Many such statues were even exhibited in Greece and Asia Minor, where this type of ruler portrait was surely quite alien. The pious princeps got what he wanted or, looking at it from the position of the dedicators, many eagerly seized the opportunity to honor him in this modest form. This new type of honorary statue was a brilliant choice. It obviated entirely the delicate question of Augustus's political power and the problem of its visual expression. It was the most striking

a   b   c

Fig. 103. *a*) Denarius of C. Antistius Vetus, Rome, 16 B.C. The sacred utensils designate the four major priesthoods to which Augustus belonged. *b–c*) Denarius of C. Marsius, Rome, 13 B.C. Portrait of Augustus with *lituus*. Augustus with veiled head and *simpuvium*.

Fig. 105. Statue of a *luper-cus*. These priests conducted an archaic ritual clad only in a short skirt and holding a whip made of goat's hide.

Lares on the Velia as a model and probably then encouraged the introduction of new cults of the Lares at the central crossroads of the new *vici*. But the actual construction was undertaken by the inhabitants of each district, particularly by the four *magistri* and four *ministri* who were each elected to a one-year term.

The extraordinary achievements of some of the *magistri* of individual *compita* in this regard are illustrated by the lavishly decorated marble fragments of a building found in 1932 during construction of the Via dei Fori Imperiali (fig. 106). Built in 5 B.C. as the *Compitum Acili,* as the magistrates who dedicated it proudly refer to themselves, the sanctuary has a dedicatory inscription on which Augustus is named as consul. On the architrave the *magistri* proudly record their sponsorship of the building (fig. 107).

In the years just after the founding of these small sanctuaries the *magistri*

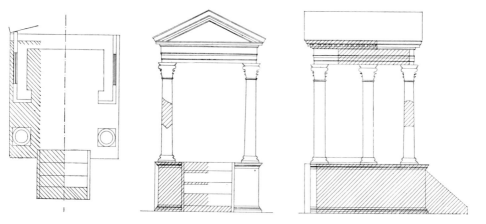

Fig. 106. Compitum Acili. Example of a shrine of the Lares. Reconstruction of the small aedicula.

seem often to have endowed altars as well and to have used the occasion to include pious images of themselves performing sacrifice. On the Lares altar of the Vicus Aescletus (A.D. 2), now in the Conservatory Palace, the four *magistri* are represented on the most prominent side, at the moment of sacrifice (fig. 108). To the accompaniment of flute players they pour their libations simultaneously over the altar. Bull and boar stand ready for sacrifice, made absurdly small by the sculptor to emphasize the *magistri*. A lictor alludes to the pseudomagisterial rank of these local *magistri*. At cultic ceremonies they were entitled to be attended by one lictor; consuls were accompanied by twelve, the praetors by six.

Worthy slaves also served at the same shrines as *ministri*. They too won thereby the status of holding public office within the community of their local district, and could show off their status on such occasions as public processions on imperial feast days (fig. 110). They too dedicated offerings and altars in their capacity as public officials. On one such altar are depicted three *ministri*, modest in scale and wearing slave dress (a shirtlike garment), receiving reverentially the statuettes of two Lares from the hands of a much larger togate figure (fig. 109).

Probably the togatus is none other than Augustus himself, accompanied by the two princes Gaius and Lucius. The fact that the two Lares alone are depicted, but not the Genius of Augustus, also supports this interpretation, since Augustus could not be handing over the statue of his own Genius.

Thus even slaves could contribute to the *pietas* of the new age, and even their humble dress received official recognition in the service of the gods. Augustus's relations with his fellow Romans revolved to a great extent around this exemplary and didactic *pietas*, as is most evident in the worship

Fig. 110. Excerpt from a large sacrificial procession. *Ministri* of a sanctuary of the Lares carry the statuettes of both Lares and of the *genius Augusti*. Early Imperial.

statue or a votive statue in the little sanctuary, and the *magistri* or *ministri* respond with the dedication of a votive altar or yet another statue of a god or goddess. The latter is frequently a personification of political signifi-cance, such as Concordia, Pax, or Securitas. Inevitably these are combined with the epithet *Augustus* or *Augusta,* as an explicit way of honoring the princeps. We have, for example, no fewer than three dedicatory statues—to Venus Augusta (fig. 112), Mercurius Augustus, and Hercules—erected by one N. Lucius Hermeros Aequitas, during his several terms as *magister* of a sanctuary of the Lares. This religious give-and-take created a direct link between ruler and *plebs,* one in which the more ambitious of the lower classes, even slaves, could participate.

In earlier times the district and guild cults had sometimes degenerated into unruly mobs. As late as 22 B.C. Augustus had issued a ban on them, but by 7 B.C. the reconstituted religious associations had become the focal point of communication, along lines of cult, between the ruler and his people. The cults of the compital, at the busiest intersections and squares of the various districts, became the centers of social activity for the local pop-

Fig. 111. Votive altar from the sanctuary of a *collegium* of woodworkers. Augustus hands over a statue of Minerva to the *magistri* of the *collegium*.

ulation. The effectiveness of the new visual imagery found its principal outlet here in the many rituals and public festivals.

PUBLICA MAGNIFICENTIA

> But I observed that you cared not only about the common life of all men, and the constitution of the state, but also about the provision[3] of suitable public buildings; so that the state was not only made greater through you by its new provinces, but the majesty of the empire also was expressed through the eminent dignity of its public buildings. . . .
>
> Since, then, I was indebted to you for such benefits that to the end of life I had no fear of poverty, I set about the composition of this work for you. For I perceived that you have built, and are now building, on a large scale. Furthermore, with respect to the future, you have such regard to public and private buildings, that they will correspond to the grandeur of our history, and will be a memorial to future ages.
>
> Vitruvius *On Architecture*

"The Roman people hate private luxury, but love richness and splendor in their public buildings (*publica magnificentia*)." This is how Cicero once

Fig. 112.   Base from a votive of the *magister* N. Lucius Hermeros to Venus Augusta (cf. figs. 99, 220*b*).

described an ideal of the old Roman way of life, but in his own time exactly the reverse obtained, the state projecting an image of impoverishment, while private wealth was all too ostentatiously displayed (cf. pp. 15ff.). Fierce criticism of Late Republican society was further sharpened by emotional sloganeering. Clearly the princeps would have to take a stand. It was obvious that in the "restored Republic" the mansions with enormous atria and extensive *horti* (i.e., gardens—an archaizing and euphemistic name for the luxurious villas on the outskirts of the city) still dotted the hillsides of Rome. Only the names of their owners had changed, to those of Augustus's principal supporters, who amassed vast fortunes in his service and lived like princes in Rome, their wives decked out in millions of sesterces worth of jewelry. A major change in the distribution of wealth was unthinkable, but the princeps could put up splendid recreational buildings for the Roman people and at the same time make statements as to the immorality of *privata luxuria*. The tentative sumptuary legislation, with which he tried to curb the extravagance of banquets and even women's clothing, naturally had no real effect, but only served to improve his image. Yet certain other actions and types of visual symbolism in the city of Rome do seem to have had a profound impact.

The Princeps Sets an Example

In the year 15 B.C. Vedius Pollio, a man from a family of freedmen who was later promoted to equestrian status, died and, as was a common practice, bequeathed to Augustus a portion of his vast estate (including his mansion in Rome), with the wish that he use it to erect a splendid building for the people of Rome. Vedius had served Augustus well as financial adviser in the economic reorganization of Asia Minor, but in ethical matters he had a dubious reputation. It was even rumored that he punished slaves by feeding them to his man-eating pet fish. His city mansion, in the crowded *Subura* (Esquiline), described by Ovid as "larger than many a small city," was a conspicuous example of private *luxuria*. Here was a perfect opportunity for a significant and visible gesture. The entire palace was leveled to the ground then "returned to the people," and in 7 B.C. Livia and Tiberius built on the site the spectacular Porticus Liviae. Even the onerous association with Vedius Pollio would be consigned to oblivion. "Thus is the office of censor carried out, thus are *exempla* created," commented Ovid (*Fasti* 6.642). Not far from the new porticus were the extensive Gardens of Maecenas, whose exquisite refinement and taste for luxury no longer suited the princeps's new image. The contrast helped heighten the effectiveness of Augustus's gesture.

The Porticus Liviae is represented on a fragment of the Forma Urbis, the marble plan of Rome from the time of the emperor Septimius Severus (fig. 113). The huge structure, measuring about 115 by 75 meters, lay in the midst of a warren of irregular streets in the old quarter. Here we can gain a clear impression of the size and conspicuous location of Vedius's palace, how recklessly he built over the old streets, even setting one corner of it on a main thoroughfare.

The Porticus Livia occupies the entire site of Vedius's palace, but the imperial architect did not interfere with the existing network of streets. The district retained its old character, and the ostentation of *publica magnificentia* was here limited to the building itself.

Augustus's reuse of the four columns from the atrium of M. Aemilius Scaurus's luxurious palace was a gesture of a different sort, but no less effective. The columns, unusually large and expensive, had been brought from Greece for Scaurus when he was aedile in 58 B.C. Together with other works of art they once filled the *scaenae frons* in his famous wooden theater, as advertisements for his reelection campaign, though later he had them incorporated into his private palace. Again the princeps had part of the palace torn down and returned the offending columns to the Roman people by setting them up in the central arch of the *scaenae frons* in the Theater of Marcellus (cf. fig. 154), where they were both impressive and a constant reminder to the people of Augustus's benefaction.

Fig. 113. Rome, Porticus Liviae. Ground plan, on fragments of the Forma Urbis (third century A.D.). This huge structure arose on the site of the palace of Vedius Pollio, torn down by Augustus, in the midst of the mazelike ancient city.

The Porticus Liviae must have been a most welcome landmark for the residents of the Subura, who could leave behind their dark houses and the chaos of the narrow little alleys to enjoy the glorious colonnades, filled with works of art, the light and fresh air, fountains and grape arbors. Other such complexes had always been in the Campus Martius, near the Circus Flaminius, but now the imperial house had made the pleasures of the aristocracy available to the common man. Like all earlier porticoes this one was also a reflection of the patron, but the style of this one had a new element, exemplary and didactic. In this otherwise secular structure Livia dedicated a sanctuary of Concordia, deliberately initiated on the feast day of the mother goddess Mater Matuta (June 11). Unlike in her cult in the Forum, Concordia was to be worshipped here as a goddess of family happiness, and the imperial family as the model of marital harmony. In later years young married couples would make an offering before a statue group of the emperor and his wife in the guise of Mars and Venus (cf. fig. 154).

Agrippa's Building Program: A Villa for the Masses

Augustus beautified the city, whose appearance had in no way reflected its greatness and glory and was besides constantly plagued by floods and fires, and so utterly remade it, that he could justly boast that he found Rome a city of brick and left it a city of marble. (Suetonius *Augustus* 28)

Along with the new temples, it was primarily the buildings for entertainment and recreation that transformed the face of Rome. But whereas Augustus personally took charge of building the sanctuaries, for secular projects he let himself be assisted by both family members and by friends, among whom the most important was Agrippa. In his unwavering loyalty Agrippa was again ready to be Augustus's right-hand man. He dedicated both his organizational talent and his huge fortune to the rebuilding of the city. In the years after Actium he fulfilled, one by one, all the extravagant promises made in 33 B.C. His first project was the complete reorganization of the water supply. Soon fresh water flowed into the city in abundance through repaired or newly built aqueducts, into 130 reservoirs and hundreds of water basins (*lacus*; according to Pliny 700 new ones were built). The mighty arches of the aqueducts helped shape the image of the city and, together with the hundreds of new fountains, proclaimed the blessings of fresh water to every dank corner of the metropolis.

The new Aqua Virgo, dedicated in 19 B.C., fed the baths built by Agrippa on the west side of the Campus Martius, near the Pantheon, the first public baths in Rome (fig. 114). Compared with those of later imperial baths, the sauna rooms and warm-water baths here look rather modest. With its extensive gardens, artificial lake (Stagnum Agrippae) serving as a *natatio,* and athletic facilities, the whole complex recalls the gymnasia of Greek cities. This was deliberate, even if the name itself was not borrowed, as is apparent from the Apoxyomenos of Lysippus (Pliny *N.H.* 34.62), which Agrippa set

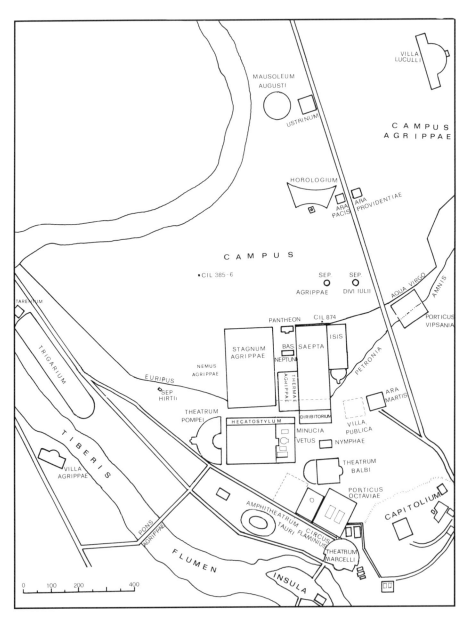

Fig. 114. Rome, Campus Martius at the time of Augustus.

up in the main building. In the creation of the new Rome, one more important gap had been filled.

The baths lay in the middle of the *monumenta Agrippae*. To the east were the Saepta Julia, to the north the Pantheon. Further east, beyond the Via Lata (the present-day Via del Corso), lay the Campus Agrippae, a park renowned for its beautiful laurel trees, and the Porticus Vipsaniae, named for Agrippa's sister. To the west was Agrippa's villa, together with race courses and a training ground for the horses. There was plenty of room for all this on Agrippa's personal property—most of which had previously belonged to Marc Antony and, before that, to Pompey.

The huge recreational area before the walls served as a kind of villa for the common people. At any rate, they could enjoy here all the pleasures traditionally associated with aristocratic villas: parks, promenades alongside flowing streams (*euripus*), warm baths, exercise areas, and, scattered throughout, masterpieces of Greek art. Agrippa decorated his springs and fountain houses with Greek columns and statues, including the famous "Hydria" in the Forum (Pliny 36.121). This accorded with his programmatic address of 33 B.C. "on the need to display publicly all Greek statues and works of art." Pliny, who knew the speech, called it "magnificent and worthy of the finest citizen," clearly contrasting its vision with the *exilia* of works of art in the villas of the rich that had been the rule up to then (Pliny 35.26). The term *exilia* (exile) had often been employed in attacks on the Late Republican aristocracy, and the princeps and his friends were conspicuous in their opposition to it. There was of course no question of a systematic appropriation of art works in private hands; only a few significant gestures needed to be made. It was not so important that more art actually be made available to the public than ever before, but only that this seem to be a matter of policy. The "policy" apparently worked, for the people really did feel as if they owned these great works. This was made clear in the (successful) outcry of the *plebs* when Tiberius tried to move the Apoxyomenos of Lysippus into his own palace (Pliny 34.62).

The centerpiece of Agrippa's building program, the predecessor of the Hadrianic Pantheon, was another reminder of the ruler even here in this recreational area. Originally a statue of Augustus was meant to be displayed among those of his patron deities in the temple cella, for in keeping with Hellenistic tradition the Pantheon was conceived for the cult of the ruler and his gods. But after the constitutional watershed of 27 B.C. Augustus required a change of plan to accord with his new image. His statue could not stand beside the gods, but would have to be moved into the pronaos, alongside that of Agrippa himself. But in the end this gesture did not alter the purpose of the building. The pediment was probably decorated, like that of the later Pantheon, with Jupiter's eagle holding the *corona civica* (cf. fig. 77).

The building which underwent the greatest expansion in Rome was the Saepta, a voting place for the *plebs* which had been planned already by Julius Caesar and was carried out by Agrippa along with his other projects (fig. 114). The actual voting area was now paved in marble and was framed by two marble colonnades 300 meters long and a 95-meter-wide building for the tallying of the votes (*diribitorium*). In 26 B.C. Agrippa dedicated the building as the "Saepta Iulia."

The structure became a vast monument to the dignity of the Roman people, although in fact they were summoned to the balloting urns increasingly seldom and soon not at all. Indeed, the Saepta was later used as a setting for games (gladiatorial combats and mock sea battles are attested). But the imperial house also enjoyed inviting the people here for grand ceremonial events. So, for example, Tiberius received an enthusiastic reception here after his victory in Illyria.

Like many other colonnades, the Saepta was also taken over as a bazaar by all sorts of merchants and was frequented all day long by those with nothing better to do, who could take in the famous works of art. Among others, Agrippa set up here two Hellenistic statue groups that are known in multiple copies: the centaur Chiron instructing his pupil Achilles and Pan teaching the young Olympus to play the syrinx (Pliny *HN* 36.29). Perhaps

Fig. 115. Pan with Olympus or Daphnis. Marble copy of Imperial date after the Hellenistic original once exhibited in the Saepta Iulia. Here in a drawing of Poussin (ca. 1620).

the two pairs of teacher and pupil allude to the lessons which surely also took place in the area of the Saepta. That Agrippa's taste in art was not constrained by moral strictures in the choice of subject matter is evident from the homoerotic nature of the Pan and Olympus group (fig. 115).

Agrippa modestly referred to his own achievements only rarely. The fresco cycle of the Voyage of Argo in one of the long colonnades and the name Basilica Neptuni probably contain an allusion to his service as admiral, for which Augustus had already bestowed on him a *corona rostrata* adorned with ships' prows (cf. fig. 168a) after the Battle of Naulochoi. But it is significant that Agrippa did not give the building his own name, but instead named it Saepta Iulia.

Those with time on their hands could also contemplate the map of the world which was commissioned by Agrippa and later transferred to the Porticus Vipsaniae. It was intended to give the Roman people an idea of "their" empire and heighten their awareness of being *princeps terrarum populus* (Livy *Praef.*). We need only think of the impressive marble plan of the Imperium Romanum which Mussolini had placed on the ancient ruins along the Via del Impero. In 20 B.C., as part of his program of road building, Augustus had placed a gilded milestone (*Milliarium aureum*) near the time-honored monuments of the Forum Romanum, symbolizing Rome's position as the center of the world.

It was Agrippa's wish that even the import of grain into Rome serve to remind her people of their position of power. The Horrea Agrippiana behind the Forum, only recently fully studied and reconstructed, was built only of travertine, but with strikingly impressive decoration, even including Corinthian columns. No one implemented the idea of *publica magnificentia* more fully or consistently than Agrippa (Seneca *De ben.* 3.32.4). After his death a well-organized force of 240 men was put to work by the state just for the maintenance of the water supply system he created (Frontinus *De Aquis* 116).

Augustus's Family: A Ubiquitous Presence in Rome

Some buildings he put up in the name of others, for example his grandchildren, his wife, or his sister, such as the Porticus Gaii et Luci Caesaris (in the Forum), the Porticus of Livia and that of Octavia, and the Theater of Marcellus. (Suetonius *Augustus* 29)

Augustus himself was the only rival to Agrippa in matters of *publica magnificentia*. But his secular buildings served a more immediate political purpose. He completed Caesar's major projects (the Basilica Iulia and Forum

Iulium), restored at great expense the Theater of Pompey and such smaller buildings as the Porticus Octavia, laid out the park around his Mausoleum, created an artificial lake for *naumachiae* in the midst of the Nemus Caesarum (in present-day Trastevere), paid for the new markets on the Esquiline (Macellum Liviae), and much more.

The gigantic Solarium Augusti, dedicated in 10 B.C., lay north of Agrippa's building projects, perhaps within the park surrounding the Mausoleum (fig. 116). It was the largest sundial ever built. A 30-meter-tall Egyptian obelisk served as pointer (*gnomon*), casting its shadow on a distant network of markings which probably functioned equally as clock and calendar (fig. 117). The inscription on the base of the obelisk contains a reference to the "victory over Egypt" twenty years earlier. Interestingly, the obelisk was also a dedication to the sun god Sol. It was so contrived that on Augustus's birthday the *gnomon* pointed to the nearby Ara Pacis Augustae, recalling that at his birth the constellation of stars had already determined his reign of peace: *natus ad pacem*. The sundial was an incredible monument, and one can easily imagine what fun it must have been to stroll around its huge network of markers. The inscriptions were also given in Greek, apparently as a gesture to the many residents and visitors to Rome from the East.

South of the buildings put up by Agrippa, above the Circus Flaminius, were the temples and porticoes erected by triumphators of the second century B.C. (fig. 118). These were taken over and restored as monuments to the imperial house, the memory of their original Republican patrons largely disappearing in the process. The Porticus Octavia, for example, had been erected in 168 B.C. by Cn. Octavius after his naval victory over the Macedonian king Perseus. It was especially famous for its lavish bronze capitals. Augustus restored the building at his own expense, and this was one case where the "modest" refusal to rename the building after himself was no hardship (Suetonius *Augustus* 31; *Res Gestae* 19), since it already bore his name. In the restored colonnade he displayed the standards he had recaptured from the Dalmati and in the Illyrian Wars.

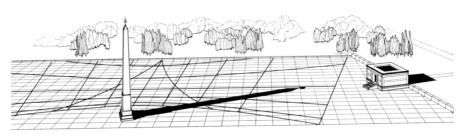

Fig. 116. Rome, Solarium Augusti, ca. 10 B.C. Reconstruction by E. Buchner. On Augustus's birthday, the obelisk cast its shadow toward the Ara Pacis Augustae.

Fig. 117. Obelisk in front of the Palazzo Montecitorio in Rome. The obelisk was carried off by Augustus from Egypt and used as the pointer for the monumental sundial.

Similarly, the Porticus Metelli, built in 147 B.C. by Q. Caecilius Metellus, another victor over the Macedonians, had to make way for the Porticus Octaviae. Augustus financed the rebuilding in honor of his sister, who later endowed here a *schola* and library in memory of her son Marcellus, after his death in 23 B.C. (Augustus had married his only daughter Julia to Marcellus and from 29 B.C. on treated him as his successor.) In the changeover, the famous works of art also dedicated by Metellus automatically adjusted themselves to the new Augustan program. Statues of Venus and Eros, as well as a multifigure equestrian monument by Lysippos depicting Alexander and his twenty-five companions at the Granicus, could all be seen as references to Augustus. After all, he adorned many of his own monuments with images and reminders of the great Macedonian and even used Alexander's likeness as his seal.

The Porticus Metelli was surely only one example among many. Augustus called the tune, and all Rome now danced to it.

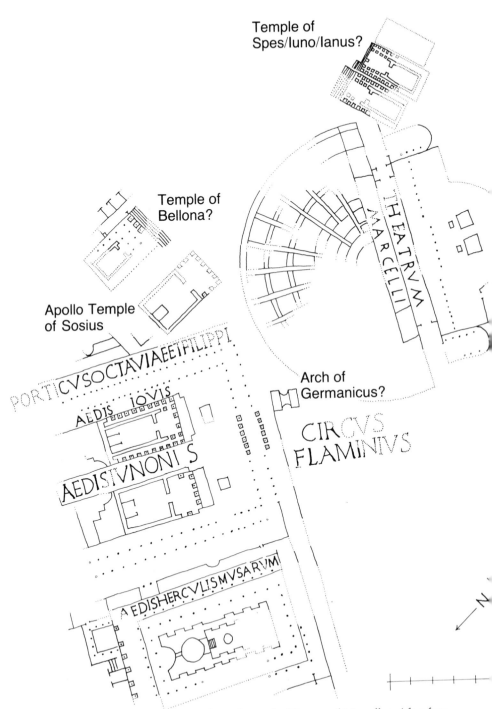

Temple of
Spes/Iuno/Ianus?

Temple of
Bellona?

Apollo Temple
of Sosius

PORTICVSOCTAVIAEETFILIPPI

AEDIS IOVIS

AEDIS IVNONIS

Arch of
Germanicus?

CIRCVS
FLAMINIVS

THEATRVM MARCELLI

AEDIS HERCVLIS MVSARVM

N

Fig. 118. Rome, porticoes and temples at the Theater of Marcellus. After fragments of the Forma Urbis.

Status and Applause: The Theater as Meeting Place of Princeps and People

Two new theaters went up in the immediate vicinity of the porticoes: the Theater of Marcellus, built by Augustus (fig. 119), with about twelve to fifteen thousand seats, and the somewhat smaller theater of the Younger Balbus. With the renovated Theater of Pompey, a total of at least forty thousand people could be accommodated at one time, on special occasions when all three theaters were in use. In addition there were two other theatral areas nearby, the Saepta and the Amphitheater of Statilius Taurus. In the course of fifteen years a virtual entertainment center had arisen in the Campus Martius (cf. figs. 114, 118).

The prospect of the Roman populace sitting in the theater did not worry Augustus as it had the Senate. On the contrary, he welcomed this opportunity for contact. The greetings and applause he received expressed the general mood of support and were a vivid confirmation of his power. Even the occasional protests against specific measures—the Equestrians opposing the financial restrictions of the marriage law of A.D. 9 or the people protesting the removal of Lysippus's Apoxyomenos—were regarded as a healthy way of blowing off steam. They gave the appearance of a real "dialogue" between the ruler and his people. It has been rightly observed that such political statements in the theater during the Empire to a great extent took the place of popular assemblies or elections and in a symbolic way expressed the popular consensus in support of the Principate. The masses were delighted when Augustus shared their entertainment and watched even the most tedious routines with evident interest, or made apologies when he could not attend (Caesar, on the other hand, had answered his mail during these shows).

The games themselves were a major part of Augustan *publica magnificentia*. "He surpassed all his predecessors in the number, variety, and splendor (*magnificentia*) of his games" (Suetonius *Augustus* 43). A distinction was drawn between the annually repeated games, which formed part of the religious calendar, and the extraordinary ones. In the time of Augustus the days with regularly scheduled games numbered sixty-seven. These were the responsibility of certain officials, who could add up to three times the publicly budgeted sum from their private funds. Not infrequently Augustus himself made up the difference for those who were not so wealthy. In his autobiography he claims to have given gladiatorial games eight times, with a total of ten thousand combatants, and animal games twenty-six times, with thirty-five hundred animals killed in all (*Res Gestae* 22f.). Together with horse races in the Circus these were the most popular games. The figures, however, belie the fact that in reality Augustus was not that enthusiastic about such mass entertainment. Trajan, by contrast, sponsored more

Fig. 119. Rome, Theater of Marcellus. Model. In the center of the stage backdrop Augustus had the Greek columns from the house of Scaurus set up.

games on his own initiative than took place during the entire forty years of Augustan rule. A large stone amphitheater is conspicuous by its absence from the many public buildings erected by Augustus (the small Amphitheater of Statilius Taurus is earlier and apparently not part of the Augustan building program). It was not until the reign of the otherwise parsimonious Vespasian that the Colosseum was built to house mass entertainment in the form of gladiatorial and animal games. This cautiousness, however, seems to have been due to the special status of Rome itself. In the planning of Augustan *coloniae,* as at Emerita Augusta (Merida, in Spain), an amphitheater was included from the very beginning.

But there were certain occasions when the princeps did pull out all the stops. For the dedication of the Forum of Augustus and the Temple of Mars Ultor, for example, he put on circus games in which 260 lions were killed, as well as the Trojan Games in the Forum, in which the prince Agrippa Postumus participated, gladiatorial combats in the Saepta, and a hunt featuring thirty-six crocodiles in the Circus Flaminius. For the same occasion he also created a huge *naumachia* on the other side of the Tiber and staged a reenactment of the Battle of Salamis between Athenians and Persians, with a total of three thousand combatants, thirty large ships and many smaller ones, all to commemorate his own naval victory at Actium. For such ideologically important public events the princeps spared no expense "to fill the hearts and eyes of the Roman people with unforgettable images" (Velleius Paterculus 2.100.2).

But in general Augustus gave most support to the theater, which besides serving as a point of contact between princeps and people also had an important cultural and didactic function. The new Rome had to have impressive theatrical performances above all because the dramatic stage had been such an important element in the Greek cities, especially in Classical Athens. Without theater, Rome's claim to being the cultural center of the Empire would carry little conviction. Behind the lavish support for the theater surely lay the desire to equal the Greeks, and the great athletic games in Greek style staged three times by Augustus could be similarly understood. Augustus boasts of these in the *Res Gestae* (22), although they were even less compatible than the theater with the traditions of his Roman forefathers.

We know that the works of patriotic Roman poets were performed in public theaters, that Augustus awarded prizes to certain favorite plays, such as the "Thyestes" of Varius, and that Vergil was especially honored. It would be fascinating to know what other plays were performed, in order to see to what extent the dramatic reworkings of Greek myth were politicized. But this aspect of Augustan imagery is almost entirely lost to us. We may be sure, however, that the pretensions of "high culture" did not last long in the theater and that burlesque and pantomime soon took over.

The new theaters also contributed significantly to the consolidation of the new social order. Here the Roman was made aware of the organization by rank of his entire society, and on each visit he saw clearly his own place in it. As early as the second century the Senate had reserved for itself the front rows (i.e., the orchestra), then later alotted the next section to the Equestrians. Segregation of undesirables in the theater was already practiced in the Late Republic, for Cicero (*Phil.* 2.44) reports that there was one section where all who were broke had to sit. Augustus then expanded this principle in his *lex Iulia theatralis*. This apparently designated all the rows and seats, giving preferential seating to some and discriminating against others. Senators sat in the orchestra, among these priests and magistrates in places of honor. Then followed Equestrians with a net worth of over 400,000 sesterces. Then came free Roman citizens in the broad middle section, arranged by tribe, as in the distribution of grain: *panem et circenses*. At the rear sat noncitizens, women, and slaves, when they were permitted to attend the theater at all. Unfortunately the details are not fully and unambiguously recorded, but we do know, for example, that soldiers and civilians sat separately and that adolescent boys had rows set aside for them and their guardians. Thanks to Augustus's laws on marriage, those who were married with many children were entitled to better seats, while recalcitrant bachelors were sometimes banned from the theater altogether. The various guilds also seem to have had their own sections.

Given the tremendous social importance of the games, these forms of favor or discrimination, of mingling or separation, were crucial in defining how every Roman citizen saw himself. The clear differentiation of seats, which was recognized by everyone in the audience and enforced by a kind of mutual surveillance, insured that the system worked smoothly. Outside the theater as well, the princeps carefully observed distinctions of social

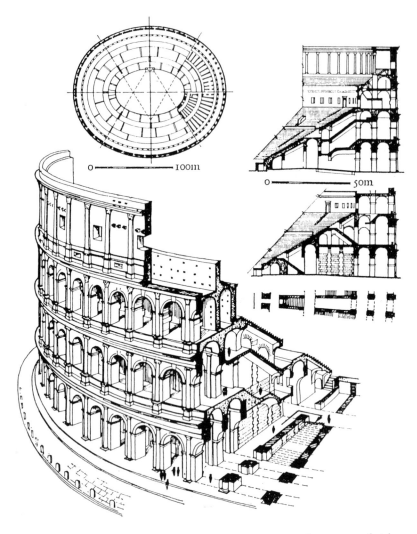

Fig. 120. Rome, Colosseum. Begun after A.D. 70. By a complex system of aisles and stairways the visitors to a Roman theater or amphitheater were conducted to seats assigned according to social standing.

rank, as for example in his invitations to dine with him (freedmen were never included). But at the same time, he made sure that every social class had its particular responsibilities and honors, so that upward mobility was always possible. For this reason the rigid pyramidal structure of Roman society was to a great extent accepted by its members. The common experience of rituals and festivals, which brought all Romans together, was essential in imbuing each individual with a sense of the social order.

Even the architecture of the theater helped to inculcate and make visible the principles of social stratification (cf. fig. 255). In the course of renovation and new construction the different sections were demarcated more clearly than before, and this was not just a visual effect. The cleverly contrived substructure beneath the semicircular *cavea* (auditorium) became an instrument of social classification. The network of arched passageways and staircases served not only to insure an easy flow of traffic in and out of the theater, but to separate the audience according to rank. Thus the "better" sort needed to have no contact at all with the common folk, whose seats were at the very top, just as in the opera houses of the nineteenth-century bourgeoisie. In Vespasian's Colosseum this system can be observed in its most perfected form (fig. 120).

As the seating arrangement in the Augustan theater shows, the creation of a monarchy in Rome did nothing to alter the pyramidal stratification of society (fig. 121). Indeed, class distinctions became even more rigid under Augustus. The economic basis upon which an individual's wealth was measured was, as it always had been, land, together with agricultural produce. The prerequisite for membership in the three *ordines* that constituted the upper class—Senators, Equestrians, and the local aristocracy of cities outside Rome (*decuriones*)—was a fortune of a certain size. Occasionally Augustus would even help out a Senator by making up the difference, to insure the continuity of the highest class. But wealth was not the sole ingredient in determining social status; family background and respect (*dignitas*) were equally important. The aristocratic principle was thus maintained, and the Roman "revolution" kept its conservative stripe.

The boundaries between upper and lower class, between those in the top three *ordines* and the rest of the population, were essential to upholding social *dignitas*, even more than economic prosperity. So, for example, a man who was not freeborn, no matter how wealthy, was excluded from certain state and local offices and thus from one of the *ordines*. In the theater, even the wealthy freedmen sat in the back rows. It was virtually impossible to make the transition from lower to upper class in a single generation, but for the sons and grandsons of a prosperous slave it was different. Here wealth was the principal determinant.

If the monarchy served to consolidate the old class distinctions, it nevertheless created new outlets to ease social tensions and opened new paths to social advancement, thus bringing about a gradual transformation of society.

The distribution of old and new priesthoods, usually associated in some way with the ruler cult, illustrates how a bond was created between the emperor and all social classes. Of course this meant primarily the most outstanding members of each class. Their services to the emperor led to social recognition and thus to the opportunity for advancement. Equestrians had major responsibilities in the administration of the provinces and in the army, which could ultimately gain them admission to the Senate. The local *Decuriones,* through similar service in their own communities, could rise to positions in provincial administration and to the Senate, whose composition shifted first in favor of Italians, then of provincials. Imperial slaves and freedmen naturally enjoyed a status far above that of other members of their class. These were roughly comparable to the wealthy freedmen in the cities of Italy, known as "Augustales" (again in the service of the ruler cult), who succeeded in creating for themselves a new social class, between *decuriones* and *populus.* We shall see how these groups striving for social ad-

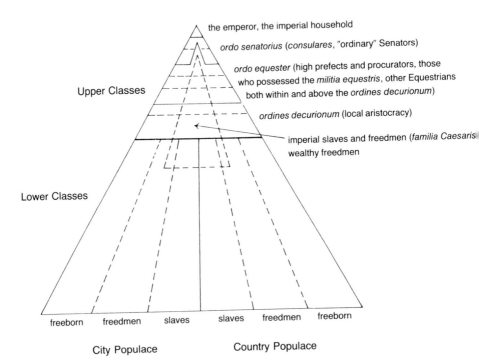

Fig. 121. The pyramidal structure of Roman society in the Imperial age. Model, G. Alföldy (1984), showing the fully developed society of the High Empire.

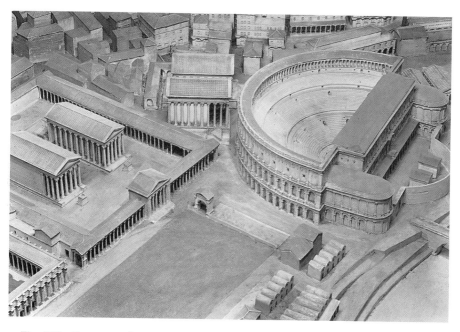

Fig. 122. Rome, southern part of the Campus Martius. Temples with porticoes next to the Theater of Marcellus. In front lay the Circus Flaminius (cf. fig. 118).

vancement are reflected in the visual arts and how they too helped spread the new pictorial imagery.

Ideology and the Image of the City

The large theaters were conspicuous hallmarks of Augustan Rome, and for the theatergoer both the Theater of Marcellus and that of Balbus evoked most impressively the *pietas* and *publica magnificentia* of the renewed city. The two semicircular auditoria were so situated that those who strolled through the outer walkways during intermission, or looked out the windows on the second floor, enjoyed a view out over an extraordinary cityscape, composed entirely of marble sanctuaries and lavish secular buildings (fig. 122). From the Theater of Marcellus one could see the renovated porticoes of the second century B.C., with their temples and gardens, the Circus Flaminius, with its honorific monuments, Sosius's new Temple of Apollo, and the Temple of Bellona, so close that from the arcades one could almost reach out and touch it, and, when one moved farther along, towering in the distance, the Temple of Jupiter Capitolinus. From the passageways of the Theater of Balbus could be seen the temples in the "Area Sacra" (the present-day Largo Argentina). These were views to warm the heart of the princeps.

Interestingly, fully a third of Strabo's description of Late Augustan Rome is devoted to the Campus Martius. This eyewitness observer from the Greek East was more impressed by the marble pleasure palaces than by the fora, the new temples, the Capitol, or the Palatine.

> The size of the Campus Martius alone [he means the northern part] is astonishing. It is spacious enough to allow chariot races and at the same time all other equestrian sports without any interference. Nearby are hordes of wrestlers and others playing ball or with hoops. Works of art adorn all the paths, and the lush gardens are in bloom at every season. The hilltops, which stretch to the Tiber, create a remarkable cityscape, a pleasure of which the eye never tires. Nearby is a second field [the southern part of the Campus Martius], in which the many porticoes, sacred groves, lavish temples, three theaters, and one amphitheater are all laid out in a semicircle. Here everything is so crowded, one upon another, that the rest of the city seems only incidental. (Strabo 5.3.8)

Strabo saw Augustan Rome when most of the building program was already finished, but contemporary Romans watched it being built. Vergil's description of the building activity in Dido's royal city of Carthage (*Aeneid* 1.418ff.) mirrors the feeling of excitement and optimism that must have permeated Rome in the 20s B.C., with new buildings going up all over. It was a community effort, as in a beehive, industrious craftsmen everywhere at work. The essential mandate, that the majesty of the Roman Empire must be reflected in public architecture (Vitruvius *Praef.*), was realized before one's very eyes. The emotional impact of this experience can hardly be overestimated.

But in spite of its marble temples and extravagant recreational buildings, the new Rome did not look like a Hellenistic city. This had been Julius Caesar's intention. If his plans had been carried out, the course of the Tiber would have been altered, and on the thus enlarged Campus Martius a preplanned city constructed, with a network of streets all at right angles and carefully proportioned *insulae*. From a huge theater on the slope of the Capitol one would have looked out on this perfectly organized new city. Later Nero would have a similar dream, but this was not Augustus's way. A radical remaking of the city would have contradicted the principal themes of his program. *Pietas* required that the old cult places be respected, his political style precluded interfering with private property, and the *mores maiorum* dictated the simplicity of residential neighborhoods.

The result was that the street system remained unchanged in many places. Tiny streets and alleys, which had grown haphazardly over centuries, are still quite evident in the Forma Urbis (third century A.D.), especially in the densely populated old residential quarters, as we have already seen in the area of the Porticus Liviae (cf. fig. 113).

The princeps did, however, reorganize the city, though on a different level. Rome was divided into fourteen *regiones* and 265 *vici* (districts). Each *vicus* elected its own "administration," made up of the *magistri* and *ministri* whom we discussed in connection with the Lares cults and the worship of the emperor. They also were in charge of other modest security measures, helped in fighting fires, insured peace and quiet, and supervised the building codes formulated by the princeps. Houses could be no higher than seventy Roman feet (about twenty-one meters), and probably such requirements as the thickness of supporting walls were also specified. The principal dangers in the old residential quarters were fire and flood. The princeps tried to alleviate these problems by creating his own fire department organized along military lines—seven cohorts of one thousand men each—and by attempting to shore up the banks of the Tiber. Order and security, also in the matter of insuring the regular supply of grain, did much to improve the "quality of life" in the various districts. The Compital cults of the *vici*, with their New Year's and Summer festivals, developed into social centers and true neighborhoods, which in turn facilitated a kind of mutual sense of protectiveness.

All these measures no doubt contributed to a better life for the inhabitants of Rome, but they did nothing to alter the essentially primitive appearance of the residential districts. Strabo was in fact right, that from an aesthetic viewpoint the old-fashioned residential Rome seemed like a mere appendage of the new marble city. And this was exactly in keeping with the ideology of Augustus's regime, as is illustrated, for example, by the great wall surrounding the Forum of Augustus, a remarkable monument which has justifiably continued to astonish ever since it was built (fig. 123).

Today one can still observe how this enormous wall, made of finely carved and ingeniously layered blocks of tufa and in places reaching a height of thirty-three meters, towered even above the roof of the Temple of Mars Ultor. From the streets and houses of the nearby Subura one could see nothing whatever of the spectacular marble buildings in the Forum. Although from inside the Forum one scarcely noticed the wall, its monumental barrier blotted out all the residential houses. Of course the wall also served a practical purpose, to protect the precious sanctuary from the frequent outbreaks of fire in the Subura. But its very form, both monumental and old-fashioned in character, took on an unmistakable symbolic importance within the plan of the entire city.

The wall was like a dividing line between the simplicity of residential neighborhoods and the *maiestas* and *magnificentia* of temples and other public buildings. In another way it also made visible one of Augustus's tenets: its irregular course, with many twists and turns, is evidence of the painful precision with which he avoided trespassing on private property. "He built his Forum somewhat smaller than originally planned, because he did not dare encroach on the property of neighboring houses" (Suetonius *Augustus* 52.2). Naturally the princeps could easily have acquired the pieces of property in question. But he was more concerned to set an example and to show that Augustus himself was bound by the same laws that he required his "fellow citizens" to obey. If we look back to the Rome of the Late Republic, the transformation of the city within the span of a single generation is almost incredible. Perhaps nothing had so powerful and positive an impact on the Roman people as what was accomplished here. Following this example, the creation of hundreds of Roman cities in the Western half of the Empire gave visible form to the spread of Roman culture (p. 307).

MORES MAIORUM

Simplicity and self-sufficiency, a strict upbringing and moral code, order and subservience within the family, diligence, bravery, and self-sacrifice: these were the virtues that had continually been evoked in Rome with the slogan "mores maiorum," ever since the process of Hellenization began. Yet in reality this archaic society and its values were receding ever more rapidly. Nevertheless, the belief in the necessity of a moral renewal was firmly rooted. Without a return to the ancestral virtues there could be no internal healing of the body politic.

Such dramatic appeals had surely been heard many times before, and, inevitably, they are vague, short-lived, and out of touch with reality. But despite this, their emotional impact can often be amazingly deep. They are an indispensable element in the eternal longing for a "brave new world."

Augustus's Legislation on Morals

"O most immoral age! First you tainted marriage, the house, and the family. Now from the same source flows pollution over fatherland and people," lamented Horace (*carmen* 3.6) in 29 B.C. Along with godlessness, immorality was regarded as the greatest evil of the past and the reason for the collapse of Rome. Augustus believed that he could bring about a fundamental change in this area as well, and through rewards and punishment even improve sexual ethics and inspire upper-class Romans to produce more chil-

Fig. 123. Rome, Forum of Augustus. The enclosure wall (H: ca. 30 m) protected the building from fire and at the same time marked a symbolic boundary. L. Rossini, ca. 1810.

dren. His first, unsuccessful attempt at such legislation was, significantly, directly linked with the program for *pietas* in 29/28 B.C. The famous laws on marriage and morals of 18 B.C. were to serve as ideological preparation for the Secular Festival of the following year, and were accompanied by a rigorous purge of the Senate. The Leges Iuliae, which prescribed criminal prosecution for adultery, major penalties for those who remained unmarried (e.g., in the disposition of their inheritance), as well as rewards and privileges for parents of several children, were conceived by Augustus as a key aspect of his program of renewal.

It was difficult to give visual expression to this campaign, but the princeps did what he could. Up to the end of his life he continued to search out effective *exempla*.

He did not hesitate to read to the Senate a speech of the censor Q. Metellus from the year 131 B.C., "On Increasing the Birthrate," "as if it had just been written" (Livy Per. 59; Suetonius *Augustus* 89). An especially fertile slave woman received a statue. An old codger from Faesulae, together with all sixty-one of his descendants, was officially received on the Capitol, made a sacrifice there, and the whole event was even recorded in the *acta*, the official records (Pliny *N.H.* 7.60). In A.D. 9, when the Equestrians protested in the theater against the (already modified) marriage laws, especially the tax disadvantages linked with them, "he [Augustus] had the children of Germanicus brought in, held one in his arms, and had the others sit in their father's lap, and by his expression and gesture demonstrated that they should take the young man as their model" (Suetonius *Augustus* 34).

Poets in Augustus's circle were also asked to contribute to the campaign. They were meant to show how closely the dawning of the new age was bound up with and necessitated improved moral conduct. Horace's dry verses on the subject reveal how unwillingly he must have churned them out.

> Now the bull pastures safely in the fields.
> Ceres nourishes the soil and gives blessed harvest.
> Ships fly over the peaceful sea,
> And marital fidelity shrinks from guilt.
>
> The pure house is no longer sullied by adultery.
> Law and custom have tamed unclean lust.
> Mothers are proud of legitimate children.
> Punishment follows on the heels of guilt.
>
> *carmen* 4.5

Unlike the programs of religious renewal and *publica magnificentia,* the social legislation, with its penalties and pressure, was of course misguided. In particular, the call for more children, no matter how positively received, was a failure. Those whom Augustus particularly had in mind—the upper classes—simply shook their heads. There was much sarcastic comment, and people like Ovid could not resist the temptation of a little wicked parody. Basically, this attempt at regimentation and meddling in private affairs did not fit the style of the new regime. Augustus was trapped in his own sense of mission and in his vision of an inner renewal. It is a peculiar image: the cool, calculating realist turned indefatigable moral preacher, who at every opportunity recited *exempla* to be followed, which he had pulled out of ancient writers, then circulated them to his provincial governors (Suetonius *Augustus* 89). It was because he identified himself so fully with this program, which was nevertheless an utter failure, that he behaved so monstrously toward his daughter and granddaughter, the two Julias. Their loose living hit him where he was most vulnerable.

Those same artists who had so enthusiastically taken up the motifs of religious renewal apparently came up with nothing appropriate to this theme. Naturally on the Ara Pacis the children of the imperial family (un-

Fig. 124. Rome, Ara Pacis. Antonia minor with Drusus maior and their children; behind, other members of the Imperial house.

fortunately there were not many) were placed in the foreground (fig. 124), and later glass medallions with images of the imperial princes and their children were distributed in the army (fig. 125). But even this is deceptive. Themes like "the moral marriage" or "the blessings of children" could not be directly translated into visual terms. But, as we shall see, they did reappear in subliminal form in the imagery of the Golden Age, which would soon become so pervasive.

The Princeps as Model

Augustus offered himself as the greatest *exemplum* and tried in his private life and public appearance to be a constant advertisement for the *mores maiorum*. If the reality did not match the image in *him*, then where else? His public style had a winning simplicity and dignity, from his gait to his manner of speech, from his friendly intercourse with the humblest people to his deference toward the Senators, and especially his discipline and self-control. Visitors reported on the simplicity and old-fashioned modesty of his private rooms at home. It was said that he had himself melted down the last gold dinner plate, and it was well known that he had no use for luxury villas (though he did, however, retain all of Capri as his private refuge). He also let it be known that his toga, simply tailored and reserved in its tokens of high rank, was woven by hand by his wife and granddaughter (amid hundreds of imperial slaves).

The modesty and simplicity of the princeps's style are most evident with respect to the honors he continually received. We have already noticed how from ca. 20 B.C. virtually all monuments erected in his honor had a votive or religious character. The new style is especially striking in architecture. The modest proportions of the Ara Pacis Augustae (fig. 126) reproduce those of the Altar of the Twelve Gods in the Athenian Agora, of the fifth century B.C. The Ara Fortunae Reducis (19 B.C.) was probably smaller (fig. 127*a*), and other altars, erected later on, were certainly no larger. Yet these altars are the largest monuments erected by the Senate and people to honor Augustus after the "turning point." What a contrast to the Altar of Zeus in Pergamum, or to the emphatic self-aggrandizement of the *divi filius* in the 30s B.C.

Augustus's modesty and his continual references to the *mores maiorum* may have offered some reassurance to a few Senators, especially as there was no lack of indications that they would still have opportunities for fame and self-fulfillment beside the princeps in the *res publica restituta*. From 19 B.C. young aristocrats serving as mint master could again put the name and insignia of their families on coins. The praetor C. Naevius Surdinus could erect a huge inscription in the midst of the Forum recording that he had paid for the new pavement (ca. 10 B.C.). The impoverished M. Aemilius Lepidus was able, with financial help from the princeps, to restore the old

Fig. 125. Glass medallion for metal setting. Tiberius or Drusus minor with two princes. This military in-signe refers explicitly to the next generation of the Imperial family.

Fig. 126. Rome, Ara Pacis Augustae, 13–9 B.C. The actual altar is located in the interior of the marble enclosure.

Basilica of the Aemilii in the Forum, and Balbus the Younger was even permitted to celebrate a triumph and with the spoils build a theater, just like the princeps himself. (A Spaniard of undistinguished family, Balbus was clearly no competition.) Little wonder that men so privileged by Augustus reciprocated with appropriate acknowledgments. Lepidus decorated his basilica with defeated barbarians in expensive colored marbles, and most coins honored Augustus on both obverse and reverse.

One mint official even celebrated the new social legislation by depicting the unchaste Vestal Tarpeia, who betrayed Rome out of love for the enemy Sabine king, buried beneath the enemy's shields (fig. 127b). The mint master did not, however, invent the motif, for it seems to have been known to the poets in the circle of Maecenas. At any rate, Propertius surprisingly dedicated an entire elegy to the story of the unhappy Vestal (4.4) and interpreted it in this way, as an explicit example of what happens when religion and morality are despised.

A new portrait of Augustus was probably created around the time of the Secular Games (fig. 128). The changes appear minor, but convey an interesting message. In place of the artfully constructed countenance and deliberately classicistic forms of the years around 27 B.C. (cf. fig. 83), there now appear more marked physiognomic traits, recalling the early portraits (cf.

a   *b*

Fig. 127. *a.*) Denarius of Q. Rustius, 19 B.C. Altar of Fortuna Redux, set up on the occasion of Augustus's successful return from the East. *b*) Denarius of P. Petronius Turpilianus, Rome, 16 B.C. The unchaste Vestal Tarpeia is buried alive with shields. The image, in the context of Augustus's moral legislation, alludes to the *mores maiorum*.

fig. 39). In particular, the severe Polyclitan arrangement of the hair with forks and tongs is given up in favor of a more realistic coiffure. The beauty and agelessness of the face are preserved, but it is no longer that of an aloof, eternally youthful hero. The revised portrait was, however, only sporadically copied. Workshops continued to use the familiar type, for by then the aesthetically unsurpassed image of the eternal youth had precluded depictions of an aging and often sickly man.

The desire for a more modest portrait must also be understood in the context of Augustus's rejection of the old-style honorific statue in favor of one showing him veiled and togate. Even the handwoven toga was an acknowledgment of tradition, a promise to respect the *res publica*. For those who endowed such statues, it was a fulfillment of these expectations.

Toga and Stola

Augustus succeeded in making the toga a kind of unofficial Roman state dress and a symbol of the proper attitude, a reminder of their own worth to those who wore it on specific occasions. Horace goes so far as to mention the toga in the same breath with the sacred guarantors of the Empire (*Odes* 3.5.10f.).

In the Late Republic, the cut and design of the toga were essentially the same as those of a Greek himation (cf. fig. 10*a*). But now, probably due to the example of Augustus and his advisers (cf. fig. 104), more elaborate models became fashionable, which had to be worn differently, in a more complicated arrangement with *sinus* and *balteus*. This produced a much more impressive effect, but putting it on and wearing it correctly were rather la-

Fig. 128. Portrait of
Augustus, after a proto-
type probably created
about 17 B.C.

borious. Over the years artists evolved explanatory models of the proper
way to wear such a toga. The voluminous material was shaped into an
aesthetic structure, the play of folds entirely concealing the body beneath
(figs. 129, 130). The symbolic meaning of the garment became more important than its functional aspect or outward appearance.

Freedmen were among the earliest exponents of the new fashion, as their
grave reliefs show. For them the toga was a sign of the citizenship they had
struggled so hard for, the symbol of their success in life. But in general
people were reluctant to wear this uncomfortable and easily soiled white
outfit. Augustus had to give them a push.

He took pains to revive the dress and the form of public appearance of
Rome's forefathers and to honor them. When he saw a group of people
at a public assembly wearing dark everyday clothes, he rose and cried
out, "Look, the Romans, masters of the world, people of the toga" (Vergil *Aeneid* 1.282). He commanded the aediles to allow no one into the
Forum or its vicinity unless he had removed his cloak and wore a toga.
(Suetonius *Augustus* 40)

The same rule obtained in the theater (Suetonius *Augustus* 44). But at
least on certain official occasions the princeps was anxious that the actual

Fig. 129. Statue of one of the leading men of Formiae. A new, more voluminous toga is now in fashion.

Fig. 130. Statue of a man with "Senator's shoes." He displays two wax ancestor portraits. He is most likely a *novus homo*.

appearance of the Roman people approximate the vision of the poets. As a result, the sight of the white *togati* in the theater and in the popular assembly must have been a proud one. And this in turn will surely have had an effect on the individual participants. The regulations on the wearing of the toga were only part of many similar measures. At the same time "true Romans" with full citizen rights received various privileges—in the theater, when there were handouts of money, and at the distribution of grain (membership in the *plebs frumentaria* was limited and strictly controlled)— which bolstered their pride in belonging to the *populus Romanus.*

   In any event, the case of the toga offers a particularly instructive example of the varieties of interaction that gave rise to the rich vocabulary of the new pictorial language. First the poet evoked a suggestive image in his na-

Fig. 131. Statue with *stola*, the long over-garment with shoulder straps that designates married Roman women and was supposed to "protect" them (cf. fig. 253).

tional epic. This led to a disturbing comparison with real life and in this instance provoked a political response from Augustus himself. In general, however, the process will have been more complex, the inspiration less poetic, and the intermediary stages more numerous.

Married women also had a special form of dress that was meant to reflect the new spirit of morality in Rome. This was the *stola*, a long, sleeveless overgarment with narrow shoulders, which probably carried woven stripes indicating the matron's social status, as on the *toga praetexta*.

This garment is frequently found on honorary statues and portrait busts of the Early Imperial period (fig. 131), sometimes in combination with a woolen fillet (*vitta*) wound in the hair. Originally the *stola* would have stood out from the *tunica* and mantle through the application of paint. In the context of the social legislation the *stola* became a symbol of female virtue and modesty. For the dignified matron, wearing the *stola* was not only an honor but a "protection from unwanted attentions." Ovid, who would later ruefully acknowledge himself the "teacher of hideous adultery" (*obsceni doctor adulterii* [*Tristia* 2.212]), wittily makes fun of this tacit significance of the garment. The first few verses of his "Art of Love" are full of ironic allusions to official morality as made manifest in the *vitta* and *stola:*

> Away with you, fillets (*vittae*), you sweet tokens of shame;
> Away with you, *stola*, trailing down to the feet.
> I sing of carefree love, of legal thievery.

It must have been hard enough for upper-class women to exchange their elegant gowns of transparent fabric for the plain, shirtlike *stola*. Now too, as Ovid would have them say, with the new legislation of morality they must stay outside the bounds of the "art of love." The young man after an amorous adventure, according to Ovid, had to limit himself to lower-class women not legally married, young freedwomen, slave girls, or foreigners. Ovid was surely not the only one who drew the inevitable consequences of the morality laws.

Chapter 5

The Mythical Foundations of the New Rome

AUREA AETAS

After ten years of religious and moral renewal, the festivals and sacrifices, buildings and images, now visible everywhere in Rome, began to take effect. Confidence in the ability of the restored Republic to stand firm and faith in its leader grew apace. Attempts to overthrow him had failed, his military prowess had been tested against the Cantabri and Parthians, and the peace within Rome had proved itself a stable one. The successes of the new regime had had an impact on every individual. It was now time to give permanent expression to this mood of optimism, to create a new imagery that would transcend reality and eternalize the happiness of the present moment. The state needed a myth, and here again Augustus was able to latch onto something that was already in the air before he came along. For years people had fantasized about the imminent dawning of a new "Saturnian" age of happiness. Another comet was expected in the year 17 B.C., so what better time simply to proclaim that the long awaited new *saeculum* had arrived? From May 30 to June 3 the great Secular Games took place, heralding the beginning of the new age.

The Golden Age Is Proclaimed

It is fascinating to consider how systematically the public was prepared for the event. First the disgrace with the Parthians was made good, then the Senate purged, finally the laws on morals passed in 18 B.C. *Virtus, mos maiorum,* and the blessings of children became the key leitmotifs of the festival and of the new imagery arising from it. From the official records of the festival, happily preserved in an inscription, and from Horace's poem for the occasion, the *carmen saeculare,* we get a good idea of the planning and the activities of the various participants. The *XV viri sacris faciundis* formulated the guidelines under the direction of Augustus and Agrippa, who had had themselves elected *magistri* of the *collegium* for the year 17 B.C. C. Ateius Capito, a specialist in sacral law, translated these guidelines into a complicated ritual, undoubtedly making extensive use of Varro's writ-

ings. The program consisted of lengthy preparations, the actual festival lasting three days, followed by several days of games of all sorts. Starting
months in advance, heralds in old-fashioned dress announced "a festival
such as no one has seen before and no one shall see again" (Suetonius *Claudius* 21).

Coins minted in the year of the festival show these heralds on the reverse
(fig. 132). On the obverse they have a youthful head of the deified Caesar
wearing a laurel wreath and, above, the symbol of the comet expected that
summer, a clear reminiscence of the *sidus Iulium* and the events of twenty-
seven years earlier, when the young Octavian had made his first public appearance.

Selected groups of people carried out certain prerequisites for the ceremony. Shortly before the start of the festivities, the *XV viri*, including the
princeps, distributed instruments of expiation and purification, such as sul-
fur, tar, and torches, with which everyone had to cleanse himself in a private
ritual. The sight of the princeps himself working tirelessly for hours in this
solemn ceremony made a considerable impression, commemorated by the
mint master for the following year (fig. 133). On the day before the festival,
priests officially received firstfruits from the people on the Aventine (as if
they were still the peasants of a bygone age and not full-fledged urbanites).
Later these fruits would be redistributed during the festival. The Roman
populace also played a direct role in the ritual itself, and even those unmarried, whom recent legislation had barred from the theater and other festivals, were permitted, "*propter religionem*," as the princeps put it.

The festival itself was a series of visually spectacular events, enacted at
various sanctuaries and cult places. The official records, as well as the *Carmen Saeculare*, show that the principal themes of the archaic rituals that
were performed, in contrast to previous Secular Festivals, were concerned
not with the propitiation of underworld divinities, but with a guarantee of
health and fertility, that is, with cultic approval for the new morality and

a   *b*

Fig. 132. Denarius of M. Sanquinius, Rome, 17 B.C. *a*) Divus Iulius with *sidus
Iulium. b*) Herald in archaic dress with enormous messenger's staff.

Fig. 133. Aureus of L. Mescinius Rufus, Rome 16 B.C. Before the Secular
Games, Augustus personally distributes
the *suffimenta* (for purification).

Fig. 134. Denarius of C. Antistius Vetus, Rome, 16 B.C., commemorating the
legendary treaty with the Gabini: sacrifice of a pig in Archaic ritual.

the new Roman state. Sacrifices were made to the Moirai, the Eileithyiai,
and Terra Mater in three nighttime ceremonies. On the first night, the Fates
received nine sheep and nine goats, as Augustus recited an elaborate, archaizing prayer for the *imperium* and *maiestas* of the Roman people, for the
health, well-being, and victory of the people and legions, for the increase of
the Empire, for the priesthoods, and finally specifically for himself, his
house and family. On the next two nights, the Eileithyiai, as helpers in child-
birth, and Terra Mater, as goddess of fertility, were invoked. To the latter
Augustus himself sacrificed a pregnant sow.

No one who witnessed this scene would easily forget it. A similar scene
of an archaic ritual slaughter and sacrifice appeared soon after on a series
of coins (fig. 134).

The daytime activities were scarcely less impressive than these nocturnal
scenes. The first two days saw sacrifices on the Capitol, first to Jupiter, then
to Juna Regina, and on the third day Apollo, Diana, and Latona received
sacrifices on the Palatine. Again Augustus and Agrippa made the sacrifices,
two oxen for Jupiter, two cows for Juno, and cakes for Apollo and Diana.
A chorus of 110 select matrons and three other choruses, each composed of
seven youths and girls clad in white, played a major role in these rituals.
The mothers sought blessings, especially from Juno, for state and family,
while the children, in their festive white costumes, sang before the Temple
of Palatine Apollo the poem *Carmen Saeculare* composed by Horace for the
festival:

> Phoebus, and Diana in woodlands regent.
> Glories of the sky, to be held in future
> Honor as in past: we entreat you on this
> Sacred occasion

When the Sibyl's chanted instructions call for
Chosen maidens chaste and unwedded youths to
Sing this hymn to gods in whose sight our seven
    Hills have known favor.

Sun of bounty who, with your shining chariot,
Bring and close the day, ever new yet changeless.
May no greater thing than this Rome, our City,
    Rise in your prospect.

Duly open wombs at their proper season,
Ílithýia, gently attending mothers,
Or, with your approval, be named Lucína
    Or Genitális.

Goddess, rear our children, uphold the laws our
Leaders have enacted to govern wedlock,
Laws we pray may yield generations also
    Fruitful in offspring,

So that through eleven recurrent future
Decades there may be, without fail, repeated
Hymns and games of holiday thrice by daylight,
    Thrice after nightfall.

Destinies you uttered proved true, O Parcae;
What you so ordained, may the fixed and changeless
End of time preserve, and let blessings past be
    Ever continued.

May our Earth, abundant in fruits and cattle,
Yield the headed grain as a crown for Ceres;
May our crops be nurtured with wholesome rains and
    Jupiter's breezes.

With your bow laid down, and benignly lending
Ear to boys entreating you, hear, Apollo!
Harken, queen of stars and the two-horned crescent,
    Luna, to maidens!

If the gods willed Rome into being when they
Bade the walls of Troy win Etruscan shores and

Bade the nation's remnant transplant its hearths by
    Rescuing voyage;

If unscathed from Ilian flames, Aeneas,
Blameless chief survivor of perished homeland,
Led the way, predestined to found a city
    Greater than ever:

Then, O gods, give young people taintless morals,
And, O gods, to tranquil old men give peace, and
To the race of Romulus give all glory,
    Riches, and offspring;

Grant the pleas submitted with votive bulls by
Venus' and Anchíses' exalted scion,
He who first wars enemies down, then lets them
    Live in his mercy.

Sea and Land acknowledge his hand of power,
By the Alban axes the Medes are daunted,
Scyths and Hindus, haughty not long ago, now
    Seek his pronouncements.

Trust and Peace and Honor and ancient Manners
Venture back among us, and long-neglected
Upright Conduct; Plenty comes too, and brings her
    Horn of abundance.

Prophet god resplendent with bow of silver,
Phoebus, welcome chief of the ninefold Muses,
Master of the skills that relieve the human
    Body of sickness,

If you find our Palatine altars pleasing,
Prosper Roman power and Latium's fortunes,
Five years more extend them, and thence forever
    Down through the ages.

Áventine and Álgidus Ridge, Diana,
Hold your shrines; the Board of Fifteen implore you:
Hear their prayers and harken with gracious ear to
    Prayers of these children.

Homewards now I carry my trust that Jove and
All the gods have heard these entreaties: I am
Phoebus' and Diana's instructed chorus,
Hymning their praises.

The poem's themes and imagery refer to the rituals just enacted in the previous few days, and images of Apollo and Diana and of the astral divinities identified with them, Sol and Luna, could be seen by the participants in the festival all over the temple precinct. By this time the Sybilline Books had most likely already been purged by the *collegium* of the *XV viri* and were in the cella of the temple. They were kept in two golden containers in the base of the cult statue group; on the base a kneeling Sibyl stood for the power of the prophecies as guarantors of the future (cf. fig. 186). But the state's real hope for the future, its children, was vividly embodied in the moving image of the young singers. Each element was bound up with the others, forming a *Gesamtkunstwerk* at every level of meaning. This one example gives us some notion of many other, now lost festivals and rituals.

The Imagery of Fertility and Abundance

Over the next several years a new set of images symbolizing the blessings of abundance appeared on the most varied monuments. As in the rituals of the Secular Festival, the focus was on the promise of fertility in nature—and of course in men and women too. If Roman society was not prepared to accept the political program of moral renewal, either directly or as expressed in terms of the blessings of children, it took up enthusiastically the vision of the *aurea aetas*. The campaign to encourage the procreation of children failed, but in the visual imagery it was maintained at a subliminal level. The process is here indicative of what the future would hold. Whether a political act of Augustus was a success or failure was of secondary importance; the imagery of lasting happiness transcended any reality and eventually came to shape the common perception of reality. The earliest and most elaborate composition of this type is the so-called Tellus relief on the Ara Pacis (figs. 135, 136).

A matronly deity in classicizing drapery sits in dignified posture on her rocky seat. She holds in her arms two babies who reach for her breast, while her lap is filled with fruit and her hair adorned with a wreath of grain and poppies. More corn, poppies, and other plants are prominently displayed growing behind her. The woman's physical presence, her posture and garment are evidently intended to invoke many different associations in the viewer. But whether we wish to call this mother goddess Venus, because of

Fig. 135. Rome, Ara Pacis. Pax, goddess of Peace. Detail of figure 136.

Fig. 136. Ara Pacis. Pax with symbols of fertility. Pax is likened both to the earth goddess Tellus and to Venus who dispenses fertility.

the motif of the garment slipping off the shoulder, Ceres, on account of the veil and stalks of grain, or the earth goddess Tellus, because of the landscape and rocky seat, it is immediately obvious that she is a divinity whose domain is growth and fertility.

The many-sided and eclectic iconography of the figure realizes in visual terms the varied promise of similar divinities in Augustan poetry. She is also typical of the new personified deities of Augustan religion, who had no traditional mythology. In the conventional iconography of the gods, a specific position (e.g., Demeter sitting on the ground), dress or attribute was sufficient to evoke in the viewer an entire myth. These new gods, however, embodied powers and values that could only be approximated in attributes.

In the case of our nature or mother goddess the repertory of attributes is especially rich. The composite figure is surrounded by a lush landscape which is meant to illustrate her powers. The artist has placed beneath the goddess's seat, on a much smaller scale, a sheep grazing and an ox at rest, symbols of the increase of herds and flocks and of the blessings of country life. But the figures on either side of her, *aurae,* are drawn from Classical Greek iconography. They are twin embodiments of the winds on land and sea. The former rides upon a goose over a stream, represented by an upended water jar, its banks thick with reeds. The sea breeze, however, sits on a submissive sea monster, a symbol that even such wild creatures have become tame and peace-loving in the new age. The *aurae,* which bring warmth and rain, are thus also tokens of increase and fertility, hence closely connected with the goddess to whom they respectfully turn. This artistic landscape is not mere scenery, but rather a symbolic setting, whose various elements could be read one by one, the scale of any one of them altered by the artist to suit his purpose. The few plants, for example, are overly large in relation to the animals, the stalks of grain shooting up as if before the goddess's very eyes. In this setting even the reeds could be seen as a symbol of life-giving moisture. The whole composition is like a kind of icon, or devotional image, in which each element would evoke manifold associations in the viewer. The enumeration of the goddess's many qualities was intended to lead to the veneration of her powers—and those of Augustus.

Much has been written about the identification of this goddess. Tellus, Venus, Italia, and Pax can all be supported with appropriate passages in Augustan poetry. But since these same poets use the same motifs for a variety of mythological and allegorical figures, and since the scene deliberately combines various tokens of blessing and happiness, the image itself can offer no definitive proof for the correct identification. Perhaps the best candidate is Pax Augusta, especially since the panel decorates the Ara Pacis and, as a pendant on the opposite side, Roma is depicted enthroned on a mound of armor. The viewer was meant to read the two images together and understand the message, that the blessings of peace had been won and made secure by the newly fortified *virtus* of Roman arms. The same association is made in more abstract terms on an altar in Carthage (cf. fig. 247). In a different context, the goddess with suckling babies and fruits can indeed represent Tellus, Italia, or Ceres. On the cuirass of the Augustus from Prima Porta (fig. 137), for example, the same figure is clearly marked as the earth mother by her reclining posture and the whole arrangement of the composition. But at the same time, of course, she also stands for the peace and prosperity of the new age as well. Only here the symbols of her power are collected in a cornucopia, as also in the case of the goddess on the Gemma Augustea (cf. fig. 182). The mother goddess of Augustan art, whatever we call her, always embodies the same ideas.

The image of Pax (if that is who she is), though filled with symbolism and capable of conjuring up so many associations, was nevertheless easy to read, thanks to the clearly organized composition. Many of the individual elements were already quite familiar to the contemporary Roman, while others had made a lasting impression in the recent Secular Festival. The happily grazing sheep and the prominently raised stalks of grain had al-

Fig. 137. The earth goddess Tellus, with cornucopia and children, wearing a wreath of grain. Detail of the cuirassed statue, figure 148*a*.

ready appeared on coins of 27/26 B.C. as symbols of the promised peace (cf. fig. 36*c*). One stanza of the *carmen saeculare* reads like a poetic paraphrase of the Pax relief, as if Horace and the sculptor had planned it this way:

> May our Earth, abundant in fruits and cattle,
> Yield the headed grain as a crown for Ceres;
> May our crops be nurtured with wholesome rains and
> Jupiter's breezes.

There can be no doubt that the key elements of this vision originated in Augustus's inner circle and are closely bound up with the program for the Secular Festival.

In the *carmen saeculare*, the promise of fertility is a direct consequence of political policy; it calls for concrete realization (lines 17–20), and is tied directly to Augustus's marital legislation. The sculptor of the Ara Pacis, however, was able to make the same imagery more palatable. It is true that the celebration of childbearing is brought to the center of his composition, but it is incorporated into a more general vision of happiness. The princeps's political program is translated into an image of affecting beauty to which every viewer could respond.

The various tokens surrounding the mother goddess illustrate how all of nature is a paradise blessed with this same fertility. Their symbolism was evidently so familiar to the Romans that they could be used or simply alluded to in the most varied settings, *pars pro toto*. A good example are the three concave reliefs that once decorated a public fountain in Praeneste. Their high quality suggests that they originated in one of the leading workshops in Rome (fig. 138*a–c*).

The theme here is the joy of motherhood and the blessings of offspring in the animal kingdom. On each relief a mother suckles her young, while beside the group is a spring alluding to the fountain's purpose. As on the Pax relief, the symbolic meaning is emphasized by an original composition. Each animal group appears self-contained, within a cave, and is pushed into the foreground. But above the caves, significantly enlarged symbols allude to other messages: the princeps's oak leaves together with reeds (a symbol of fertility) above the bristling wild sow (fig. 138*a*); the laurel, along with a rustic shrine richly decked out with offerings, an altar, and relief, above the lioness (fig. 138*b*). Above the mother sheep, a shepherd's purse and a sheep pen proclaim the simple and happy peasant life (fig. 138*c*), though the artist has inadvertently betrayed how far from reality his bucolic idyll is by depicting the pen with layered marble slabs, as if it were one of the smaller temples in Rome.

Thanks to their generalized and universal character, such peaceful scenes of animal life could always be used to invoke the myth of the new age. These symbols of motherhood could be juxtaposed with tokens of *pietas*, with a paean to the simple rustic life, or with allusions to Augustus—the combination was always right. Since these same and similar tokens were constantly used in changing contexts, the programmatic themes they represented mingled easily and freely with one another in the mind of the thoughtful observer. The sheaf of grain, for example, could stand for the fertility of the fields, for the Arval Brethren, for peace, or even for the princeps's efforts to guarantee the grain supply in Rome. The chief characteristics of the Augustan pictorial vocabulary are its broad spectrum of associations and the general applicability of the individual symbols, but also a corresponding lack of specificity in any one particular case. Even a seemingly innocuous plant, as on the relief from Falerii (fig. 139*a*), takes on far-reaching associations, thanks to the didactic plan of the composition and the juxtaposition of various plants that never occur together this way in nature.

The plants are arranged in mirror-image pairs, but each grows in isolation, so that the viewer is forced to consider each one as an individual. Again corn stalks and poppies are rendered on an enlarged scale. The symbolism of the reed is here further emphasized by the presence of water birds:

a

Fig. 138. Three reliefs from a fountain in Praeneste, Early Imperial. Symbolic images of fertility and peace in nature. *a*) Wild sow. *b–c*) Lioness and sheep.

streams water the earth, making the young shoots grow. In the midst of all this, however, is a more playful allusion to fertility and procreation: three hungry young sparrows are fed by their protective parents (fig. 139*b*).

Even the genre motif of the birds is by no means a spontaneous creation of the author of this relief, but an image already familiar from public monuments of the period. It was already known in Hellenistic art, but acquired the ideological baggage first in Augustan Rome. The precise meaning of the motif, however, varies according to the purpose of each monument that it

c

decorated. On the base of a statue that the *magister* of a sanctuary of the Lares in Rome dedicated to Venus Augusta, the birds are clearly meant as tokens of the goddess (cf. fig. 112). But on the base of an Apolline tripod, together with the wreath of grain, they probably refer to the theme of fertility central to the Secular Festival (cf. fig. 99*a*), while on a marble ash urn they might be generalized symbols of happiness, as we shall see presently (cf. fig. 220*b*).

The Vines of Paradise

The old decorative motif of the vine now took on a more specific meaning within the context of the promulgation of a *saeculum aureum*. As a symbol of growth in nature the vine was among the most frequently repeated elements of the new pictorial vocabulary. Indeed, it is hard to find a building of the Early Empire, whether in or outside Rome, where it does not turn up. In the carefully planned decorative program of the Ara Pacis, vines and garlands occupy more than half the surface of the altar enclosure (fig. 140).

On the exterior walls the vines grow from broad acanthus calyxes into treelike forms, which send out new shoots in all directions, leading the eye through an endless pattern of infinite variety. Signs of fertility and abundance are set directly into this framework, though the viewer only becomes aware of these as he nears the monument. Jagged leaves, flowers of all sorts, and fruits and plants both real and fantastic, even crawling little creatures,

a

Fig. 139. *a*) Birds and animals in a wet patch of reeds. Through the isolation and enlargement of individual elements, the symbolic significance of the image is impressed upon the viewer. Early Imperial relief from Falerii. *b*) Detail, with bird feeding her young (cf. fig. 112).

all suggest nature's growth, so alive that it seems to be real (fig. 141). But when one steps back again and takes in all the vines at once, one has the strong impression of a strictly observed order governing every detail. In fact, allowing for minor variations, the vines do adhere to a precisely calculated arrangement in mirror image. However wildly the plants and blossoms seem to burst forth and grow, every tendril, every bud and leaf has its prescribed place. To our eye it seems curious and unexpected that these symbols of the unrestrained growth of nature combine into a model of perfect

b

Fig. 140. Ara Pacis Augustae. Excerpt from one of the vine clusters. The abundance of nature is rendered in strictly symmetrical arrangement.

order. Perhaps this peculiar phenomenon reflects on the aesthetic level the almost fanatical preoccupation of the Augustan Age with law and order.

The symbolic use of the vine had a long tradition in art, probably rooted in the "nature" of the motif. On South Italian vases of the fourth century B.C., for example, spiraling tendrils are combined with the head of Persephone emerging from the earth. Even on the earliest Augustan buildings vines are more than just a favorite decorative motif. On one of the friezes on the Temple of Caesar in the Forum, the goddess of victory rises from the vines, and on the door of the Temple of Apollo, as we have seen, the vines are rooted in the bowls of the tripods (p. 86).

But these early Augustan vines still have the abstract spiraling form of Classical art. It is only in the context of the subsequent programmatic use of the fertility theme that the branches and leaves imitate Hellenistic models and are more realistically depicted to simulate living plants. The overall impression is shaped above all by the tangible leaves and large, blossoming buds. In this way Augustan artists again tried to highlight a certain meaning through a purely formal change. Another innovation was the combining of real and imaginary plant species. Grapes, figs, and palmettes all growing out of acanthus branches; ivy and laurel spiraling between heavy volutes; garlands bearing all manner of fruit; all this was meant to characterize the new age as a paradise on earth (cf. Vergil's Fourth Eclogue).

The function of the vine as symbol of the *saeculum aureum* was made

Fig. 141. Detail with miniature animals, including a snake slithering over a bird's nest.

clear to the Roman viewer through a variety of suggestive juxtapositions. When, for example, on a relief in Naples (fig. 142), the vine grows behind a conquered people sitting dejectedly on the ground, one was inescapably reminded of the slogan "through just war to the blessings of peace." The two centaurs on a cuirassed statue in Chercell (cf. fig. 178) express the same idea. A sea centaur holding a rudder recalls the foundation myth of the new Rome, the Battle of Actium, while a normal centaur holds a cornucopia and his body ends in a tangle of vines.

The Ara Pacis is of course also not without its own specific references to the *saeculum aureum*. On a frieze between vine branches bearing new shoots sit Apollo's swans: *iam regnat Apollo* (Vergil *Eclogues* 4.10). The vine by itself is celebrated and worshiped like a cult object on terra-cotta plaques of the period (fig. 143).

For Augustan artists the vine was of course a most welcome motif. It could be used virtually anywhere, on a frieze, ceiling coffer, or door frame, and could be fitted into even the most awkward places. Down to the pattern work on the sandals of the gods and cuirassed generals, it proclaims the fertility and prosperity of the new age. But the vine also transcended any other symbol as an inspiration for ever more imaginative elaboration.

In the private sphere, the wall paintings and silver vessels of the Augustan period give the impression that the inventiveness and playful wit of Augustan artists could only fully express itself when they were not constrained by

Fig. 142. Relief with two entablature supports in Classical style. In the middle, the personification of a conquered nation, with plants growing up in the background (inscription modern). Early Imperial.

official propriety and decorum. An example are the vines on the great silver krater from the treasure at Hildesheim (fig. 144). On the one hand, they are thoroughly indebted to the political symbolism of the times. The vines themselves grow out of the wings of a heraldically arranged pair of griffins, and the putti (without wings) are inevitably connected with the theme of the blessings of children in the *aurea aetas*. But other elements—the transformation of the carefully and symmetrically arranged branches into abstract linear design, the children riding on pencil-thin stalks and fishing for shrimp—replace the world of official iconography with one of artistic fancy. To the modern eye, Augustan art is at its best in works like these, rather than in the academic perfection of the Ara Pacis.

Happiness Born of Victory

Augustus's victory over the Parthians had already taken place in the year 20 B.C. But since its role in Augustan ideology only developed in the context of the proclamation of the *saeculum aureum*, we have saved until now a discussion of the imagery it inspired. This event was endowed with an extraordinary significance. As we have already seen, it was regarded as one of the prerequisites for the opening of the Golden Age. But at the same time,

less important than forging the link between military victory, internal order, and happiness in general.

The Romans had been preparing for a new campaign against the Parthians since the mid-20s B.C. The slogans that this must have engendered are reflected in the poets: Romans should remember the disgrace of 53 B.C., when Crassus (a member of the First Triumvirate) lost the standards and eagles, and the prisoners too, who were purportedly still in captivity. Without restoring the honor of Roman arms, the restoration of the state itself would be incomplete. A passage was even found in the Sibylline Books, hinting that the Golden Age would dawn only after the conquest of the Parthian. Caesar had been murdered before his planned campaign in the East, and Antony had proved himself incompetent. Now Augustus would march to the East, like a new Alexander, and prove that the reborn Roman *virtus* was worthy to be set beside the bravery of their forefathers.

The campaign itself was rather unspectacular. After some threats and a marshaling of the troops, a diplomatic settlement was negotiated. The Parthian king Phraates returned the standards and later sent a few of his wives and children to Rome as hostages, acknowledging Rome's hegemony and promising future cooperation.

This time Augustus was utterly restrained, in contrast to his behavior after Actium. He even refused the triumph which the Senate had already decreed. He agreed only to display publicly the recaptured eagles and standards, hastily building an impressive setting for them, a small round temple to Mars the Avenger (Mars Ultor).

The round temple, with the *signa* and an archaistic statue of Mars, is represented on a number of coins (fig. 145*a, b*). The choice of location, on

a   *b*

Fig. 145. The return of the standards from the Parthians was commemorated in many coin types. *a*) Cistophorus, Pergamum, 19 B.C. Small round temple for Mars Ultor on the Capitol in Rome. *b*) Denarius, 17 B.C. Archaistic cult statue of Mars Ultor with the recovered *signa*.

the Capitol, was a stroke of genius. Not only were the *signa* thus displayed as votives for Jupiter, but at the same time they made unmistakably clear the victor's own self-esteem. The little temple was right next to two other sanctuaries closely linked with Augustus, the temple of Jupiter Feretrius, first dedicated by Romulus but rebuilt by Augustus, and that of Jupiter Tonans, built by Augustus just four years earlier (cf. p. 108). The latter recalled how Jupiter had with his thunderbolt designated the victor over the Parthians as his chosen deputy. In the Temple of Jupiter Feretrius, however, stood the *spolia opima* of Romulus and Marcellus, which now received competition in the recaptured standards. The significance of all this was well understood. A series of coins shows the new Temple of Mars, with the *signa*, along with the Temple of Jupiter Tonans (cf. fig. 89).

All other commemorations of the victory over the Parthians took the form of honors for Augustus. The Senate took the lead in this, employing the traditional imagery of triumph. Over Augustus's objections, the Senate Fathers erected an arch with three portals and the triumphal chariot of the victor, right next to the Temple of the Divus Julius (Cassius Dio 54.8). On the arch were depicted the defeated Parthians, either as retreating archers or handing over the *signa* to the victor (both types are attested on coins: fig. 146*a*).

The image of the defeated Parthian, originally created by the Senate, was especially popular. Large issues of denarii had a kneeling Parthian handing over the standards (fig. 146*b*), even as Horace described Phraates "on his knees accepting the right and rule of Caesar" (*Epodes* 1.12.27). People even wore this image on rings, as we can see from a glass paste showing kneeling barbarians together with Victoria on the globe (fig. 147). Finally Augustus himself took up this fine image and made it his own: "I compelled the Parthians to return the spoils and standards of three Roman armies and humbly to beg the friendship of the Roman people" (*Res Gestae* 29).

The kneeling barbarian remained for many years an inordinately popular image and to a great extent shaped the Romans' view of their relationship to those peoples living on the borders of the Empire. Once they had felt the power of Rome, they were supposed to honor Rome's rulers and ask for *amicitia*. This is most beautifully expressed on one of the Late Augustan silver bowls from Boscoreale (cf. fig. 180*b*).

But war itself is not a subject of Augustan art, as it would be later under the Empire. There are no references to the difficult and protracted campaigns in Spain, Illyria, and Germany. Indeed, the emphasis on scenes of peace and security helped wipe out the memory of these wars. Later Tacitus (*Annals* 1.9.5; 10.4) would remark with sarcasm on the contrast between the official imagery and reality: *pacem sine dubio . . . verum cruentam.* Peace there was, without question, but a bloody one.

a   b

Fig. 146. *a*) Aureus, Spain, 19/18 B.C. Triumphal arch for Augustus as victor over the Parthians, *b*) Denarius of M. Durmius, Rome, 19 B.C. Kneeling Parthian with standards.

Although the theme of victory over the Parthians is expressed in similar terms in all artistic media, there is no evidence that this was so planned or required. No one prevented the mint master of 19 B.C. from reviving an old tradition in comparing the victor in Parthia with Hercules and even with Dionysus, celebrating his triumph in a chariot drawn by elephants. But the comparison with Dionysus was clearly inappropriate, in the wake of Antony's abuses, and it was never repeated. Those whose assignment it was to praise the emperor generally knew how to stay within bounds and did so without the need for regimentation.

The Parthian motif is surely most elaborately expressed on the famous cuirassed statue of Augustus from Livia's villa at Prima Porta (fig. 148*a*). This is a marble copy of a bronze statue which must have been made in the years immediately following the victory over the Parthians. This much is clear from the intimate association between the imagery of the breastplate and certain motifs in Horace's *carmen saeculare*. Whoever commissioned the statue (perhaps the Senate) or advised the commissioner thus surely belonged to the princeps's inner circle. That it found favor with the imperial

Fig. 147. Two Parthians kneel with standards held up before the Victoria of Augustus. Impression from a glass paste.

family is evident from the findspot and the fact that the copy can be shown, on the basis of certain details, to have been made not long after the original. Although it was in just these years that Augustus cultivated a more modest image than ever and commissioned a less emphatic portrait, the Prima Porta statue does not hesitate to celebrate the radiant conqueror and make clear reference to his divine ancestry. In his left hand he held a spear, in the right perhaps the recaptured *signa*. His footwear, deliberately not that of a mortal, recalls the imagery of gods and heroes, while the Eros riding a dolphin is unquestionably an allusion to his ancestress Venus. Not only the portrait, but the entire body imitates the Classical forms of Polyclitan sculpture, which are intended to elevate the figure onto a higher plane (cf. p. 245). But it is the reliefs on the cuirass that convey a totally new conception of victory (fig. 148*b*).

In the center of the composition, the Parthian king extends the legionary eagle, attached to a battle standard, to a cuirassed figure in military pose, either a representative of the Roman legions or perhaps the embodiment of Mars Ultor himself. This perfectly straightforward, historical event is, however, only the centerpiece of an image encompassing heaven and earth. Two mourning women sit on either side of the central scene, representing peoples whose relationship to Rome was either that of conquered provinces (the woman holding an empty sheath) or client states (the other, holding a sword). The figure at right, distinguished by a dragon trumpet and boar's tail, should stand for the conquered Gallic tribes in the West, especially in Spain, while the despondent but not yet disarmed figure at left could represent the tributary peoples serving as buffer states in the East or in Germany. This would correspond to Horace's succinct summary of the various victory slogans of this period:

> So that you may remain *au courant* with the progress of Roman affairs. The *virtus* of Agrippa has brought the Cantaber to his knees, that of Claudius Nero [Tiberius] the Armenian. On his knees did Phraates accept the right and rule of Caesar. Golden abundance (*aurea copia*) scatters her fruits from overflowing horn over all Italy. (*Epistles* 1.12.25–29)

Similarly, on the cuirass relief the victory over the Parthians is celebrated as the culmination of a perfect world order. Mother Earth reclines beneath the central scene, her attributes essentially the same as those of Pax on the Ara Pacis (cf. fig. 137). Both goddesses stand for the *aurea copia* of the new age. This theme is further alluded to in the figures of Apollo and Diana, riding on the animals associated with them in Greek iconography, griffin and hind. These two divinities are in turn closely connected, as in Augustan poetry and at the Secular Festival, with the astral deities above the central

a

Fig. 148. *a*) Cuirassed statue of Augustus from the Villa of Livia at Prima Porta. Marble copy of a bronze original. After 20 B.C. *b*) Detail of the cuirass of the statue, with cosmic representation of the new ideology of victory.

b

group. The sun god Sol in his chariot appears above Apollo, the moon goddess Luna above Diana, and between them Caelus spreads out the canopy of the heavens. Only the upper part of Luna is visible; the rest is hidden (or outshone) by the winged figure of Dawn, who pours the dew from a jug. The artist has characterized Luna as *noctiluca* or *lucifera* (cf. the verses of Horace cited below) through the addition of a torch. The torch also emphasizes her association with Diana, who, quite uncharacteristically, holds one alongside her quiver. The reference is to a particular quality of the two goddesses, Luna/Diana, who in just these years coalesced into one:

> Sing, as is fitting for the son of Leto [Apollo],
> Sing of Luna, the brightness of the night, with her torch.
> She who grants us fruit and guides the hastening
> Course of the months [toward maturity or birth].
>
> Horace *carmen* 4.6.37–40

Another principal leitmotif of the Secular Festival is thus also present in the imagery of victory.

The astral gods, with their perpetual rising and sinking, symbolize eternity. Together with the sky god and the earth goddess they emphasize the cosmic character of space and time on the relief. The two sphinxes sitting on the epaulets of the cuirass are the guardians of this world (we shall hear more of them presently). The victory in Parthia is thus celebrated as both the prerequisite and the consequence of the *saeculum aureum*. The unique historical event is turned into a paradigm of salvation, in which the gods and the heavens act as guarantors, but need not intervene directly. Interestingly, the only figure in the scene who is not immobilized is the Parthian, looking up respectfully at the Roman eagle.

The princeps who wears this new image of victory on his breastplate becomes the representative of divine providence and the will of the gods. It is not a question of heroic deeds; through his very existence, the offspring of the gods guarantees the world order. The harmony between the state and the gods is embodied in him by virtue of his divine ancestors. In spite of the glamorous appeal of this statue, it is not incompatible with the many images of the togate Augustus with veiled head. He had no need to present himself as military victor in a series of new and spectacular exploits, for he possessed this quality permanently by virtue of his close relationship to the gods. The later imagery of victory will show how quickly this new conception took root in the visual arts (cf. fig. 178).

MYTH IN PAST AND PRESENT

The Rome of Augustus, the marble city filled with images of the *saeculum aureum,* was in itself impressive enough, but there was also a glorious past. The princeps's great act of 27 B.C. was one of "restoration," not innovation, and wherever possible he invoked Rome's forefathers. The new state and Augustus's dominant role in it required a legitimacy drawn from the past.

The great aristocratic families still defined themselves in terms of the old freedom of the Republic and might naturally have regarded the Principate as an exceptional and temporary circumstance of a sort with which Roman history was filled. For Augustus it was important to dispel this idea. The past had to be incorporated into the myth of the present new age, for the sake of Rome's future.

In the same year as the Secular Festival (17 B.C.), Augustus's daughter Julia, the widow of Marcellus and now wife of Agrippa, had given birth to a second son. The princeps adopted both this baby and his brother, older by three years, in the same year. The official names of these two were now *Gaius* (and *Lucius*) *Caesar, Augusti Caesaris filius, Divi Julii nepos*. Once the new state had been established, it was of course essential to insure that it would last. Legitimizing the rule of a Julian dynasty was a principal element in the creation of the new official mythology. It is no accident that the image of the deified Caesar with the *sidus Iulium* reappears on coins for the first time in this same year, 17 B.C. (cf. fig. 132*b*).

Augustus's Family and Rome: Growth of a Myth

When the *divi filius* first appeared to claim his inheritance, he had seized upon the mythical tradition of the Julian family, effectively capitalizing on his supposed descent from Venus and Aeneas (cf. fig. 27*b*). Then, however, he cast himself as savior and as protégé of Apollo, with no precedent in Roman history. It was only with the naming of his grandchildren as successors that the use of family mythology was revived, though not this time for personal self-glorification, as in the struggle with Marc Antony. In the interim, Vergil had written the *Aeneid*—at the instance of Augustus (29–19 B.C.)—and imbued the myth of Venus, the Fall of Troy, and the wanderings of Aeneas with a new meaning, in which not only the future rule of the Julian house, but the whole history of Rome was portrayed as one of predestined triumph and salvation. In the *Aeneid* the age of Augustus is adumbrated in visions and, in the mythological context, is celebrated as the ultimate realization of an all-encompassing world order. By virtue of his powerful and evocative imagery, Vergil created a national epic that was perfectly designed to bolster the Romans' self-confidence.

Just as with the building of temples and Augustan *publica magnificentia*, the public's response to the *Aeneid* was largely conditioned by its perception of the cultural superiority of the Greeks. In 26 B.C., after hearing a recitation of several books of the *Aeneid*, Propertius had written that the poem would surpass Homer's *Iliad*. The fame that Vergil enjoyed during his lifetime illustrates the readiness of his fellow Romans to identify with the na-

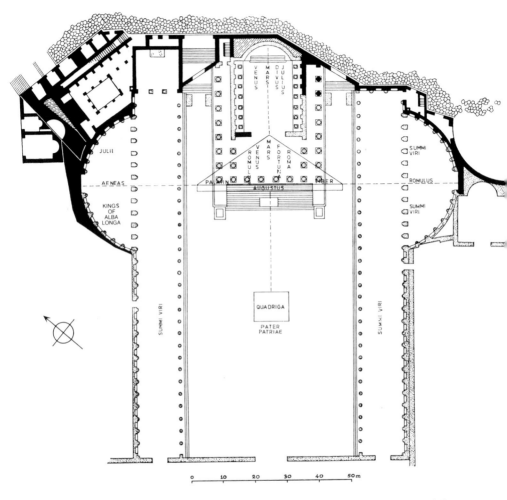

Fig. 149. Rome, Forum of Augustus. Ground plan, with reconstruction of the sculptural program. The southern part of the square is still unexcavated.

tional myth he had forged. Tacitus reports that "the people, when they heard his verses in the theater, all rose and cheered the poet, who happened to be present, as if he were Augustus himself" (*Dialogus* 13).

The monument which most fully expresses the new mythology is the Forum of Augustus (fig. 149). Octavian had vowed a temple to Mars Ultor during the battle against the assassins of Julius Caesar at Philippi (42 B.C.), but the sanctuary was finally dedicated only forty years later. By then Mars had proved himself Rome's avenger a second time, against the Parthians. This is why the recaptured *signa* were permanently displayed in the cella of the new temple. Identifying Mars Ultor with this later occasion, as well as with other deeds of Augustus's armies and generals, was a convenient way of forgetting the association with the civil war.

The temple was built by Augustus on his personal property (*in privato solo*) and financed by the spoils of war. He was thus clearly responsible for this monument, as was not the case with the Ara Pacis or the Prima Porta statue, and, as in the sanctuary of Apollo twenty-six years earlier, the program of the Forum of Augustus expresses his own ideas. Borrowed from Vergil's imagery, myth and history are woven together into a vision of salvation. Only instead of looking toward the future, as in the epic, here we are directed from the present back into the past. Forum and temple were conceived as emblematic of the new Rome, and their decorative programs were intended to educate her people. In keeping with his political style Augustus avoided any direct references to himself, though, conditioned by thirty years of praise for the ruler, people could hardly have failed to see hints and allusions everywhere. But even the most adamant opponent of Augustus would have been hard pressed to find any signs of unseemly self-promotion. As we shall see, even in the Forum of Augustus it remained for the Senate to put the capstone in the arch of a new national mythology, one that focused both myth and history on Augustus himself.

Venus and Mars

The mythological aspect of the Augustan program consisted of relatively few figures and contained basically no new elements. The essential element was the combination of two myth cycles, the legend of Troy and the story of Romulus. According to the myth of Rome's foundation, in the version employed by Vergil, Mars had seduced Rhea Silvia, daughter of the king of Alba Longa, and had thus become father to the twins Romulus and Remus and ancestor of the Romans. But Rhea Silvia belonged to the Trojan family of Aeneas and could therefore be incorporated into the family tree of Augustus (for this reason she is referred to by Augustan poets as Ilia, from Ilium [Troy]). Venus and Mars were then both ancestors of the Romans, though by different partners—something Ovid would turn into an ironic comment on the marriage legislation. Together Mars and Venus would watch over and protect their own. Mars guaranteed the Romans *virtus,* while Venus granted fertility and prosperity. The myth of the Julian family thus became the centerpiece of the new national myth. From now on the statue of the goddess of love would always stand beside that of the war god, even though this inevitably recalled the story of their adulterous affair in Greek mythology. But under Augustus this issue was skirted and the myth

Fig. 152. Bronze statue of Victoria with shield. Early Imperial. The statue copies a Greek model, figure 153, which represented Venus Genetrix. She celebrates the victories of her descendants by recording them on the shield of Mars.

Fig. 153. So-called Venus of Capua. Roman copy of a Greek original of the fourth century B.C. Venus is reflected in the shield of Mars.

which is copied from a work of the fifth century B.C. (fig. 154). In the use of two Classical prototypes in the same group, the symbolic meaning of the pair is rather blatantly expressed. The focus, however, is no longer on the mythological love affair, but on the deeper meaning which the new national mythology conferred on Venus and Mars. Significantly, later copies of this group, like the one illustrated here, substitute the portrait features of the imperial couple, who thus embody the moral values associated with the image.

For Ares, as ancestor of the Romans, appropriately impressive new images would also have to be created. The cult statue in the temple, probably executed in gold and ivory, is reflected in a colossal marble copy (fig. 155a). As earlier on the Ara Pacis, the god was depicted as a dignified father figure. Not many years before, in 20 B.C., in the round temple on the Capitol he

Fig. 154. Statue group of Mars and Venus, after an original of Augustan date. The bodies are copies of Classical statue types of divinities. The embrace makes manifest ideological associations. Later, the group was completed, as here, with portrait heads and thus served to convey the self-image of both imperial and private individuals. This group dates to the reign of the Emperor Commodus (A.D. 180–92).

was still shown youthful and nude, in an archaistic striding pose (cf. fig. 145*b*). Now he wears a richly decorated breastplate, a splendid helmet and greaves, and holds spear and shield.

While the breastplate is in the style of the period, the helmet imitates that of the Athena Parthenos of Phidias, with sphinxes and pegasoi. Beard and face are also in High Classical style, inspired by an Attic *strategos* portrait. But the breastplate and the shield are filled with images that allude to the

Fig. 155. *a*) Copy of the cult statue of Mars Ultor. *b*) Detail of the cuirass. The association of griffin and vegetal ornament has a symbolic character.

a

present. A large *corona civica* gleams on the shield (cf. fig. 151); that it really belonged to Augustus as "savior" would have been clear to anyone standing in the temple cella, for the recaptured eagles and standards were displayed like holy relics on the stepped base of the cult statue group (*Res Gestae* 29). The breastplate was dominated by two heraldic griffins. These and the Gorgoneion refer to the arms of Mars that spread terror (to the Romans the griffin was the animal not only of Apollo, but of Nemesis as well). The elephants' and rams' heads on the *pteryges* (leather lappets) are also to be understood as symbols of might. Yet the griffins sit on a large palmette with vines, and between them grows a plant arrangement like a candelabrum (fig. 155*b*). On the shoulder flaps appear crossed cornucopiae: the fatherly Mars has become a guardian of peace.

In the middle of the temple pediment, however, a more aggressive Mars was represented. Nude to the waist, he set his foot on the globe in a triumphant gesture and held sword and spear (cf. fig. 152). The two different images—the fatherly protector and the mighty conqueror—have deliberately been juxtaposed in this one temple. The latter aspect reflects Augustus's perception of his responsibility as ruler to enlarge the Empire. It is no wonder that later on the deified ruler himself was portrayed in the same statue type.

In fact, the Mars in the temple pediment is already connected indirectly with Augustus through the figures on either side of him. We have already mentioned Venus Genetrix and Eros; opposite her stood Fortuna holding rudder and cornucopia. The Senate had erected an altar to Fortuna Augusta in 19 B.C., after the princeps's return to Rome. Then come the seated figures of Roma and Romulus as an augur, then the reclining Tiber and Mons Palatinus, on which Romulus had built the first city wall and where Augustus was now living.

The composition of this pediment typifies the dignity and solemnity at which the new public art aimed, as well as the use of mythical figures and personifications to convey a message in terms of set slogans. The pediments of Classical and Hellenistic temples had usually either narrated a myth or dramatized a battle. Even in the Temple of Quirinus begun by Julius Caesar, several mythological events were depicted, including Romulus's *augurium*. Now, however, the figures are simply arranged beside one another in axial symmetry and represent either an abstract meaning or indirect references to the princeps.

Aeneas and Romulus: Old Myths in a New Guise

The same principle is true of the few narrative subjects that were chosen for representation from the repertoire of heroic myth. In the Forum of Augustus, in the central niches of the two large exedrae, Aeneas and Romulus stood as counterparts of Mars and Venus (cf. fig. 149). Venus's grandson was depicted fleeing from Troy in flames, the son of Mars as *triumphator*. The juxtaposition was not intended to measure the two heroes against one another, but to celebrate their deeds as the embodiments of two complementary virtues.

The statues themselves do not survive, but statuettes, reliefs, and wall paintings give us a good idea of their appearance. Aeneas carries his aged father Anchises and leads his little son Ascanius by the hand (fig. 156a). He also rescues the precious household gods, or Penates, held by the old Anchises. These were worshiped, along with the Palladium, in the Temple of Vesta, as guarantors of Rome's safety. Julius Caesar had also placed himself under the protection of Aeneas: a coin of his shows the hero fleeing with the

Fig. 156. Wall paintings from a house facade in Pompeii, with reflections of the statue groups in both exedrae in the Forum of Augustus. *a*) Aeneas with his father Anchises and the little Ascanius. *b*) Romulus with the arms of the enemy chief defeated in single combat (*spolia opima*).

archaic idol in his hands (cf. fig. 27*b*). But in the statue group in the Forum of Augustus, as on the coin, the dramatic story is not what is most important. Within the context of the new official mythology, Aeneas is presented as a paradigm of *pietas* toward the gods and his own father in time of need. For this reason the artist has incorporated in the image a series of allusions that, strictly speaking, have nothing to do with the narrative. The young Trojan hero, barely out of Troy, is depicted as a future Roman, wearing not only Roman armor, but, as ancestor of the Julian clan, even patrician footwear. By contrast, the little Ascanius is represented like a Phrygian shepherd, in long-sleeved garment and pointed cap, and, curiously, he carries a stick of the sort used in hunting rabbit. This is evidently an allusion to the tradition that the Trojan youth were shepherds on Mount Ida, where the boy's grandfather Anchises had his amorous encounter with Venus. In this scene, however, Anchises is the pious old man, his head veiled like that of Augustus and many other priests in Rome at this time. There is no room left for spontaneous artistic inspiration when every detail has a specific reference and a specific place in the overall design. A comparison with a coin minted for the young Octavian in 42 B.C. shows to what extent the later relief conforms to the new interpretation of myth under Augustus. In the earlier scene (cf. fig. 27*b*), Aeneas was shown nude, as in Greek iconography, carrying Anchises, who turns to look back apprehensively at his pursuers. The Penates themselves were apparently not yet considered so important and are omitted.

In the center of the opposite exedra, Romulus was shown with a *tropaion* (fig. 156*b*). If Aeneas was the *exemplum pietatis,* the image of protection from suffering and want, Romulus is the *exemplum virtutis.* He is celebrated as Rome's first *triumphator,* in accordance with the official reckoning of the *fasti,* which the Senate had recorded on long marble slabs and affixed to the triumphal arch of Augustus next to the Temple of Caesar. Happily, the beginning of these lists is preserved. The triumph of "King Romulus, the son of Mars" over King Akron of Caenina is precisely dated and fixed "in the first year of the state." Romulus was said to have defeated this enemy chief single-handedly and dedicated his armor as *spolia opima* in the Temple of Jupiter Feretrius, which Augustus would later rebuild before the Battle of Actium. This proud beginning under the "father of the city and of *virtus*" (Propertius 4.10) reached its culmination in the triple triumph of Augustus. These victories were celebrated in the arch where the triumphal *fasti* were displayed.

The juxtaposition of Aeneas and Romulus also occurs on the reliefs on the front side of the Ara Pacis. These scenes are different from those in the sanctuary of Mars in that there is no action, and instead of showing exemplary deeds they express the divine providence that governed Roman history from the beginning. To the right of the entrance is depicted Aeneas's arrival in Latium (fig. 157), to the left, the she-wolf with the twins.

The pious Aeneas, after much wandering, has finally found beneath an oak tree the sow with her young which had been prophesied (Vergil, *Aeneid* 3.390; 8.84). Here, according to the oracle, he was to build a temple to the Penates at the future site of Lavinium, and here the refugees from Troy would find a new home.

A simple stone altar has already been built in several courses and decorated. Wreathed attendants hold the sow ready for sacrifice, along with a large plate of fruit, while Aeneas himself, his head veiled, pours the libation. But he seems to be sunk deep in his own thoughts, and in fact the entire action looks curiously frozen. Even the attendants seem to gaze far into the distance, as if they were experiencing a vision. The thoughts of the viewer are likewise directed beyond the actual event portrayed. And the more deeply he immerses himself in the details of the scene, the more associations it evokes.

In order to endow the figure of Aeneas with a special dignity, the artist has rendered his head and torso in the manner of an Early Classical statue

Fig. 157. Rome, Ara Pacis Augustae. Aeneas sacrifices to the Penates rescued from Troy, after the landing in Latium. The Penates already appear in the temple first vowed only now. In front of him, the sow from Lanuvium prophesied by the oracle.

and dressed him in a mantle of "old Roman" style, which would have been familiar from the ancient statues of the Roman kings on the Capitol (Pliny *N.H.* 34.23). Like these figures, Aeneas holds a spear as token of his rule. Far different from the young warrior and savior portrayed in the Forum of Augustus, he is here the pious *pater Aeneas* who has endured a thousand trials. Ascanius, however, of whom only a small part is preserved, still wears Trojan dress and carries the shepherd's staff, though he has now grown into a youth. Aeneas's gaze is directed toward the handsome youths before him. These are idealized versions of the brave and pious youth Augustus wished for Rome's future, dressed as contemporary sacrificial attendants and holding the same paraphernalia one could see at the nearly daily religious rituals in Rome.

Aeneas offers the sacrifice not to Juno, as in Vergil, but to the Penates rescued from Troy (Dionysius of Halicarnassus 1.57). Thus the connection is made both to the image of Aeneas with the Penates in the Forum of Augustus and to the family of the princeps. On the Ara Pacis relief the little

Fig. 158. The shepherd Faustulus finds the she-wolf with the twins. Terra-
cotta revetment plaque.

marble temple, already built of fine ashlar blocks, appears on a height, the
two enthroned Penates looking down with favor on the sacrifice. This is of
course another reference to Rome's new *aurea templa* and to Augustus, who
in fact is himself shown with his head veiled and attending a sacrifice elsewhere on the same monument (cf. fig. 100*a*).

The associations multiply. Augustan artists created an utterly new narrative technique, in order to join together past and future in a single image.
Even more powerfully than in the allegorical Pax relief, the panel has the
effect of an icon, and the "arrested" movement in itself would have induced
in the viewer a contemplative mood. Observing the countless oak wreaths
and branches, he could not fail to realize that the oak tree is central to the
composition not only as a topographical indicator, but as a symbol of salvation directed at the present: from the very beginning, *fata* and the gods
were watching over Augustus.

The pendant to the Aeneas relief unfortunately survives only in fragments. Here too a sacred tree occupied the middle of the composition. This
time it is the fig tree (*ficus ruminalis*), beneath which the shepherd Faustulus
discovers the she-wolf with the twins. In the branches perches Mars's wood-

pecker, which had also helped nourish the babies. This peaceful scene was observed by Faustulus and Mars, standing calmly, almost reverentially before the miracle, as on a terra-cotta relief (fig. 158). Again the picture is more an "icon" than a narrative scene. Mars's head conveys a good impression of the mood of the entire panel (fig. 159). Like the viewer himself, he and Faustulus marvel at the workings of providence, under whose protection Rome has always stood. Contemporaries were aware that Augustus had rebuilt the supposed site of this miracle, the Lupercal at the foot of the Palatine, and every year they could experience the ancient ritual there discussed earlier. Once again the present was intimately linked to the mythical beginnings of Rome.

It is remarkable how on Augustan monuments the two most important mythological cycles have been reduced to so few images. By contrast, Pergamene sculptors had rendered much more colorfully and in greater detail the legend of the founding of Pergamum, which was likewise tailored to the needs of the ruling family. Even in the frieze of the Basilica Aemilia (34 B.C.?), stories of early Rome had been vividly narrated. Now, however, the didactic intentions took precedence, and the narrative content became wholly subsidiary. Significantly, there are virtually no figural friezes in Augustan art. Mythological subjects are restricted to just a few individual scenes, whose form and composition are made to suit the needs of the offi-

Fig. 159. Rome, Ara Pacis Augustae. Head of Mars. The artist has employed High Classical forms, as for the Aeneas (cf. figs. 157, 204).

Fig. 160. Temple of
Vesta, with oak tree
with symbolic meaning.
Marble relief, Early Im-
perial.

cial mythology. In this imagery, Aeneas and Romulus no longer come across
as living, breathing mythological figures, but as intellectualized and idealized paradigms. And since the campaign for moral renewal was built
around only a few leitmotifs, the corresponding mythological imagery focused on two key concepts, *pietas* and *virtus*. The exemplary behavior of
the heroes is displayed as a model and wherever possible linked with the
living *exemplum* of the princeps. Augustus in turn modeled his own behavior on the mythical *exempla*, creating once again an association between the
real life of the present and the mythological past.

Another good example of this is evident in the particular care that Augustus lavished on the cult of Vesta. Once he had finally become Pontifex
Maximus, after the death of Lepidus in 12 B.C., he built a sanctuary of the
goddess in his own house on the Palatine (so that he would not have to
occupy the priest's headquarters in the Regia). Thus when Augustus, as the
descendant of Aeneas, conducted a sacrifice in front of the Temple of Vesta,
where the Palladium was with good reason displayed, it was as if the myth
of the Penates and Palladium being rescued were recreated. Augustus *had* in
fact rescued the images of the gods—from neglect and oblivion. No wonder
that in one representation of the Temple of Vesta an oak tree protrudes quite
meaningfully from behind the temple (fig. 160).

Particularly characteristic of Augustan mythological imagery is the emphasis on the workings of predestination and providence. This was supposed to induce in the viewer a meditative and quasi-religious mood, which

a

Fig. 161. *a*) The Muse Klio (?) leaning on an elaborate vessel. Next to her, a globe carried by a winged creature. Marble relief, Early Imperial. *b*) Detail of the vessel, with abduction of a woman and Diomedes carrying the Palladium.

would make him receptive to otherwise rather vague intimations of divine salvation.

On a relief preserved in two copies (fig. 161*a*, *b*), the Muse Klio appears *in propria persona* above a scene of the destruction of Troy, deep in contemplation. She leans thoughtfully over a large vessel, on which a scene of rape (Ajax and Cassandra?) is depicted. Again a finger is pointed to direct our attention, lest we miss the meaning. Diomedes, his back to the tumult, holds the large Palladium: Troy must fall, so that Rome may be founded and her present greatness realized. The figure of Diomedes is also important elsewhere in Augustan art, because of both the rape and the rescue of the Palladium. Just as once Diomedes (or Aeneas) had rescued the Palladium that was now worshiped in the Temple of Vesta, so had Augustus saved it, as Varro would say (cf. p. 103) through his preservation of the Roman state. For this reason he and later emperors were sometimes represented as Diomedes. As in the scenes of Aeneas's flight from Troy, here too an image of suffering is incorporated into the story. It seems that Vergil's epic once again had an impact on the artists or their patrons.

But artistic imagery seldom required the viewer to be so learned as in this instance. Most mythological scenes were easy to understand, especially since they usually came down to the same message: Aeneas, Vesta, Diomedes, or the emperor himself associated with the Palladium; Venus or Aeneas symbolizing the divine ancestry of the imperial house; or Apollo, the tripod, the sphinx, or the sibyl all alluding to divine providence.

What makes many modern, overly learned interpretations of Augustan iconography so tedious reflects an important characteristic of the works of art themselves: their unrelentingly didactic intent, manifested in constant repetition, similies, and equivalences.

To the more perceptive observer, even then, it all became too much. He tried to find respite in irony and humor. Ovid's ambiguous and sometimes malicious verses apparently found a responsive audience, and there were occasionally even caricatures of the sacrosanct mythological images. The owner of a villa near Stabiae, for example, had painted on his wall a parody of the often copied Aeneas group in the Forum of Augustus, with the heroic ancestors of the princeps depicted as apes with dogs' heads and huge phalloi (fig. 162). And this is not a unique example, for Winckelmann mentions a bronze statuette of the same subject.

Yet these were still minority voices. In general the new mythological im-

Fig. 162. Caricature of the Aeneas group from the Forum of Augustus (cf. fig. 156a), as dog-headed apes. Wall painting from a villa near Stabiae.

Fig. 163. Tombstone of Petronia Grata. The image was chosen by her daughter, to express their close relationship.

agery was widely spread through Roman cities, and not only in the public sphere. It played an important part in private commissions as well and penetrated into the consciousness of a wide spectrum of the population. We may perhaps wonder how many people, as they enjoyed an evening's entertainment at home, sang, like Horace:

> Let us by ancient custom recall great men
> In song sustained by Lydian flutes: let us
> Of Troy and of Anchíses sing, and
> Bountiful Venus's high descendants.
> *Odes* 4.15.29

The motif of Aeneas and his family was also widespread on finger rings, lamps, and in terra-cotta statuettes, and undoubtedly served as a token of loyalty. It was not long before this same group was employed in the private sphere as a symbol of *pietas*. Those who commissioned grave reliefs like the one illustrated here (fig. 163) had apparently assimilated the moral content of this originally political image and used it to express the *pietas* of the deceased or the bond between the dead and the living (cf. p. 278).

Summi Viri: A Revised Version of Roman History

In antiquity there was no clear distinction between myth and history. The deeds of one's heroic ancestors were considered no less "historical" than those of more recent generations. On the contrary, the former were especially prized for their value as *exempla*. It was thus no departure from tradition when Augustus set up statues of the worthiest men in his family beside the Aeneas group in the exedra and colonnade to the left of the Temple of Mars Ultor (cf. fig. 149). Roman aristocrats had for years called attention to the importance of their *gens* with statues of their distinguished ancestors. But this had never been done on such a scale as in the unparalleled "gallery of worthies" of the Julian family in the Forum of Augustus, going from Aeneas and Ascanius and the other kings of Alba Longa, to the important members of the clan in the Early Republic and down to the present. Even the father of Julius Caesar, a man of no consequence, was honored here with a statue. Naturally certain gaps had to be filled with second- or third-rate individuals, in order to create the impression that the family had continually distinguished itself throughout all of Roman history. But the most original and suggestive aspect of the whole program was that the counterpart to this Julian family portrait gallery, to the right of the temple, was a row of carefully selected great men of Rome (*summi viri: Historia*

Augusta Alexander Severus 28.6). These stood beside Romulus and the kings of Rome in the opposite colonnade. The juxtaposition of the two portrait galleries thus justified the position of the princeps's family in the new Rome by proclaiming its unique historical importance. The reality of competition between Rome's leading families stretching back for centuries, all the ups and downs, and the relative insignificance of the Julii from the fourth to second centuries B.C. were all thereby utterly obscured. In this version, the Julii had always been Rome's most important family, for this family would produce her savior. A similar interpretation was already to be found in the poetry of Vergil.

The criteria used in selecting the greatest figures of Roman history made it possible to eliminate certain periods better forgotten, especially those of internal conflict, and to present a consistently harmonious picture. Individuals singled out for inclusion were above all those "who had brought the Roman people from its modest beginnings to its present position of greatness and world rule" (Suetonius *Augustus* 31).

By this criterion, the greatest Romans were the imperialists, generals, and triumphators. The display of statues in the sanctuary of Mars suggested a coherent overall view of Roman history. Onetime enemies stood united in this national Hall of Fame: Marius beside Sulla, Lucullus beside Pompey. The youngest of the "empire builders" was Augustus's stepson Drusus, who fell in 9 B.C. while on campaign in Germany. Only the dictator Julius Caesar himself was missing from the gallery of Julian worthies, for as a god he could not be included among the mortals. Instead, a place within the temple was reserved for the Divus Julius.

Beneath each statue was a brief *titulus* giving the name and *cursus honorum* of the honorand, as well as a longer *elogium* recounting his greatest services to the state (fig. 164). Among these were also recorded the nonmilitary achievements of the *summi viri*. Appius Claudius Caecus, for example, is celebrated for his victories over the Samnites and Sabines, for building the Via Appia, the aqueduct bearing his name, and the Temple of Bellona, and for having successfully prevented the Romans from making peace with King Pyrrhus of Epirus! This cataloglike inscription would have reinforced the impression that those honored with statues here were truly the greatest. The preserved fragments in marble include several figures in cuirass or toga (figs. 165–66). Most likely the type was chosen in each case to reflect the individual's principal accomplishments. Older statues also seem to have been incorporated into this gallery. The fragmentary foot of a figure wearing the *calcei patricii* testifies to the extraordinarily high quality of the new marble statues.

These portrait galleries thus offered a revised version of history suited to the purposes of Augustan Rome, conveyed equally in image and text. Ro-

Fig. 165. Fragment from the foot of a portrait statue in the Forum of Augustus. The sculptor has carefully depicted the double laced "Senatorial shoes," a significant sign of high social status. Each loop is decorated with a stylized classical palmette.
Fig. 164. Rome, Forum of Augustus. Statue from the gallery of *summi viri*, with *titulus* and *elogium*. Reconstruction.

man history was reduced to a single, continuous process of the growth of empire up to the present. This impression resulted necessarily from the abbreviated accounts of each individual's greatest achievements.

There can be no doubt that Augustus participated directly in designing this program and in the selection of the *summi viri*. According to Pliny (*N.H.* 22.6.13), he was even thought to have composed the *elogia* inscribed below the statues himself. We need not take this literally, for he surely had many advisers, and the arrangement of the places of honor will certainly have engendered long and lively discussion. There is good reason to believe, for example, that C. Julius Hyginus, a freedman of Augustus who ran the library in the Temple of Apollo, played an important part in designing the program. He would have been considered an expert in such matters, for he had written a book *De Familiis Troianis*, as well as a commentary on Vergil's *Aeneid*. But the basic idea no doubt originated in the great scene in

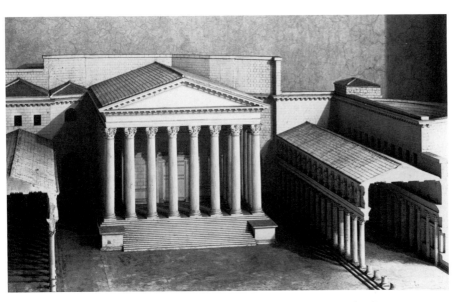

Fig. 166. Forum of Augustus. Detail of model. The statue niches for the *summi viri* are visible on the rear side of the colonnades to the right of the Temple of Mars.

book 6 of the *Aeneid*, when Anchises in the underworld shows Aeneas the great Romans of the future, down to Caesar Augustus: "He brings the golden age back to Latium, Saturn's onetime realm" (*Aeneid* 6.792).

The Romans would later witness the whole panorama of this Roman Valhalla once again after Augustus's death, in his funeral procession.

His burial now followed. The bier was made of gold and ivory, adorned with a purple shroud. The body itself was hidden from view, in a sarcophagus. But one could see a wax image of him in the garb of the triumphator. This was brought from his house on the Palatine by the consuls designated for the following year and carried at the head of the procession. A second statue, of gold, came from the Curia, and a third was brought on a triumphal quadriga. Then followed the "images" [*eikones:* probably individuals carrying the appropriate portrait masks] of his ancestors and deceased relatives, with the exception of Julius Caesar, who was included among the heroes. [For this reason his statue probably stood in the Temple of Mars Ultor; cf. fig. 151.] There then followed the *eikones* of all those Romans who had distinguished themselves in any way, at the head of the procession Romulus himself. Even Pompey was among them, and all the peoples conquered by Augustus, each in his native dress. (Dio Cassius 56.34)

But long before this mute tableau with masks, it was clear that the gallery of heroes in the Forum of Augustus was directly linked to Augustus himself. He had explained the significance of the visual program in an edict on the occasion of the Forum's dedication, to make everything perfectly clear: "It had been his thought that the Roman people should judge him, so long as he was alive, and then future *principes* by the standards of these men" (Suetonius *Augustus* 31).

This was very much in keeping with Augustus's practice of using arguments grounded in the laws and the very words of earlier generations. The response to this challenge from Augustus was immediate: the Senate erected an imposing honorary monument in the form of a triumphal quadriga, whose inscription proclaimed the new honorific title Pater Patriae which he had been granted in the same year his Forum and the Temple of Mars were dedicated.

In my thirteenth consulship, the Senate, equites, and the entire Roman people conferred on me the title "Father of the Nation" and determined to place an appropriate inscription in the entrance to my house, in the Curia Iulia, and beneath the quadriga which the Senate had erected to me in the Forum (*Res Gestae* 35)

The inscription also recorded all of Augustus's victories (Velleius Paterculus 2.39), and these clearly showed him to be the greatest of the great.

The comparison between past and present greatness invited by Augustus was not merely for rhetorical effect. The ceremonies of state which Augustus initiated in connection with the new Forum and Temple of Mars insured that in the future the glory of the present would be enacted against the background of the Roman past, now so neatly reorganized. Here young men when they came of age would put on the toga and were inscribed in the military lists. In the Temple of Mars the Senate officially proclaimed war, peace, or triumphs. From here provincial governors departed on campaign, and here returning victorious generals laid down the insignia of victory. Here barbarian princes swore their friendship and allegiance to Rome. The Temple of Mars thus took over certain distinctions that had previously been reserved for the Capitoline Temple of Jupiter. In short, the new Forum of Augustus became the showplace of Rome's "foreign policy," for everything associated with *virtus* and military glory.

When we hear how Caligula explicitly directed those bringing his letters from Gallia to carry them first through the Forum Romanum, dismounting at the Curia, then finally present them to the assembled Senate in the Temple of Mars (Suetonius *Caligula* 44), we can imagine the elaborate ceremony which must have accompanied truly important occasions, such as triumphs or the reception of foreign royalty.

In the future, victorious generals were to be honored with a bronze statue in triumphal garb in the Forum, and arms and insignia captured from the defeated enemy would be displayed here. This much was laid down by Augustus, and indeed we know the names of several men who did receive this honor by order of the emperor. But Augustus's zeal in trying to inspire imitation of the great men of the past by honoring each in accordance with his service to Rome was largely disregarded. The statues of worthy generals of the present were relegated to spaces between the columns or on the edge of the square, while for the imperial princes Germanicus and Drusus Minor Tiberius erected a triumphal arch beside the Temple of Mars in A.D. 19, in direct imitation of the arches of Augustus beside the Temple of Caesar.

THE ASSIMILATION OF AUGUSTUS'S SUCCESSORS INTO THE NATIONAL MYTHOLOGY

The fusion of myth and history was realized in the creation of a timeless present. A concept of the future, in the sense of a further development, did not exist in this system. The *saeculum aureum* had dawned, and it was only a question of maintaining and repeating it. After a period of rapid and drastic change, Rome had arrived at a state of equilibrium, a timeless and mythically defined present. Internal harmony and external strength, fertility and prosperity, would all continue unabated, at least so long as the Julii ruled and both princeps and people made sure to worship the gods as was proper and live according to the ways of their forefathers.

Gaius and Lucius Caesar as Descendants of Venus

He never commended his sons to the people without adding "if they are worthy." He always lamented bitterly that whenever these youths appeared, the whole people stood up and applauded. (Suetonius *Augustus* 5.6)

Promoting his successors effectively was one of Augustus's chief concerns as he got older. In so doing he had to maintain his image as *primus inter pares* but at the same time make it clear that the successor could only be a member of the "chosen people," the Julian family. With the apportioning of roles now widely accepted, Augustus's two grandsons Gaius and Lucius

Fig. 167. Two denarii of C. Marius. Rome, 13 B.C. *a–b) Augustus Divi F(ilius),* Julia with her sons Gaius and Lucius Caesar. *c)* head of Diana/Julia with quiver and Augustan coiffure.

could be groomed for succession years in advance. While the Senate, equites, and people applauded and awarded them honors and high public office when they were under age, the princeps kept his distance, consented only reluctantly—but all the same carefully selected the boys' public appearances. The older of the two, Gaius, was presented to the public for the first time at age seven, in 13 B.C., when he took part in the Trojan Games. In the same year the *tresvir monetalis* C. Marius struck a coin with busts of the two boys with their mother Julia (fig. 167*a, b*).

Above Julia's head hovers the *corona civica* as a dynastic symbol and proof of direct descent from Augustus. On the reverse of a second coin the same bust appears alone, here linked with Diana's quiver (fig. 167*c*). The implication is that the goddess herself had attended the birth of the two boys. We are reminded here of the opening verses of the *carmen saeculare*. The services of the boys' real father Agrippa are also celebrated in the same series of coins more prominently than ever before, especially in references

Fig. 168. Two denarii of C. Sulpicius Platorinus. Rome, 13 B.C. *a)* Agrippa, as general and admiral, wears the "crown" with battlements and ships' beaks awarded him by Augustus. *b)* Agrippa next to Augustus on the chair of office (*bisellinum*). The podium is decorated with the ships' beaks, probably one of the two speakers' platforms in the Forum Romanum.

Fig. 169. Rome, Ara Pacis Augustae. Detail of the procession on the south enclosure wall. The little Gaius Caesar clings to the toga of his father Agrippa (cf. fig. 100).

Fig. 170. Detail from the procession on the south enclosure wall: Lucius Caesar with family members, precisely opposite his brother. The two boys are perhaps depicted as little Trojans by their dress and neck-ring (*torques*).

to the Battle of Actium. Agrippa sits beside Augustus on the *rostra* and his likeness bears the *corona rostrata* (fig. 168).

The Senate also honored the young princes in this same year, on the Ara Pacis. They occupy a prominent position, though depicted in an unusual form, as little Trojans or "Trojan riders" (figs. 169, 170). Just at that point where the two processions join, those of members of the imperial family and of the various priesthoods, two boys, one older than the other, are represented on either side of the altar enclosure. Unlike the other children on the frieze, who wear the toga, these two wear a short *tunica* and have long hair (the older, Gaius, with a headband). Both are clearly marked out by the *torques,* a braided ring about the neck. The "Troy Game" was an ancient religious competition on horseback favored by the youths of the Roman nobility. In the Augustan period it was integrated into the myth of Troy and particularly encouraged by Augustus as a way of promoting military training among the youth. Vergil describes the game in the *Aeneid* and even specifically mentions the *torques* (5.556). Once Augustus awarded a golden torque to a boy who had been injured in the contest, which was rather dangerous. Probably the Senate, as sponsor of the Ara Pacis, chose to have the young princes depicted in a costume familiar to the Romans from the Troy Games, perhaps even from the historical procession itself.

This interpretation is still controversial. Some scholars object that the boys on the frieze are too small to represent Gaius and Lucius, who were seven and four when the Ara Pacis was dedicated, and suggest instead that they are barbarian princes raised at the court of Augustus. As so often absolute certainty is impossible, but several points argue in favor of calling them Gaius and Lucius. They occupy a prominent position in a procession which is otherwise, as far as we can tell, composed solely of members of the imperial house arranged according to the order of dynastic succession. The way that the older boy clutches the toga of Agrippa is especially striking. Furthermore, the two boys are the only ones whose lively, childlike expressions bring some variety to the solemn procession and thus call attention to themselves. As on other occasions, the winning charm of the outgoing little princes is exploited to gain support for the ruling family, and in this context it is perfectly understandable that they should be represented a little younger than they really were.

A few years later Gaius was presented to the legions on the Rhine. Here again the young prince, now twelve years old, had to display his courage in a similar kind of equestrian game. The event was subsidized by a donation from Augustus, and the mint at Lugdunum recorded it for posterity (fig. 171). The great impression that the boys made on the troops is illustrated, for example, by a scabbard ornament depicting the two princes as officers, wearing the cuirass, flanking their mother (fig. 172).

Not long after this their public careers officially began. In 5 B.C., Augustus had himself elected consul for the first time in seventeen years, so that he could personally escort the fifteen-year-old Gaius, who had already received the *toga virilis,* to the Forum and into the Senate. It must have been an impressive and memorable scene. At the same time Gaius himself was named consul-designate for the year A.D. 1, and the equites elected him *princeps iuventutis,* which had no concrete political significance but quickly became a kind of official title for the successor to the throne. The previous year Augustus had rejected a resolution of the people to elect Gaius consul, but now this too was accomplished, accompanied by great ceremony. There was a distribution of money (sixty denarii per person), and official delegations came to Rome from distant parts of the Empire. From now on, whenever possible the two princes accompanied the princeps at all his public appearances (cf. fig. 109).

On a coin minted at Lugdunum between 2 B.C. and A.D. 11 (fig. 173), the two *principes iuventutis* are shown with the honorary tokens conferred

Fig. 171. Aureus, Lug-
dunum/Lyon, 8 B.C.
Gaius participates in
equestrian games. He
wears the *bulla* around
his neck and holds in his
left hand shield and
sword. A battle standard
indicates the camp.

Fig. 172. Decoration of an Augustan scabbard. Julia between her sons Gaius and Lucius, both represented as generals in cuirass.

on them by the equites, a silver shield and silver lance. Above their heads
are tokens of the priesthoods to which they belonged, Gaius as pontifex,
Lucius as augur. The message of these routine symbols is the same as that
of the many honorary monuments and decrees issued throughout the Empire after the tragic and premature deaths of both youths (Lucius in A.D. 2,
Gaius in A.D. 4): the same virtues that marked their father also marked the
two princes.

Augustus had taken a great interest in these boys from the time they were
infants and even made sure that they learned to imitate his handwriting
(Suetonius *Augustus* 64). As they grew up, official portraits were created,

Fig. 173. Denarii and Aurei, Lugdunum, 2 B.C. Gaius and Lucius Caesar in togas
with honorific shield and spear. The legend calls them "sons of Augustus, consuls
designate, and *principes iuventutis*."

Figs. 174 (left) and 175 (right). Portraits of Gaius or Lucius Caesar, most likely posthumous. The facial features and their hairstyles imitate portraits of Augustus. The heads belong to nude "hero"-statues in Classical style.

which could then be used as models by the workshops commissioned to produce honorary statues and busts. These depict boys whose faces seem to come from the same mold as Augustus's (figs. 174, 175). They are classicizing, somewhat artificial faces filled with a grave dignity, no less stylized than the portrait of Augustus. The two are differentiated only by the different arrangements of forks and tongues in the hair across the brow. The portraits of their brother Agrippa Postumus, by contrast, who was not at first admitted into the Julian family, resemble those of his real father (fig. 176).

By now the holy aura that had grown up about the Julian family for nearly half a century had created a certain atmosphere. Alongside Venus and Aeneas, Julius Caesar now received renewed honors. A coin minted in 12 B.C. recalls the beginning of Octavian's career, when he laid a star on the statue of Caesar after the appearance of the *sidus Iulium* (cf. fig. 25*a*). But significantly, the mint master now has the princeps, holding his *clipeus virtutis*, represented larger than the newest member of the Roman pantheon. Even images of Caesar's apotheosis were now openly displayed. An altar of the Lares of about 7 B.C. preserves a modest copy of such an image, joining the young princes with the Divus Julius and their ancestor Venus (fig. 177).

Fig. 176. Bust of Agrippa Postumus. In contrast to the portraits of his brothers, who were admitted to the *gens Iulia,* his physiognomy is not idealized in classicizing style, but is likened to the portrait of Agrippa.

The deified Caesar ascends to heaven in a chariot drawn by winged horses. Venus Genetrix greets him with one hand and with the other embraces a small togate figure, while a second, even smaller, clings to her. These are the two princes, shown under the protection of their ancestor. (Their own mother, Julia, received at this time honorary statues in the guise of Aphrodite in the Greek East.) A third togate figure stands behind the chariot with right hand raised in prayer, most likely Augustus. The reason for his modest role here may be that he himself dedicated the original of this relief to the Divus Iulius.

The two princes, in whom Augustus placed so much hope, were thus elevated even while still alive to extraordinary heights, and after their early deaths were incorporated permanently into the new national myth. They were honored throughout the whole Empire as new heroes. They received triumphal arches, public buildings, altars, and even temples, such as the famous Maison Carrée in Nîmes (cf. fig. 201). In Rome the voting precincts were named for them and their names were added to the sacred songs of the dancing priests known as Salii. Augustus also gave their names to the Basilica Iulia in the Forum and to the large park near the Naumachia in Trastevere (Nemus Gai et Luci Caesaris). In front of the Basilica Aemilia arose a new and lavishly decorated portico bearing the names of the two brothers, and the Senate also erected a major honorary monument in the Forum. A

Fig. 177. Augustan altar of the Lares, ca. 7 B.C. Apotheosis of the Divus Iulius. In the foreground, Venus Genetrix with the two princes C. and L. Caesar. Behind the chariot, Augustus before a temple structure (column). The missing heads were originally inset.

huge inscription belongs to this monument (*CIL,* VI, 36908), but, aside from recording that the boys belonged to the imperial family, it contains only the information that Lucius was already designated consul at age fourteen.

The princes did not live to celebrate a triumph over a conquered foreign people, the crucial act by which imperial rule was legitimized, but at least Gaius could be celebrated posthumously as new victor over the Parthians and Armenians. Augustus had sent him, at age twenty, to resolve a conflict over the throne of Armenia and put down uprisings in Parthia (1 B.C.). Among his staff were the finest experts on Eastern affairs, and all was carefully planned in advance. Augustus's prayers for his son were virtually programmatic: the wisdom of Pompey, the bravery of Alexander, and his own Fortuna (Plutarch *Moralia* 2.98.10). No wonder poetry and epigrams on Greek statue bases celebrated him as a new Ares as he made his way to the East. Like Alexander and Augustus before him, he would march to the East and earn his title *princeps designatus* (*CIL,* XI, 1420). The undertaking was only a partial success. At the siege of Artagira, which he did eventually take, Gaius was mortally wounded and died on the journey home.

Among the posthumous monuments honoring Gaius is probably the over life-size cuirassed statue found in the theater of Jol-Caesarea (modern Cher-cel, in Algeria), capital city of the kings of Mauretania. It may have been set up by King Juba II, who grew up at the court in Rome together with Gaius. Since, however, the decorative program of the cuirass is closely related to that of the Augustus from Prima Porta (cf. fig. 148*b*), we may suspect that the Chercel statue is one of several copies of a major monument created in Rome.

On both statues, the reliefs on the cuirass celebrate a military victory. On the statue of Gaius (fig. 178), a heroized member of the imperial house hands over to Venus Victrix a figure of Victoria with *tropaion*. The youthful hero is represented in the same statuary pose as the Divus Iulius in his temple in the Forum Romanum (cf. fig. 26). Later this pose will be used frequently to represent heroized emperors and princes after their death, sug-gesting that the figure on the cuirass is also deceased (cf. fig. 194). In addi-tion, since the decorations of the shoulder flaps appear to be stylized heads of orientals, it is tempting to associate the victory alluded to here with Gaius Caesar's victories in Armenia and Parthia.

The young scion of the Julian house piously hands over the tokens of his victories to the family's ancestress. Since she is depicted armed, we may call her Venus Victrix. The god of war himself appears above the scene in the form of a large bust, which is clearly derived from the cult statue of Mars Ultor dedicated in 2 B.C. (cf. fig. 155). Eros with the bow stands behind Venus, and a Victory holds the *corona civica* over the head of the prince and designated successor. This is analogous to honorary inscriptions that refer to the *iam designatus . . . princeps* (CIL, XI, 1421).

What makes this ostensible image of Gaius as victor so interesting for our discussion, however, is not so much the way it is taken for granted that the young prince assumes the role of Augustus, but the allusions to the victory at Actium and the Golden Age, in the form of sea centaurs holding rudders and regular centaurs whose tails end as vines (fig. 178). In other words, the new victory of Gaius assures the continuity of the well-being first created by Augustus at Actium. The old slogans of the early Augustan Age have coalesced into an ideology of victory, and the princeps's early victories are treated like heroic deeds of the mythological past.

Tiberius and Drusus as Commanders of the Imperial Army

At the time Augustus adopted his two grandsons, Tiberius and Drusus, his two stepsons, were twenty-five and twenty-one years old. They were never considered primary candidates as successors to the throne, but instead played an important role as military commanders. As such they contributed

Fig. 178. Posthumous cuirassed statue of Gaius Caesar (?). As on the cuirass of Augustus (fig. 148*a*), the victory is placed in a cosmic setting. The prince victorious in the East extends his Victoria to his ancestress Venus. Below, a sea centaur and a land centaur embody the happy fruits of victory. The bearded heads of barbarians on the leather lappets allude to the conquered Parthians. Above, Mars Ultor.

Fig. 179. Coin series, Lugdunum (Lyon), 15 B.C. *a*) Tiberius and Drusus hand over their palms of victory to Augustus. *b*) The bull as symbol of Mars Ultor. *c–d*) Apollo Actius and Diana Sicilia, recalling the earlier victories of Augustus at Naulochoi and Actium. *e–f*) Quinarius. Augustus and Victoria sitting on the globe.

to the glory of the dynasty, as well as their own, long before Augustus reluctantly made Tiberius his successor after the deaths of his two grandsons. Like other commanders, Tiberius and Drusus were *legati* of Augustus, but as "princes" they of course held a special rank. This quickly evolved into a kind of official position as "acting" emperor and became a permanent part of the ideology of rule. When the princeps was not able to take the field himself, the princes fought in his place. Their victories were his victories, for he alone possessed the power of commander-in-chief, *imperium maius*. This juridical situation took on a mythical dimension through the medium of artistic imagery.

The first occasion requiring the new imagery was the wars of expansion carried on by Drusus and Tiberius against the Alpine tribes. The mint at Lugdunum, which was governed by the princeps himself, commemorated the first successes against the Vindelici with a very revealing series of denarii and aurei. The principal motifs show either Drusus alone or Drusus and Tiberius, both dressed as generals, handing over to Augustus the palm branches of victory (fig. 179a). He wears the toga and sits on the official seat (*sella curulis*). Though this is set on a high podium, he is nonetheless still depicted as a magistrate, in accordance with the "constitution" of the Principate. But the four remaining types in this series elevate the same occasion into a universal statement of divinely sanctioned Augustan rule (fig. 179*b–e*).

The figures of Diana and Apollo, with the inscriptions SICIL. and ACT., recall the victories that started it all, at Naulochoi and Actium. The charging bull, an image once carried by Caesar's legions on their flags, symbolizes the unstoppable power of the Roman Mars. Victoria, however, does not fly as on earlier coins, but rather sits calmly on the globe, her hands folded in her lap. Roman rule is secure and will remain so. The portrait of the princeps, now age fifty, appears as usual on the obverse, but he looks unusually youthful, and for the first time in years his titulature includes "Divi Filius."

Under pressure from Augustus (cf. Suetonius *Vita Horatii* 31f.), Horace also commemorated the deeds of the two stepsons, in two long odes. The Drusus ode (4.4) celebrates primarily the glory of the Claudian family and the perseverance of their forefathers in times of hardship, while Augustus is the focus of the Tiberius ode, "the greatest of all rulers (*principes*) as far as the sun's rays reach" (4.14.5f):

> With forces you had furnished, advised by you,
> With gods of yours presiding; for since the day
>   When Alexandria surrendered
>   Harbor and tenantless royal palace
>
> Fortuna has consistently prospered you
> And granted happy outcome to all your wars,
>   Conferring glory and a hoped-for
>   Honor upon your achieved dominion.
>
> The hitherto unmastered Cantabrian.
> The Mede, the Hindu, even the nomad Scyth.
>   Defers to you, O shielding presence
>   Over our Rome and the land Italian;
>
> The Nile, of sources hidden in mystery,
> The Danube, and the Tigris of rapid flow,
>   The monster-teeming waves of Ocean
>   Bursting in thunder to far-off Britons
>   *Odes* 4.14.33–48

The poet and the coins issued at Lugdunum make use of the same *topoi*. The Senate too erected the great Tropaeum Alpinum near Nice, not in honor of the victorious generals, but for the commander-in-chief, "quod eius ductu auspiciisque gentes Alpinae omnes quae a mari supero ad inferum pertinebant sub imperium populi Romani sunt redactae . . ." because under his leadership and his auspices all the peoples of the Alps down to the sea were brought under Roman rule (Pliny *N.H.* 3.136; *CIL*, V, 7817).

If we compare the official image of Augustus's stepsons with that of his grandsons, especially Gaius, the hierarchy is very clear. While the *principes iuventutis* received constant honors as the designated successors, even as young boys, and, both in official imagery and in reality, stood beside Augustus, the commanders Drusus and Tiberius, who had truly earned such honors, are blatantly portrayed as subservient to the commander-in-chief. The consistency of honorific formulas illustrates how the princeps, while remaining in the background, was able to set the proper tone. A comparison with the reaction to the earlier Parthian victory of Augustus shows that those who might have been expected to take the lead in celebration of the ruler now much more cautiously waited to follow signals from above. Their unanimity is impressive—the prime example is the change in his position to which Tiberius had to adapt.

Tiberius as Successor to the Throne

Augustus's pleasure in his young imperial commanders was short lived. Drusus died in Germany, while Tiberius had been estranged from Augustus since 7 B.C. and remained so for eleven years. Offended at the way Augustus allowed his adolescent grandsons to be celebrated as successors, he went into voluntary exile on Rhodes and lived there as a Greek, wearing chlamys and sandals and gathering a circle of poets and philosophers around him. (For him, too, Greek culture was a means of escape from the "real" world.) Only after "grim Fortuna" had "deprived" Augustus of his sons (thus the beginning of the *Res Gestae*) was he forced to settle for this new successor. Tiberius was thus adopted and, for his part, had to adopt Drusus's son Germanicus and Agrippa Postumus, born after his father Agrippa's death. Unlike the deceased grandsons, Tiberius, as a member of the proud Claudian *gens,* could not be assimilated into the family mythology of the Julians. Instead, his qualities as a military commander would have to be the focus. As early as 7 B.C. he had celebrated a triumph over the Germans, and after his adoption he won victories in Pannonia and Dalmatia, receiving a triumph in A.D. 12.

Unfortunately there is no direct evidence to be found in the form of monumental public art of the later years of Augustus's rule. But two silver cups found in a small villa at Boscoreale, near Pompeii, reflect in four related comiastic poetry. The most important figure is Venus, to whom Augustus turns as she places a Victory on the globe that he already holds. Thus his ancestress confers on him power and the assurance of victory. Behind him come the Genius Populi Romani, with cornucopia, and Roma, who sets her foot on a pile of enemy arms, a symbol that all is well with the state. From the other side Mars leads the personifications of subject and pacified provinces before the "throne." The gods of the new Rome are represented distinctly smaller than the ruler, as if they were in his service. Many elements alluded to, or hinted at through juxtaposition, in the decorative scheme of the Forum of Augustus are here transformed into an all-out panegyric of the ruler. But in both the message is essentially the same.

It is characteristic of the deliberate timelessness of the new imagery that the narrative scenes are not presented as onetime occurrences, but rather as exemplary and endlessly repeating actions or events. As in the quiet, contemplative mythological scenes, the didactic purpose here comes to the fore and suppresses narrative specificity in favor of emphasizing the suggestive and emblematic.

The great men of the Late Republic had always stressed what was unique or special in their achievements, but emperors and princes had above all to play their well-defined respective roles. As princeps-to-be, Tiberius still had to demonstrate his *virtus* in specific deeds, to play the heroic man of action. But as ruler Augustus acts as the contemplative counterpart, the personification and guarantor of a just and unperturbed order. He oversees and guides everything; everything centers around him. The presentation of his successor as victor and *triumphator* necessarily places the ruler himself in a transcendent position.

Augustus in the Guise of Jupiter

Ever since Alexander the Great, the Hellenistic world had rendered its rulers in the guise of Zeus, and, as we shall see, Augustus was no exception. It is even more significant, however, that in Rome too this image found a place within the newly created mythology. But then, how better could Augustus's supreme and all-encompassing rule be expressed in immediate, visual terms?

On the Gemma Augustea of about 10 B.C. (fig. 182), Augustus in the guise of Jupiter is enthroned beside Roma, but instead of the thunderbolt he holds the augur's staff. His gaze is directed toward Tiberius as he descends from a chariot driven by Victoria. The *lituus* in Augustus's hand thus indicates that Tiberius's victory was won under the auspices of Augustus. The young Germanicus stands armed next to Roma, ready for the next cam-

Fig. 182. Gemma Augustea. Augustus enthroned, like Jupiter, beside Roma. He
holds the *lituus* as token of military high command, for the princes before him
wage wars under his orders. Behind the throne, personifications of the peaceful
and joyous earth. Below, Roman soldiers and personifications of auxiliaries with
subjugated barbarians. Ca. A.D. 10.

paign. The two princes are emissaries of the universal ruler; his invincibility
is transferred to them like a discreet entity. This is why Roma looks admir-
ingly at Augustus and not at the actual victors. Victory is as predictable as
the movement of the stars through the heavens. Above Augustus's head, the
Capricorn shines against a disk (the sun?) and a star in the background, all
three symbols of mythic and cosmic predestination. From behind Augustus's throne representatives of this blessed world look up toward him. Italia,
wearing around her neck the *bulla* (actually the token of a freeborn youth!),
sits on the ground, surrounded by children and holding a cornucopia. Behind are Oceanus and Oikoumene, the latter crowning Augustus with the
corona civica. The personification of the inhabited world wears a mural
crown, thus representing the flourishing cities of the Empire (cf. fig. 184).

a

Fig. 183. So-called Sword of Tiberius, after 16 B.C. *a*) In the center, medallion
with portrait of Augustus. Six *coronae civicae* perhaps refer to military distinctions
of the owner. Below, a sanctuary of the Lares and an Amazon as symbol of barbarian enemies. *b*) Detail: Tiberius, enthroned, receives a prince, probably Germanicus, who hands over his Victoria to him. Beside him are Mars Ultor and Victoria.
On the shield of Tiberius: FELICITAS TIBERI.

Below this spectacular panegyric, a specific event is referred to, by which
once again the power of Roman arms has upheld the divinely ordained
world order. In the left half of the scene, Roman soldiers erect a *tropaion*,
and the scorpion, Tiberius's zodiac sign, is visible on one of the shields. The
reference is probably to the victory over the Illyrians, following which Tiberius returned to Rome—not long after the annihilation of Varus's legions
in the Teutoburg Forest. From the right two personifications drag recalcitrant, perhaps Germanic barbarians to the victory monument. The woman
carrying spears probably symbolizes Spanish troops, the man in broad-
brimmed petasos, Thracian. This scene would then allude to future victories
of Tiberius in the North.

As in the scenes on the silver cups from Boscoreale (cf. figs. 180, 181),
the specific is overshadowed by the paradigmatic. The stability of the Empire has been achieved, but there will always be revolts to be suppressed on
one or another of the borders. This princeps will be followed by another
with the same qualities, and at his side will stand yet another young prince.
It is worth taking a closer look at those figures that are new on the Gemma
Augustea, Oikoumene and the personifications of the Roman legions in the
costumes of their native provinces. With the latter, for the first time the
perspective of political imagery in the visual arts is extended beyond Rome
itself to the Empire. In the Forum of Augustus, the iconographic program
was still purely a product of the city of Rome and its traditions, and the
Empire treated as an object of repeated conquest. On the Gemma Augustea,
by contrast, the new personified provinces have an active share in the victory and in honoring the ruler.

Scholars have had difficulty coming to grips with the notion of Augustus
in the guise of Jupiter, because it is such a flagrant contradiction of his

b

"Republican" style. But it cannot be easily explained away by either of the arguments usually adduced, viz. that the Gemma Augustea should be dated posthumously, and thus represents the deified emperor, or that it was a luxury item intended to be seen only by an "inner circle," a playful piece of court art not to be taken seriously as a political statement. But after the death and deification of Augustus, Tiberius also took on the role of Jupiter—again while still alive—as evidenced not only on the famous Grand Camée de France, but also on a scabbard found in Roman Germany (fig. 183).

On the latter, Tiberius is enthroned in the manner of Jupiter and holds in his left hand a shield with the inscription *Felicitas Tiberii*. He welcomes back a young prince standing before him, either Germanicus or the younger Drusus. The emperor is flanked by Mars Ultor and the Victoria of the Augustus. The patron gods of the Emperor had stood by the prince in battle, who now returns Victoria—it is again that of the Augustus.

The equation with Jupiter must, accordingly, have been more than a rhetorical flourish occasionally employed by court poets and artists. Soon portrait statues in the guise of Jupiter would be dedicated in temples, shrines, and statue galleries, not only in the East or for the army, but in the cities of Italy as well. And these depict not only deified principes, but those still very much alive and in power. In a few instances this was true even for Augustus (cf. p. 318), though he apparently made sure that this did not happen in Rome.

This does not mean, of course, that Augustus's admirers genuinely equated him with Jupiter or that he felt himself to be a new Jupiter. It took the deranged mind of a Caligula to go that far. Even in old age, the *pater patriae* remained true to his conception of the Principate, and up to the end he appeared to the people as *pontifex maximus* and to the Senate as a duly elected magistrate. The comparison with Jupiter is rather an allegorical symbol of his rule, celebrating it as just, final, and all-embracing, like that of the supreme god. Augustus was the gods' representative on earth. The image itself had a long and distinguished tradition and better than any other conveyed the dazzling religious aura of the ruler. It was, however, a borrowed image, and, like so many that came with the Hellenization of Rome, its meaning in the Roman context was not quite compatible with its original connotation. In Rome it did not connote the physical presence of divine power, as in the depiction of Hellenistic rulers.

The image of Jupiter/Augustus must be understood within the context of the interwoven patterns that comprised the new mythology, alongside such other types as the *togatus capite velato*. Both images present the ruler as emissary, whether of the state or of the gods, and his rule is equally suited to this dual role. The *lituus* that he holds on the Gemma Augustea alludes to his role as intermediary between heaven and earth. Even in official inscriptions toward the end of his reign he is referred to as *custos* and *praeses totius orbis* (*CIL* 10.1421).

The image of Augustus as Jupiter is hardly a unique instance within the new mode of glorifying the ruler. Female members of the imperial house were also likened to all manner of divinities. This was true even on coins minted in Rome itself, as we have seen in the case of Diana/Julia (cf. fig. 167c). The purpose of this, however, was not so much to express through the comparison specific qualities attributed to the subject (as in the Greek world), as to stress the association of the various goddesses with the imperial family. On a well-known cameo (fig. 184), Livia, enthroned like a goddess and holding a bust of the deified Augustus as if she were his priestess, is simultaneously likened to three different, though related, deities. The mural crown and *tympanon* link her to Cybele/Magna Mater, the sheaf of grain to Ceres, and the garment slipping from her shoulder to Venus. At the same time she also wears the *stola* of the proper Roman matron. Even if the multiplication of divine attributes seen here is rare and reflects the exaggerated panegyric of the court style in carved gems, the same basic phenomenon is evident in statues of women of the imperial house in divine guise throughout the Empire. In the theater at Leptis Magna, for example, stood a figure of Ceres Augusta in mural crown, with the clear portrait features of Livia (fig. 185). Whether the goddess was Venus, Diana, Ceres, Concordia, Pietas, or Fortuna Augusta, she could always be intimately linked to the

Fig. 184. Sardonyx in modern setting, after A.D. 14. Livia enthroned, as both priestess and goddess. She holds the bust of the deified Augustus. Stalks of wheat, tympanon, and diadem with battlements liken her to the goddesses Ceres and Magna Mater.

imperial house through the hairstyle or facial features of one "princess" or another (cf. fig. 196).

The ruler had been chosen by the gods for his role and enjoyed success in it thanks to his own qualities and those of his family; his power was thus inseparable from political custom and moral virtue. The Romans repeatedly witnessed the ceremony of rulers and princes performing sacrifice, departing on campaign, and returning victorious. But on these occasions they did not masquerade as gods, as the Hellenistic kings and later Antony and Cleopatra had done. This would have flouted Roman tradition and the style of the Principate, and when later Caligula, Nero, and Domitian tried it on even a modest scale, it contributed directly to their downfall. The political style of the Principate required the emperor and his family to appear as Roman citizens, in toga and *stola*. The strict separation between the live appearance and self-image on the one hand, and the rhetorical, artistic comparisons with divinities on the other, gave these mythological images a rather cool and abstract quality, unlike the emotional image of the godlike Hellenistic ruler. For the Romans, the gods were used like poetic epithets, an intellectualized formulation of virtues, not, as in Hellenistic art, as the direct realization of the divinely inspired ruler.

This concept was of course not limited to words and pictures, but extended to cult as well. Even in Augustus's lifetime every city had temples and shrines where his *genius* and *numen*, his virtues and his patron gods, indeed his very person were worshiped, usually together with Roma. The nians, instead of bowing to the will of the world ruler, withdrew entirely from his influence. But apparently none of these facts impinged upon the consciousness of the Romans themselves. To them, an image was more powerful than the reality, and nothing could shake their faith in the new era.

Chapter 6

Form and Meaning of the New Mythology

In the introduction to his treatise "On the Ancient Orators," Dionysius of Halicarnassus speaks with great admiration for his own age, for the art of oratory had just experienced a tremendous revival. A new literary culture had arisen, so he believed, through imitation of the finest Attic authors of the Classical Age in Greece, which was worthy to stand beside the best of the past. The unwavering devotion to the Classical or Atticizing model is balanced by vehement attacks on the baroque Asiatic taste, which had distorted the entire culture with its shameless theatricality, aimed only at stirring up the basest instincts. Its ostentation and glittering vulgarity, he writes, had even turned the once refined Athens into a bordello.

Like many other Greek writers and artists, Dionysius had come to Rome in 30 B.C., just after the decisive Battle at Actium. His somewhat crude polemic is characteristic of the volatile mood that governed Rome at the time of the Secular Games (17 B.C.). For Dionysius, more is at stake than just styles of rhetoric. The Atticizing style is for him both an element in and the expression of a whole new kind of education, of a new moral standard. He himself acknowledges that the cultural turnaround is directly linked to the political situation. He sees the cause of the miraculous "turn" (*metabole*) in Rome's worldwide empire and in the moral and cultural standards set by the rulers at Rome. It is only thanks to them that this turn for the better has been achieved so rapidly and so far afield. Only in a few remote cities of Mysia, Phrygia, and Caria are vestiges of the old, wicked ways to be found. And that is surely no surprise, since the Orient had always been the source of all evil.

A sudden change in political imagery, as abrupt as that in artistic style, can also be observed. We need only recall how the new portrait of Augustus, composed of quotations from Classical sculpture, replaced the more emotional portrait of his youth (cf. fig. 83), how honorary statues showing off the glories of the male nude were replaced by the togate figure with veiled head, or how images of the carefree Aphrodite in Asiatic splendor were replaced by icons heavy with symbolism.

The intention was to create a kind of "superculture," which would combine the best traditions of both Greek and Roman culture, Greek aesthetics

Fig. 187. Pediment of a tetrastyle Ionic temple, from the relief of a large altar. The structure probably represents, like figure 86, one of the new marble temples built under Augustus. The pedimental figures seem to have been Classical originals, as on the Apollo Temple of Sosius. Claudian period.

four bulls or cows by Myron appeared before the Temple of Apollo. This "Myronian flock" (*armenta Myronis*, Propertius 2.31) stood around a statue of Apollo of Actium pouring a libation at an altar (cf. fig. 68), possibly itself a Classical statue, to judge from the evidence of coins.

But the judgment of Late Hellenistic artistic theory, which ranked Classical sculpture above all other, was surely not the only standard by which the works in the Apollo Temple were chosen. This is clear from the use of Archaic sculpture as well, which this school considered stiff, old-fashioned, and aesthetically inferior. According to Pliny (36.5.12) Archaic works by Bupalus and Athenis, sons of the great master Archermus of Chios, were used even in the pediment (*in fastigio*) of the temple. The pediment of the contemporary Apollo Temple of C. Sosius boasted an Amazonomachy originally carved for a Greek temple of the fifth century B.C. Booty of Archaic and Classical Greek sculpture adorned other Augustan sanctuaries as well (fig. 187).

Only a few years ago was a precious fragment of a small Archaic statue of Athena found on the Palatine recognized, on account of its Ionian style, as possibly belonging to the works of the sons of Archermus (fig. 188). These Archaic sculptors were also extremely famous. They were even familiar in literary circles because of their well-known quarrel with the poet Hipponax. One of their works had been in the possession of Attalus II of Pergamum (d. 134 B.C.), and Augustus seems to have particularly admired them. Pliny even claims that he exhibited works of the sons of Archermus "in almost all his temples" (*in omnibus fere aedibus;* 36.5.12). He was interested not just in these particular artists, but, as other sources, as well as the monuments themselves make clear, the Archaic style as such. Why, then, this special fondness for Archaic form, alongside the Classical, even in spite of its inferiority in the view of Hellenistic aesthetic theory?

Archaic Form: Intimations of the Sacred

In the fifth century B.C., the Archaic style was already on occasion revived in certain religious contexts because of its hieratic connotations. Even in the Hellenistic period this meaning was not forgotten, even as the Late Archaic style was appreciated for its exaggerated, mannered quality. Well into the period of the High Roman Empire, Archaic forms were still thought to possess a special religious aura. Pausanias, for example, notes that an ancient and artistically quite undistinguished statue of Heracles had a "somehow holy" effect (2.4.5). This old belief would surely come to the fore within the context of Augustus's program of religious revival. In Rome, ancient clay images of the gods had been especially revered at least since the time of Cato the Elder. Writers took up the same idea and endowed it with the appropriate tag words: Cicero, for example (*De Oratore* 3.153) says that the use of archaic words makes a speech "more impressive and dignified," while for Quintilian, the archaisms in Vergil's vocabulary lend him "just as in the visual arts that inimitable dignity (*auctoritas*) of age"

Fig. 188. Fragment of an original Late Archaic statuette of the Palladium, from the Palatine. Ca. 520 B.C.

Fig. 192. This head gives some idea of the lost archaistic head of the statue of Priapus. The mannered clarity and ornamental character of the archaic forms reflect Augustan taste.

Fig. 191. Archaistic statue of Priapus. Kid, animal hide, and garlands of fruit (originally in metal, now lost) are traditional attributes. The little children, however, are an innovation representing a specifically Augustan prayer to the old fertility god. Early Imperial.

Treatises on aesthetics written in the classicistic atmosphere of the late second century B.C. had for the first time begun to look at a work of art not only through the eyes of the artist, with his formal criteria, but from the standpoint of the lay viewer or art lover. This led to an increasingly vague definition of aesthetic criteria, which evolved naturally into moral categories. Concepts derived from a work's effect on the viewer, such as *decor, auctoritas,* or *pondus,* were now used to define formal qualities, which in

Fig. 193. Apollo and Hercules struggling for the Delphic tripod. The symbolic character of the tripod adorned with Victories is emphasized by the heraldic composition. Revetment in the novel, eclectic style combining Early Classical and Archaic elements. From the excavations at the Temple of Apollo on the Palatine, ca. 30 B.C.

turn determined the ranking of the Classical masters. At the top of the list stood the art of Phidias and Polyclitus. In the age of Augustan reforms, this system of aesthetic ranking, which had been developed by and for art critics, was borrowed and applied to the selection of specific works for use in an artistic program defined primarily by moral and political objectives.

This is not simply a matter of conjecture. Treatises on rhetoric, principally that of Dionysius of Halicarnassus but also the *Ars Poetica* of Horace, give us some idea of the field of associations in their day. Indeed, they are particularly relevant in this context, since they occasionally drew explicit parallels between literary and artistic style. For example, Dionysius of Halicarnassus, in the work quoted at the beginning of this section, "On the Ancient Orators," a kind of handbook of style, tries to define the specific stylistic qualities of individual Classical authors. In so doing he characterizes each one's qualities with a single term, precisely echoing the ethical standards of his age. Virtually every author is praised for either simplicity, clarity, precision, or purity of style. These are exactly the qualities which the most characteristic works of Augustan art so brilliantly display: clarity of outline, precision of form, and simplicity and clarity of composition.

Dionysius also gives some indications of the criteria by which Augustan artists chose Classical models for specific occasions, since he praises the particular advantages of each author with a view toward how and when he might be used. So, for example, the orator Lysias (late fifth century B.C.) is singled out not only for clarity and simplicity, but also for "lightness" (*leptotes*) and grace (*charis*), though criticized for a lack of verbal force. Isocrates, a contemporary of Lysias about 400 B.C., lacks Lysias's *charis* but may be more impressive through his grandiosity of style. This would correspond to a heroic rather than mortal nature, as Dionysius puts it, and he adds:

> In my opinion it would not be incorrect to liken the speaking style of Isocrates with the art of Polyclitus and Phidias, with respect to *to semnon* (holiness), *to megalotechnon* (grandeur), and *to axiomatikon* (dignity). Lysias's style could be compared with that of the sculptors Callimachus (late fifth century B.C.) and Calamis for *leptotes* and *charis*. (*Orat. Vett. Isocr.* 4)

Dionysius has clearly borrowed the judgment of Late Hellenistic, classicistic art critics, who regarded Polyclitus and Phidias as the highpoint in the rendering of the human and divine figure. But the values assigned to them are here no longer aesthetic, but explicitly ethical in nature. In the passage just quoted, it is revealing that all three traits attributed to Isocrates—and to Phidias and Polyclitus—mean almost the same thing, and in all three the overtones of the sacred are unmistakable.

It appears that the choice of Classical sculpture was indeed made according to these criteria, at least in the formative stage of Augustan public art. We have already noted the portrait types of Augustus and the young princes, with their artificial, classicizing facial features (cf. figs. 174, 175). But also the bodies of statues portraying deceased rulers and princes, where these are exposed, often follow precisely Classical proportions and are set in a Polyclitan stance.

Fig. 194. Statue of Tiberius. The body follows a new Augustan model, which was intended to replace the Hellenistic schema, as in figure 195. The corporeal forms are copied from Classical works of the fifth century B.C.

Fig. 195. Statue of Agrippa in the Hellenistic manner (arms restored). Ca. 30 B.C.

This is especially clear in the type probably first created for a cult statue of the deified Julius Caesar, with nude torso and mantle draped about the hips in the Classical manner (fig. 194). This type was then used for statues of deceased princes and emperors, who were in this way characterized as "heroic." In the provincial cities of Italy, the local nobility then borrowed this grandiose form for their own posthumous statuary, apparently not considering it the private preserve of the imperial house.

This image is a typical compromise between Hellenistic/Late Republican traditions and the values of the new Rome. In the 30s Octavian and Agrippa still had no compunctions about having themselves represented in Asiatic style, completely nude, in dramatic movement, with fluttering mantle and swelling muscles (fig. 195). After the "turnaround," there was still a desire to retain the nude statue type, which had become quite popular, as a sign of special honor for certain dead heroes. But the requirements of the new morality dictated at least a partial covering up of the body. With its Classical forms, the half-nude body need no longer connote an emphatic assertion of power, but could be understood as an acknowledgment of the new system of moral/aesthetic values.

Quintilian calls the Doryphorus of Polyclitus, *"vir gravis et sanctus"* (5.12.20). The same words could serve as a worthy description of Augustus. That artists and patrons did in fact take up this idea is well illustrated by the case of King Herod of Judaea. In his new showplace Caesarea, named for Augustus, he built a temple of Roma and Augustus dominating the harbor and set within it a cult statue of Augustus copying the Chryselephantine Zeus of Phidias at Olympia and one of Roma based on Polyclitus's Hera at Argos (Josephus *Bell. Jud.* 1.408). We may suspect that Augustus was not entirely happy with the cult statue of himself, but it is clear that Herod's conception was perfectly in keeping with the tenets of official Roman classicism.

In the same category belong statue types of various female abstract personifications, such as Fortuna, Concordia, Pietas, Pax, and Felicitas Augusta, as well as the honorific statues, hardly distinguishable from these, of female members of the imperial family. These were also based on Classical models, but not so much of the Severe Style or High Classical as of the late fifth and fourth centuries. The decisive criterion in this choice was probably *charis,* as Dionysius defines this quality in the style of Lysias and Callimachus. A beautiful statue of Tiberian date, for example, represents one of these personifications with the portrait features and coiffure of Livia (fig. 196). The casual stance and lively, clinging drapery of the so-called Rich Style of the late fifth century are typical of the "Callimachean manner." While statues of emperors and princes had to express above all stateliness and dignity, these female divinities were imagined to dispense gifts from their cornucopia with delicacy and grace. The addition of portrait features, however, makes it clear, with no great subtlety, that the true source of all these good things is the imperial house.

The more eclectic artists—following the precepts of atticizing rhetorical theory—thought they could heighten their aesthetic achievement through the combination of several derivative styles. We have already encountered examples of this in the use of Archaic images ennobled with Classical forms (cf. fig. 193). A similar approach can be detected in the charming Diana Braschi in the Glyptothek, Munich (fig. 197). The effectiveness of this divine

Fig. 196. Statue of an Augustan goddess with portrait features and hairstyle of Livia. Body and drapery after Classical models of the late fifth century B.C. Ca. A.D. 40.

Fig. 197. Diana with hind. An original creation of the Early Imperial period, in the characteristic style of mixed Classical and Archaic elements.

image, a brilliant creation of Augustan art, is largely indebted to the dynamic movement of the Callimachean manner. *Leptotes* and *charis* are the perfect attributes for the delicate maiden goddess. But at the same time the artist was striving for a hieratic dignity, through allusions to Archaic form. The stiff, elongated gait, the addition of the diminutive deer as an attribute, the locks falling stiffly to the breast, and the perforated crown with animal frieze are all archaizing elements that serve this purpose.

In order to surpass the Greeks, one must not limit oneself to imitating one single model. Rather, only by borrowing a little of this and a little of that can one achieve a greater perfection. (Quintilian 11.2.25f.)

Statue groups in particular became an opportunity to display a stylistic combination of two different Classical models into a single composition. We have already observed the most interesting example of this, though unfortunately preserved only in late copies (cf. fig. 154). Here Venus, in the form of a *Late* Classical Aphrodite, embraces Mars, in the form of a *High* Classical Ares, who, faithful to the model, stares angrily at the ground, despite the warm embrace. This would have been perceived by the new aesthetic standard as an appropriate, even exemplary application of artistic method, no matter how hard it may be for us to appreciate it as such. The primary aim was to translate into visual terms the central mystery of the new official mythology. The use of Classical forms elevated the image into a sacred realm where it would conjure up the desired effect.

"Atticizing" Compositions

Thus far we have considered only the choice of sculptural forms and the criteria for their selection. But new kinds of compositions and modes of representation contributed equally to the effectiveness of the new style. On the cuirass of the Augustus from Prima Porta (cf. fig. 148a), for example, the various figures are arranged in an extremely simple grouping around the key scene in the middle. Each one is like a cut-out figure set against an empty background. This accords with the "solemn" style (*to semnon*) of now lost Early Classical wall painting, some reflections of which can be found in Attic vase paintings of the period ca. 450 B.C. All movement is dispensed with, and the composition is limited to relatively few images. This was intended to lead the viewer to a slow and careful contemplation of the whole. But whereas the quiet mythological scenes of Classical painting contained a powerful psychological tension, here the primary purpose is to indicate meaningful associations. This is even more evident in the purely symbolic or allegorical scenes, such as the Pax relief on the Ara Pacis (cf. figs. 135, 136), which is "put together" from interchangeable elements into a strictly axial-symmetric composition. We can almost imagine exactly how this came about, or what the conversation must have sounded like between patron and artist, the one insisting that certain leitmotifs of the *saeculum aureum* be included, the other left with little chance to exercise his own imagination, being required to arrange the various symbols into an immediately intelligible composition. The image radiates the cool, calculated rationality of Augustus's political program. Only when we look closely at excerpts and details (cf. fig. 141) do we gain some access to an appreciation of the masterly technique and artistic skill.

The icon of Aeneas performing a sacrifice (cf. fig. 157) is built upon much the same simple principles. But thanks to the element of mythological narrative, the overall effect is here not one of pure dogma, in spite of the heavy burden of symbolic associations. The introspection in this scene creates a solemn mood, which surrounds Aeneas with an aura of mystery and profundity. The remarkable impact of the relief on the viewer was no doubt a prime achievement of neoclassical compositional principles. The quiet tone was apparently appreciated by art lovers for what they perceived as its aesthetic charm and for this reason quickly adopted for private art. Whether designing a mythological genre scene for a wall painting or an episode of Homeric inspiration for a silver cup, artists invariably tried to create the simplest and most lucid compositions and thus evoke a meditative mood. This even extends to the popular erotic subjects, which appear already in Hellenistic relief pottery (fig. 198). While the earlier scenes depict a more immediate intimacy, those on early Arretines bowls show couples in positions that could almost be called dignified (fig. 199). Purity of line and classicizing proportions predominate, creating even here a model of the new morality. Such scenes are a good example of how artistic form, with its ideological trappings, can take precedence over narrative content.

Lack of narrative and an intellectualized symbolism lend classicistic imagery a remarkable "openness" of interpretation. Evoking a whole field of associations was more important to the artist than iconographic precision. This is why some figures, like the Pax on the Ara Pacis, cannot be easily identified.

In the private sphere this approach to imagery not infrequently turns into a kind of erudite puzzle. A deliberate ambiguity must have been contrived by the artist as part of the image's appeal. A splendid example is the famous Portland Vase (fig. 200*a*, *b*)—why else would the artist have failed to give

Fig. 198. Fragment of a Hellenistic clay vessel. Pergamum, second century B.C.

Fig. 199. Mold for Arretine terra-cotta bowls, ca. 20 B.C. A comparison with the Hellenistic example illustrates the typical classicism of the Augustan style.

his figures any identifying attributes? The blue glass vessel is a model of this peculiar narrative style. The two three-figure compositions balance each other perfectly, and almost every individual figure is derived from a well-known Greek statue type. These puzzling scenes have so far inspired two dozen interpretations of all sorts, while fevered scholarly brains still seethe. As often in Augustan art, two images are presented as a significant contrasting pair. In both the focus is a female figure, on one side in anticipation of a happy erotic liaison, on the other sunk in mourning. The first is joined with a sea monster and joyously greets a young hero accompanied by Eros, while the second is portrayed in a gesture of grief and holding a down-turned torch, having turned away from her hero. Could the vessel have been a wedding gift decorated with mythological similes?

Quotation from Classical Art for Symbolic Value

Naturally not every image in Augustan art was affected by the decision to employ archaizing and classicizing styles for ideological reasons. In many areas style and iconography remained unchanged, such as garden sculpture, and above all in the handling of subjects like the Dionysiac sphere, for which the only available models were Hellenistic. Even in official monuments artists occasionally indulged in thoroughly unclassical styles and

Fig. 200. *a–b*) Portland vase. Dark blue glass vessel with white overlay, in which   *b*
the scene is carved. The two mythological scenes are associated with each other
through formal correspondences. Augustan.

modes of representation. We need only recall the landscape elements (cf. fig.
136) and vegetal friezes on the Ara Pacis or the crowd of figures in deep,
receding planes on the silver cups from Boscoreale (cf. figs. 180, 181). Most
of all, the major religious architecture of the Augustan Age, so fundamentally different from Classical Greek temples, shows that we cannot begin to
talk about an all-embracing classicism or archaism. It was precisely because
Augustan classicism had a more intellectual than aesthetic character that it
could adapt itself to other formal traditions, even the Hellenistic. What
governed the choice in each instance was the means of best displaying ethical values.

   In the case of temples and other public buildings, the specific value that
these embodied was called *publica magnificentia,* as we have already seen.
The marble structures of the new Rome were intended to rival those of
Greece, even of Athens. The *maiestas imperii* would be expressed in the
egregiae auctoritates of these temples, as Vitruvius writes, echoing the official terminology. This was above all defined by the use of the most expensive
building materials, the most lavish decoration, and the most impressive effects.

   The Doric order, which the Greeks still used occasionally as a reminis-

Fig. 201. So-called Maison Carrée, Nîmes. The new marble temples combine traditional architectural forms dictated by Roman cult practice with Greek ornamentation and references to Classical art.

cence of past glory and which had earlier been used often in Italy, was no longer adequate. Both it and the Ionic order were now almost totally superseded, at least in temple architecture, by the more sumptuous Corinthian.

The style of the new temples in Augustan Rome was intentionally a *mixtum compositum* (fig. 201). Podium, porch, and tall, heavy pediment all belong to the Italic religious tradition, while the height of the columns, the capitals, and the organization of the facade are derived from Hellenistic models. The lavish materials, however, including even the gilding of individual elements, outdid anything that the past had to offer. But above all, the soaring constructions of gleaming, carefully hewn marble stood out dramatically amid the old tufa temples (cf. fig. 85).

The total effect of such temples is utterly unclassical, yet architects and patrons nevertheless wanted them to bear the "Classical" seal of approval. In the first instance the ostentatious use of marble fulfilled this desideratum. But in addition, the frequent Classical quotations in the ornament convey a clear message. The most obvious example of this is the Forum of Augustus, with its exact, to-scale copies of the Erechtheum caryatids in the attic of the

Fig. 202. Caryatids in the attic of the colonnades in the Forum of Augustus (cf. fig. 166). The female figures holding up the entablature were exact copies of the korai of the Erechtheum on the Athenian Acropolis (ca. 415 B.C.).

colonnades (fig. 202; cf. fig. 166). But several other quotations have been pointed out on the temple itself. The profile of the column bases, for example, copies that in the Propylaea on the Acropolis, and an Ionic capital is a replica of one in the Erechtheum. Also, both types of lion's head water spouts, as well as ceiling coffers and ornamental bands, seem to be quotations.

Such quotations can be found on every temple of the Early Imperial period, even amid the gaudy exuberance of the sima and entablature on the Temple of Concord, which as a whole looks so unclassical (fig. 203). The large dentils framed by Lesbian and Ionic cymas prove to be a classical quotation when compared with the narrow rows of dentils hidden in the shadows of Hellenistic temples. The heavy console cornice is, however, an innovation of Augustan architecture. Interestingly, even here the basic form was inspired by that favorite Classical model, the Erechtheum, but the Classical design of the console was inadequate. It had to be elaborated with added decoration in the form of ornamental bands, themselves Classical in origin. Above the consoles rose a steep wall composed of four ornamental bands, utterly obliterating the Classical arrangement of geison and sima.

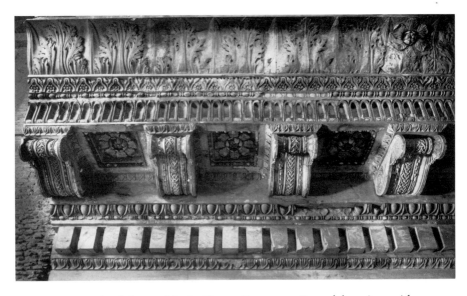

Fig. 203. Temple of Concord in the Forum Romanum. Part of the geison with sima. A.D. 12. A splendid example of the great elaboration and eclectic style of Augustan temple decoration.

This type of brim is in itself rather an archaism. Thus it is no accident that just above sits the row of spikes familiar from the terra-cotta roofs of ancient Italic temples.

The choice of ornament varies from temple to temple, but none lacks classical quotations or archaizing elements. The meaning of these quotations is unmistakable: the new temples embody the best of native tradition, yet at the same time the best of the Greek tradition as well. In this way can the new temples far surpass even the most grandiose Hellenistic marble creations.

There is abundant evidence that this principle was not limited to architectural ornament, but underlay the configuration of all art forms. There is scarcely a single figured scene with "political" content that does not offer an appropriate quotation at some crucial spot. We need only think of the image of Aeneas sacrificing on the Ara Pacis, his head and body both rendered in Early Classical style (fig. 204). Here too the Classical quotation takes on a symbolic function, in endowing the figure of Aeneas with *to semnon* and *to megalotechnon*, of which Dionysius of Halicarnassus speaks. But even in the realm of more playful ornament, as on candelabra (fig. 205) or elaborate marble bases, the Classical Greek "seal of approval" is conveyed by the quotation of at least one Classical ornamental motif.

Fig. 204. Head of Aeneas on the Ara Pacis (cf. fig. 157). The sculptor employed Early Classical forms for facial features and hair.

Fig. 205. Augustan candelabrum base. The lotus-palmette frieze and the rams' heads are quotations from Classical models.

Not only individual elements, but the very clarity of precision of form also carry a symbolic meaning, which is especially striking in the architectural ornament, whose ethical connotations we have already considered.

"vos exemplaria Graeca nocte versate manu, versate diurna.
[You must take Greek models in hand, day and night.]
                                        Horace *Ars Poetica* 268

Hard work and perseverance—*labor* and *mora*—these are the requirements for immersing oneself in the arts of the Greeks. He who does not engage himself with these models intensively, down to the finest detail, will not be able to surpass them, according to Dionysius of Halicarnassus. Of course teachers have always given their pupils such advice, usually with not much success. It is thus all the more astonishing that Augustan artists made this credo their own and lived by it with such determination. Every acanthus leaf on the column capitals of major buildings (cf. fig. 87), every lock of hair on every finely carved head attests to a total identification with this ethical and artistic dogma. The techniques of Augustan artists have often and justifiably been likened to the precision of the metalsmith. Never before had copies of Classical masterpieces been made with such exact "purity" in

Fig. 206. Detail of the bronze Doryphoros herm, fig. 84. The most careful Roman copies of Greek masterpieces come from the Augustan Age. In the precise rendering of individual forms they sometimes surpass even their models.

every detail (fig. 206). This was not the result of a natural stylistic development growing out of the so-called neo-Attic art of the Late Hellenistic Age, as is sometimes maintained. It was, rather, the result of a complete change in mentality, a *metabole*. Such precision and love of detail are unimaginable without presupposing some kind of identification between the artist and the spirit of the new age, and with his role as one individual contributing to the realization of a cultural program.

The emphasis on the idea of a new age dawning—and the classicizing and archaizing styles closely associated with this idea—were not long lived and were above all a phenomenon of the city of Rome. But at the same time, the consequences for Imperial art were profound. Of course the traditions of Hellenistic art lived on and in some areas even experienced a renaissance. But the notion of the immediacy and corporeality of sculptural form did not survive. The great works of the fifth and fourth centuries remained the models for art on public display. Sculptural workshops were geared to the Classical style, even when they were not making copies. The regular and abstract forms of Classical art gradually became the automatic and universal medium of expression. For this reason, even copies of Hellenistic works made during the Empire are blunted in their effect by the interpolation of Classical quotations. Thanks to Augustus's cultural program, classicism was destined to shape Imperial Roman art into the early third century. If Marc Antony had won the Battle of Actium, would Roman ateliers not probably have continued working in the Late Hellenistic style?

At the end of this section we may take a brief look at Athens. The city whose Classical culture provided the model for Augustus and his circle would early on feel the effects of Rome's worldwide power and her cultural pretensions. At first Augustus himself avoided the city that had so warmly welcomed Antony, but by about 15 B.C. Agrippa was active in the Athenian Agora as a major benefactor. He stood in a long tradition, but unlike the Hellenistic kings and Roman aristocrats before him who came only as admirers and patrons, the number two man in Rome came with a didactic purpose. He set his massive Odeum in the middle of the square, which for centuries had remained open, directly in front of one of the busiest colonnades (fig. 207). The latter-day Athenians, economically devastated and, in Augustus's eyes, morally wanting, were to be reminded of the great days of their own culture. Here they would honor the great Classical writers, watched over by several copies of Augustus's much admired Classical sphinx (cf. fig. 212). But it must also be impressed upon the Athenians that the high culture of their ancestors was built upon religious piety. Thus a temple of the period of the Parthenon, transported from its original location somewhere in the Attic countryside, was reconstructed likewise in the middle of the Agora, aligned with the Odeum. Again Classical form took on symbolic meaning, for the temple was dedicated to Ares, the war god. The Athenians understood on whose side the god now stood, when they dedicated a statue to Gaius Caesar, the emperor's son, as the "new Ares."

Agrippa's activities in Athens were not without impact. Here too the "moral rearmament" was unavoidable. A much discussed inscription (IG II 1035) refers to a program to renew eighty ruined temples throughout Attica. This seems to be directly inspired by Augustus's campaign for the restoration of temples in Rome. In the same years Julius Nicanor, a Syrian with Roman citizenship, bought the island of Salamis back for the Athenians and in return had himself honored as a new Thucydides and a new Homer— itself a form of classicism. It was a disgrace that the place where the Persians had been defeated had been seized by foreign hands. For his part, Augustus forbade the selling of Athenian citizenship. All this made a considerable impression and wrought many changes. Old letter forms were revived in stone inscriptions, the so-called Roman Agora was outfitted with architec-

Fig. 207. Athens, Agora. The traditional political character of the square was lost in the erection of the Temple of Mars and the Odeum. Augustus's program of cultural renewal had a strong impact even in the Greek East.

tural ornament of the Periclean Age, and occasionally even the Classical system of clamps and dowels was employed in laying courses of marble blocks.

Athens is not the only city in the Greek East where the effects of the Augustan program of religious renewal, together with a programmatic classicism in artistic style, can be observed. In the great sanctuaries of Greece we find new building activity and an increase in cult activity and dedications. Even in the ancient shrine of the Corycian Cave on Crete a significant increase in votive gifts in this period has been ascertained, and in Tarentum, the old center of Greek culture in South Italy, early Imperial imitations of Classical votive terra-cottas have been discovered. The classicism stipulated by the new regime in Rome spread, at least in outward form, throughout the Empire. It not only created an aesthetic fashion, but inspired a whole new way of thinking, if not a genuine expression of religious reawakening.

Chapter 7

The New Imagery in the Private Sphere

It was inevitable that the radical change in political imagery would have an effect on art in the private sphere as well. If an aesthete and keen observer of his environment, killed at the Battle of Actium, had returned from the dead at the end of Augustus's reign and visited Rome and Italy, he would not have believed his eyes. For the appearance and decoration of private residences, even of burial places was totally changed. Wall paintings, which dominated a room far more strikingly than do our carpets, were in an utterly new style. Not only walls, but furniture and other objects were decorated with new motifs, often borrowed from political iconography. This was as true in more modest houses as in the grandest. But the presence of tripods, sphinxes, Victories, and symbols of the *aurea aetas* did not necessarily mean that the resident was a fanatical supporter of the princeps. Rather, the new mentality of Augustan Rome had brought about a revolution in taste as well.

Unfortunately, there is too little evidence that is securely dated and attributable to a specific social context to allow a detailed analysis of the relationship between public and private forms of display and visual imagery. Nor is it possible to follow step by step the adaptation of each individual symbol or the rise of the new taste in interior design, or to define clearly the connection between general outlook and artistic taste.

Allegiance and Fashion

First comes the direct takeover and use of political images as expressions of loyalty and allegiance. The Roman who set up portraits of Augustus and his family in the atrium of his house—quite a common practice—acknowledged his support for the new regime even at home. The poet Ovid, exiled to the Black Sea, had a particular reason for the reverence he showed for the imperial house, since he was hoping for a pardon and a return to Rome. Nevertheless, his household shrine, which included silver busts of Augustus, Livia, Tiberius as successor to the throne, and the princes Germanicus and Drusus—an exact reflection of the sculptural program of public galleries in Rome—was certainly no different from thousands of other "house aediculae," where sacrifices were performed on imperial feast days and when company came (*Epistulae ex Ponto* 2.8.1ff.; 4.9.105ff.). Likewise, the Roman who wore a seal ring with the image of the emperor or a symbol such as Capricorn, a ship's prow, Mars Ultor, or a kneeling Parthian (cf. fig. 63ff.) identified himself with the new state as clearly as the owner of silver utensils like the bowls from Boscoreale (cf. fig. 180). Thanks to the mass-produced copies of such objects in cheaper materials, e.g., gems copied in glass paste or silver copied in clay, the spread of the new imagery was limitless. Soon political symbolism could be seen on every imaginable object made for private use, indeed on virtually everything that could be decorated at all: jewelry and utensils, furniture, textiles, walls and stuccoed ceilings, door jambs, clay facings, roof tiles, and even on tomb monuments and marble ash urns.

Naturally we cannot tell whether the buyer or recipient of any particular work really intended to advertise the political message of a certain image, or whether he simply accepted a mass-produced object that was the workshop's current offering. This is, to be sure, an oversimplification of the complex interactions within the marketplace. It is, in the end, of little importance whether the initial impetus for the borrowing of certain imagery or symbolism came from manufacturers or from customers. As long as an image was still relatively new, its use in the private sphere implies in every instance a conscious decision on the part of all involved. When the average man in the street bought himself a clay lamp with an image of the *corona civica*, Victoria on the globe (fig. 208), the *clipeus virtutis*, or Aeneas fleeing from Troy, instead of one with a chariot race or an erotic scene, he was making a deliberate choice. The same is true for the Arretine bowls with Apollonian subjects (cf. fig. 69).

For wealthier Romans, who include not only the residents of the grand villas, but also the owners of small houses in Pompeii, there are varying testimonia. The owner of the Villa at Torre Annunziata, who in the years around 30 B.C. had the Apollonian tripod so prominently painted on his walls (fig. 209), or the Consul C. Piso Frugi Pontifex, who bought for his villa copies of several statues in the Danaid cycle that Augustus had dedicated in the Temple of Apollo, were certainly no supporters of Antony, any more than the citizen of Pompeii who put an archaizing statue of Apollo or Diana in his garden (cf. fig. 189), instead of the more common Dionysus or Venus. The question remains open, of course, whether the patron's interest was more in the new artistic style alone, or in the particular divinities and ethical qualities associated with Augustus.

After the dedication of the Temple of Apollo in 28 B.C., there were apparently many prosperous Romans who wanted to surround themselves with the imagery of the new religious program, whether at banquets and sympo-

Fig. 208. Clay lamp with Victoria over
the globe (cf. fig. 62b).

sia or for private enjoyment and contemplation of a single work, such as an
archaistic statue or a carved gem. Evidence for this is the work of silver-
smiths, impressions of which we have observed on Arretine terra-cotta
bowls (cf. fig. 69), or gems and cameos. It is striking how often the latter
display divine or mythological subjects with political associations. Frequently these images are marked by an unmistakable artistic form. A head
of Mercury, for example (fig. 210), is very consciously Polyclitan. The experienced viewer is reminded automatically of the Classical, stylized countenance of Augustus's portraits, even though this image has in fact hardly
any specific physiognomic traits.

Such observations lead to the conclusion that at the beginning of Augustus's reign, a spontaneous interest in the new political imagery arose among
patrons and buyers. Workshops responded to this interest by acquiring the
appropriate models and producing to meet the demand. Naturally it must
have started with certain influential individuals, whose behavior inspired
imitation. When a prominent Roman commissioned from the leading atelier
a set of new silver decorated with tripods, candelabra, sacrificial scenes, and
the like, and used it at his banquets, the market would respond rapidly to
such an impetus. Perhaps the owner of the major ceramic workshop in Arezzo belonged to the inner circle of Augustus and inspired the potters to
imitate silver vessels, some examples of which he himself could provide. It
would only have required a few initial moves of this sort to create a demand
and set the natural workings of the marketplace in motion.

The new images must have been created by just a few leading artists,
who designed them for Augustus's temple projects or for the major monuments erected in his honor. Predictably, the more modest workshops will
have geared themselves, consciously or unconsciously, to the latest trends.
We need only think of the rapid changes in fashions in our own day. Impor-

Fig. 209. Wall painting with architectural fantasies. The gigantic golden tripod in the center of the picture was probably inspired by the votive tripod that Augustus set up in the Temple of Apollo. Ca. 25 B.C. From the great villa at Torre Annunziata.

tant "political" architecture had become by far the most interesting source of iconographic and stylistic innovations, which could enliven the traditional repertoire of a workshop and thus give it a competitive edge. Hence the borrowing of a new motif, at least after the first few years, the "incubation" period, need not necessarily be attributed to a specific commission. Other artistic, technical, and commercial factors surely also played a major role in this process. So, for example, the vine motif offered artists an ideal, all-purpose ornamental element, and the sphinx, quite apart from its considerable symbolic value, was a versatile supporting figure (figs. 211, 212). Neither the artist nor the customer necessarily thought he was advertising the *saeculum aureum* by using these images. They had simply become ubiquitous and extremely popular. The wall painter, when he used miniature tripods, candelabra, sphinxes, griffins, hippocamps, swans, or goddesses entwined in vines, to elaborate the elegant new decorative style, was surely not consciously celebrating Augustus and the Principate. In the workshops of Arretine pottery, motifs associated with the worship of Apollo and other "political" themes actually disappear from the repertoire relatively quickly, nor do these seem to have been replaced by new ones commemorating the Parthian victory, the opening of the *saeculum aureum*, or the successors of Augustus. This suggests a rapid loss of interest in explicit political imagery on the part of the buyers, at least of clay vessels, but does not mean of course that such imagery had no lasting effect. On the contrary, it was fully assimilated and later turns up again on funerary altars and ash urns.

At the same time, it is striking that those pieces of furniture, utensils, or silver objects bearing unmistakable elements of the new pictorial vocabulary that happen to be preserved are as a rule of very high quality, leading one to suspect that the customer did make a deliberate choice. A marble table foot, for example, with two sphinxes as supports, was undoubtedly made in one of the leading sculptural workshops in Rome (fig. 211*a*, *b*). Such marble tables were part of the furnishing of the atrium in a wealthy

Fig. 210. Reddish-brown agate, formerly in the Marlborough Collection. Mercurius/ Augustus. High Classical formal elements seem to be combined with physiognomic traits of the portrait of Augustus. Augustan period.

a

Fig. 211. *a*) Marble table leg with sphinxes and vines. Ostentatious furniture with such pictorial symbols was popular in the Early Imperial period. Augustan.
b) Detail of figure 211. This excerpt shows how precisely the Early Classical forms of the model were imitated.

home. In the Late Republic these were often imported from the East, and the supports were traditionally lions or lion griffins. In the Augustan period the iconographic repertoire was gradually expanded to include motifs such as cornucopia or globe, and often, as here, the lion was replaced by the more suggestive sphinx. This rather conspicuous motif seems to reflect more than just an ordinary change in fashion.

Ever since the 30s B.C., the sphinx had been a symbol of hope. Under

b

Fig. 212. Marble base in the form of a sphinx. Copy after the same Early Classical work that also inspired figure 211.

Julius Caesar it was already paired with the Sibyl on coins, and Octavian then used the sphinx as his seal. After Actium, the creature associated with oracles and riddles appears on coins in the East (cf. fig. 36b), and after the victory in Parthia she turns up, for example, on the shoulder lappets of the Augustus from Prima Porta (cf. fig. 148b). We can then trace her career, in combination with other symbols, on candelabra, bronze utensils, in wall painting, and on funerary altars and marble urns. What makes the sphinx on this table foot so interesting is that she is apparently an exact copy of an Early Classical Greek original. The sphinx on various coins, gems, candelabra, and table feet seems to be derived from the same model. Judging from the finest copies carved in the round, the original was a "life-size" standing figure (fig. 212). Its tremendous influence in the minor arts suggests that the original was a famous monument in Rome. Could it perhaps have been one of the votives dedicated by Augustus in the Temple of Apollo on the Palatine? The sphinxes on the table foot are clearly marked as symbols of the new age, not only by their Classical style, but by the luxuriant vines accompanying them, which grow out of a broad calyx and fill the entire picture field.

In a case like this, we are probably dealing with a deliberate borrowing of "political" imagery, at least in the creation of the model for the series. The same is true of an object like the bronze coal basin from Pompeii (fig. 213), which is also supported by three sphinxes, or a table ornament in the form of a Victory on the globe (fig. 214). In both cases the workshop must have been catering to high aesthetic standards, for the sphinxes are in that subtle, eclectic style mixing archaizing and classicizing elements that we have earlier discussed, and the Hellenistic drapery of the Victory has been replaced by Early Classical. In such conscious use of particular styles, the

Fig. 213. Bronze support for a basin, with three archaistic sphinxes. The mannered combination of several different stylistic elements presupposes patrons with high standards and a fine aesthetic sense. The basin, also Augustan, stood on a now lost support.

workshops were in close conformity with the official classicism of public monuments.

For silverware, "political" motifs were sometimes displayed quite blatantly, at other times used with a more capricious sense of fashion. Whoever used the pair of cups from Boscoreale (cf. fig. 180) was of course identifying himself closely with the regime, the more so when we think of how such cups would have been passed around the table at a banquet. For as the cup was turned, the scenes would come to life as one saw the entire composition. We might imagine that such a pair of cups was used especially on imperial feast days, when, for example, at the beginning of the meal the customary toast was made to the emperor. On the other hand, looking at the beautiful garlands and fantastic play of vines on an object like the silver

Fig. 214. Bronze table support, with Victoria upon a globe, holding a tropaion.

Fig. 215. Silver bowl. Detail of figure 144. The children of the Golden Age balance on slender plant stems and hunt for fish and shrimp. Augustan.

krater from Hildesheim (cf. fig. 215), one could easily lose sight of the political message. This is even more true of vessels decorated only with leaf patterns or sacrificial equipment.

But whatever the case with a particular object—whether the owner sought to proclaim his political loyalty or wanted only to enjoy the latest in artistic fashion—the cumulative effect of the new political imagery, echoed in Roman houses on every level of society, must have been inescapable.

We must of course keep in mind that many decorative motifs inherited from Hellenistic art continued to be employed, and that within the decorative program as a whole in most houses the new motifs were no more than a way of enriching the traditional repertoire and making it *au courant*. But when we recall the principles on which modern advertising is based—the

Fig. 216. Clay lamp. Victoria holds the   Fig. 217. So-called New Year's lamp.
clipeus virtutis. Early Imperial.   Victoria with *clipeus virtutis* and
                                               money pieces.

subliminal absorption of an image through constant repetition, regardless of the context—we can believe that the long-term effect on the Romans, even when unconscious, was not inconsiderable.

The Final Stage: From Internalization to the Private Message

No one could escape the impact of the new imagery, whether he consciously paid attention to it or not. This is clear from a variety of forms of assimilation and internalization, and here we come to perhaps the most interesting phenomenon in the entire process. But we should start by considering a concrete example.

The Victory on a *clipeus virtutis* appears on terra-cotta lamps at first as an unambiguous sign of loyalty and esteem for Augustus. On the early lamps the legend *ob cives servatos* stands on the shield (fig. 216). These are thus reflections of the famous honorary shield in the Curia. Soon, however, lamps with the same motif start to carry an inscription with totally different connotations. *Annum novum felicem mihi et tibi* ("Happy New Year to you and me") appears, in abbreviated form (fig. 217). The lamps are New Year's gifts, and the goddess of victory and the emperor's honorary shield have

Fig. 218. Gladiator's helmet from Pompeii. In front
of the visor, a small copy
of the Mars Ultor from the
Forum of Augustus (cf. fig.
155). Arms and armor
were decorated with a
whole variety of symbols
and imagery from official
art.

become the bearers of personal greetings and private aspirations. Coins scattered in the picture field leave no doubt that the wishes are meant in a quite material sense. No wonder the same motif also appears on the Roman equivalent of piggy banks!

Such assimilation could also be occasioned by one's job or profession, as in the case of gladiators' helmets from Pompeii. One of these, for example, has an image of Mars Ultor in a prominent position (fig. 218). The god of war is not only the helper of emperors and princes; the gladiator too hopes for victory by this sign. For this purpose the figure of Mars is not essentially different from other symbols that are apotropaic or incorporate the idea of bravery. Even the spreading oak or laurel decoration on greaves implies an association between the glorious though deadly skill of the gladiator and the now much-admired *virtus*. The gladiatorial profession claimed respect and recognition, and for this made use of the same imagery that celebrated the savior of the Roman state.

Just as on public monuments, these helmets often present symbols in meaningful pairs. Griffins, for example, are paired with Erotes, Mars with Dionysus. In other words, successful combat is viewed as the prerequisite for a happy life, just as the princeps's victories make possible the blessings of the Pax Augusta. Such objects give the impression that here for the first time certain complementary patterns of thought and image have been taken over from official iconography and transplanted in the private sphere. The effectiveness of imagery in shaping the perceptions and values of the contemporary Roman is here immediately apparent.

The impact of the *corona civica* and of the laurel wreath, whose meaning is often the same, merits special consideration. We have already seen how this honorific symbol, implying "the salvation of the citizens and the state," quickly became one of the most ubiquitous shorthand expressions of praise for the emperor, applicable to every object in any context, at times even approaching the status of an insigne of empire (cf. fig. 167*b*). In spite of this, there was no question of its being the sole prerogative of the emperor. By the Tiberian and Claudian periods there is evidence for the use of essentially the same imperial wreath in the private realm, to convey a personal and utterly nonpolitical message. The first to use it may have been freedmen connected with the imperial house, who used this imperial symbol to advertise their recently elevated status. The members of the collegium of Augustales in Pompeii, for example, placed enormous *coronae civicae* on their funerary altars (fig. 219), sometimes even above the doors of their houses. Imperial freedmen made the same use of them. Soon, however, oak and laurel wreaths became, in the context of funerary art, generalized symbols of past service and recognition, similar in meaning to the typical formulas in grave inscriptions, such as *optimus* or *bene meritus*.

The marble funerary altars and ash urns from Rome are in general our best means to following the gradual acceptance and then assimilation of official imagery. First, largely nonspecific motifs are borrowed from the imagery of *pietas,* such as bucrania, garlands, sacrificial instruments, torches, and branches. These in turn lead us to suspect that the very form of these grave monuments is significant. The earlier urns often imitated temple forms (fig. 220*a*), while the funerary altars are apparently modeled on Augustan sacrificial altars, like those of the Lares. In other words, the new burial customs were directly inspired by visual manifestations of the revived religion and must be considered, as a whole, as an expression of *pietas* now fully assimilated into private life.

The new type of funerary urn was also adopted by some prominent citizens of provincial Italian cities. One good example contained the remains of one of the leading men of Perugia, whose name, P. Volumnius A.f. Violens, is inscribed on the architrave of his marble urn, like that of a temple dedicator. On one of the long sides, bucrania and garlands are clearly inspired by public monuments like the Ara Pacis, while on the other appear props from a luxurious garden (fig. 220*b*). Among these the motif of a bird drinking out of a krater is especially prominent. We have already encountered this in the context of the theme *saeculum aureum* and as a symbol of Venus Augusta (cf. fig. 112). Here the lighthearted image has nothing to do with the grave *pietas* of the new age, but is rather to be seen as a sign of the

Fig. 219. Pompeii, street of tombs before the Herculaneum Gate. Funerary altars of freedmen who belonged to the *collegium* of Augustales. In the foreground, altar with large *corona civica;* behind, altar with the chair of office that the deceased was permitted to occupy as *augustalis.*

good life in prosperous and cultivated surroundings, the kind of life which the deceased had enjoyed and which, perhaps, he hoped to continue in the afterlife.

Gradually, as these private monuments become more and more geared to the idea of *familia,* they take over even more elements from the official pictorial vocabulary: eagles, heads of Ammon, Victories, armor, tripods, swans, sphinxes, and all manner of fertility symbols. They take on a broad and indistinct range of meanings, embodying personal values and aspirations, equally applicable to the dead and their survivors. The tripods, for example, which in the more extravagant examples are joined with lushly growing vines, surely have little connection with Apollo, but rather stand

a

Fig. 220. Marble ash urn of P. Volumnius from Perugia. *a*) The urn takes the form of a small temple. The pictorial images are largely borrowed from official art. *b*) Park motifs, including a marble basin from which birds drink (cf. figs. 99, 112).

for personal *pietas* and for a wealthy, religiously correct burial. Direct references to death are, by contrast, extremely rare on the urns and altars. Even ships' prows were displayed as a particularly worthy motif, not because they alluded to the Battle of Actium (fig. 221*a*, *b*), but simply because ships' prows looked so impressive on official monuments.

The result of all this is that, owing to the dominance of official imagery, it became impossible to find a means of individual expression. Sculptors and patrons had to try to formulate personal sentiments, if this was the goal at all, using the language of imperial politics. Thus the scene of Aeneas and his family is employed on grave monuments as a symbol of personal piety and devotion (cf. fig. 163), while the she-wolf with the infants Romulus and Remus, the embodiment of Roman pride and self-assurance, is transferred to funerary altars as a symbol of selflessness and love within the family.

The private use of images and symbolism from Augustan public art reached its culmination only in the Flavian period. Evidently the process of assimilation moved slowly and in small steps, and the new imagery retained its popularity, even in the private realm, for generations.

b

Taste and the New Mentality

We must return to the origins of Augustan art to understand how the spirit of the new age penetrated the private home, not simply in the form of new visual images, but as a totally changed mentality that led to the creation of a new domestic decorative style. In the 40s and 30s B.C. the extravagant Architectural Style in wall painting was still favored, with its use of expensive materials and realistic simulation of colonnaded courtyards, gardens, and the most luxurious refinements (cf. figs. 21, 22).

Then about 30 B.C. there began to appear more mannered forms, which did not do away with the extravagance, but rather made it more and more eccentric (cf. fig. 223). Conservatives like the architect Vitruvius (perhaps expressing the opinion of a large group of the upper class) rejected this diversion from time-honored aesthetic standards as nothing less than immoral. This in itself suggests a relatively sudden change in taste.

They now prefer to paint monstrosities (*monstra*) on plaster rather than faithful copies of natural objects. In place of columns they put fluted reed stalks with curling leaves, and, in place of pediments, volutes and candelabra bearing little aediculae. On their pediments grow tender blos-

Fig. 221. *a*) Roman funerary altar. Claudian period. The imagery of official art has here been "internalized" and used partly for specific, partly for very generalized types of personal messages. *b*) Detail. Candelabra stand on *rostra,* which here serve as tokens of social status without any further significance.

soms, whose stalks twist in and out and on which sit utterly meaningless little figures. They paint stalks of plants with half-figures, some with human heads, other with animal heads. Such a thing has never existed and never will. (Vitruvius 7.5)

If we consider the wall as a whole, the mannered elongation of columns and the exaggeration of decorative motifs into the realm of the fantastic actually resulted in a decided reduction in the oppressive luxury and crass ostentation of painted architecture. Admittedly, certain paintings, like those in the Villa Farnesina (ca. 20 B.C.) surpass the earlier walls in the wealth of detail, but the extravagance is now reserved more and more for the ornament. The illusion of breaking through the wall is no longer sought—rather its integrity is emphasized—and the viewer is meant to focus on the meaning of just a few images that dominate the room. This development is also accompanied by iconographic and stylistic changes, which once again seem to be associated with moral principles. Evidence for this can be found in one of the principal rooms in the excavated section of Augustus's house on

Fig. 222. Wall painting from the House of Augustus on the Palatine. Ca. 30 B.C. The relatively uncomplicated walls are dominated by large pictures; in the center of each is depicted a cult object, here a so-called baitylos (cf. fig. 73).

the Palatine (fig. 222). The wall is articulated with striking simplicity, like a stage, helping to intensify the impact of the landscape panoramas. But each of the three scenes is subsidiary to a mysterious cultic or votive object pushed into the foreground. Undoubtedly the religious elements in the decorative program are due to the influence of the patron.

The response of aesthetic sensibilities to the changing cultural situation moved astonishingly quickly. The painted rooms in the House of Livia and the House of Augustus (ca. 30 B.C.), even those in the Farnesina (ca. 20–10 B.C.), are still executed in the old manner (fig. 223). But in spite of this, eccentric mannerisms, restrained use of color, and an emphasis on the central pictures all lend these walls a novel quality. Apparently, different workshops were all searching simultaneously for new means of expression, but as yet no revolutionary solution had been found. What all these attempts have in common, however, is that they avoid the impression of a conscious display of luxury and great expense, which must now have been perceived as undesirable and tasteless. The objective was to find simpler and more artistic solutions, instead of the blatant overkill of earlier architectural extravaganzas. Naturally there were also other stimuli for formal change: the desire of the viewer for variety and the desire of the workshops for innova-

Fig. 223. This wall painting imitates a pinakotheke, with ancient Greek paintings. Ca. 20 B.C. From a villa situated on the Tiber, beneath the present-day Farnesina.

tion. But it is hardly coincidental that these changes took place simultaneously with Augustus's efforts to bring about a "moral turnaround." In short, an altered mentality brought about a change in public taste and aesthetic sensibility, that is, in everything that was considered pleasing or beautiful.

The new taste found its clearest expression in the decorative system of the so-called Third Style (fig. 224*a*). This new "Style" does not seem to me the result of a gradual process, as it is usually represented. It is rather an eclectic but nevertheless unified artistic creation, blending old and new in a novel synthesis of forms. The formative models must have appeared first about the time of the Secular Games. It is sometimes referred to as the "Candelabra Style," owing to the frequency of this motif borrowed from the realm of the sacred. This too suggests the mentality that gave rise to the new style.

Once invented, the new decorative system spread quickly, for it clearly expressed prevalent notions of taste. In Pompeii, for example, many owners of even more modest houses had their rooms painted in the new style. A good example of the Third Style in its purest form is preserved in a villa at Boscotrecase (ca. 10 B.C.), which probably belonged to the family of Agrippa (fig. 224a). Columns and architectural prospects have been turned into narrow and elegant ornamental friezes, which articulate the entire wall in exquisitely subtle and balanced proportion. Only when we look up close (fig. 224b) do we see that the column shafts and moldings are decorated with the most lavish and extraordinary ornament and that the decorative bands, despite their diminutive width and immaterial impression, are actually composed of columns, entablatures, pilasters, or candelabra.

Though these framing elements may be considered still within the tradition of mannerist architectural wall decoration, the large expanses of monochrome wall on which our eye comes to rest represent a major innovation. The striving for intelligibility, the clear delineation of socle, wall, ornament, and picture field, and a uniform, quiet color scheme in the individual rooms betokens a new longing for calm, order, and clarity.

The lavish, exuberant decoration prevalent just a few years earlier is now strictly limited to miniature friezes or is unrolled along the narrow borders of the monochrome wall as neatly drawn, almost calligraphic ornament, all exhibiting a single-minded devotion to the new concept. There is good reason to believe that the first patrons of this style belonged to the inner circle of the court. Otherwise it would be hard to explain the style's extremely high quality of execution and rapid spread, which must be due to both the importance and the high visibility of the first houses decorated in the new style.

The painters who developed the new style were apparently trying to give expression not only to a changed aesthetic taste, but the new system of values. This is most evident in the moral implications of the imagery about which the consciously "simple" walls and carefully ordered artistic scheme are built. It would, however, be mistaken to talk in terms of a specific "program." The new political order is reflected only indirectly in roughly equivalent aesthetic attitudes. But of course, conversely, the altered appearance of the houses gradually had its own effect on the public mentality.

Two types of pictures are especially popular on the walls of the Candelabra Style: mythological scenes and "sacral-idyllic" landscapes. Examples of the former can already be found on walls of the earlier mannerist style, for example in the House of Livia. The subjects are mainly derived from models in Classical Greek monumental painting, thus echoing in this respect the classicism of official art in this period. Furthermore, they often

a

Fig. 224. *a*) Wall painting in the new decorative style. Characteristic features are the large monochrome wall surfaces and the narrow little columns and moldings. From a villa belonging to the family of Agrippa near Boscotrecase. Ca. 10 B.C. *b*) Detail of one of the wall paintings from Boscotrecase. The wealth of ornament is now revealed in miniature pictures.

display in their narrative technique the paucity of action characteristic of the mythological "icons" of public monuments. In both cases relatively few gestures and expressions communicate to the viewer a deeper and paradigmatic meaning, without always elucidating a specific content. Thus the scene of the baby Dionysus entrusted to the nymphs becomes an emblem of the worship of the divine child, the fall of Icarus signifies mourning for the youth's death, and the punishment of Dirce is a symbol of hubris. The invitation to ponder these meanings is unmistakable. Occasionally it is hard to ascertain whether the Augustan artists have made any changes in adapting their Classical models or not, but just by their choice of subjects and the careful arrangement of the wall decoration they betray a different attitude

b

toward the content of the scenes. This is particularly striking in the self-conscious imitations of Archaic and Classical painted panels (*pinakes*). The "picture gallery" on the walls of the Villa Farnesina, with its imitations of ancient paintings, takes on the ambience of a sanctuary filled with precious votive *pinakes* (cf. fig. 223). These wonderfully fresh paintings could be understood both as an expression of the officially promoted *pietas* and as an example of the private sphere's adaptation of programmatic archaism and classicism. They are in any event a major work embodying the fully eclectic artistic taste of the period. Only the central pictures—the votive *pinakes* and large "Classical" painting of Dionysus and the nymphs—pay homage to the new ideological style. In the subsidiary decoration—supporting figures and highly mannered architectural ornament—the artist indulges in an uninhibited eclectisism, employing much of the Hellenistic "baroque" tradition.

Bucolic Fantasies

Pietas is also the principal message of the novel landscape scenes with predominantly sacred and bucolic subject matter that were introduced along with the new decorative system and appear on many walls of the Candelabra Style (fig. 224*c*). These carry the viewer off into a world of peace and calm. Meadows and ancient trees, rocks and streams, here and there fishermen or shepherds with their flocks, as well as satyrs and nymphs, evoke thoughts of the carefree life in "unspoiled nature," though in reality the compositions consist of parklike settings with garden architecture, little temples and colonnades, even villas in the background. The focal point is

Fig. 224c. View of a sacral-idyllic landscape (detail of fig. 224a). Sacrifice before an enthroned goddess; cult buildings and tokens, with a herdsman and his goats in the middle. In the background, temple and grounds of a villa.

always an artfully constructed shrine, with small sanctuaries, votive offerings, and statues of the gods, before which stand worshippers performing a sacrifice. Of the latter some are simple country folk, others festively attired priestesses. In this setting even the satyrs leave their maenads unmolested and instead piously bring offerings to Dionysus or Priapus.

The pastoral idyll was in fact already part of the thematic repertoire of earlier wall painting, but merely as a genre scene, one of several kinds of landscape. Now it becomes the principal subject, and always associated with statues of divinities, altars, votives, and cult activities. At least as early as Vergil's poetry the bucolic world had been burdened with "political" symbolism. In the *Georgics,* the simple life of Romulus and his shepherds, its unspoiled piety, is celebrated. For other Augustan poets as well, the pastoral idyll always represents a longing for escape from city life, with its daily stress, ostentation, and moral decay (e.g., Horace *Epodes* 2.1.140). Ever since the happy shepherd and his peacefully grazing flock had become symbols of the *saeculum aureum,* visual imagery focused on the praise of simplicity and unaffected piety, turning the subject into a deliberate metaphor. We need only recall the grazing animals in the Pax relief on the Ara Pacis (cf. fig. 136).

The little landscapes are remarkably constructed. The individual elements do not compose a unified pictorial space, but are simply set beside one another, as in Chinese landscape painting. As a result the views have a peculiar, floating quality, and the lack of a frame gives them the character of a vision or epiphany. Artists were more concerned with communicating a certain atmosphere than with rendering specific details.

But these new idylls are full of contradictions. In this highly sophisticated society, sated in luxury, painters could only imagine the simple pastoral life against a background of elegant parks and villas. The simple stone altar stands in front of extravagant and exotic religious architecture and lavish votive offerings. These views of country landscape never reveal Roman peasants at work or the fertile Italian soil so rapturously celebrated by Vergil. We see only satyrs vintaging, not men and women. This vision of agriculture is unencumbered by the Augustan moral campaign, which only succeeded in redefining the imagery of escape into a world of *otium.* In place of the almost palpable luxury of the Late Republic, we are presented with nostalgic visions combining the very real urge for a quiet weekend in the country villa with the imagined longing for a simpler and harmonious way of life. Rustic piety and the pastoral idyll are the poetic metaphors for this life. The problems of daily life, the pressures and anxieties, which Augustus's program for moral renewal called attention to without actually solving, are here nowhere in evidence. Instead, the new system of values has, as elsewhere, simply been assimilated. Political ideology and longing for personal fulfillment play upon each other, but the gap between both of these and daily reality becomes ever greater.

In place of painted landscapes, relief panels could also be set into the wall. The sculptural technique of these small-scale reliefs, which are mostly of unusually high quality, required a terse and concentrated formulation in comparison with painted panels. They lack therefore the "suspended" quality that makes the small wall paintings such a welcome relief from the calculated rationality of Augustan state art. The carved reliefs are more didactic and emphasize their programmatic character—even when the subject matter is erotic.

Fig. 225. Satyr and nymph before a rustic sanctuary, with goats and other references to the herdsman's life. The mythical landscape reflects new values. Such reliefs could be set into a wall in place of painted pictures.

A relief in Turin (fig. 225) celebrates the amorous pleasures of nymphs
and satyrs. But unlike in the erotic groups of Late Hellenistic art, with their
direct sensuality, here the lovers turn away from the viewer. The nymph's
protestations against the importunate satyr rival the elegance of a shepherd
and shepherdess in a painting of the ancien régime. The lovers, as if sur-
prised by the viewer, look toward the impressionistic, sacral landscape,
where our gaze is also directed. The statue of a rustic divinity looks out
gravely from his little sanctuary. At the left stands a mysterious holy shrine
hung with fillets, and in the center of the picture a large laurel tree rises up,
a shepherd's pouch hanging in the branches. The flock is indicated in the
form of two disproportionately large goats. Nature assures those who remain true to her everything in abundance, effortlessly. What is all the wealth
of the modern world against this, asks the sculptor, as tendentiously as the
poets in Augustus's circle.

Fig. 226. Old peasant with cow before a rustic sanctuary. The aboriginal piety of one's ancestors was sought in the country, among the simple shepherds and peasants.

No less dogmatic in its own way is a fine, small relief in Munich (fig. 226). Amid this ostensibly innocent and loving view into a world of personal fulfillment, there is scarcely a single detail that does not function like a little didactic signpost. An old peasant drives his cattle to market. But unlike Hellenistic artists, whose detached studies of half-starved, scruffy fishermen and peasants bore a distinctly negative connotation, our sculptor is at great pains to show how the farmer prospers. His well-nourished cow carries two fat sheep, while the old man himself carries a hare over his shoulder and originally held a fruit basket. This is all portrayed as the reward not so much for hard work, but rather for the proper way of life. The background is dominated by an ancient sanctuary. We can make out the wall and gate of the sacred precinct, an altar with torch and cult vessels before it, and, in the distance, a small shrine of Priapus. From the middle of this round structure of marble ashlar blocks, a pillar soars up, supporting the Dionysiac grain basket with mystic tokens, the phallus, and bunches of

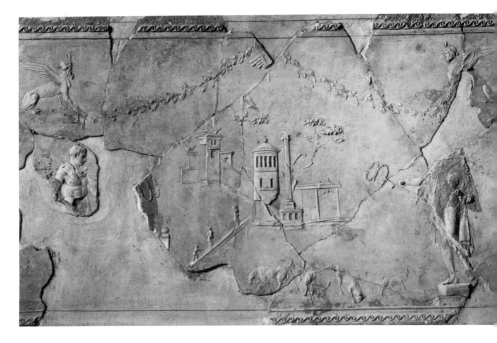

Fig. 227. Stuccoed ceiling from the villa beneath the "Farnesina" (cf. fig. 223). View into a sacral-idyllic landscape framed by two statues of Mercury holding oversized caducei, symbols of peace and prosperity. Ca. 20 B.C.

fruit. As if this were not enough, the ancient tree, which has long ago already grown up through the gate, now miraculously spreads its fresh, luxuriant oak branches precisely over the holy objects. In the decaying state of the sanctuary we may suspect an allusion to the *deserta sacraria* (Propertius 3.13.47), which—until Augustus appeared on the scene—were tended to only by the unspoiled farmers and shepherds. The iconography of a scene like this is no less complex and richly textured than the bucolic imagery of Augustan poets.

Occasionally, interior decoration refers directly to the new mythology of the Golden Age, as on the vaulted ceiling frescoes in the Farnesina, a villa on the far side of the Tiber. Within the traditional pictorial field on one ceiling, a full-scale "program" has been constructed, including rustic sacrifices, initiation in a Dionysiac mystery cult, hortatory mythological *exempla* (e.g., Phaeton), as well as hovering Victories, looking pointedly at weapons, and of course scenes of the promised land in the *saeculum aureum* (fig. 227). As in the wall paintings, fattened flocks graze before a background of shrines and temples. Here, however, two griffins and two statues of Mercury frame the scene. Their oversize *caducei*, prominently displayed, would have been universally recognized as tokens of peace and prosperity. Modern commentators have seen a reference to the likeness of Augustus in the figures of Mercury. This may indeed have been the intention of both patron and artist.

It is possible to imagine these wall paintings and ceiling frescoes, along with furniture and utensils, as a kind of decorative ensemble entirely comparable to those of the Age of Napoleon. The Empire Style in France was created by only a few ateliers working for the court and its immediate circle. A similar situation seems to have obtained in the time of Augustus. In both cases, the rapid transmission of the new style depended upon an aesthetic receptivity, which was in turn anchored in a new way of thinking, the result of a complex set of interactions. The transformation of the political system was but one of several contributory factors that made possible the coalescence of already existing tendencies into a directed program.

Tomb Monuments and Portraiture: Expressions of a New Self-Awareness

In concluding this chapter, we may take a brief look at a few of the many tomb monuments and anonymous portraits of the Early Empire, in order to illustrate how the change in taste and outlook affected the way people at all levels of society thought of themselves.

In Rome itself and other Italian cities, the type of ostentatious tomb monument, represented by the Mausoleum of Caecilia Metella or that of the master baker Eurysaces (cf. figs. 13, 14), gradually fell out of favor in the course of Augustus's reign. So too the countless houselike single tombs of freedmen, with which they took part in their own way in the competitive atmosphere of Roman society in the last decades of the Republic, proudly displaying themselves and their families along the roadside (cf. fig. 12). Now, in place of elaborate individual tombs practically accosting the passerby, burial precincts were created, walled off from the street, their decorated side facing into the interior.

For the old aristocracy, and even for those who now rose within the imperial administration, the urge to show off became pointless, at least in Rome itself. The fact that Augustus now dispensed public honors and determined who would receive a statue in the available space still remaining in the Forum Augustum obviated any desire for extravagant self-glorification. Munatius Plancus, for example, built his imposing mausoleum not in Rome, but near Gaeta, though still in a conspicuous setting. C. Cestius, a minor political figure who was evidently not so sensitive to the changed political and aesthetic climate, set his great tomb-pyramid before the Ostian Gate in A.D. 11, but was one of the last practitioners of the old, ostentatious style. There are, to be sure, some even later examples of monumental grave monuments for private individuals, but then always for "outsiders," not major politicians or members of the old aristocracy.

The new taste among the upper class now dictated, instead of large tomb monuments, simpler family burial plots, within which each member received a modest funerary altar and portraits and ash urns were displayed in correspondingly modest tomb structures. The altar in particular was now the most characteristic and significant feature of funerary art. On the tombs of the Augustales in Pompeii (cf. fig. 219), in the last decades before the city's destruction, the altar is prominently placed on a socle over the tomb itself. This type of tomb prevalent in Pompeii must represent an imitation of a practice that originated in Rome: pretentious self-advertisement replaced by a return to a modest *pietas*.

The changed social structure in Rome is vividly illustrated by the sometimes enormous columbaria put up by guilds of freedmen and artisans. This new form of common burial was initiated by freedmen of the imperial house. A modest entrance led into a large underground vault, with niches sunk into the walls, as in a pigeon coop (*columbarium*) (fig. 228). Within each of these standardized niches, members could place the ashes of their loved ones in a marble urn or other container, and, if they chose, also display a portrait in marble. Only those few who had held positions of honor within the group received a more prominent burial place. The spirit of competition, of trying to promote oneself at the expense of others, which in the Late Republic had resulted in all sorts of hybrid tomb monuments, at all levels of society, essentially disappeared. One now sought a burial the way one found one's seat in the theater: a clearly designated place in one's own social class, with the appropriate, standardized appurtenances.

The many marble portraits of the period illustrate, in their own way, the desire of a broad spectrum of society to identify with the imperial family and the new spirit in Rome. The pyramidal social structure meant that the ruler and his family automatically became the models of all things to all people. They had a palpable presence in even the tiniest communities, in the form of honorary statues bearing their physiognomy and hairstyles. So, for example, the coiffures of Julio-Claudian women quickly set the fashion throughout the Empire. When Livia gave up the style with complicated braids in favor of a more "classical" one with central part, women copied her, just as they later copied Agrippina Minor, when she adopted a more elaborate look with three rows of curls. The assimilation of private portraits to the hairstyles and physiognomies of the court is sometimes so extreme

Fig. 228. Rome, Columbarium of the freedmen of the imperial house. The niches were used to house ash urns. The imperial freedmen were the first to organize themselves into such burial societies and thereby created an alternative to the ostentatious individual tomb monument (cf. figs. 12, 13).

that the scholar is hard-pressed to decide whether an individual portrait depicts the wife of the emperor or an anonymous woman. The very same is true of fashions in clothing. In distant Spain, Roman women had *stolae* made for themselves, and sculptors then had to adapt even their busts to display the shoulder strap (cf. fig. 131).

In male portraits, there is more emphasis on individualized facial features than for the women. But again there is a pronounced stylization of the hair, which frames the forehead and keeps it in just the right proportion to the face, quite independent of how the subject's hair actually grew (fig. 229*a–d*). Not surprisingly, there are virtually no more bald heads or jowly faces among Early Imperial portraits. But most strikingly, in their facial expression and the tilt of the head these likenesses echo precisely the stereotypical formulas of portraits made to honor Augustus and the Julio-Claudian princes (cf. figs. 83, 174f.) We are reminded of the conventional poses and expressions of portrait photographs of the 1930s, especially when we see the difference in portraiture of the Late Republic (cf. figs. 5–8): locks of hair

a

Fig. 229. *a–d*) Portraits of anonymous Romans from the Augustan/Tiberian Age. Dress, bearing, and style all express a new self-image.

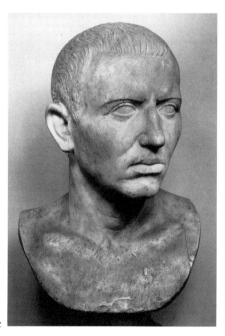

c

now perfectly ordered across the brow, instead of free to move; smooth cheeks instead of lines, wrinkles, and warts; only classically proportioned faces instead of the whole gamut from fat to skinny, elderly to youthful; and a single dignified, detached, uniform expression, instead of vivid, theatrical movement. The much-admired portrait style of the imperial house apparently inspired the most conscientious imitators to suppress even their own individual features in favor of depersonalized formulas expressing dignity and moral worth.

When we consider that the average person past a certain age is extremely loath to be parted from those things that belong to his personal style and image, such as his accustomed clothes and haircut, then we may begin to realize just how powerful the interaction must have been among changing fashions and taste, the influence of the imperial house, and the ordinary Roman's whole conception of himself.

Chapter 8

The Roman Empire of Augustus:
Imperial Myth and Cult in East and West

Up to now we have been concerned almost exclusively with the city of Rome and have glanced only incidentally at other cities of the Empire. This is perhaps inevitable, insofar as the new visual language arose in Rome and from there spread to the rest of the Empire. We must, however, make a fundamental distinction between the Greek East and the Roman West. The East, rich in its own traditions, would necessarily react differently to the new political situation. But in both East and West it was the rapidly spreading cult of the emperor that was the principal vehicle for propagating the Augustan program and its attendant imagery.

The Greek Reaction

"The whole of humanity turns to the *Sebastos* (i.e. Augustus) filled with reverence. Cities and provincial councils honor him with temples and sacrifices, for this is his due. In this way do they give thanks to him everywhere for his benevolence."

With these words, Augustus's contemporary Nikolaos of Damascus described the spontaneous reaction of the Greek world to the creation of a monarchy after the defeat of Antony. Unlike Rome, the Greek East needed no newly invented symbols or visual imagery of empire. It could apply the old and ingrained "language" of the Hellenistic ruler cult to this new monarch, whose power to bring peace and restore order were everywhere visible, to greet him "with the honors usually accorded the Olympian gods" (Philo *Legatio* 149–51).

Although the outward forms of the new imperial cult were essentially the same as those with which Greek cities had earlier honored Alexander and the Hellenistic kings, later Roma and individual Roman generals, in its proportions and the extent of its spread it did indeed represent a new phenomenon. Previously, the ruler cult was instituted sporadically in one city or another, usually for a particular occasion. But now it appeared everywhere, almost simultaneously, not only in "free" cities, but in the administrative centers of the provinces, and even in settlements without civic status. The imperial cult rapidly became the most widespread of all cults.

The form and scale of worship naturally varied from city to city, depending on the financial resources of individual patrons and the size and status of the community. The cult of Augustus might be attached to already existing cults and festivals of the gods, but often it was housed in structures built for it alone. "In cities old and new, they build temples, propylaea, sacred precincts, and colonnades for him" (Philo *Legatio* 149–51). These new sanctuaries for the emperor were often larger and grander than those of the traditional gods, but were otherwise indistinguishable in their outward appearance. There was usually a freestanding, peripteral temple, surrounded by colonnades, or a round temple and monumental altar. But the new style Roman marble temple, with tall podium, heavy pediment, and exuberant decoration, occurs in the East, if at all, only in new Roman foundations. Elsewhere, the use of old and familiar architectural forms reassured the Greeks of the intimate association between traditional religion and the worship of the emperor.

The physical setting of the cult of the emperor was usually in the middle of the city, integrated into the center of religious, political, and economic life. So, for example, a round Temple of Roma and Augustus was built on the Athenian Acropolis, very near the Erechtheum and Parthenon. In Ephesus, the Temple of Augustus lay in the midst of the Upper Square, a new urban center that grew up around the foundation of the ruler cult. King Herod chose a particularly imposing spot for the Temple of Roma and Augustus in the newly founded city of Caesarea (named in honor of the emperor). Set on a high podium, the temple dominated the harbor and shaped the whole outline of the city (Josephus *Jewish Antiquities* 15.339).

In some places, there was more than one cult place for the imperial house. In Eresos, on the island of Lesbos, for example, a wealthy citizen erected not only a Temple of Augustus at the harbor, like Herod, but also a sacred precinct for C. and L. Caesar in the Agora, then yet a third sanctuary, for Livia. Altars erected for the cult of the emperor were evidently often inordinately lavish, like the one in the Hellenistic bouleuterion of Miletus which has only recently been reconstructed (fig. 230). All of this was a constant visual reminder to every city-dweller of the importance attached to the worship of the emperor. It also expressed a new consciousness within cities of the Greek East, which could identify much better with the monarchy than they had with the large and continually changing administration of the Republic. Direct communication with the emperor, through the medium of cult, gave rise to a new and positive sense of belonging to the Roman Empire.

Greek ruler cults had, since the fourth century B.C., linked the ruler, as the incarnation of earthly power, with the traditional cults of the gods. Usually sacrifices were made to the old gods *for* the ruler, but occasionally people might entreat him directly. Even Augustus and his successors were not treated as fully equal to the gods, despite the extravagant temples and ritual. But the emperor was set beside the gods, as a power that penetrated into every aspect of the life of the city and its people. Historians of religion have often questioned the depth of emotional and religious experience in the ruler cult and dismissed it as a routine expression of allegiance to the state, a view which stems from the Christian conception of religion as faith. But, whatever Greeks in the time of Augustus may have thought or experienced in a sacrificial procession in honor of the emperor, such rituals were linked with parades, public meals, and lavish games. Imperial feast days became the high points of the entire year, when the citizenry could experience a sense of community. As part of the excitement, people streamed in from neighboring towns, markets were held, and self-important embassies came from distant parts. An imperial feast day was also a bright spot in the lives of the poor. Rituals performed for the emperor in faraway Rome blended with high spirits and pride in one's own city. For prominent citizens, it was an opportunity to show off their own status and how much they could afford to lavish on honors for the emperor and enjoyment for their fellow citizens.

But every day of the year, a permanent architectural stage set, against which people played out their lives, was a constant reminder of the emperor. One encountered pictures and statues of him everywhere, and there were also, of course, the coins with his likeness, minted in almost every city (fig. 231a–c). This in itself represented a unique means of honoring the world ruler on a scale never seen before. At first, however, the coin portraits were

Fig. 230. Altar of Augustus in the bouleuterion of Miletus. The imperial cult penetrated to all the cities' religious and political centers.

Fig. 231. Examples of coins minted in honor of Augustus in the cities of Greece and Asia Minor. *a*) Pella (Macedonia). The victor of Actium above a large ships' beak. *b*) Teos (Ionia). Portrait in the temple to the emperor. *c*) Avados (Phoenicia). City goddess with smaller portrait of Augustus.

not by any means uniform. A thorough study of these could ascertain interesting gradations and emphases in the praises thereby accorded the emperor.

While the architecture, as well as forms of ritual and ceremony, were largely traditional, honorific statues for the emperor and his family were apparently most often imitative of models originating in Rome. The widespread togate statue with veiled head presented the emperor as pious Roman (figs. 232, 233), an appropriate counterpoise to the many cult statues. In his images, Augustus was thus manifest as both god and man, corresponding precisely to his special status in the imperial cult. But other types of statues seem also to have been taken over more or less directly from Rome: the figure with garment about the hips, the cuirassed statue, and the heroic nude in Classical style. The same is true of female divinity types, used to celebrate women of the imperial family as a new Aphrodite, Hera, or Hestia, sometimes also as personifications, as was done in the West. In short, the visual language used to express the myth of the emperor shared many common elements in East and West.

Nevertheless, it is probably still true that in the East the emperor was linked more directly with the ancient myths of gods and heroes than in the West. This is, at least, the implication of various later monuments, such as one erected ca. 170 to Lucius Verus in Ephesus, commemorating his victory in Parthia, and a building belonging to the imperial cult recently excavated at Aphrodisias, dating to the Early Empire.

The latter was decorated with two series of large-scale relief sculpture. One series presents familiar mythological subjects—Meleager's hunt, Leda with the Swan, et al.—while in the other, the emperor himself appears in various mythological guises. For example, he subdues Britannia like a new

Figs. 232 and 233. Portraits of Augustus from Corinth (fig. 232, left) and Samos (fig. 233, right). They match the Roman model exactly (cf. fig. 83) and belong to togate statues with veiled head.

Achilles, the composition borrowed from the familiar group of Achilles and Penthesilea (fig. 234). Several of the reliefs depict him as victor, surrounded by divinities and personifications. In these scenes, the ruler is shown either nude or wearing a cuirass, both reflecting statue types then popular in the West. The various personifications, such as the Genius Senatus and the Genius Populi Romani, are also represented in the standard Roman way. The female deity who crowns Nero accords perfectly with the new type of "political" divinity in Rome, both in her classicizing pose and in the fact that she bears the portrait features and hairstyle of an empress, in this case Agrippina Minor, the wife of Claudius and mother of Nero (fig. 235).

These examples illustrate how East and West early on were able to make use of the same formulaic expressions of praise for the emperor, and how Roman personifications and symbolic depictions of the emperor in mythical guise were easily attached to much older Greek myths, so that the former, in the eyes of the Greek viewer, took on at least some of the same qualities.

Portraits of the emperor and of his family are also usually faithful to models originating in Rome, sometimes extremely so (cf. figs. 232, 233). There are, to be sure, instances where the Roman model has been adapted to the emotional style of Hellenistic portraiture or even assimilated to earlier ruler portraits, but these are quite rare. The question is, why did the Greeks imitate so slavishly their Roman models? Were there no artists whose imaginations were sparked by the new ruler? Or was their intention simply to reproduce his "authentic" features, which were by now so well known from numerous statues in both East and West and from so many coin portraits?

In any event, the result of the copying process was that, thanks to the abundance of honorific statues, a uniform conception of the emperor's appearance and that of his family prevailed, and these images in turn, owing to the new political order, became models for clothing and hair styles—in life no less than in art—throughout the Empire. From the time of Augustus, private portraits, even in the East, consistently display the hairstyles favored by the emperor and other women and men of his house. This in itself was a significant step toward the creation of a uniform imperial culture.

The Imperial Cult: Competition Among Cities

Cults and honors for the emperor spread rapidly and had a momentum of their own. Only rarely did Augustus himself or members of his circle take the initiative. The erection of altars of Roma and Augustus for the new provincial assemblies of Gaul and Germany, in Lyon (fig. 236) and Cologne, constitute an exception, whose purpose was primarily to convey the permanent bond between the imperial house and the leading men among the recently subjugated peoples. Mostly, however, Augustus made a modest impression and never tired of reassuring his fellow Romans that he was a mere mortal and that they should reserve divine honors for the gods. As "princeps," he could not do otherwise.

Yet once Augustus had granted permission, in the winter of 30/29 B.C., to the provincial assemblies of the Greeks in Bithynia and Asia for cult worship of his person—with, however, the conditions that the goddess Roma must be associated with him in the cult and that he not be named explicitly as a god—there was no turning back. Here too, the various roles were clearly defined. For the emperor's subjects, it was an opportunity to express their allegiance, while he himself had constantly to impose restrictions, occasionally refuse to allow excesses, or even forbid certain forms of worship altogether. Cult worship created a direct link to the emperor. On those occasions when he granted petitions for support or special privileges, when he proclaimed a victory, when a death or birth in the imperial family was announced, when the anniversary of his rule came around, or anything else of the sort, he might expect even more elaborate honors than usual. We

g. 234. The Emperor Claudius subju-
ites Britannia. The model was the Hel-
nistic group of Achilles and Penthesilea.
phrodisias (Asia Minor), from a build-
g used in the imperial cult.

Fig. 235. The Emperor Nero crowned
by a divinity with the portrait features
of his mother Agrippina. This artist
has employed the same iconographical
schemata that were being used in
Rome. Aphrodisias, from the same
building as figure 234.

Fig. 236. As, Lugdunum, 10–7
B.C. (?). Provincial altar for
Roma-Augustus. On the altar, a
corona civica and small laurel
trees, with Victoriae on tall columns at the sides. On the altar itself, two shrines for Roma and
Augustus; alongside, perhaps
busts of the imperial family. This
coin type was minted in large
quantities over an unusually long
time.

are reminded in a way of the practice of reciprocal gift-giving in archaic religion.

Unlike the provincial assemblies, the big cities were largely independent of Rome in managing their own affairs. They could decide for themselves whom they wished to honor, and how, and as a rule did not need to seek Rome's approval. They were just as free as any private individual to accord the emperor religious honors, and Augustus had no reason to stand in their way. This was as true in the West as it was in the East. The only place where he made sure that no temples were built to him while still alive was in Rome itself. For here decisions were taken by the Senate, and Augustus was the Senate's most prominent member. But we may still ask how much difference it made for the worshiper—aside from the question of labels—that the *genius* of Augustus, and not Augustus himself, was worshiped together with the Lares in the local district sanctuaries of Rome.

In any case, the imperial cult did spread throughout the West, only not quite as early on as in the East. Yet by the end of Augustus's reign, there was probably not a single Roman city in Italy or the western provinces that did not enjoy several cults linked directly or indirectly to the imperial house. There was, however, no tradition of a ruler cult in the West: on the contrary, Italic religion made a much sharper distinction than Greek between mortal and immortal. There must, therefore, have been powerful social and political pressures operating here. Naturally, we should also take account of the substantial Hellenization of the West. But in any case, the imperial cult became a pillar of the new order in every Roman city in the West.

At first, cities in the West drew inspiration from models in the East, sometimes quite directly. In 27 B.C., when the city of Mytilene on Lesbos voted a whole series of honors for Augustus—temple, priests, games, statues in the temples of the ancient gods, monthly sacrifices of a white bull on the day of Augustus's birth, and more—the local magistrates proudly sent an embassy to Rome to announce all this and, in addition, set up copies of the honorary decree not only in the house of Augustus on the Capitoline, but in a variety of cities all around the Mediterranean.

One copy of the decree which chances to survive, though not complete (IGR IV 39), names the following cities: Pergamum, Actium, Brundisium, Tarraco, Massilia, and Antioch in Syria. All these cities were important administrative or commercial centers or harbors, where the inscription would surely be read by many. We happen to know that in one of these cities, Tarraco (Tarragona), an altar to Augustus with appropriate ritual was set up at about this very time. Of course we cannot be sure that the display of the Mytilenian inscription was the immediate stimulus that galvanized the people of Tarraco into action. There were literally hundreds of cities all around the Mediterranean that set up altars and temples to Augustus at this time. But in general it seems clear that mutual competition among cities played a decisive role in the swiftness with which the imperial cult spread.

But this is not all we know about the altar at Tarraco. Among all such altars it had a special distinction in that a miracle was associated with it: in the course of time a palm tree grew up on it, all by itself! The city council of Tarraco excitedly sent messengers to inform the emperor of the miracle, but he replied dryly, "one can see how often you have lit the sacrificial fires" (Quintilian 6.3.77). Beside attesting to Augustus's remarkable wit, the response indicates clearly how he took such sacrifices for granted. The miracle of the palm nevertheless enjoyed a certain recognition, for the city of Tarraco later minted coins with the altar and palm tree, in order to boast of the miracle to other cities (fig. 237).

There is epigraphical evidence to suggest that the practice of sending such embassies to Rome and to allied cities was quite common. For the leading men of provincial cities, this presented a unique opportunity to establish personal contact with Augustus. The real reason behind these embassies was not simply the hope of receiving certain privileges, financial support for building projects, or help in times of need, but also the chance for the city to present itself as an important, well-run, and loyal member of the Empire. Copies of honorary decrees in Rome could be read by envoys from throughout the Empire, when Augustus granted them an audience, or when they conducted sacrifices in the Temple of Jupiter on the Capitol. In other provincial allies as well, these inscriptions were displayed in prominent places.

Competition among cities in the worship of the emperor leaves little doubt how fully accepted the monarchy was everywhere. Through the imperial cult, ties with and orientation toward Rome took on a new dimen-

Fig. 237. Tiberian coin of the city Tarracco, with altar of Augustus. On the altar, the miraculous palm tree. Bucrania, a garland, and, behind, what is probably an oversized offering bowl can be made out. Under the pulvini is a frieze of vines.

sion. In the early years, we can still observe efforts at originality in the various initiatives of some cities, but the trend very quickly became one of standardization and uniformity. The story of the contest sponsored by the provincial assembly of Asia provides a good example. In 29 B.C., a golden wreath was offered to whoever could invent the greatest honor for the new god. When the prize was finally awarded twenty years later, it went to the Roman proconsul Paullus Fabius Maximus (Consul in 11 B.C.), for, of all things, his suggestion that the solar calendar be introduced in the province of Asia and that in future the new year begin on Augustus's birthday.

In earlier times, cities in the East and in the West had competed among themselves, in central Italy, for example, where they built the great terraced sanctuaries to proclaim their self-assurance. The intention was to impress the visitor on his arrival and so to enhance the prestige of the sanctuary. This type of competitive spirit was now a thing of the past. Every city directed itself primarily to the emperor, and only as an afterthought considered its own needs or its immediate rivals.

It was then not long before the most important stimuli came not from within the cities themselves, but from Rome. In the first instance, the Senate determined which deeds or events in the imperial house should be celebrated or mourned, then individual cities followed suit, more or less voluntarily and each according to its means. Just recently, substantial parts of an inscription were found near Seville, preserving a decree of the Roman Senate and people (*tabula Siarensis*), part of which was already known from other inscriptions. All the fragments now constitute one of the longest known Latin inscriptions. It concerns the enumeration of honors that the Roman Senate and people voted after the death of Germanicus in A.D. 19. These include monumental arches, whose sculptural decoration is described in detail, statues of Germanicus in triumphal garb, which were to be added to several already existing portrait galleries of the imperial family in Rome, annual sacrifices, and much else. The most interesting passage in the present context is the provision that copies of this decree be set up in all the *municipia* and *coloniae* of Italy, as well as in all *coloniae* in imperial provinces. The recent discovery in the remote province of Baetica proves that this provision was indeed carried out. Thus, by this time, the Senate was proceeding as earlier the city of Mytilene had, only much more systematically. Accordingly, what emanated from Rome as "inspiration" was perceived in the provinces more as requirement and obligation. And in fact, arches and statues in honor of Germanicus were erected, just as cults and altars had been instituted everywhere some twenty years before, after the early deaths of Augustus's grandsons Gaius and Lucius, the Senate in Rome leading the way.

Figs. 238 and 239. Altars for the divinities Pax (fig. 238, left) and securitas Augusta (fig. 239, right). The altars were erected by order of the town council and people of Praeneste, probably in the Forum. Augustan period.

The Imperial Cult in the West

In the Roman cities of the West, especially in Italy, approval for the new regime and the desire to work together toward a brighter future were even stronger, since it was their own country that was at stake. Rich and poor, slaves, freedmen, and the old aristocracy were all equally relieved when the civil wars were finally over. Apart from the nobility in Rome, no one mourned the passing of the Republic. Some may even have regarded this turn for the better as a kind of miracle. When, for example, the citizens of Praeneste walked past the altars of Securitas and Pax (figs. 238, 239) dedicated by the *decuriones* (local Senate) and *populus*, or contemplated the fountains with carved friezes heavy with symbolism (cf. fig. 138*a*–*c*), they saw them as much more than aesthetic objects. And the next generation in Praeneste will have well understood why, after the death of Augustus, a third altar for the deified emperor was added, with his portrait surrounded by cornucopiae (fig. 240).

The religious revival movement in Rome had quickly spilled over into other Italian cities. We encounter evidence for the renewal of cults and temples everywhere. But outside Rome, from the very start, *pietas* was di-

Fig. 240. Altar of the deified Augustus, after A.D. 14. The portrait of Augustus was adorned with a bronze crown of rays. The cornucopiae proclaim him founder of the general prosperity. Palestrina, Museo Barberiniano.

rected less at the traditional divinities than at Augustus himself. Forms of worship were more restrained and less explicit than in the East, but for that no less numerous and, in their own way, elaborate. Although the living emperor was not addressed as a god, everyone of course knew that after his death he would be worshiped as an official deity of the Roman state, just like the Divus Iulius. Many sacrifices and festivals focused not directly on Augustus, but on personifications that stood for the achievements and divine powers of the imperial house. But in reality these naturally honored above all the princeps, no less than the altars set up in honor of the young princes after their deaths. This is clear in the very scale on which these indirect cults of the emperor were sometimes carried out. So, for example, the splendid Maison Carrée in Nîmes (cf. fig. 201), the best preserved of all Roman temples and probably the largest one in that city, was dedicated not to the Capitoline Triad or to Mars, but to C. and L. Caesar after their premature deaths.

A glance at the Forum in Pompeii (fig. 241) illustrates the steady growth of the imperial cult to major proportions during the Early Imperial age, even in a small country town of about twenty thousand inhabitants. In the middle of the square's east side, two new sanctuaries were reserved exclusively for the cult of the emperor. Further, a large aedicula for this purpose was installed in the new market, Eumachia's building was dedicated to Con-

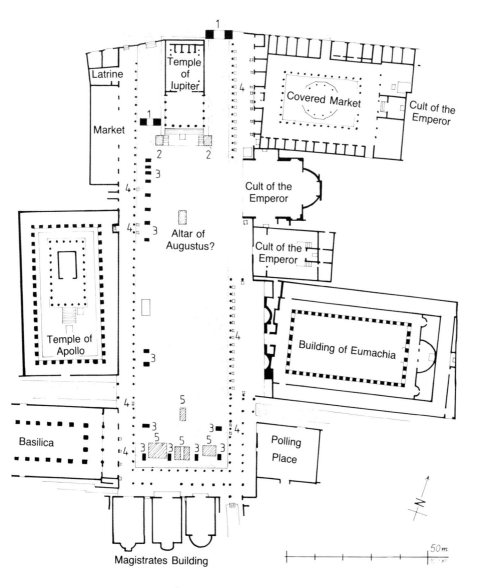

Fig. 241. Pompeii, Forum. Before A.D. 63. 1, Arch; 2, equestrian statue of the imperial princes (?); 3, equestrian statues of local magistrates; 4, simple honorific statues; 5, imperial monuments.

cordia and Pietas Augusta, and a Temple of Fortuna Augusta stood in the northern extension of the Forum, at one of the busiest intersections.

Pompeii was one of the first cities in Italy to be strongly Hellenized and already in the second century B.C. boasted an impressive city plan and world-class architecture. This was not, however, the case in most cities in the West, where the new temple for the imperial cult was often the first marble structure of any sort. In Pompeii, some of the new buildings for the imperial cult in the Forum could not enjoy the optimum visual effect, due to an older portico, part of which stood in the way. But elsewhere, when there were no such restrictions, the new temple was given a position of particular prominence. In Ostia, for example, the marble Temple of Roma and Augustus competed directly with the old Capitolium and indeed far surpassed it in its elaborate decoration (fig. 242). The temple serving the imperial cult in Leptis Magna was the largest of several sanctuaries in the old Forum. The same was true in Terracina, and in Pola too, the Temple of Augustus, together with another, dominated the Forum (fig. 243).

These new temples were mostly built of marble, unlike earlier temples in the West, or at least with a marble facing. As in Rome, this had an impor-

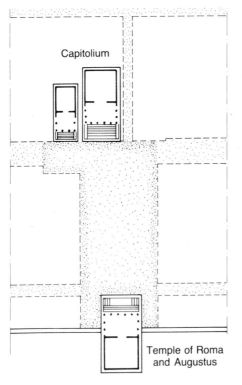

Fig. 242. Ostia, Forum of the Early Empire. The new temple for the imperial cult, sheathed in marble, came to dominate the square, while the old Capitolium was overshadowed.

tant symbolic value, but it also created problems for the local or itinerant masons' workshops, for, except in Rome itself, they did not have the necessary experience with marble that their counterparts in the East had. We can tell from the workmanship on individual elements and in the overall plan of a number of temples that the workshops were often put together on an ad hoc basis, with craftsmen of varying backgrounds and levels of skill, and that the architects too had little experience in marble construction.

It was impossible to imitate the great sanctuaries that Augustus had built in Rome; architects had to design projects appropriate to local resources. Only gradually were new elements of architectural ornament taken up. We can trace how at first certain technical features and decorative elements were adopted, and only later whole architectural members, such as the standard Corinthian capital.

Temples built during the Early Empire are in general immediately recognizable, whether they be in Campania, North Italy (fig. 243), southern France (cf. fig. 201), Spain, or North Africa. No matter what differences there may be in detail, the overall impression is always the same, always bearing the stamp of the *aurea templa* built by the princeps in Rome. These temples are always set on a podium, with grand staircase, tall Corinthian columns, richly ornamented entablature, and elaborate roof cornice. The impressive effect of the facade is always especially sought after. Even without specific models, the key principles of the new sacred architecture were everywhere fully assimilated: the most expensive possible materials and skillful execution. The exquisite Corinthian capitals suggest how well it was understood that these principles had an exemplary significance. They are invariably unstinting with the complicated leaf pattern of the calyx, the helices and volutes (fig. 243*b*). It was thus no accident that occasionally a patron, like C. Calpurnius, in the dedicatory inscription on his temple in Puteoli, specifically added *cum ornamentis,* since these were the most expensive part. The *ornamenta* included also the friezes and pedimental sculpture, in short all forms of decoration, and even the altar.

There were, thus, plenty of surfaces for figured decoration. But this does not mean that a varied iconography developed outside Rome, any more than an original architectural ornament. Rather, sculptors again looked toward Rome, and there is scarcely a single motif that is not borrowed directly from the new pictorial vocabulary created in Rome. If anything, the need to be selective and to simplify made this vocabulary, as it was employed outside Rome, even easier and more accessible. The most popular elements included the vine friezes, motifs of the sacred, laurel or oak leaves, and arms and armor (fig. 244). Local museums in virtually every Roman city in the West are filled with such bits and pieces, and with few exceptions, all are of the Early Imperial period.

a

Fig. 243. *a*) Pola, Temple of Roma and Augustus. Between 2 B.C. and A.D. 14. *b*) Detail. The rich architectural ornament is typical of the buildings of the imperial cult in East and West.

The specific meaning of these symbols was readily understood everywhere, at least at the beginning of the new age. Even an unlettered viewer could hardly fail to grasp the message, thanks to the constant didacticism presented by deliberate combinations of signs and symbols. In the Forum of Cumae, for example, was found a statue of a beautiful woman nude to the waist (fig. 245*a, b*). She holds a suckling child and sits on a rocky seat completely overgrown with vines. As on the Ara Pacis, the branches rise up from an acanthus calyx. She must be the same figure as that on the Pax relief of the Ara Pacis (cf. fig. 136). The message concerns the blessings of the new age, mirrored in an image of fertility. In this instance the interpretation is also confirmed by a dedicatory inscription. Cn. Lucceius, a member of one of the leading families in Cumae, dedicated her to Apollo as god of the new age: The words *Apollini sacrum* appear on the vine-covered rock. Since there exist several replicas of the same statue type, we may presume

b

that the original, perhaps a masterpiece of the Classical period, stood in Rome.

Examples of such imitations of major monuments in Rome are familiar from many cities throughout Italy and the western provinces, but, just as with portraits of the members of the imperial family, we do not know exactly how the process of transmission worked. It seems likely that both patrons and workshops were equally involved. The local aristocracies would have known some of the Roman monuments firsthand and may have occasionally commissioned portraits or architectural ornament directly from Roman ateliers. Then local workshops will have quickly developed the means of turning out the repertoire borrowed from Rome, to meet the widespread demand for this limited body of subjects.

Naturally, many different variations and combinations were possible. On

Fig. 244. Frieze of weapons from an Augustan marble building in Turin, perhaps an honorific arch.

a

Fig. 245. *a–b*) Statue of a female divinity with child from the Forum of Cumae, embodying the peace and prosperity of the *saeculum aureum*.

a copy of the Pax relief in Carthage (fig. 246), for example, the central image is an exact replica, while the two *aurae* have been replaced by more obvious figures, probably because the original motif was too "learned." Instead, a Triton capers in the sea on one side, and on the other a female divinity with torches appears above the fertile land. Perhaps she is Diana *Lucifera*, whom we have already met in the context of the imagery of birth and fertility (cf. p. 216).

Fig. 246. Relief of Pax (?), from Carthage. A variant of the figure on the Ara Pacis in Rome (fig. 136).

Also in Carthage, the freedman P. Perelius Hedulus instituted a cult of the *gens Augusta*, which he presided over as *sacerdos perpetuus*. One side of the large altar depicts Hedulus himself performing a sacrifice, while the other three constitute virtually a textbook summary of Roman official iconography (fig. 247): Aeneas fleeing from Troy, Apollo with the tripod, and Roma seated on a pile of weapons, as on the Ara Pacis. The Roma relief is particularly noteworthy, for it shows how provincial artists were able to both simplify and elaborate their Roman models at the same time. In her hand is a Victory that not only holds a shield, but also hovers above a pillar. This is of course an allusion to the *clipeus virtutis* and the monument in the Curia at Rome. In addition, the Victory flies toward a curious object composed of globe, cornucopia, and caduceus, while Roma herself also looks toward this "monument." The whole composition is best understood as a simplified version of the two complementary scenes of Pax and Roma on the Ara Pacis. Pax herself is replaced by symbols of peace and worldwide prosperity. Instead of figures of poetic inspiration, these more pedestrian symbols of commerce and material well-being embody the tangible results of Augustus's reign. This is presumably in keeping with the taste and personality of the donor, who must himself have been a businessman.

Fig. 247. Altar from a sanctuary of the *gens Augusta* erected by the freedman P. Perellius Hedulus. Roma with Victoria before a monument celebrating worldwide peace and general well-being. Early Imperial.

The Local Elite and the Augustan Program

The various examples of cults and honors voted by city councils should not obscure the fact that most public building activity, whether religious or secular, was sponsored by private individuals. This quickly led to competition and pressures within every social class, which contributed significantly to the rapid and natural spread of the imperial cult and to the "spontaneous" takeover of the Augustan cultural program in the West. Many people felt they had to put up a building or make a dedication, simply because someone else had done it.

Leading the way were of course the local aristocracy in each city, but they competed not only against members of their own class. As in Rome, wealthy freedmen in the provinces used the imperial cult to win for themselves public recognition and honors, even though they were excluded from holding office. For such "social climbers," the need for recognition in society was of course especially great, and they were among the first to seize upon the new opportunities. It is conceivable that these freedmen, many of whom will have come from the East originally, were in some cities the first to set up, on their own initiative, a cult of the emperor, thus forcing the local aristocracy to come up with a similar undertaking.

A particularly revealing example is known to us from the excavations at Tibur (modern Tivoli). There, a freedman named M. Varenus, who served as *magister Herculeus*, set up a small shrine in the Forum "with his own money," on the occasion of the safe return of the emperor, as the dedicatory inscription informs us: *pro reditu Caesaris Augusti* (fig. 248). The reference must be to Augustus's travels either in 19 or 13 B.C. On those two occasions the Senate and people in Rome had erected the famous altars of Fortuna Redux and of Pax Augusta, both of which, along with the later honors for the deceased princes, were especially influential in the provinces. A broad statue base is preserved in the apse of Varenus's little shrine, and on it a finely carved seated statue of a well-known Jupiter type (fig. 249). Unfortunately, the head does not survive, but judging from the style and findspot, this was in all probability the statue of Augustus dedicated by Varenus.

The freedman thus celebrated his emperor in the guise of world ruler, as was commonplace by now in Rome, and probably with a private cult as well, just as Herod was doing, albeit on a grander scale, at the same time in Caesarea (cf. p. 250). It is of course true that the statue is something of a

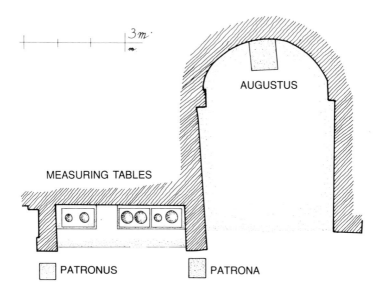

Fig. 248. Ground plan of the dedications of the freedman Varenus in the Forum of Tibur (Tivoli). 20–10 B.C.

Figs. 249 and 250. Statues of the deified Augustus (fig. 249, left) and the reigning Emperor Claudius (fig. 250, right) in the guise of Jupiter. From the Forum at Leptis Magna. Claudian period.

contradiction of the image of the princeps as pious worshiper that he had propagated in Rome, which only shows that Varenus was not bound by any rules or restrictions. Indeed, the princeps himself, as well as his successors, evidently had no objection to this rather grandiose image, as long as it was not displayed directly under his nose, in Rome. This much, at any rate, can be inferred from the numerous statues of the emperor in the guise of Jupiter, many of which bear the portrait features of Tiberius or Claudius and were certainly put up while the subject was still alive. So, for example, the only difference between the statue of the deified Augustus and that of the living princeps Claudius in the Forum of Leptis Magna is the raised left hand of Augustus holding a divine scepter (figs. 249, 250). In portrait galleries of the imperial house, whose presence in many cities in the West is attested by surviving fragments, the sculptural type of Jupiter was readily used to signal the preeminent rank of the princeps, above the younger princes, as we have already seen is the case on the Gemma Augustea (cf. fig. 182).

It is surely no accident that a man like Varenus threw himself into the worship of Augustus so early on and with such abandon. To a freedman, the old traditions of the Republic meant little or nothing, whereas the power of Augustus meant everything. Besides, none of the *decuriones* on the city council was about to say no to his request for a site in the Forum for this particular purpose.

Our wealthy freedman, for whom all public offices and honors were inaccessible, was evidently at great pains despite this to call attention to himself. This is clear from the marble tables (*mensae ponderariae*) which he set up just next to the shrine of Augustus, practical and hence surely much-used objects on which the donor's name appeared twice, rather conspicuously. But in addition, on either side of these *mensae*, Varenus put up statues of his *patrona* and *patronus*. The honorific inscription for his former owners gave him another opportunity to include his own name, along with the fact that the site had been granted him by decision of the *decuriones*. The one thing he could not put up was a statue of himself, but he did everything possible to turn this double monument into a monument to himself.

Perhaps it was such cults sponsored by individual freedmen that gave Augustus the idea of encouraging district cults of the Lares in Rome. The next step was the creation of the *augustales* as cult associations patterned after the model of the Roman *compital* cults. This gave wealthy freedmen the opportunity to make public appearances, usually in a *collegium* of six. The imperial cult thus allowed them to sponsor games and public meals, and, in this capacity, to enjoy, if only temporarily, certain prerogatives of public officials, such as the *toga praetexta*, an honorary seat, and official attendants. Later, on their tomb monuments, they boast of the games they paid for and recall those cherished moments when they were allowed to sit on a tribunal in official garb. In this manner the freedmen could try to establish themselves as a kind of recognized class, second to the *decuriones*, at least in outward appearance. Membership in the college of *augustales* was the greatest goal a freedman could attain.

The little temples and local cults associated with this remarkable social and political institution were usually located in the Forum, and thanks to the frequent and highly visible festivals and cult activities they became way stations in the transmission of the imperial mythology. In Rome, the shrines of the Lares served a similar purpose. The extraordinary prestige that the *augustales* attached to their own office is illustrated by the enormous oak wreaths that they had carved not only on altars for the emperor and for the divinities associated with him, but also on their own funerary altars and above the doors of their houses (cf. fig. 219).

As important as the activities of the freedmen may have been, the cults they established did much less to shape the overall appearance of a city than those of the *domi nobiles*, or local aristocracy. Statistical studies have at-

tempted to compare the extent of private donations made by the two principal social classes. These suggest that the leading families, which held political office, spent on average at least twice as much money for public
construction and other dedications as the middle class, comprising primarily successful freedmen. The archaeological evidence, though of course subject to accidents of preservation, presents a roughly analogous picture. As a
rule, the *decuriones* had a say in the size and setting of each dedication, and
they will have seen to it that the proportions of a building accurately reflected the social status of the benefactor.

In Pompeii, we can reconstruct to a great extent the competing activities
of the leading families and their important role in the life of the city. The
four major, identifiable donors, two men and two women, all belong to the
top level of the local aristocracy, and all four held priestly office. The men
were both priests in the imperial cult and were also leading political figures
in the city. The first initiative was probably taken by M. Tullius M. F., with
his temple of Fortuna Augusta, which lay outside the Forum. He was three
times *duumvir* and later held the highest local office of *quinquennalis,*
which was occupied only every fifth year. In addition, he was *augur* and
bore the honorific title *tribunus militum a populo* (military tribune by rec-
ommendation of the people), granted by the emperor at the suggestion of
his fellow citizens. Mamia, a *sacerdos publica,* put up a temple *Genio Augusti solo et pecunia sua,* which we know only from the dedicatory inscription. It was probably part of one of the two sanctuaries of the imperial cult
on the East side of the Forum (cf. fig. 241). But by far the grandest new
building in the Forum, far surpassing the Augustus temples of Tullius and
Mamia, was put up by the rich widow Eumachia L. F. and dedicated to
Concordia and Pietas Augusta (fig. 251).

This building was an expression both of worship of the emperor and of
publica magnificentia. It served as a kind of "recreation center," with an
entrance hall decked out with statuary, a cult area, colonnades, and cryptoporticoes (galleries). It is possible that commercial enterprises were also
integrated into this pretentious marble structure. Eumachia was evidently
trying to imitate Livia, who had dedicated the Porticus Liviae on the Esquiline in Rome in 7 B.C., together with Tiberius (cf. fig. 113). The decoration
of Eumachia's building also shows the influence of Roman models. The
marble door frames, for example, with their luxuriant vines, look as if they
could have come from the same workshop responsible for the Ara Pacis (fig.
252*a, b*). In the chapellike apse in the center of the building stood the statue
of Concordia or Pietas Augusta, of which only the gilded cornucopia has
been recovered. Perhaps, like many such female personifications, she bore
the portrait likeness of Livia (cf. fig. 196).

When the fourth of the great patron families in Pompeii, represented by

the brothers M. Holconius Rufus and M. Holconius Celer, began its building activity around the start of the Christian era, there was probably no
large site still available in the Forum. So, following the example of the princeps, they decided in favor of a different form of *publica magnificentia*, with
the restoration, expansion, and beautification of the theater. It seems likely
that the bill for all this was even bigger than Eumachia's. M. Holconius
Rufus occupied the same offices as M. Tullius, only about a generation later,
and he too received from the emperor the honorific title *tribunus militum a
populo*. But his services to his city seem to have surpassed even those of
M. Tullius, for the Pompeiians conferred on him the title *patronus coloniae*,
the highest honor they could bestow.

Such local worthies, always striving to outdo one another, were not only
the focus of city politics, but as priests invariably played the leading roles at
imperial festivals, performed rituals, and inaugurated the games. They were
the *principes* of their local communities, as Augustus and his family were in
Rome. In this role they were also responsible for translating the new values
into action and seeing to it that the program of cultural renewal was carried
out as effectively in the western provinces as it was in Rome.

In return for their services they were accorded appropriate honors. Statues of them were put up in public places, especially, of course, in the buildings they had dedicated. In the Temple of Fortuna Augusta and in the mar-

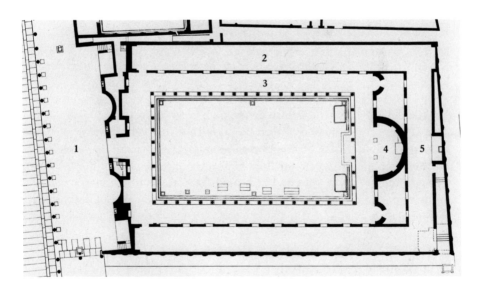

Fig. 251. Ground plan of the building erected by the priestess Eumachia in the
Forum of Pompeii. 1, chalcidicum; 2, cryptoporticus; 3, porticus; 4, statue of Concordia; 5, statue of Eumachia.

a

Fig. 252. *a*) Marble door frame from the building of Eumachia. Pompeii, Forum. *b*) Detail. The marble work probably comes from a workshop in Rome.

ket-aedicula in Pompeii, statues of the patron stood in the cella (fig. 253) and were thus neighbors of the emperor and the imperial divinities, just as in Rome statues of Augustus stood in temples of the traditional gods. Eumachia's building makes clear how important such honors in the form of statuary were (cf. fig. 251). In the niche behind the cult image, the fullers' guild "spontaneously" dedicated, after the completion of the building, a statue of their patroness Eumachia, which in reality had been planned from the start.

The statues of these local benefactors betray in their very form how they conceived of their role, for the types are the same employed to honor the emperor and his family. Instead of the nude, dramatic figure so popular in the previous generation, they chose a togate statue with veiled head (cf. fig. 129). And of course priestesses had themselves represented just like the

b

Fig. 253. Statue of a public priestess from Pompeii. She wears the *stola* over her dress. The statue stood in a shrine of the emperor in the market building (cf. fig. 241). Neronian period.

pious and chaste women of the imperial house, wearing a veil and the virtuous *stola*, performing a sacrifice (fig. 253; cf. 131).

Cities of Marble: The New Self-Assurance in the West

It is primarily due to these local aristocracies and their new self-image that the face of many Roman cities in the West was fully transformed in the Early Empire. The leading families could boast of having done for their cities what Augustus did for Rome: turning them to marble, at least their temples, public buildings, piazzas, and monumental gateways. In some instances they had help from the emperor or a member of his family, or another of the Roman nobility. Such occasional subsidies were most likely to

Fig. 254. Roman theater at Arausio (Orange/Provence). This photo illustrates the monumental effect of a theater in its original setting.

go to the *coloniae* founded by Augustus himself. But for the most part, local *domi nobiles* had to rely on their own resources to bring about an architectural revival patterned on that in Augustan Rome. If we discount for the moment those cities of Campania and Central Italy that had been Hellenized as early as the second to first century B.C., then indeed most cities in Italy and the western provinces received their first public buildings in marble, streets, squares, and gateways at all comparable with those of the average Greek city only at the time of the Augustan revival.

The building activity for the imperial cult that we have just considered will have made clear how closely the architectural revival was linked to the new political situation and the sense of excitement that went with it. Even purely aesthetic refinements or, at the other extreme, mundane engineering projects involving road- and bridge-building or the water supply system cannot be fully divorced from the ideological foundations of the Augustan cultural program.

A particularly important component in the architectural renewal in every city, not only in Rome, was the theater, whose significance went far beyond its practical purposes. As in Pompeii, so too in almost every city in the West a theater was either newly built or enlarged or renovated during the Early Empire. Unlike in colonies founded during the Republic, the theater was now usually a conspicuous part of any new city founded under Augustus.

Fig. 255. Reconstruction of the theater in Pompeii after the Augustan expansion and restoration by the Holconii.

The theater was regularly situated at a central or easily accessible site, its soaring facade, clad in marble and richly ornamented, towering over the surroundings (fig. 254). As in Rome, seating was by social status, so that the *cavea*, when full with spectators, presented a vivid reflection of the carefully structured social hierarchy within each city. At the front were seats for city magistrates, priests, and *decuriones*, as well as others which by law had to be kept free in the event of Senators from Rome passing through the city. Stalls separated the seats in the middle area, reserved for the *plebs*, from those of the nobility, which in Pompeii occupied twenty rows. In some cities, the forward section will probably have had further subdivisions, though good evidence for this is lacking. Those at the bottom of the social ladder— women, foreigners, and slaves—sat at the very back (fig. 255).

At the rear of the theater in Pompeii, at the uppermost section of the *cavea*, the brothers Holconii built a vaulted passage (*crypta,*) which contained additional, tightly packed rows of seats. This is surely more than a routine expansion to meet local needs and is not typical. Augustus's policies were based on a clear separation of social classes, but they nevertheless strove to include all those on the fringes of society in greater numbers than ever before. This is evident not only in the imperial cult, but at games and festivals as well.

The princeps was of course unable to appear in person in all these local theaters, as he did in Rome. This may help explain how the custom arose, as early as the time of Augustus, of placing statues of him and his family in the *scaenae frons,* the colonnaded facade behind the stage, where previously figures of gods, muses, and Greek masterpieces were displayed.

In the building inscription at the theater in Pompeii, the Holconii brothers make reference to another of the improvements they made, the *tribunalia.* These are seats reserved for the magistrates in charge of the games, located over the barrel-vaulted side entrances to the orchestra, and with their addition, the essentially Hellenistic theater of Pompeii was turned into a Roman one. The particular importance of this feature for the Augustan Age is evident in Leptis Magna, where the dedicatory inscriptions are displayed just here, on the *tribunalia.* Leading magistrates appeared on these elevated seats before the populace like statues on a triumphal arch come to life. Thus the local powers were also incorporated into the stage set, though in a clearly subsidiary position to the statues of the emperor in the *scaenae frons.*

The Augustan theater was surely no place to go to forget politics and lose oneself in a spontaneous, Dionysiac entertainment. We do not know whether even outside Rome one was required to wear a toga to the theater, but certainly the ennobled spirit of the new age was ever-present in the form of statues and other images. Everywhere were carved altars, little temples, Victories, arms and armor, and vines. In Rome, later on, the theater curtain was even decorated with pictures of bound barbarians. Symbols of the imperial cult were on hand on various forms, some more blatant than others. So, for example, above the auditorium of the theater in Leptis Magna stood a small temple with a statue of Ceres Augusta with the coiffure and portrait features of Livia (cf. fig. 185). Similarly, the famous altar with the swans of Apollo stood in the theater at Arles (fig. 256).

In the construction of any theater or other public building, the decorative scheme was of course an integral part of the planning, by both patron and architect, from the start. But in public squares, especially in fora, on the other hand, honorary statues and other monuments accumulated gradually. Even allowing for the fact that most of these were put up on an ad hoc basis, there emerged a distinctive and expressive whole, which was fundamentally different from a public square of the Republic.

We must again turn to Pompeii to gain an impression of such a square in its full effect. The Republican Forum had apparently been characterized by monuments of roughly equal size, to judge from the socles of equestrian statues along the west side (cf. fig. 241). On the south side, in front of the administrative buildings, more monuments were originally lined up in this same egalitarian arrangement, until they had to make way, first for a monumental arch, probably to Augustus, then for two colossal bases for other

Fig. 256. Altar from the
Roman theater at Arles.
The swans of Apollo (cf.
fig. 140) carry garlands.

imperial monuments, perhaps triumphal chariots. Not long after, an oversize equestrian monument was set up before the arch of Augustus. All these
new monuments naturally relegated the equestrian statues of local nobility
to secondary importance. That the hierarchy of status according to size of
monument was everywhere an important principle during the Early Empire
is confirmed by a charge against the proconsul Marcellus, reported by Tacitus (1.74), that he set up his own statues higher than those of the *caesares*.
It is also striking that bases for equestrian statues were more prominently
displayed than those for simple standing figures (*statuae pedestres*). In Pompeii, *statuae pedestres* now no longer stood in the square, but in the porches
of the new buildings. Socles of the same type were probably erected simultaneously in front of the Macellum and in the Chalcidicum of Eumachia's
building, to carry older images of local worthies, following the model of the
summi viri displayed in the Forum of Augustus. Although these *statuae pedestres* imitate the body types, hair styles, and even expressions of statues
of the imperial family, their scale and location, relative to those of the overwhelming imperial monuments, indicate clearly their true rank in society.

This picture of the Forum in Pompeii would be incomplete without the
two honorific arches on either side of the Temple of Jupiter. They may have
been among the honors voted after the early deaths of the princes Gaius and

Lucius, or Germanicus. Augustan models for the linking of temple facade and honorary arches can be found in the Forum Romanum and later in the Forum of Augustus as well. Similarly situated arches of early imperial date have also been found in other cities, as in Spoleto. It need hardly be emphasized how such a setting enhanced the effect of such arches, with their statues, tropaea, or quadrigas. The sacred aura of the temple facade was thus pressed into the service of whichever member of the imperial house was honored by the arch.

Theater and public square were the places where the ordinary citizen lingered the longest, apart from the baths. In both places he was confronted with an impressive collocation of imagery, which vividly illustrated for him not only the power structure and social organization of the state, but also his own place within society.

But it was not only the cities themselves that were transformed, but their surroundings as well. The traveler along the roads of Italy in the first century A.D.—roads largely built by the princeps, with a pillar set up every mile to proclaim in big letters to whom it was owed—would have continually encountered new city walls and towers. Augustus and Tiberius personally gave many Italian cities the money to build such walls, even in peacetime. Why, we may ask, just when the Empire was enjoying the much-touted Pax Augusta?

In the Late Republic, the city wall had become in many parts of Italy an important element of self-promotion. Now, in changed circumstances, it became a symbol of defense, particularly defense of the *virtus* recently restored by the princeps. In places like Hispellum (Spello) in Umbria, the prospect of a city protected by great walls, carefully staged by the layout of the road network, turned Vergil's poetic vision into a reality. *Mores* and *moenia* went together (*Aeneid* 1.264; 6.403), and the new walls gave proof of the new spirit.

In reality, the young men of Italy were being called upon less and less for active military service. But the militarization of visual imagery, for which a whole series of other examples could be cited, was intended at least to instill in them, through the appropriate symbolism, the correct mentality. The military towers in the city gates of Spello or Turin (fig. 257) are the outward expression of military preparedness. As in Saepinum (fig. 258), which received money from Tiberius to build walls and towers, in many other towns statues of captured barbarians recalled not only the victories of the imperial house, but more generally, the self-appointed mandate of the Romans as world rulers. That M. Holconius Rufus, patron of the theater in Pompeii, chose to be honored with a cuirassed statue of himself (fig. 259)—a copy, in fact, of the statue of Mars Ultor in Rome (cf. fig. 155)—should be understood in the same context. The fact that Holconius had never won military

Fig. 257. Augustan gate house in Turin, model. The extravagant and menacing towers have a primary symbolic character, since the gate itself was not secured by the corresponding defensive installations. Similar illusory towers are not uncommon elsewhere.

laurels, perhaps never went on campaign at all, was not as important as projecting the proper attitude. The emperor had recognized this in him and therefore rewarded him with the honorific title. The people of Pompeii apparently saw nothing incongruous in this treatment of their leading man, indeed they seemed to have liked seeing him in this military pose.

There is evidence that city dwellers were fully aware of and enjoyed the transformed appearance of their towns. The people of Verona, for example, had many opportunities to admire their city, taking it all in from a bird's eye view. At intermission in the theater, every time they came out of the *cavea,* which was set on the slope of a mountain, climbed up to the two superimposed porticoes, and promenaded back and forth, they enjoyed a view out over the whole city, with its ring of walls, regular streets, and handsome marble buildings. In other places as well, aesthetic and moral values intersected in the component parts of an integrated city plan: walls of regular ashlar blocks, strong city gates, the orderly layout of the streets and of the construction within them, the dominating site of the temple, and the luxury of country estates (fig. 260).

Fig. 258. Gate of the small city Saepinum (Molise). The walls and gates were donated by Tiberius and Drusus. The statues of barbarians are associated with the victories of the donors in Germany. 2–1 B.C.

This necessarily abbreviated glimpse over the Empire shows how, from the foundation of the monarchy, a uniform visual language began to develop, one based almost entirely on forms of paying homage to the imperial house. As in Rome, this followed a course of natural progression, without the need for explicit directives from above. After Actium, both East and West must have felt an overwhelming need to establish direct contact with Augustus, with the one individual who, for the first time in the history of the Mediterranean world, had created a stable and recognizable universal rule. Only the East, however, had an instrument already in place for establishing lines of communication, in the form of the ruler cult. There, people had long felt the lack of a genuine ruler and of an empire with which they could identify.

Fig. 259. Cuirassed
statue of M. Holconius
Rufus. The body is a
copy of the cult statue
of Mars Ultor (fig. 155).
After 2 B.C.

It was inevitable that the West would take over the ruler cult, since it gave local aristocracies a new vehicle for expressing and maintaining their positions of power. The integration of the ruler cult into traditional religious ritual allowed each individual, and the community as a whole, to share the feeling of participation in the restoration of the state.

The new monarchy also inherited, along with the Hellenistic ruler cult, a fully developed system of visual communication, into which the specifically new imagery and symbolism were easily integrated. Viewed somewhat dif-

Fig. 260. Fragment of the representation of a city with streets at right angles. The gate is open, and the walls are depicted for their aesthetic qualities.

ferently, the entire sequence of events is a further stage in a gradual process of acculturation in Rome. The adoption of the ruler cult represents a new watershed in the Hellenization of the Roman cities in the West.

The pictorial vocabulary that evolved in Rome was inextricably linked with the current situation there and with the city's political traditions. For this reason, certain elements of it, such as the "Principate style" and the imagery of cultural renewal, were irrelevant in the East. Here its impact centered on those aspects directly associated with the person of the emperor or with particular points in his program that struck a responsive chord. Such might be the case in an area like that of religious revival or, in a city like Athens, the new classicism.

The leading families in each city, in both East and West, were those who contributed most to the ruler cult and also profited most from it. Those in the West had the added advantage that they could, as Romans, identify personally with Augustus's program of cultural renewal. In these areas, the imperial cult went hand in hand with the visual expression of new moral values, especially in the complete architectural remodeling of the cities themselves. The impact of the new imagery in the West thus presupposed the acceptance of a complete ideological package. Temples, theaters, water systems, and city gates, all of specifically Roman type, gave every city in the West a uniform look, one which remained essentially unchanged.

The unavoidable need to simplify, excerpt, and trivialize both artistic form and iconography actually strengthened the effectiveness of the few visual formulas in which the myth of empire was expressed. Outside of Rome itself, skill in execution, learned allusions or clever genealogies, self-conscious archaism or classicism all had minimal importance. But even in

Rome, the future was hardly to move in the direction of increased refinement and elaboration. The simplified visual language gradually taking root in Italy outside Rome held its own and sometimes even had an influence back in Rome.

Conclusion

As we look back on the *saeculum augustum,* it was certainly a decisive turning point, not only for all forms of art and architecture, but for the entire system of visual communication. Structures that came into being then took root and shaped the character of Roman cities well into Late Antiquity. Only the great ages of transition at the end of the Greek Archaic Age and in the Early Hellenistic are comparable in the scale and depth of change. In these two earlier periods as well, new forms of artistic and visual expression had arisen in the wake of fundamental political change.

The power of visual imagery was by no means the least of the forces that propelled Rome into the world of Hellenistic culture and contributed to the dissolution of the old Republican order. From the second century B.C., the whole spectrum of Greek art and architecture stood at the disposal of culturally starved Romans. The choice was wide open, limited only by the demands, needs, and means of the recipient. The processes of adaptation and assimilation may have operated very differently in different artistic media, but throughout artists found themselves challenged by the new patrons and commissions, producing exciting and appealing new formal combinations, innovation, and elaboration of received models. From this point of view the Late Republic has rightly been called the Golden Age of creativity in Roman art.

With the establishment of one-man rule, however, there began in every cultural sphere a comprehensive move toward standardization within fixed norms. Up to this time, the various centers of Hellenistic art had each exerted its varied influence on the Romans, but now Rome itself became the home of a uniform culture gradually evolving and emanating outward. Prior to Actium, the monuments of rival strongmen had determined the character of public space, and the pervasive mood of competition had further heightened the formal diversity of Late Hellenistic art. In the face of this, an integrated system of shared values could scarcely emerge within the pictorial world of the Late Republic.

In the standardized visual language of Roman Imperial art, the emperor and the state stood at the center. As we have seen, this was true in every respect, not just those areas directly concerned with the celebration of the ruler and his cult. Since the compact, pyramidal structure of Roman society was entirely oriented toward its apex, the image of the emperor easily became the model for every individual. This applied not simply to an immediate impact on fashions in clothing and hair, or to the assimilation of bourgeois portraiture to the physiognomy of the reigning emperor. At another level, the imagery of the imperial mythology could, through symbolic adaptation, be employed to convey a range of civic virtues and values.

The use of political imagery in everyday civic life extended with time to ever broader spheres. So, for example, a man's diligence and fortitude in life could be commemorated on his sarcophagus by means of a heroic battle scene, even if he had never served in the army, the deceased himself portrayed in the role of the victorious emperor. For women the phenomenon was a comparable one: tombs of middle-class women without any social standing employing the same forms created to honor those of the imperial family. The modern viewer is apt to be put off by the depiction of an older woman as Venus, Concordia, or Pietas, but for her contemporaries this was evidently perceived as a dignified means of celebrating the deceased for her beauty, her devout and peaceful nature. Only when we view this visual language as a whole, reflecting both the political system and the societal compulsion to conform, can we fully grasp the meaning of such forms of internalization.

Alongside the "imperial mythology" there was a second basic ideology that informed the whole system of values and, with it, the artistic vocabulary: a belief in the uniqueness of "Classical" Greek culture and in the present age as a kind of renaissance in which the best of that culture was combined with a world dominance based upon the highest moral principles and universal prosperity. The groundwork for this ideology was also laid in the Augustan period. The two foundations of the program of cultural renewal—*publica magnificentia* and "classicism"—though at first directed only toward Rome itself, led to a homogeneous pictorial language that enabled all inhabitants of the *Imperium Romanum* to participate in the revival of Classical culture and its ethical values while still preserving their national identity.

The canvas on which this ideology was drawn was even broader than for the imperial myth. It took in everything from the Classical skyline of provincial cities to the pictures and sayings of Greek philosophers on tavern walls. The fascination of "Greek" style marble architecture with its rich decoration continued unabated into the third century, in the wealthy cities of Africa and Syria, with their ostentatious columned streets. Such building projects had little to do with actual needs. Rather, these endless rows of Corinthian columns had become a symbol for one's claim to a share in Roman Imperial culture.

Augustus's program of renewal and rebuilding had put an end once and for all to the earlier political opposition in Rome to the *luxuria* of Greek culture. The new culture of the *saeculum aureum* included the heritage of Greece in its "purified" form. In the process, the stimulating and creative tension between public and private space, which had characterized the era of acculturation in the Late Republic, was dissipated. From now on, Greek sculpture, painting and architecture were equally prominent in both private and public places. The philhellenes and aesthetes of the Empire, whatever they built or put on display in their private villas, were automatically in accord with the prevailing political climate and contributing, whether consciously or not, their approval of the new age.

Once the emperors themselves paid homage to Greek culture or, in the case of Hadrian or Marcus Aurelius, even actively placed it at the center of their own programs, many strata of society began to equate Greek myth, Classical art, and especially the "philosophical way of life" with the most sought after lifestyle. No matter how modest the cultural horizon of the individual actually was or how impoverished its artistic or literary expression often seems to us, there was nevertheless something of fundamental value thus transmitted to the public consciousness. The result was men and women who had themselves depicted as philosophers or Muses, furnished their public and private rooms with copies or paraphrases of Classical masterpieces, and adorned their houses and tombs with representations of Greek myth.

We have observed how many elements of political imagery reaching back to the early Empire were gradually internalized. The same thing happened with the quotations from and copies of the Greek artistic legacy. These too were employed to express a private message, for example to convey feelings of love or pain on a sarcophagus through the medium of Greek myth, or to celebrate the courage, beauty, or virtue of the deceased. As much as the imperial mythology, this cultural ideology echoes through all spheres of life and all levels of population, becoming inextricably bound up with the personal values and concerns of the individual.

The visual language of the High Empire did not, however, evolve into a totally rigid system, but was rather subject to continual expansion and changes in accentuation. So, for example, the qualities of the emperor as field marshal and the preparedness of the army came to play an ever more important role, while the civilian side of the princeps necessarily retreated to a more subsidiary position. Most of the change, however, was in the form of greater simplification, clarification, and above all sheer proliferation. The rituals of the imperial cult and its festivals, as well as their architectural settings, became increasingly lavish and, thereby, more alike. On relief sarcophagi, the values illustrated were even more strongly emphasized, their application to the deceased made even more direct. As a result, from the late second century mythological narratives, classical iconography, and classicizing style all become gradually somewhat secondary. But viewed as a whole, the system and its basic structures remained unchanged for two centuries after Augustus, since they reflected both a form of monarchy and a stable societal order that were themselves unchanged.

Given such a system, all change and innovation in pictorial imagery had to originate at the top and could as a rule emanate only from Rome. It was of course sometimes possible for an individual group within society, such as a philosophical school, to propagate a new set of imagery. But this could then go on to win general acceptance only when taken over by the imperial house or the highest strata of society.

That this system did not give rise to a kind of uniformity of mass culture in the modern sense is largely due to the process of independent momentum that we have observed so often throughout this book. Nothing was explicitly prescribed, nothing supervised, and there were no advertising campaigns. For this reason certain patterns, once accepted, could persist over generations, even when the original model was long out of fashion. As one example, older men were still styling their hair like that of the emperor Trajan even down to the time of Antoninus Pius.

There were some areas in which innovation was entirely precluded: columns of the traditional architectural orders, the selection of Greek myths and masterpieces, or the decorative ornament of wall painting. The notion of having arrived at a state of perfection and of the absolute worth of the inherited models must have made the static quality of Roman culture itself seem like a value and cast doubt on any change. Likewise, the artistic style associated with the Classical models was altered over generations only with respect to technical execution. The consequence was that artistic and architectural forms could not go out of style. New monuments might be more costly or ambitious than the old, or they might be better able to convey particular messages, but they always spoke the same language. Thus the visual arts contributed measurably to the remarkable stability of the sociopolitical system.

At this point we must nevertheless ask at what cost this culture of uniformity and prosperity, in which so many could participate, was achieved. A comparison with the culture of the Early Hellenistic Age suggests itself and reveals in almost every sphere of intellectual activity—philosophy, rhetoric, poetry, scientific research, and technology—the same process of standardization and stagnation as in art and architecture. Intellectual progress, artistic creativity, the evolution of rational thought and technical change came to a virtual standstill during the Empire, and in some areas ground was actually lost. Instead the arts of copying, compilation, and technical virtuosity flourished. During the first two centuries after Augustus, impressive creative achievements can be found only in the application of power to military and economic systems and communication, especially in keeping the urban masses who were to enjoy the general prosperity organized, well supplied, and entertained. Architecture and city planning were pivotal in this process. But to justify that statement and fully document it would be the subject for another book.

Notes and References for Further Reading

The following references have been kept as brief as possible. An overview of historical scholarship of the past several decades is given by D. Kienast, *Augustus* (Darmstadt, 1982). N. Hannestad, *Roman Art and Imperial Policy* (Aarhus, 1986) now provides a general survey of the subject. His extensive bibliography may be used to complement the sources cited here. Erika Simon's thoroughly illustrated *Augustus: Kunst und Leben in Rom um die Zeitwende* (Munich, 1986), organized according to artistic media, appeared while this book was in press and could not be cited on specific points.

Abbreviations used here are in general those of the German Archaeological Institute (cf. *Archäologischer Anzeiger* 1985, 757ff.). For further information on the illustrations, including location, dimensions, etc., see Illustration Sources. Abbreviations for frequently cited works follow.

AA	*Archäologischer Anzeiger*
ABr	*Griechische und Römische Porträts,* ed. P. Arndt and F. Bruckmann ("Arndt-Bruckmann")
ActaAArtHist	*Acta ad archaeologiam et artium historiam pertinentia*
AJA	*American Journal of Archaeology*
AM	*Mitteilungen des Deutschen Archäologischen Instituts, Athenische Abteilung*
ANRW	*Aufstieg und Niedergang der römischen Welt*
ArchCl	*Archeologia classica*
BCH	*Bulletin de correspondance hellénique*
BdA	*Bollettino d'arte*
BJb	*Bonner Jahrbücher des Rheinischen Landesmuseums in Bonn und des Vereins von Altertumsfreunden im Rheinlande*
BSR	*Papers of the British School at Rome*
BullCom	*Bullettino della Commissione archeologica comunale di Roma*
CIL	*Corpus Inscriptionum Latinarum*
Coarelli, *Foro*	F. Coarelli, *Il Foro Romano,* vols. 1–2 (Rome, 1984)
Crawford	*Roman Republican Coinage* (London, 1974)
CVA	*Corpus Vasorum Antiquorum*
Fittschen-Zanker	K. Fittschen and P. Zanker, *Katalog der römischen Porträts in den capitolinischen Sammlungen,* vol. 1 (1985)

Foto Inst.   Photo Institut für Klassische Archäologie (Munich)
Fototeca Unione   Fototeca Unione presso Academia Americana, Rome
Giard   J. B. Giard, Bibliothèque Nationale. *Catalogue des Monnaies de l'Empire Romain*, vol. 1 (Paris, 1976)
Gros, *Aurea Templa*   P. Gros, *Aurea Templa: Recherches sur l'architecture religieuse de Rome à l'époque d'Auguste* (Rome, 1976)
Guida, Ruesch   A. Ruesch, *Guida illustrata del Museo Nazionale di Napoli* (Naples, 1908)
Gymnasium   *Gymnasium: Zeitschrift für Kultur der Antike und humanistische Bildung*
Helbig   W. Helbig, *Führer durch die öffentlichen Sammlungen klassischer Altertümer in Rom*⁴, vol. 1 (1963); vol. 2 (1966); vol. 3 (1969); vol. 4 (1972)
HBr   P. Herrmann, *Denkmäler der Malerei des Altertums* ("Herrmann-Bruckmann")
Hölscher, *Victoria*   T. Hölscher, *Victoria Romana* (Mainz, 1967)
Hölscher, *Staatsdenkmal*   T. Hölscher, *Staatsdenkmal und Publikum* (Constance, 1984)
INR   Photo Deutsches Archäologisches Institut Rom, Neg. No.
IstMitt   *Istanbuler Mitteilungen*
JdI   *Jahrbuch des Deutschen Archäologischen Instituts*
JRS   *The Journal of Roman Studies*
Kienast   D. Kienast, *Augustus*, EdF, (Wiss. Buchges. Darmstadt: 1982)
MemAmAc   *Memoires of the American Academy in Rome*
MdI   *Mitteilungen des Deutschen Archäologischen Instituts*
MEFRA   *Mélanges de L'Ecole française de Rome, Antiquité*
MM   *Madrider Mitteilungen*
MuM   Münzen und Medaillen AG (Basel)
Nash, *Bildlexikon*   E. Nash, *Bildlexikon zur Topographie des antiken Rom*, vol. 1 (1961); vol. 2 (1962); originally published as *Pictorial Dictionary of Ancient Rome* (London, 1961)
NSc   *Notizie degli scavi di antichità*
Niggeler   MuM Auktion 1966 Part 2
Platner-Ashby   S. B. Platner and T. Ashby, *A Topographical Dictionary of Ancient Rome* (1929)
RE   *Paulys Realencyclopädie der classischen Altertumswissenchaft.*
RevNum   *Revue numismatique*
RIA   *Rivista dell'Istituto nazionale d'archeologia e storia dell'arte*
RM   *Mitteilungen des Deutschen Archäologischen Instituts, Römische Abteilung*

Schneider   R. M. Schneider, *Bunte Barbaren* (Worms, 1986)

Torelli   M. Torelli, *Typology and Structure of Roman Histori-*
                         cal Reliefs (Ann Arbor, 1982)

Zanker, *Apollontempel* P. Zanker, "Der Apollontempel auf dem Palatin," in
                         Città e Architettura nella Roma Imperiale, Anal. Rom.
                         suppl. no. 10 (1983): 21–40

Zanker 1983   P. Zanker, "Zur Bildnisrepräsentation führender Män-
                         ner in mittelitalischen und campanischen Städten zur
                         Zeit der späten Republik und der julisch-claudischen
                         Kaiser, in "*Les Bourgoisies" municipales italiennes aux*
                         IIᵉ et Iᵉʳ siècles av. J.-C. Int. Colloquium Centre Bérard,
                         Naples, 1983 (Naples and Paris, 1983), 251–56

Introduction

H. Jucker, *Das Verhältnis der Römer zur bildenden Kunst der Griechen* (Frankfurt am Main, 1950); O. J. Brendel, *Prolegomena to the Study of Roman Art* (1953; reprinted New Haven, 1979); R. Bianchi Bandinelli, *Rome: The Center of Power* (New York, 1970; P. A. Brunt, *Social Conflicts in the Roman Republic* (London, 1971); E. Gabba, *Esercito e società nella tarda repubblica romana* (Florence, 1973); C. Nicolet, *Le métier de citoyen dans la Rome républicaine* (Paris, 1976); K. Christ, *Krise und Untergang der römischen Republik* (Darmstadt, 1979); C. Meier, *Res publica amissa*² (Frankfurt, 1980); G. Alföldy, *Römische Sozialgeschichte*² (Wiesbaden, 1984); E. Rawson, *Intellectual Life in the Late Republic* (London, 1985).

Acculturation: P. Veyne, "The Hellenisation of Rome and the Question of Acculturation," *Diogenes* 106:1–27; *Modelli etici, diritto e transformazioni sociali*, ed. A. Giardina and A. Schiavone (Bari, 1981); cf. in particular the essays by G. Clemente (luxury and sumptuary legislation) and A. La Penna.

Chapter 1

The Problem of Nude Honorific Statuary

On the bronze statue, figs. 1–2, in Rome: J. Ch. Balty, *MEFRA* 90 (1978): 669–86. R. Lullies, *Griechische Plastik*⁴ (Munich, 1979), pl. 274f. A. Giuliano, ed. *Museo Naz. Rom. Le Sculture*, vol. 1, pt. 1 (Rome, 1979), 198, no. 124.

On the Arringatore, fig. 4: T. Dohrn, *Der Arringatore* (Berlin, 1968). On the tokens of social class and the dating: K. Fittschen, *RM* 77 (1970): 177–84, pls. 74–76. M. Cristofani, *I Bronzi degli Etruschi* (Novara, 1985) no. 129, p. 30.

T. Hölscher, *RM* 85 (1975): 315–57. G. Lahusen, *Untersuchungen zur römischen Ehrenstatue in Rom* (Rome, 1983). Idem, *Schriftquellen zum römischen Bildnis*, vol. 1 (Bremen, 1984). Zanker 1983, 251–66. K. Stemmer, *Untersuchungen zur Typologie, Chronologie und Ikonographie der Panzerstatue* (Berlin, 1978), 133ff. L. Giuliani, *Bildnis und Botschaft: Hermeneutische Untersuchungen zur Bildniskunst der römischen Republik* (Frankfurt, 1986).

On the portraits, figs. 5–8: Caesar: F. Johansen, *Anal. Rom.* 4 (1967): 34, pl. 16. P. Zanker, *AA*, 1981, 349–61. Pompey: V. Poulsen, *Les Portraits romains,* vol. 1 (Copenhagen, 1973), no. 1; Giuliani, loc. cit., passim. M. L. Crassus: D. Boschung, *JdI* 101 (1986): 284ff. Giuliani, 233ff. Anonymous subject in Cagliari: S. Angiolillo, *RM* 78 (1971): 119ff., pl. 70f.

Family Propaganda and the Collapse of the Aristocracy

T. Hölscher, *JdI* 95 (1980) 271–81.

On the "language" of Late Republican coins: T. Hölscher, in *Proc. 9. Int'l. Congr. Numismatics* (1979), 269–82. For Republican coinage see M. Crawford's outstanding work, *Roman Republican Coinage* (London, 1974).

On Fig. 10a–b: H. Kähler, *Seethiasos und Census* (Berlin, 1966). T. Hölscher, *AA,* 1979, 337. For the interpretation advocated here, and for the significance of genealogy in general: T. P. Wiseman, "Legendary Genealogies in Late Republican Rome," *Greece and Rome* 21 (1974): 153ff.

Funerary monuments: J. Toynbee, *Death and Burial in the Roman World* (London, 1971). M. Eisner, *Zur Typologie der Grabbauten im Suburbium Roms* (Mainz, 1986). H. v. Hesberg and P. Zanker, eds., *Römische Gräberstassen,* Bayerische Akademie der Wissenschaflen Abhandlungen, n.s., 96 (1987).

Tombs of freedmen: P. Zanker, *JdI* 90 (1975): 267–315.

Monument of Eurysakes: P. Ciancio Rossetto, *Il sepolcro del fornaio M. V. Eurisace* (Rome, 1973). Eisner, op. cit. 92ff. For the interpretation as a grain silo: L. Castiglione, *Acta Arch. Acad. Scient. Hungaricae* 27 (1975): 157–61.

Monument of Metella: Eisner, op. cit., pp. 36, 204, pl. 9. C. Hülsen, *Neue Heidelberger Jahrb.,* 1896, 50–58.

Grave monument of the consul C. Hirtius: Nash, *Bildlexikon,* vol. 2, 341.

Monument of the Julii at St. Remy: G.-Ch. Picard, *Les Trophées Romaines* (1957), 195ff. P. Gros, *Revue Arch.,* 1986, 65–80.

The City of Rome as a Reflection of State and Society

P. Gros, *Architecture et société* (Paris and Rome, 1978); F. Coarelli, "Public Building in Rome between the Second Punic War and Sulla," *BSR* 45 (1977): 1–23; D. E. Strong, "The Administration of Public Building in Rome," *Bull. Inst. Class. Studies London* 15 (1968): 101ff.

Literary sources for buildings mentioned in Platner-Ashby. References on the monuments: Nash. *Bildlexikon.*

The "Gardens" on the Pincio: F. Coarelli, in *Architecture et Société,* (Rome, 1983), 191–217.

On living conditions: Z. Yavetz, "The Living Conditions of the Urban Plebs," *Latomus* 17 (1958): 513. B. W. Frier, *Landlords and Tenants in Imperial Rome* (Princeton, 1980).

Theater of Pompey: Gros, *Aurea Templa,* 69. A. Rumpf, *MdI* 3 (1950): 45. J. A.

Hanson, *Roman Theater-Temples* (Princeton, 1959), 43–55. H. Drerup, "Architektur als Symbol," *Gymnasium* 73 (1966): 181–96. Giuliani, op cit.

On the decoration of theaters with works of art: M. Fuchs, *Untersuchungen zur Ausstattung römischer Theater in Italien und in den Westprovinzen des Imperium Romanum* (Mainz, 1987).

On the coins, fig. 17: F. Prayon, in *Festschrift U. Hausmann* (Tübingen, 1982), 320. H. Drerup, *Zum Ausstattungsluxus in der römischen Architektur* (Münster, 1957).

On the decoration of the buildings in the Campus Martius: M. Pape, *Griechische Kunstwerke aus Kriegsbeute und ihre öffentliche Aufstellung in Rom* (Hamburg, 1975).

Relief from the amphitheater in Capua: G. Pesce, *I rilievi dell'anfiteatro Campano* (Rome, 1941), pl. 15*a*. *Guida,* Ruesch, 173, no. 609f.

On the Forum of Caesar: Gros, *Aurea Templa*, 70–72. Coarelli, *Foro* 2:233 ff.

On Caesar's plans: literary sources collected in Z. Yavetz, *Caesar in der öffentlichen Meinung* (Düsseldorf, 1979), 159ff.

The Villa and the Creation of Private Space

J. D'Arms, *The Romans on the Bay of Naples: A Social and Cultural Study of the Villas and their Owners from 150 B.C. to A.D. 400* (Cambridge, Mass., 1970); idem, *Commerce and Social Standing in Ancient Rome* (Cambridge, Mass., 1981); H. Drerup, in *Marburger Winckelmannsprogramm*, 1959, 1–24; P. Zanker, *JdI* 94 (1979): 460–523; H. Mielsch, *Die römische Villa: Architektur und Lebensform* (Munich, 1987).

Otium and negotium: J. M. André, *L'otium dans la vie morale et intellectuelle romaine des origines à l'époque augusteenne* (Paris, 1965), 287.

R. Neudecker, *Die Skulpturenausstattung römischer Villen in Italien* (Mainz, 1988).

Sperlonga: B. Conticello and B. Andreae, "Die Skulpturen von Sperlonga," *Antike Plastik* 14 (1974).

Villa dei Papiri: D. Comparetti and C. De Petra, *La villa ercolanese dei Pisoni, i suoi monumenti e la sua biblioteca* (Turin, 1883). Reconstruction of the villa in Malibu: N. Neuerburg, *Herculaneum to Malibu: A Companion to the Visit of the J. Paul Getty Museum Building* (Malibu, 1975).

On the sculptures: Neudecker, op. cit., G. Sauron, *MEFRA* 92 (1980): 277–301. R. Wojcik, *La Villa dei Papiri ad Ercolano* (Rome, 1986).

On wall painting of the so-called Second Style, the fundamental work is H. G. Beyen, *Die Pompejanische Wanddekoration vom zweiten bis zum vierten Stil* vol. 1 (1938); vol. 2 (1960). See also A. Barbet, *La peinture murale romaine. Les styles decoratifs pompéens* (Paris, 1985); B. Wesenberg, *Gymnasium* 29 (1985): 470; K. Fittschen, "Zur Herkunft und Entstehung des 2. Stils," in *Hellenismus in Mittelitalien*, ed. P. Zanker (Göttingen, 1976), 539–63; E. W. Leach, "Patrons, Painters and Patterns," in *Literary and Artistic Patronage in Ancient Rome*, ed. B. K. Gold (Austin, 1982).

The Casa dei Grifi: Rizzo, *Monumenti della pittura* vol. 3, pt. 1 (Rome, 1936).

Boscoreale: P. W. Lehmann, *Roman Wall Paintings from Boscoreale* (Cambridge, Mass., 1953).

Villa of the Mysteries: A. Maiuri, *La villa dei Misteri,* 2d ed. (Rome, 1947). On the interpretation of the famous frieze see most recently M. G. Sauron, in *Comptes Rendues de l'Académie des Inscriptions et Belles-Lettres* (1984), 151–76, with earlier references and, in my opinion, an interpretation that goes too far.

Romans in Greek dress: Suetonius *Tiberius* 13; Tacitus *Ann.* 2.59 (Germanicus); Cicero *in Verrem* V. 13. 31, 16.40, 52.137; Val. Max. 3. 6. 3 (Sulla).

On the reused statue of Poseidippos: Helbig vol. 1, no. 129. The "Senatorial shoes" were subsequently deepened, the laces added in bronze. The face was recut about 50 B.C.

On the so-called Greek Orator: Naples, Nat. Mus. 6210. D. Comparetti and De Petra, op. cit., pl. 17.3. R. Wünsche, *Münchner Jahrb. bild. Kunst* 31 (1980): 25f. For comparable hairstyles cf. Fittschen-Zanker, vol. 1, no. 19.

Chapter 2

Divi Filius

R. Syme, *The Roman Revolution* (Oxford, 1939); K. Scott, "The Political Propaganda of 44–30 B.C.," *MemAmAc,* 1933, 7–49; A. Alföldi, *Oktavians Aufstieg zur Macht* (Bonn, 1976); Kienast, 1–66; S. Weinstock, *Divus Iulius* (Oxford, 1971); A. Alföldi, "La divinisation de César," *RevNum* 15 (1973): 99–128, pls. 4–13.

On the coin with the Temple of Caesar: F. Prayon, op. cit., 322, pl. 71.6.

On the Hellenistic tradition of the *sidus Iulium:* H. Kyrieleis, in *Festschrift F. Hiller* (1986), 55 ff. D. Kienast, "Alexander und Augustus," *Gymnasium* 76 (1969): 431–56.

On the slaughter at Perugia: H. Strasburger, *Gymnasium* 90 (1983): 49, 52.

The Imposing Statues of the Young Caesar

Equestrian statue of 43 B.C.: D. Mannsperger, in *Festschrift U. Hausmann* 331–37. T. Hölscher, *RM* 85 (1975): 315ff. I owe many important references to the unpublished dissertation of J. Bergemann on Roman equestrian monuments (Munich, 1987).

On the coins with statues in the "Neptune-pose": Crawford no. 511.3 K. Kraft, *Zur Münzprägung des Augustus* (Wiesbaden, 1969), 207.

The statue of Caesar in the same pose: Weinstock, op. cit., 40ff. On the statuary pose cf. Helbig vol. 4, no. 3028 (von Steuben).

On the sphaera: P. Arnaud, *MEFRA* 96 (1984): 53–116.

The not uncommon image of Skylla in these years (e.g., on capitals, table feet, and wall paintings) likewise probably had political connotations.

On fig. 32a: some idea of the appearance of such a statue is conveyed by the over life-sized statue of Agrippa in Venice, here fig. 195: G. Traversari, *Mus. Arch. di Venezia: I Ritratti* (Rome, 1968), no. 12.

On the portrait of Octavian, fig. 33: P. Zanker, *Studien zu den Augustus-Porträts: I. der Actiumtypus*[2] (Göttingen, 1978). Fittschen-Zanker vol. 1, no. 1. For the early dating cf. A. Alföldi and J. B. Giard, *Quaderni Ticinesi di Numismatica e Antichità Classiche* 13 (1984): 147, where the Divus Iulius issue, which had already been associated with this portrait type, is dated to the years 41 / 40 B.C.

Man and God: Role-Playing and Self-Image

On family genealogy: T. S. Wiseman, *Greece and Rome* 21 (1974): 153ff. On utopian hopes for the future: A. Alföldi, *Chiron* 5 (1975): 165ff. On Marc Antony and Hercules: D. Michel, *Alexander als Vorbild für Pompeius, Caesar und Marcus Antonius,* Coll. Latomus, no. 94, (Brussels, 1967), 114.

On the ring, fig. 35: H. P. Laubscher, *JdI* 89 (1974): 251. On the practice of wearing rings with portraits carved in the stone: M. L. Vollenweider, *Museum Helveticum* 12 (1955): 96–111; eadem, *Die Porträtgemmen der römischen Republik* (Mainz, 1974).

On Marc Antony and Dionysus: D. Mannsperger, *Gymnasium* 80 (1973): 381–404; J. Griffin, "Propertius and Antony," *JRS* 67 (1977): 17–26. On the Dionysian *tryphe* of the Ptolemaic kings: H. Heinen, *Historia* 32 (1983): 116ff.

On Octavian's role: D. Kienast, *Gymnasium* 76 (1969): 431–56.

On the miracle tokens: Scott, op. cit.; Alföldi, op. cit.

Capricorn: K. Kraft, *Jahrb. für Num. u. Geldgeschichte* 17 (1967): 17–27; Kienast, 183.

Sphinx as seal: H. U. Instinsky, *Die Siegel des Kaisers Augustus* (Baden-Baden, 1962).

On the glass cameo, fig. 39: E. Zwierlein-Diehl, in *Tainia, Festschrift R. Hampe* (Mainz, 1980), 410ff.

On Augustus's identification with Apollo there is extensive literature; cf. the summary, with references, of Kienast, 192ff.; Schneider, 67ff. and, in particular, E. Simon, *Die Portlandvase* (Mainz, 1957), 30ff.

G. Carettoni, *Das Haus des Augustus auf dem Palatin* (Mainz, 1983); Zanker, *Apollontempel.*

The Programmatic Silver Coinage of Octavian

On the dating of the series of denarii (Giard, pl. 1ff.): D. Mannsperger, in *Festschrift U. Hausmann,* op. cit., 331; J. B. Giard, *RevNum* 26 (1984): 78.

On the pictorial program: K. Kraft, *Zur Münzprägung des Augustus* (Wiesbaden, 1969).

On Jupiter Feretrius, fig. 44, cf. Wissowa, in *RE* 6 (1909): 2209f. Octavian's assimilation to a god in fig. 44 was apparently not the only instance. In the library on the Palatine stood a statue of Apollo which bore his features. Probably this too belongs to the period before or just after Actium: Sch. Horace, *EP.* I.3.17 (ed. Keller, p. 225); Servius on Vergil *Eclogue* 4.10.

Antony Betrayed by His Own Image

K. Scott, *MemAmAc,* 1933, 7–49; idem, "Octavianus' Propaganda and Antony's *de sua ebrietate,*" *Classical Philology* 24 (1929): 133–41.

Arretine bowls of Perennius Tigranes (fig. 45): *CVA* Metropolitan Museum IV BF, pl. 24. A. Oxé, *BJb* 138 (1933): 94. Most recently: A. C. Brown, *Catalogue of Italian Terra-Sigillata in the Ashmolean Museum Oxford* (1986), 15, no. 37.

Relief in Boston, Museum of Fine Arts: M. Comstock and C. Vermeule, *Sculpture in Stone* (Boston, 1976), no. 324.

On Anthony's partisans in Rome: J. Griffin, *JRS* 66 (1976): 87; *JRS* 67 (1977): 17; reprinted in J. Griffin, *Latin Poets and Roman Life* (London, 1985).

On the coin, fig. 48: P. Amandry, *The Israel Museum Journal* 6 / 7 (1982 / 83): 1ff.; idem, *Schweizer Numism, Rundschau,* n.s. 65 (1986): 73 ff.

On the relief with the "Arrival of Dionysus" (fig. 49): C. Watzinger, *MdI* 61 / 62 (1946 / 47): 77–87; A. H. Borbein, *Campanareliefs* (Heidelberg, 1968), 183ff.; the connection of this pictorial type with Antony had already been recognized by G. Méautis, *Arch. Ephem.* 1 (1937): 27. The figure of Paris is also among the images associated with Antony; cf. J. Griffin, *JRS* 67 (1977): 18f. A further type which was very popular on reliefs of the latest Republic and early Empire may also be relevant; on this cf. most recently H. Froning, *Marmorschmuckreliefs mit griechischen Mythen im 1. Jh. v. Chr.* (Mainz, 1981), 63.

On the archaistic reliefs with the Apollonian Triad (fig. 50) see most recently H.-U. Cain, *Römische Marmorkandelaber* (Mainz, 1985), 100f., particularly important in summarizing the results of an unpublished master's thesis by A. Wagner (Munich, 1982).

On the pictorial vocabulary of classicistic art cf. below, chap. 6.

Architecture: Competition and Innovation

A good overview of the building activity of this period in F. S. Shipley, *MemAmAc,* 1931, 7–60; Gros, *Aurea Templa,* passim.

On individual buildings: Platner-Ashby and Nash, *Bildlexikon.*

The Diana Temple of Cornificius: Gros, *Aurea Templa,* passim and pl. 20. On the location cf. *Roma: Archeologia nel Centro,* vol. 2 (Rome, 1985), 442f.

On the consoles (fig. 53): H. von Hesberg, *Konsolengeisa des Hellenismus und der frühen Kaiserzeit, RM* 24 Ergänzungsheft (Heidelberg, 1980).

On the architectural decoration of the Apollo Temple of C. Sosius see most recently E. LaRocca, in *Amazzonomachia,* exhibition catalog, Palazzo dei Conservatori (Rome, 1985), 95ff.

On the interpretation of the frieze (fig. 55): T. Hölscher, "Denkmäler der Schlacht von Actium." *Klio* 67 (1985): 84ff.

Monuments of Asinius Pollio: Pape, op. cit., 177.

On Agrippa's building activity: J. M. Roddaz, *Marcus Agrippa* (Paris and Rome, 1984), 231ff. The "dolphins" (cf. fig. 56) also turn up on the so-called Campana reliefs: H. von Rohden and H. Winnefeld, *Architekt. röm. Tonreliefs d. Kaiserzeit,* 2 vols. (Berlin, 1911), pl. 74.

The Mausoleum of Augustus

K. Kraft, *Historia* 16 (1967): 189ff.; Kienast, 340, with earlier references; D. Boschung, *Hefte des Berner Archäol. Seminars* 6 (1980): 38–41 (on the obelisks). On the decoration and inscriptions cf. the forthcoming publication of H. von Hesberg and S. Panciera. This includes the new reconstruction which H. von Hesberg has kindly allowed me to reproduce here. I am indebted to J. Ganzert and M. Pfanner for the comparison drawings.

Chapter 3

The Forum as Showplace of the *Gens Iulia*

For literature on the political situation see Kienast, 67.

On the Forum Romanum: P. Zanker, *Forum Romanum: Die Neugestaltung unter Augustus* (Tübingen, 1972); Coarelli, *Foro,* vol. 2. On Victoria on the globe (fig. 62*b*): Hölscher, *Victoria,* 6ff.

The location of the four *columnae rostratae* can be inferred from a passage in Servius's commentary on the *Georgics.* Domitian had the honorary columns removed to the Capitol. This must have been associated with the erection of a mighty equestrian monument. Accordingly, the columns will have stood originally before the Basilica Julia, perhaps at equal intervals along the whole length of the basilica.

The Temple of Saturn: P. Pensabene, *Tempio di Saturno* (Rome, 1984); K. Fittschen, *JdI* 91 (1976): 208ff. The motif of the Tritons in the spandrels of the pediments seems to have been used often; cf. the Campana reliefs of the type illustrated by Rhoden-Winnefeld, op. cit., pl. 82.

Allusions to the Victory at Actium

Hölscher, *Klio* 67 (1985): 81–102.

On the marble ship's prow (fig. 63): B. Schweitzer, in *Leipziger Winckelmannsprogram,* 1930. In Ostia, for example, one of the monumental tombs before the Porta Marina was decorated with large marble rostra (M. F. Squarciapino, *Scavi di Ostia,* vol. 3 [Rome, 1958], 194, pl. 32.3). We should like to know whether the occupant of the tomb actually fought at Actium; cf. the tomb of Cartilius Publicola: F. Zevi, in *Hellenismus in Mittelitalien,* ed. P. Zanker (Göttingen, 1976), 56ff.

On gems and seals with symbols of Actium: D. Salzmann, *BJb* 184 (1984): 158ff.

Decorated lamps: A. Leibundgut, *Die römischen Lampen in der Schweiz* (Bern, 1977). On the antefix (fig. 64): A. Anselmino, *Terrecotte architettoniche dell' Antiquarium comunale di Roma I: Antefisse* (Rome, 1977); H. Mielsch, *Römische Architekturterrakotten und Wandmalerei im Akademischen Kunstmuseum Bonn* (Berlin, 1971), 24f., no. 35.

On the pediment of the Apollo Temple of C. Sosius: E. La Rocca, in *Amazzonomachia,* exhibition catalog, Palazzo dei Conservatori (Rome, 1985).

For references on the likening of Actium to the victory of the Athenians over the Persians cf. Schneider, 64.

On the arch in Orange: R. Amy et al., *L'Arc d'Orange, Gallia,* suppl. no. 15 (Paris, 1961); I. Paar, *Chiron* 9 (1979): 215 ff.

A Change of Focus: Self-Glorification Gives Way to Religious Devotion

On the decoration of the Apollo Temple on the Palatine: Zanker, *Apollontempel;* H. Jucker, *Museum Helveticum* 39 (1982): 82–100.

Tripods: Schneider, 58 ff., with complete references. Cf. p. 82 on the painted tripod (fig. 70) and p. 75 on the association of tripod and griffin.

For tripods on Arretine bowls: C. H. Chase, *Catalogue of Arretine Pottery,*[2] Museum of Fine Arts Boston (Boston, 1975), pls. 4, 6, 10. A. Oxé, *BJb* 138 (1933): 92f. On the iconography of early Arretine: G. Pucci, in *L'Art décoratif à Rome* (Rome, 1981), 101 ff. The meaning of the tripod as a symbol of religious renewal is now thoroughly treated in a master's thesis by O. Dräger (Munich, 1987).

On candelabra: H.-U. Cain, *Römische Marmorkandelaber* (Mainz, 1985). There also recent discussion on the so-called Baitylos and on the sphinx, p. 78 ff.

On the Meta Albani: ABr, 4519–21. W. Fuchs, *Die Vorbilder der neuattischen Reliefs* (Berlin, 1959), 154. The monument could have been dedicated to Apollo, despite the Dionysiac imagery. There are numerous examples of the worship of Apollo by followers of Dionysus in the Early Imperial period.

On the so-called Campana reliefs from the Palantine: G. Carettoni, *BdA,* 1973, 75–87. On the interpretation: M. J. Strazzulla, *Ann. Perugia* 20 (1982–83): 463–87.

Res Publica Restituta

On the history and political significance of the honors of 27 B.C.: A. Alföldi, *Die monarchische Repräsentation im römischen Kaiserreich*[3] (Darmstadt, 1980); idem, *Der Vater des Vaterlandes im römischen Denken* (Darmstadt, 1971); idem, *Die Lorbeerbäume des Augustus* (Bonn, 1973). Recent references in Kienast, 67 ff.

On the coin imagery of the censor Lentulus (fig. 74): C. Vermeule, *Numismatica,* 1966, 5–11; S. Walker and A. Burnett, *The Image of Augustus* (London, 1981), 28.

On the *clipeus virtutis:* Hölscher, *Victoria,* 98 ff.; A. Wallace Hadrill, "The Emperor and His Virtues," *Historia* 30 (1981): 298 ff.

Venus on the shield: H. P. Laubscher, *JdI* 89 (1974): 255.

On the two cameos (figs. 81–82) cf. most recently T. Hölscher, *Klio* 67 (1985): 97f.; W.-D. Megow, *Kameen von Augustus bis Alexander Severus* (Berlin, 1987), 164, A 11 and pl. 7,19.

The Title "Augustus": A New Image

On the name Augustus cf. the refences in Kienast, 79 ff.

On the portrait of Augustus: *Die Bildnesse des Augustus,* exhibition catalogue,

Glyptothek (Munich, 1979), ed. K. Vierneisel and P. Zanker. Most recently: Fittschen-Zanker, vol. 1, no. 1ff.

On the Doryphorus of Polyclitus: H. von Steuben, *Der Kanon des Polyklet* (Tubingen, 1973).

Chapter 4

PIETAS

K. Latte, *Römische Religionsgeschichte*[2] (Munich, 1967), 294ff.; Kienast, 185ff.; A. D. Nock, "Religious Development from the Close of the Republic to the Death of Nero," in *Cambridge Ancient History,* vol. 10 (Cambridge, 1934), 465ff.; J. A. North, "Conservatism and Change in Roman Religion," *BSR* 44 (1976): 1–12; G. Liebeschütz, *Continuity and Change in Roman Religion* (Oxford, 1979).

On M. T. Varro: *RE,* suppl., vol. 6 (1935), 1172f. (H. Dahlmann).

Aurea Templa

Gros, *Aurea Templa.* On the highly prized nature of marble in Rome and on the beginnings of the exploitation of the distant Luni quarries cf. H.-U. Cain, *Römische Marmorkandelaber* (Mainz, 1985), 9ff.; D. and F. Kleiner, *AA,* 1975, 250ff.

On the so-called Ara Pietatis: Torelli, 63ff.; G. Koeppel, *BJb* 183 (1983): 98–116.

On the iconography: J. A. North, "Sacrificial Scenes in Roman Reliefs," in *Acta XI International Congress of Classical Archaeology* (London, 1978), 273f.

On the circle of poets: J. Griffin, "Augustus and the Poets: 'Caesar qui cogere possit,'" in *Caesar Augustus: Seven Aspects,* ed. F. Millar and E. Segal (Oxford, 1984), 189–218.

On individual sanctuaries see the references collected in Platner-Ashby and Nash; more recent literature in *BullComm* 89 (1984).

On Augustus and the Egyptian gods: P. Lambrechts, *Augustus en de Egyptische Goodsdient* (Brussels, 1956).

On Magna Mater: K. Schillinger, *Untersuchungen zur Entwicklung des Magna Mater-Kultes im Westen* (1978), 333f. Recent investigations of the temple by P. Pensabene reported most recently in *Roma, Archeologia nel Centro,* vol. 1 (Rome, 1985), 179ff. On the new appreciation of Cybele in the Augustan period cf. T. P. Wiseman, "Cybele, Virgil and Augustus," in *Poetry and Politics in the "Age of Augustus,"* ed. T. Woodman and D. West (Cambridge, 1984), 117–28.

A New Kind of Imagery

On the statuary program on the coin (fig. 90) with the Temple of Concord: Gros, *Aurea Templa,* 92; P. Zanker, *Forum Romanum* (Tübingen, 1972), 22; C. Gasparri, *Aedes Concordiae Augustae* (Rome, 1979). For the acroteria group, compare Caligula's coin issue of a trinity of female divinities in honor of his sisters: J. P. C. Kent et al., *Die römischen Münze* (Munich, 1973), no. 168.

For decorated bases similar to the so-called Ara Grimani (fig. 91) cf. H. von Hesberg, *RM* 87 (1980) 255–86.

On the Forum of Augustus (fig. 92): P. Zanker, *Forum Augustum* (Tübingen, 1968).

Festival and Ritual

The festival calendar: V. Ehrenberg and A. H. M. Jones, *Documents Illustrating the Reigns of Augustus and Tiberius*[3] (1976), 32ff.; P. Herz, "Kaiserfeste der Principatszeit," in *ANRW* II, 16, no. 2, (1978) 1135–1200; Ovid *Fasti*, ed. and commentary F. Bömer (Heidelberg, 1957); H. H. Scullard, *Festivals and Ceremonies of the Roman Republic* (London, 1981).

On interior spaces cf. Gros, *Aurea Templa*. On the decoration of the cella in the Apollo temple of Sosius (fig. 94): *Amazzonomachia*, exhibition catalog, Palazzo dei Conservatori (Rome, 1985), 91.

On *supplicationes: RE* A 4, 942ff.

Tiberius's art collection in the Temple of Concord: G. Becatti, *ArchCl* 25 / 26 (1973 / 74): 18–53.

T. Kraus, *Die Ranken der Ara Pacis* (Berlin, 1953). C. Börker, *JdI* 88 (1973): 283–317.

The sanctuary of Hercules on the Tiber (fig. 97): E. LaRocca, *La Riva a Mezzaluna* (1984), 62f. and pl. 9f.

The Chief Priesthoods

J. Scheid, "Les prêtres officiels sous les empereurs julio-claudiens," in *ANRW* 16 no. 1, (1979) 610–54; F. Millar, *The Emperor in the Roman World* (London, 1977), 355.

On the Arval Brethren: J. Scheid, *Les frères Arvales* (Paris, 1975); E. Olshausen, "Uber die röm. Arvalbrüder," *ANRW* 16,1 (1979) 820ff.

On the priesthoods represented on the Ara Pacis cf. Torelli, 27ff.; E. Simon, *Ara Pacis Augustae* (Tübingen, 1967).

On the iconography of the *X viri sacris faciundis* and on the tripod base (fig. 99): H. R. Götte, *AA*, 1984, 573–89; O. Dräger, in the master's thesis cited above. The association of Apollonian symbolism with the wreath of grain and vegetal candelabrum, as tokens of fertility, could allude to a link with the Secular Games, which were organized by the *XV viri sacris faciundis*. Since the same type of base is preserved in several identical examples, with matching iconography, they could represent a large series of votives. Perhaps these bases stood in the sanctuary of Apollo.

On the iconography of the Salii: T. Schaefer. *JdI* 95 (1980): 242–66.

On the significance of the "style" of the processional friezes: A. H. Borbein, *JdI* 90 (1975): 242–66.

On the frieze from the Porticus Octaviae (fig. 102): T. Hölscher, *JdI* 99 (1984): 204ff.

Priesthoods and Social Status

On the denarius with the attributes of the priest (fig. 103*a*): E. Zwierlein-Diehl, in *Tainia: Festschrift R. Hampe* (Mainz, 1980), 412f.
On Genius statuettes: H. Kunkel, *Der römische Genius* (Heidelberg, 1974). On the Lupercalia: C. Ulf, *Das römische Lupercalienfest* (Darmstadt, 1982); H. Wrede, *RM* 90 (1983): 185–200.
On the *compitalia* associations and the shrines of the Lares: Kienast, 164. The literature on the altars of the Lares is now collected by M. Hanno, in *ANRW* II, 16, 3 (1986) 2334–81.
On the Altar of the Vicomagistri in the Vatican (fig. 110) see most recently Hölscher, *Staatsdenkmal*, 27, fig. 35f.
On the compitum Acili (figs. 106–7): A. M. Colini and A. M. Tamania, *BullCom* 78 (1961 / 62): 147–63; *Année Epigraphique*, 1964, no. 77: 33.
On the altar of the collegium of woodworkers (fig. 111): G. Zimmer, *Römische Berufsdarstellungen* (Berlin, 1982), 162, no. 84; Helbig, vol. 2, no. 1238 (E. Simon).
On dedications by and for Augustus, such as the base of N. L. Hermeros (fig. 112): S. Panciera, in *Archeologia Laziale*, vol. 3 (Rome, 1980), 202ff.

PUBLICA MAGNIFICENTIA

For literature on Augustus's economic policies see Kienast, 311.
On Vedius Pollio: R. Syme, *JRS* 51 (1961): 23–30.
On the Porticus Liviae: M. B. Flory, *Historia* 33 (1984): 309ff.; P. Zanker, in *Urbs: Espace urbain et histoire* (Rome, 1987).

Agrippa's Building Program: A Villas for the Masses

On the Monumenta Agrippae: *RE* A 9 (1961), 1226f., s.v. "Vipsanius" (R. Hanslik); J. M. Roddaz, *Marcus Agrippa* (Rome, 1984), 231ff.
On the water supply: W. Eck, in *Frontinus, Wasserversorgung im antiken Rom*² (Munich, 1983), 47–77, with extensive treatment of private use.
On the Pantheon: F. Coarelli, in *Città e Architettura nella Roma Imperiale, Anal. Rom*, suppl. no. 10 (1983): 41–46.
On the two mythological "education"-groups: M. Bieber, *The Sculpture of the Hellenistic Age*² (New York, 1961), 135, fig. 628; HBr, 109ff., pl. 82.
On the *Horrea Agrippiana*: Kienast, 166ff.; H. Bauer et al., *ArchCl* 30 (1978): 31ff.; G. Rickman, *The Corn Supply of Ancient Rome* (Oxford, 1980), 60ff., 179ff.

Augustus's Family: A Ubiquitous Presence in Rome

For recent literature on Augustus's building activity in Rome see Kienast, 336ff.
On the Milliarium Aureum: P. Zanker, *Forum Romanum* (Tübingen, 1972), 24, fig. 41.
On the Solarium Augusti: E. Buchner, *RM* 83 (1976): 319ff.; 87 (1980): 355ff.
On the decoration of the porticoes in the Campus Martius: M. Pape, *Kunstwerke*

aus Kriegsbeute und ihre öffentliche Aufstellung in Rom (Hamburg, 1975). On the comparisons with Alexander: D. Kienast, *Gymnasium* 76 (1969): 430–56.

Status and Applause: The Theater as Meeting Place of Princeps and People

H. Kloft, *Liberalitas Principis* (Cologne, 1970); P. Veyne, *Le pain et le cirque* (Paris, 1976), esp. 701ff.; J. Deininger, "Brot und Spiele: Tacitus und die Entpolitisierung der plebs urbana," *Gymnasium* 86 (1979): 278ff.; R. Gilbert, *Die Beziehung zwischen Princeps und stadtrömischen Plebs im frühen Principat* (Bochum, 1976).

On propaganda for the regime in poetry and theater: R. Syme, *The Roman Revolution* (Oxford, 1939), especially the famous chapter "The Organisation of Opinion," 459ff.; K. Quinn, *The Roman Writers and Their Audience* (London, 1979); idem, in *ANRW* 30,1 (1982): 75ff.

On Augustus and the theater, and the *lex Julia theatralis:* E. Rawson, "Discrimina Ordinum," *BSR* 55 (1987): 83–114; Kienast, 169; T. Bollinger, *Theatralis Licentia* (1969).

On the social structure: G. Alföldy, *Römische Sozialgeschichte*[3] (Wiesbaden, 1984), with the schema reproduced here with kind permission of the author. Cf. also Alföldy's discussion in *Die römische Gesellschaft* (Stuttgart, 1986), 69ff.

Ideology and the Image of the City

T. P. Wiseman, "Strabo on the Campus Martius," in *Liverpool Classical Monthly,* July 1979, 129–34.

On Caesar's plans for a new city, the sources are collected by Z. Yavetz, *Caesar in der öffentlichen Meinung* (Düsseldorf, 1979), 159–61.

On the reform of the districts: Kienast, 164; *RE* 8 A 2 (1958): 2480, s.v. *"vici magister"* (J. Bleicken).

H. Vetters, "Die römerzeitliche Bauvorschriften," in *Festschrift B. Neutsch* (Innsbruck, 1980), 477ff.

MORES MAIORUM

On the laws of morality: H. Wallace-Hadrill, *Proc. Cam. Phil. Soc.* 27 (1981): 58–80; D. Nörr, in *Freiheit und Zwang: Festschrift H. Schelsky* (Opladen, 1977), 309–34; Kienast, 137.

On glass phalerae such as fig. 125: A. Alföldi, *Ur-Schweiz* 21 (1957): 80ff.; H. Jucker, *Schweizer Münzblätter* 25, no. 99 (1975): 50ff.; D. Boschung, *BJb* 187 (1987): 193–258.

The Princeps as Model

On the Ara Pacis and the Altar of the Twelve Gods: H. Thompson, *Hesperia* 21 (1952): 79ff.; A. Borbein, *JdI* 90 (1975): 246 with illustrations.

On the Ara Fortunae Reducis: Torelli, 28f. Cf. the fragments of yet another Augustan marble altar in the Villa Borghese: G. Moretti, *Ara Pacis Augustae* (Rome, 1948), 190f.

On the issues of the mint masters: M. Fullerton, *AJA* 89 (1985): 473–83; Kienast, 324.

On the Surdinus inscription: Coarelli, *Foro* 2:211ff.

On the statues of barbarians in the Basilica Aemilia: Schneider, 117ff.

On the Theater of Balbus: G. Gatti, *MEFRA* 91 (1979): 237ff.; D. Manacorda, *Archeologia urbana a Roma: Il progetto della crypta Balbi* (1982).

On the third portrait type of Augustus: Fittschen-Zanker, vol. 1, no. 8.

Toga and Stola

On the *toga:* F. W. Goethert, *RM* 54 (1939): 176–219. The dissertation on this subject by H. R. Götte (Göttingen, 1985) is not yet published.

On the *stola: RE* A 4 58ff., s.v. "stola" (M. Bieber); W. Stroh, "Ovids Liebeskunst und die Ehegesetzgebung des Augustus," *Gymnasium* 86 (1979): 343–52.

On the statue in fig. 131: M. Fuchs, *Untersuchungen zur Ausstattung römischer Theater* (Mainz, 1987), 104, pl. 45.

Chapter 5

AUREA AETAS

The Golden Age Is Proclaimed

On the Secular Games: *CIL* VI no. 32323; T. Mommsen, *Gesammelte Schriften* 8 (1931): 567–626; Helbig, vol. 3, no. 2400 (H. G. Kolbe); A. Wallace-Hadrill, "The Golden Age and Sin in Augustan Ideology," in *Past and Present* 95 (1982): 19–36; Kienast, 99, 187.

The translation of the *carmen saeculare* is reprinted from Charles E. Passage, *The Complete Works of Horace* (New York, 1983).

On the cult statue group in the Temple of Apollo cf. p. 241. The Sibyl is attested on the base from Sorrento (fig. 186): G. E. Rizzo, *BullCom* 60 (1932): 7ff.; M. Guarducci, *RM* 78 (1971): 90ff.

For the coin (fig. 134) cf. an archaistic relief of the same period with a sacrifice of a pig: F. Willemsem, *AM* 76 (1961): 209ff., suppl. 93.

The Imagery of Fertility and Abundance

On the so-called Tellus relief (figs. 135–36): E. Simon, *Ara Pacis Augustae* (Tübingen, 1967), 25. For the identification as Pax: Torelli, 38ff. Cf. also Tibullus 1.10.67f. or Germanicus *Arat.* 96ff.

On the so-called Grimani reliefs and the Palestrina relief (fig. 138*a–c*): V. M.

Strocka, in *Antike Plastik* 4 (1965): 87, pl. 53ff.; F. Zevi, *Prospettiva* 7 (1976): 38–41; A. Giuliano, *Xenia* 9 (1985): 41–46. A dating in the Augustan period seems to be quite possible.

On the relief with plant motifs from Falerii (fig. 139): A. Giuliano, *Prospettiva* 5 (1976): 54f.; L. di Stefano Manzella, *Pontificia Accademia Romana di Archeologia, Memorie*, ser. 3, vol 12, no. 2 (1979): 96f. The relief belonged to a larger complex, probably in a private setting.

On the Sosos Mosaic and the influence of the motif: K. Parlasca, *JdI* 78 (1963): 256–93; H. Meyer, *AA*, 1977, 104–10. On the urns: F. Sinn-Henninger, *Römische Marmorurnen* (Mainz, 1987), cat. no. 10.

The Vines of Paradise

T. Kraus, *Die Ranken der Ara Pacis* (Berlin, 1953); C. Börker, *JdI* 88 (1973): 283–317; A. Büsing, *AA*, 1977, 147–257. On the symbolism of the vines: H. P. L'Orange, in *ActaAArtHist* 1 (1962): 7ff. and, most recently, G. Sauron, *Comptes Rendues Academie des Inscriptions et Belles-Letters* (Paris, 1982), 81–101, whose interpretation in my view far exaggerates the possible impact.

On the frieze of the Temple of Caesar see most recently Hölscher, *Staatsdenkmal*, 20, fig. 28.

On the relief (fig. 142): A. Schmid-Colinet, *Antike Stützfiguren* (Cologne, 1977), 236, W 84.

K. Fittschen, "Zur Panzerstatue in Cherchel," *JdI* 91 (1976): 181, fig. 5 and, on the vine ornament on the footwear of statues of gods, 201, fig. 22.

On fig. 143: A. H. Borbein, *Campanareliefs* (Heidelberg, 1968), 193f.

On fig. 144: E. Pernice and F. Winter, *Der Hildesheimer Silberfund* (Berlin, 1901); U. Gehrig, *Hildesheimer Silberfund* (Berlin, 1967), 20, figs. 2–5.

Happiness Born of Victory

Historical sources on the so-called Parthian victory: M. Wissemann, *Die Parther in der augusteischen Dichtung* (Frankfurt, 1982); Kienast, 283f.

On the ideology of victory: Hölscher, *Victoria;* J. R. Fears, "The Theology of Victory at Rome," in *ANRW* II 17, 2 (1981): 827–948.

On the archaeological evidence pertaining to the victory over the Parthians see most recently Schneider, 29ff. and passim, with full references and a thorough discussion of the motif of falling to one's knees.

The archaistic figure of Mars (fig. 145b) is also attested in bronze and terra-cotta statuettes, on gems, lamps, and terra-sigillata vessels. The original must have been a famous work. The mixed archaizing and classical style of the better versions suggests an Augustan creation; cf. pp. 243ff.; A. Leibundgut, *Die römischen Bronzen der Schweiz*, vol. 3 (1980), no. 11. One of particular interest: catalog, Sotheby's (New York, 30 May 1956), no. 47.

On the Parthian arch in the Forum Romanum: that the arch stood *iuxta aedem*

Divi Iulii is certain (sch. Veron. Vergil *Aeneid* 7.605), but on which side of the Temple of Caesar is still disputed. Cf. the most recent and challenging suggestions of F. Coarelli, *Foro* 2:258ff., who assumes a location for the Parthian arch between the Temple of Caesar and the Basilica Aemilia, or Porticus Gaii et Luci Caesaris, and also offers a new interpretation of the coin types. His argument is accepted by P. Gros, in *Gnomon*, 1986, 58–64.

The motif on the glass paste in Berlin (fig. 147) is attested in several copies; cf. most recently Schneider, 38, 48, 91.

On the absence of battle scenes in Augustan art: a possible exception is a relief in Mantua, identified by D. Strong and J. B. Ward-Perkins, *BSR* 30 (1962): 1–30, as the frieze of the Temple of Castor and Pollux. Cf. T. Schaefer, *MM* 27 (1986): 345–64.

On the cuirassed statue of Augustus from Prima Porta (fig. 148): H. Jucker, *Hefte des Archäologischen Seminars der Univ. Bern* 3 (1977): 16ff; a good account of the dating and interpretation is K. Fittschen, *JdI* 91 (1976): 203ff. I do not find the distinction drawn by H. Meyer, *Kunst und Geschichte* (Munich, 1983), 123ff., between a Greek and a Latin conception of the relief on the curiass to be convincing, since this interpretation, in my view, isolates the imagery from the contemporary ideological context.

MYTH IN PAST AND PRESENT

On the Forum of Augustus: P. Zanker, *Forum Augustum* (Tübingen, 1968); V. Kockel, *RM* 90 (1983): 421–48 (on the reconstruction of the temple and its sculptural decoration); J. Ganzert, *RM* 92 (1985): 201–19 (preliminary publication report on the Temple of Mars Ultor).

Venus and Mars: on the relief in Algiers (fig. 151): K. Fittschen, *JdI* 91 (1976): 82ff.; Hölscher, *Staatsdenkmal*, 32, fig. 61; Meyer, op. cit., 141. The current discussion of this relief has, in my view, not produced any persuasive arguments against the old interpretation of S. Gsell, who saw in it a reflection of the cult statue group of the Temple of Mars Ultor. In the controversy over whether the figure with the mantle draped over the hips represents the Divus Iulius or a prince of the Julio-Claudian family, no distinction is made between the visual model and the function of the relief itself. It is quite conceivable that the figure on the relief represents a prince, such as Gaius Caesar after his early death, and that it comes from a monument erected in his honor. The model originating in Rome would then have been brought up to date in the provinces. The relief's function in North Africa, after all, was not as a topographical or iconographic guide to the famous sights in Rome. The same problem occurs with the interpretation of the cuirassed statue from Cherchel, pp. 192, 223.

On the Victoria in Brescia (fig. 152): T. Hölscher, in *Antike Plastik* 10 (1970): 67ff. On Venus with the shield: H. P. Laubscher, *JdI* 89 (1974): 254.

On the statue group (fig. 154): Helbig, vol. 3, no. 2132; P. Zanker, in *Entretiens Fondation Hardt* 25 (1979): 195.

On the colossal statue of Mars Ultor (Fig. 155): Helbig, vol. 2, no. 1198; U. Müller, *BullCom* 87 (1982): 135; E. Simon, *Marburger Winckelmannsprogramm,* 1981 (with very speculative interpretations that I am not entirely able to follow).

On the statue in the pediment of the Temple of Mars Ultor (fig. 152): P. Hommel, *Studien zu den römischen Figurengiebeln der Kaiserzeit* (Berlin, 1954), 22.

Aeneas and Romulus: Old Myths in a New Guise

On the transmission of the Aeneas group (fig. 156a): *Lexicon Iconographicum Mythologie Classicae* 1 (1981): 296ff. C. Dulière, *Lupa Romana* (Brussels, 1979).

On the Parthian arch in the Forum Romanum, cf. most recently Coarelli, *Foro* 2:287, with a new suggested location.

On the triumphal Fasti: A. Degrassi, ed., *Inscriptiones Italiae* XIII, 3 (Rome, 1947).

Aeneas and Romulus on the Ara Pacis: E. Simon, *Ara Pacis Augustae* (Tübingen, 1967), 23ff.; G. Moretti, *Ara Pacis Augustae* (Rome, 1948).

On the terra-cotta relief with the Lupa and Faustulus: H. v. Rhoden and H. Winnefeld, *Architektonische römische Tonreliefs der Kaiserzeit* (Berlin, 1911), pl. 127.1.

On the frieze in the Basilica Aemilia: C. Carettoni, *RIA* 10 (1961): 5ff.; Coarelli, *Foro* 2:207; Schneider, 118.

On the relief in Palermo with the vestals before Augustus: Hölscher, *Staatsdenkmal,* 31, pl. 54.

On the relief with the Temple of Vesta (fig. 160): G. Mansuelli, *Galleria degli Uffizi I. Le Sculture* (Rome, 1958), no. 143.

On the two reliefs with Klio (fig. 161): Paris, *Louvre Cat. Sommaire,* 110, no. 1891, and p. 2, no. 8; T. Schreiber, *Die hellenistischen Reliefbilder* (Leipzig, 1894), pl. 49ff., 50; S. Reinach, *Repertoire des reliefs Grecs et Romains,* vol. 2 (Paris, 1912), 283; J. Charbonneaux, *La Sculpture Grecque et Romaine au Musée du Louvre* (Paris, 1963), 94.

On Diomedes in Early Imperial art: C. Maderna, *Juppiter, Diomedes und Merkur* (Heidelberg, 1982).

On Aeneas as an ape (fig. 162): F. Canciani, *Lexicon Iconographicum Mythologiae Classicae,* 1 (1981): 388, no. 99; Zanker, *Forum Augustum.*

On the funerary altar with the Aeneas group cf. most recently P. Nölke, *Germania* 54 (1976): 434, pl. 47.2.

Summi Viri: A Revised Version of Roman History

On the "Hall of Fame" in the Forum of Augustus: A. Degrassi, op. cit.; Zanker, op. cit.; more recent literature in Schneider, 124.

On the role of C. Julius Hyginus cf. P. L. Schmidt, in *RE,* suppl. no. 15 (1978), s.v. "Victor Aurelius," 1655ff. According to these reconstructions, Augustus's direct opponents were naturally not represented. It was indeed taken for granted that Brutus and Cassius would, just like Marc Antony, be consigned to oblivion.

THE ASSIMILATION OF AUGUSTUS'S SUCCESSORS INTO THE NATIONAL MYTHOLOGY

For the sources on the problem of succession see Kienast, 107ff.

On the coin series (fig. 167a–c): M. Fullerton, *AJA* 89 (1985): 473–83.

Gaius and Lucius Caesar as Descendants of Venus

On the identification of the children on the Ara Pacis (figs. 169–70) see most recently Torelli, 49ff.; R. Syme, *AJA* 88 (1984): 583ff. In a new study, J. Pollini, *The Portraiture of Gaius and Lucius Caesar* (New York, 1987), revives E. Simon's suggestion that the two boys are barbarian princes. His most important argument is the size of the children, i.e., that they are depicted too small to be Gaius and Lucius at age four and seven. This is hardly convincing, however, since the artists of the Ara Pacis were clearly not concerned with being strictly true to life elsewhere in the representation of other figures. It was precisely their qualities as children that elicited the public's sympathy for the young princes.

On fig. 172: V. v. Gonzenbach, in *Helvetia Antiqua: Festschrift E. Vogt* (1966) 183–208.

On the portraits of the princes (figs. 174–76): Fittschen-Zanker, vol. 1, nos. 20, 21.

References on the altar of the Lares in Florence, Uffizi Museum (fig. 177): cf. p. 353.

On Gaius's expedition against the Parthians cf. the account in *RE* X (1919), 424, no. 134, s.v. "Gaius Iulius Caesar" (Gardthausen).

On the cuirassed statue in Chercel (fig. 178): K. Fittschen, *JdI* 91 (1976): 175–210.

The *corona civica* held by Victoria from behind, rather than above the head, is a strong argument in favor of the identification with Gaius. It would be most appropriate for the future princeps, but difficult to explain in this form for Caesar. If Caesar were intended, which victory are we to suppose Augustus was celebrating? Besides, the Victoria on the right hand of the presumed Gaius does not race over the *sphaera*, like Caesar's Victoria on the well-known denarius of C. Lentulus of 12 B.C. (fig. 25a).

Tiberius and Drusus as Commanders of the Imperial Army

On the wars of expansion in the North: Kienast, 293ff.

On the coin series from Lugdunum (fig. 179a–e): K. Kraft, *Zur Münzprägung des Augustus.* (Wiesbaden, 1969), 235ff.; Giard, 199, no. 1366, pl. 55.; H. Gabelmann, *Antike Audienz-und Tribunalszenen* (Darmstadt, 1984), 118ff.

Tiberius as Successor to the Throne

The Boscoreale cups (figs. 180–81): T. Hölscher, *JdI* 95 (1980): 281ff.; J. Pollini, "Studies in Augustan 'Historical' Reliefs" (Ph.D. diss., University of California, 1978), 173–255; Gabelmann, op. cit., 127f.; F. Baratte, *Le trésor d'orfèvrerie romaine de Boscoreale* (Paris, 1986). I am not persuaded by Gabelmann's dating of the cups in the Claudian period. It is based entirely on stylistic criteria, which in turn presuppose both a uniform Augustan style and a decisive stylistic "development." Everything we know from other artistic media makes this unlikely. We need only recall the varying styles alongside one another on the Ara Pacis. E. Künzl has rightly considered the possibility of large historical paintings as the models for the cups (*BJb* [1969]: 364). In each instance the style of the model will have determined that of the toreutic artist. Even if the cups were not made until Claudian times, the models must, judging from the subjects, be Late Augustan. In the time of Claudius, who would have still been interested in such specific events of the Late Augustan period?

Augustus in the Guise of Jupiter

On the Gemma Augustea (fig. 182): H. Kähler and A. Rubeni, *Dissertatio de Gemma Augustea* (Berlin, 1968); Pollini, op. cit., 173. On the history of this unique monument see W. Oberleitner, *Geschnittene Steine: Die Prunkkameen der Wiener Antikensammlung* (Vienna, 1985), 40–44. On the significance of cameos in general see H. Jucker, "Der große Pariser Kameo," *JdI* 91 (1976): 211–16; W. Megow, *Kameen von Augustus bis Alexander Severus* (Berlin, 1987), esp. 155, A 10, on the Gemma Augustea.

On the so-called sword of Tiberius (fig. 183): S. Walker and A. Burnett, *Augustus,* British Museum Occasional Papers, no. 16 (London, 1981), 49ff.; Gabelmann, op. cit., 124.

On the Livia cameo in Vienna (fig. 184): F. Eichler and E. Kris, *Die Kameen im Kunsthistorischen Museum* (Vienna, 1927), 57, no. 9, pl. 5; Megow, op. cit., 254, B 15, pl. 9.

On the colossal statue of Ceres Augusta from the theater at Leptis Magna (fig. 185): G. Caputo and G. Traversari, *Le sculture del teatro di Leptis Magna* (Rome, 1976), 76, no. 58, pl. 54f.; S. Sande, *ActaAArtHist* 5 (1985): 156f.; on the portrait type: Fittschen-Zanker, vol. 3, no. 1.

On the difficult economic situation in the later Augustan period cf. the sources collected in Kienast, 311ff.

Chapter 6

Dionysios of Halicarnassos: The Critical Essays, ed. S. Usher, vol. 1 (London, 1974); U. von Wilamowitz-Moellendorf, "Attizismus und Asianismus," *Hermes* 35

(1900): 1–52; E. Norden, *Antike Kunstprosa*² (Leipzig and Berlin, 1909); M. Fuhrmann, *Einführung in die antike Dichtungstheorie* (Darmstadt, 1974), 168ff.

On Dionysius of Halicarnassus and the controversy between the Atticizing and Asiatic schools see "Le Classicisme à Rome," *Entretiens Fondation Hardt* 25 (1979), especially the essays by T. Gelzer and G. Bowersock, for a good introduction to the issues.

Reuse of Archaic and Classical Originals

On the decoration of the Temple of Apollo: Zanker, *Apollontempel.*

On the cult statue group on the "base from Sorrento" (fig. 186): G. E. Rizzo, *BullCom* 60 (1933): 7–109; P. Mingazzini and F. Pfister, *Forma Italiae* vol. 1, no. 2 (Florence, 1948), 177, no. 16; M. Guarducci, *RM* 78 (1971); pl. 64ff.

On classicistic art theory: B. Schweitzer, *Xenokrates von Athen,* (Königsberg, 1932); idem. *Zur Kunst der Antike,* vol. 1 (1963), 105ff. F. Preißhofen and P. Zanker, *Dialoghi d'Archeologia* 4, no. 1, (1970 / 71): 100ff.

F. Preißhofen, in *Entretiens Fondation Hardt* 25 (1979): 263–82.

On the temple in fig. 187: P. Hommel, *Studien zu den römischen Figurengiebeln* (Berlin, 1954), 34ff.; Nash, 1: 74, fig. 75f.

On the Classical Amazonomachy in the pediment of the Apollo Temple of C. Sosius: E. La Rocca, in *Amazzonomachia,* exhibition catalog, Palazzo dei Conservatori, (Rome, 1985).

On fig. 187: E. Paribeni, *BdA* 49 (1964): 193–98, fig. 1ff.; E. Langlotz, *Studien zur nordostgriechischen Kunst* (Mainz, 1975), 127ff.

Archaic Form: Intimations of the Sacred

The particular qualities of the archaistic sculpture of the Augustan period have thus far not been clearly elucidated. For general literature see H. Bulle, *Archaisierende griechische Rundplastik* (Munich, 1918); E. Schmidt, *Archaistische Kunst in Griechenland und Rom* (Munich, 1922); L. Beschi, "La Spes Castelliani," in *Il Territorio Veronese in età Romana.* (Verona, 1971), 219–50; M. Fullerton, "Archaistic Draped Statuary in the Round of the Classical, Hellenistic and Roman Periods" (Ph.D. dissertation, Bryn Mawr College, 1983) with thorough bibliographies. For important references I would like to thank T. Hohoff, who is writing a dissertation on archaistic sculpture.

On the statue of Artemis (fig. 189) from Pompeii VIII, 2 or 3: F. Studniczka, *RM* 3 (188): 277; *Pompeii* A.D 79, exhibition catalog, vol. 2 (Boston, 1978), 147, no. 82.

On the sestercius of Claudius with Spes Augusta (fig. 190): Fullerton, op. cit., 295; M. E. Clark, "Spes in the Early Imperial Cult: 'The Hope of Augustus,'" *Numen* 30 (1983): 80–105.

The statue of Priapus (fig. 191): H. Brunn and F. Bruckmann, *Denkmäler griechischer und römischer Sculptur* (Munich, 1888—1900), 659; Helbig, vol. 2, no. 1699.

The head of Priapus (fig. 192): Helbig, vol. 2, no. 1512.

On the Campana plaques from the Palatine (fig. 193): G. Carettoni, *BdA* 58 (1973): 75–87. The distribution of these revetments indicates a clear concentration in imperial and other lavish buildings: cf. S. Tortorella, "Problemi di produzione e di Iconografia," in *L'art décoratif à Rome* (Rome, 1979), 61–100.

The Moral Claim of Classical Forms

On the so-called "Hüftmantel" type: H. G. Niemeyer, *Studien zur statuarischen Darstellung der römischen Kaiser* (Berlin, 1968), 54f., 101f. See also the review by K. Fittschen in *BJb* 170 (1970): 545.

On fig. 194: V. Poulsen, *Les portraits Romains,* vol. 1 (Copenhagen, 1973), no. 47.

On fig. 195: G. Traversari, *Mus. Arch. Venezia: I Ritratti* (Rome, 1968), no. 13.

On the iconography of Agrippa: Fittschen-Zanker, vol. 2 (forthcoming, 1988), no. 16.

On fig. 196: V. Poulsen, op. cit., no. 38.

On fig. 197: H. Brunn and F. Bruckmann, *Denkmäler griechischer und römischer Sculptur* (Munich, 1888–1900), 562.

On groups of Venus and Mars (cf. fig. 154): E. Schmidt, in *Antike Plastik* 8 (1968): 85f., pl. 60ff; Fittschen-Zanker, vol. 1, no. 64. On the group illustrated here in fig. 154: Helbig, vol. 3, no. 2132; R. Calza, in Scavi di *Ostia* 9 (1978), Ritratti II no. 16, pl. 11f. The individuals represented are not an imperial couple, but rather a pair of *honoratiores* from Ostia.

"Atticizing" Compositions

On the Classical painting of the period of the Parthenon, such as on vases by the Niobid and Peleus painters, cf. E. Simon, *Die griechischen Vasen* (Munich, 1976), pl. 190ff.

On erotic scenes on Arretine bowls (fig. 199): A. Greifenhagen, "Beiträge zur antiken Reliefkeramik" *JdI* 21 (1963); *Römisches im Antikenmuseum* (Berlin, 1978), 159.

On the Portland Vase (fig. 200): E. Simon, *Die Portlandvase* (Mainz, 1957); D. E. L. Haynes, *The Portland Vase²* (London, 1975), with a summary of earlier interpretations; most recently, L. Polacco, in *Alessandria e il mondo ellenistico-romano: studi in onore di Achille Adriani,* vol. 2 (Rome, 1984), 729, with references to more recent literature. Many interpreters have succumbed to the temptation to see portraits in the idealized faces of the figures. This stems from the classical stylization of official portraiture. The desperate search to find once and for all the "right" interpretation led Polacco to see an Oriental cap under the so-called Ariadne. The history of interpretation of the Portland Vase would be a worthy subject for a critical study.

Quotation from Classical Art for Symbolic Value

On Augustan temples (fig. 201): Gros, *Aurea Templa;* H. von Hesberg, in *Göttinger Gelehrte Anzeige* 233 (1981): 218–37; R. Amy and P. Gros, "La maison carée de Nîmes," *Gallia,* suppl. no. 38 (1979).

Quotations in the decoration of the Forum of Augustus (fig. 202): E. E. Schmidt, "Die Kopien der Erechtheionkoren," *Antike Plastik* 13 (1973); B. Wesenberg, *JdI* 99 (1984): 172ff.; V. Kockel, *RM* 90 (1983): 421–48; Schneider, 103ff.

On the cornice of the Temple of Concord (fig. 203): C. Gasparri, *Aedes Concordiae Augustae* (Rome, 1979). For the different selection and application of ornament on the frieze and the entablature compare the Temple of Mars Ultor (Kockel, op. cit.) and the Temple of the Dioscuri (D. Strong and J. B. Ward-Perkins, *BSR* 7 [1962]: 1f.). On the latter temple, nearly the same ornamental elements appear, but the ordering is completely different. The decorative bands could apparently be rearranged with complete freedom. An egg and dart could even crown a pillar frieze. Unlike the Temple of Concord, the sima of the Temple of the Dioscuri is decorated only with lion's head water spouts, again probably intended as a quotation. The theory of a gradual fixing of a canon of forms in the middle and later Augustan period is certainly true of the Corinthian order on the exterior of temples, but not for the totality of the ornament.

On marble candelabra such as that in fig. 205: H.-U. Cain, *Römische Marmorkandelaber* (Mainz, 1985); cf. P. Zanker, in *Entretiens Fondation Hardt* 25 (1979): 283–306.

On "purist" copies of Augustan date (as in fig. 206): H. Lauter, *Zur Chronologie römischer Kopien nach Originalen des V. Jh. v. Chr.,* (Erlangen, 1969); P. Zanker, *Klassizistische Statuen* (Mainz, 1974).

Athens: for a review of the literature see D. J. Geagen, in *ANRW* II 7, 1 (1979) 378ff.; H. A. Thompson, "The Odeion in the Athenian Agora," *Hesperia* 19 (1959): 31–141; J. Travlos, *Pictorial Dictionary of Ancient Athens* (London, 1971), 366, also for the sphinx herms of the *pulpitum,* figs. 485–87.

On the Temple of Ares: H. A. Thompson, *Agora* 14 (1972): 160. On the renovation of sanctuaries: C. P. Jones, *Phoenix* 32 (1978): 222ff.

Chapter 7

Allegiance and Fashion

For portraits of the imperial family in the atria of private houses, an early example is the portrait of Marcellus from the Casa del Citarista in Pompeii: Fittschen-Zanker, vol. 1, no. 19; R. Neudecker, *Die Skulpturenausstattung römischer Villen* (Mainz, 1988).

On carved ring stones: M. L. Vollenweider, *Die Steinschneidekunst und ihre Künstler in spätrepublikanischer und augusteischer Zeit* (Baden-Baden, 1966). Glass

364 Notes and References for Further Reading

pastes with Augustan portraits are now being studied by C. Maderna and R. M. Schneider, under the guidance of T. Hölscher. In the meantime, see the series *Antike Gemmen in deutschen Sammlungen*, (1968–) with references to other sources and catalogs.

On gems and cameos: P. Zazoff, *Die antiken Gemmen*, Handbuch der Archäologie (Munich, 1983); E. Zwierlein-Diehl, *Kölner Jahrbuch für Vor- und Frühgeschichte* 17 (1980): 12–53; cf. the references here p. 360.

On Augustan silver: E. Pernice and E. Winter, *Der Hildesheimer Silberfund* (Berlin, 1901); U. Gehrig, *Hildesheimer Silberfund* (Berlin, 1967). On silver in general: D. E. Strong, *Greek and Roman Silver Plate* (London, 1960); E. Künzl, *BJb* 169 (1969): 321ff.; idem, *Jahrbuch Röm. Germ. Mus. Mainz* 22 (1975): 62ff.; C. C. Vermeule, "Augustan and Julio-Claudian Court Silver," *Antike Kunst* 6 (1963): 33ff. It would also be worthwhile to consider in this context compositions which betray a more playful association with political imagery. The best examples are the Hoby Cups in the National Museum, Copenhagen. On these see most recently H. Gabelmann, *Antike Audienz- und Tribunalszenen* (Darmstadt, 1984), 142.

Arretine Bowls: for an overview of the literature see *M. Perennius Bargathes*, exhibition catalogue, Museo Archeologico (Arezzo, 1984), 29f. On the silver models for early Arretine: E. Ettlinger, in *Gestalt und Geschichte: Festschrift K. Schefold* (Basel, 1967), 116f.

Clay lamps: A. Leibundgut, *Die römischen Lampen in der Schweiz* (Bern, 1977).

Furniture and utensils: V. Spinazzola, *Le arti decorative in Pompei* (Milan, 1928); *Pompeii A.D. 79*, exhibition catalog, vol. 2 (Boston, 1978), ed. A. Claridge and J. Ward-Perkins; St. Adamo Muscettola, "Le ciste di piombo decorate," in *La regione sotterrata dal Vesuvio.* (Naples, 1982), 701–34.

The Final Stage: From Internalization to the Private Message

On fig. 216: D. Baily, *Catalogue of Lamps in the British Museum*, vol. 2 (London, 1980), Q 870, pl. 11; Hölscher, *Victoria*, 108ff.; idem *Klio* 67 (1985): 99.

On fig. 217: G. Heres, "Römische Neujahrsgeschenke," *Forschungen und Berichte: Staatliche Museen zu Berlin* 14 (1972): 182ff.

On fig. 218: individual gladiatorial weapons from Pompeii are frequently illustrated, but there has thus far been no investigation of all the material in the National Museum, Naples. This is now being prepared by Diana Bettinali-Graeber. Cf. Fiorelli, in *Catalogo del Museo Nazionale di Napoli: Armi Antiche* (Naples, 1869); *Guida*, Ruesch, 415f.; J. Garbsch, *Römische Paraderüstungen* (Munich, 1978); Schneider, 42.

On laurel and oak wreaths: A. Alföldi, *Die zwei Lorbeerbäume des Augustus* (Bonn, 1973), with earlier references.

On fig. 219 (tomb of the Augustales in Pompeii): V. Kockel, *Die Grabbauten vor dem Herkulaner-Tor in Pompeii* (Mainz, 1983) 37, 42, 95f.

Funerary inscriptions: H. Geist and G. Pfohl, *Römische Grabinschriften* (Munich, 1969).

On funerary altars and urns: W. Altmann, *Die römischen Grabaltäre der Kaiserzeit* (Berlin, 1905); D. Boschung, *Antike Grabaltäre aus den Necropolen Roms* (Bern, 1987). On the marble urns from the city of Rome: F. Sinn-Henninger, in G. Koch and H. Sichtermann, *Römische Sarkophage*, Handbuch der Archäologie (Munich, 1982), 41–57; eadem, *Stadtrömische Marmorurnen* (Mainz, 1987). On fig. 220: F. Sinn, op. cit., 93, no. 10, pl. 5f.; S. Panciera, *Archeologia Laziale* 3:211, n. 20.

Fig. 221: I am much indebted to the owner and to Dr. M. Anderson (Atlanta) for permission to illustrate here this previously unpublished marble altar. The private use of imperial signs and symbols, devoid of their original meaning, was of course not limited to funerary art, but was common in the decoration of houses as well. In fact, their use in household decoration may well have preceded that in funerary monuments. A fine example of the former is the bronze ship's prow in Trimalchio's "palace," donated by his accountant Cinnamus (Petronius *Satyricon* 30.1).

On the use of the group with the lupa in the private sphere cf. C. Dulière, *Lupa Romana* (Brussels, 1979).

Taste and the New Mentality

On wall painting of the Second Style see p. 28. On the new Augustan style in wall painting see F. L. Bastet and M. de Vos, *Il terzo stile pompeiano* (Rome and Rijkswijk, 1979). The series of "development" proposed there have rightly been criticized. They represent an abstract construct that does not take account of the realities of the artistic process. See now W. Erhardt, *Stilgeschichtliche Untersuchungen an römischen wandmalereien* (Mainz, 1987).

A recent survey that gives more emphasis to the spatial dimension of the paintings is A. Barbet, *La peinture murale romaine* (Paris, 1985). See also E. W. Leach, "Patrons, Painters and Patterns," in *Literary and Artistic Patronage in Ancient Rome,* ed. B. K. Gold (Austin, 1982).

On Vitruvius's criticism see most recently H. Knell, *Vitruvs Architekturtheorie* (Darmstadt, 1985), 161ff.

Fig. 222: on the paintings in the house of Augustus: G. Carretoni, *Das Haus des Augustus auf dem Palatin* (Mainz, 1983); idem, *RM* 90 (1983): 373–419.

On fig. 223: The paintings found in the Roman villa beneath the famous "Farnesina" are housed in the Terme Museum: A. Giuliano, ed., *Museo Nazionale Romano: Le Pitture,* vol. 2, no. 1, (1982) (I. Bragantine and M. de Vos).

Fig. 224: On the wall paintings from Boscotrecase: P. H. von Blanckenhagen et al., *The Paintings from Boscotrecase* (Heidelberg, 1962); K. Schefold, *Vergessenes Pompeii* (Bern, 1962), 59ff.

On the "Tending of the child Dionysus" in the Farnesina cf. Bragantini and de Vos, op. cit., 135, pl. 68.

On the "Mourning for Icarus": P. H. von Blanckenhagen, *RM* 75 (1968): 108–43.

Bucolic Fantasies

N. Himmelmann, *Uber Hirten-Genre in der antiken Kunst,* Abhandlungen der Rheinschisch-Westfälischen Akademie der Wissenschaften no. 65 (1980), 113; H. P. Laubscher, *Fischer und Landleute* (Mainz, 1982); H. von Hesberg, *Münchner Jahrb.* 37 (1986): 7–32.

Fig. 224*c*: on the nature of the so-called sacral-idyllic landscapes cf. P. H. von Blanckenhagen et al., *The Paintings from Boscotrecase* (Heidelberg, 1962), 52ff.

On fig. 225: Dütschke, vol. 4, no. 172; von Hesberg, op. cit., 20f, fig. 24.

On fig. 226: A. Furtwängler, *Beschreibung der Glyptothek* (1910), no. 455; von Hesberg, op. cit.

Other "relief pictures" of this type are collected by T. Schreiber, *Die hellenistischen Reliefbilder* (Leipzig, 1894), now out of date. Cf. the bibliographical lists of J. Sampson, *BSR* 29 (1974): 27.

Fig. 227: on the stucco ceilings of the Farnesina cf. the publication of Bragantini and de Vos cited on p. 365 and H. Mielsch, *Römische Stuckreliefs* (Heidelberg, 1975), 20, 111; Helbig, vol. 3, no. 2482 (B. Andreae).

Tomb Monuments and Portraiture: Expressions of a New Self-Awareness

On the tomb monuments cf. the references for p. 11.

On the large tomb monuments mentioned here see the references collected by M. Eisner, *Zur Typologie der Grabbauten im Suburbium Roms* (Mainz, 1986) and, on their interpretation, H. von Hesberg and P. Zanker, eds., *Römische Gräberstrassen,* Bayerische Akademie der Wissenschaften, Abhandlungen no. 96 (Munich, 1987).

W. Eck, "Senatorial Self-Representation: Developments in the Augustan Period," in *Caesar Augustus: Seven Aspects,* ed. F. Millar and E. Segal (Oxford, 1984), 129–67.

For an example of a family grave precinct of the upper class cf. D. Boschung, "Uberlegungen zum Liciniergrab," *JdI* 101 (1986): 257ff.; Nash, *Bildlexikon* 2:374.

On fig. 228 (columbaria): J. M. C. Toynbee, *Death and Burial in the Roman World* (London, 1971), 193ff. On the columbarium illustrated here see Nash, *Bildlexikon* 1:336f.

Portraiture: on female hairstyles in the early Imperial period: K. Polaschek, *Trierer Zeitschrift* 35 (1972): 141–216. On portrait styles for males cf. P. Zanker, "Herrscherbild und Zeitgesicht," *Römisches Portrait,* Wiss. Zeitschrift der Humboldt–Univ. Berlin, 2 / 3 (1982): 307–12.

Chapter 8

The Greek Reaction

On Nikolaos of Damascus: *Die Fragmente der griechischen Historiker,* ed. F. Jacoby, vol. 2, sec. A (Berlin, 1926), no. 90, p. 391, no. 125; G. Bowersock, *Augustus and the Greek World* (Oxford, 1965).

On the imperial cult in the East see now the thorough and stimulating book of S. R. F. Price, *Rituals and Power: The Roman Imperial Cult in Asia Minor* (Cambridge, 1984), where further references will also be found on the phenomena discussed in the following pages. Cf. also the contributions of F. Millar and G. Bowersock in *Caesar Augustus,* ed. F. Millar and E. Segal (Oxford, 1984). More references in Kienast. On the Hellenistic ruler cult see C. Habicht, *Gottmenschentum und griechische Städe*[2] (Munich, 1970).

On the archaeological testimonia cf. the lists of monuments in C. C. Vermeule, *Roman Imperial Art in Greece and Asia Minor* (Cambridge, Mass., 1968).

On the topographical situation of temples of the imperial cult in East and West see H. Hänlein-Schaefer, *Veneratio Augusti: Studien zu den Tempeln des ersten römischen Kaisers* (Rome, 1985), 23ff.

Ephesus: W. Jobst, *IstMitt* 30 (1980): 241ff.

On fig. 230 (Miletus): K. Tuchelt, *IstMitt* 25 (1975): 91–140, fig. 15.

Fig. 231: on local coin issues with portraits of Augustus: A. Burnett, in *Augustus,* British Museum Occasional Papers, no. 19 (London, 1981).

On fig. 232: *Corinth,* vol. 9 (Cambridge, Mass., 1931), (F. P. Johnson), 71, no. 134.

On fig. 233: B. Freyer-Schauenburg, in *Festschrift E. Burck* (Amsterdam, 1975), 1ff. On the issue in general see P. Zanker, *Provinzielle Kaiserportraits: zur Rezeption der Selbstdarstellung des Princeps,* Abhandlungen Bayrische Akademie der Wissenschaften 90 (Munich, 1983).

Portraits from Asia Minor are collected in J. Inan and E. Rosenbaum, *Roman and Early Byzantine Portrait Sculpture in Asia Minor* (London, 1966); J. Inan and E. Rosenbaum, *Römische und frühbyzantinische Porträtplastik aus der Türkei: Neue Funde* (Mainz, 1979)

On the Parthian monument in Ephesus see most recently W. Oberleitner et al., *Funde aus Ephesos und Samothrake,* catalog, vol. 2, Kunsthistorisches Museum (Vienna, 1978), 68–94.

On figs. 234–35 ("Caesareum" in Aphrodisias): K. T. Erim, *Revue Arch.,* 1982, 1, 163–68; idem, in *V. Kazi Sonuclari Toplantisi* (Istanbul, 23–27 May 1983), 525, fig. 6.1; idem, *Aphrodisias: City of Venus* (London, 1986), 106ff.; R. R. R. Smith, in *JRS* 107 (1987).

On the Agrippina Minor cf., for example, the statue in Petworth House: Fittschen-Zanker, vol. 3, (Mainz, 1983), no. 5 suppl. 6a–d.

The Imperial Cult: Competition Among Cities

On the Imperial cult under Augustus see C. Habicht, in *Le culte des souverains dans l'empire romain,* vol. 19. of *Entretiens Fondation Hardt* (Geneva, 1973), 39ff.; Kienast, 202ff. On the Imperial cult in the Roman cities of the West see the now outdated lists of L. R. Taylor, *The Divinity of the Roman Emperor* (Middletown, Conn., 1931). Recent archaeological literature may be found in Hänlein-Schaefer, op. cit.

Fig. 236: on the altar of Roma and Augustus in Lugdunum and other provincial cults in the West see Kienast, 206; D. Fishwick, in *ANRW* II 16, 2 (1978), 120ff. On the case of Mytilene and Tarraco see Price, op. cit., 127f.; Fishwick, op. cit.: idem, *MM* 23 (1982): 222ff.; Hänlein-Schaefer, op. cit., 64.

On the prize for Paullus Fabius Maximus: Kienast, 204.

On the Republican terrace sanctuaries in central Italy see P. Gros, *Architecture et société à Rome et en Italie centro-méridionale aux deux derniers siècles de la République*, Collection Latomus, no. 156, (Brussels, 1978); F. Coarelli, in *Les "Bourgeoisies" municipales italiennes aux IIe et I^e siècles av. J.-C.* (Naples and Paris, 1983), 217–40.

On the Tabula Siarensis: J. Gonzáles, *Zeitschrift für Papyrologie und Epigraphik* 55 (1984): 55–100.

On the Altars at Praeneste: F. Zevi, *Prospettiva* 7 (1976): 38–41.

On the Maison Carrée: R. Amy and P. Gros, *La maison carrée à Nîmes* (Paris, 1979), 188f.

On fig. 241 (the Forum of Pompeii): A. Mau, *Pompeji in Leben und Kunst*[2] (1908), 90ff., 129ff.; on the individual buildings see most recently Hänlein-Schaefer, op cit., 133. The dating of the buildings on the west side is to some extent unsettled and needs a new investigation. The construction of the walls surrounding the so-called Temple of Vespasian, for example, corresponds with that of the exterior south side of the building of Eumachia. The altar has been repaired, the marble sections in part renovated. This suggests the necessity of reconstruction after the earthquake of 62 A.D. Preliminary observations by M. Pfanner suggest that the eastern portico was not continuous. The facades of the two buildings belonging to the imperial cult could have stood in the open. The supposed altar in the middle before these facades cannot have been that of the Temple of Jupiter, since its altar was integrated into the stairs.

On the Temple of Fortuna Augusta in Pompeii, as well as all the other cult places associated with Augustus, such as those in figs. 242–43, see Hänlein-Schaefer, op. cit.

On the situation of the ad hoc organized and peripatetic building sheds, see the pertinent study of H. Heinrich in his still unpublished Master's thesis (Munich, 1985).

On fig. 245 (seated statue from Cumae): M. E. Bertoldi, *BdA*, 1973, 40f., figs. 6–8; *CIL*, X, 1613 and cf. 3697.

On fig. 246 ("Pax" relief from Carthage): Hölscher, *Staatsdenkmal*, 31, fig. 56; most recently, L. Berczelly, *ActaAArtHist* 5 (1985): 137, with new and, in my view, misguided interpretations of the Pax and Lupa reliefs on the Ara Pacis.

On fig. 247 (Altar of P. Perelius Hedulus from Carthage): L. Poissot, *L'autel de la gens Augusta à Carthage* (Tunis 1929); Hölscher, *Staatsdenkmal*, 31, fig. 58f.

The Local Elite and the Augustan Program

On fig. 248 (the Augustus cult of M. Varenus in Tibur): C. F. Giuliani, *Tibur*, vol. 1 (*Forma Italiae* vol. 1, no. 7 [Rome, 1970]), 62ff., 67. The statue: R. Paribeni, *NSc*,

1925, 249f., fig. 7; A. Dähn, *Zur Ikonographie und Bedeutung einiger Typen der römischen männlichen Porträtstatuen* (Marburg, 1973), 5ff., 64f.

On the statues from Leptis Magna (figs. 249-50) and the type see H. G. Niemeyer, *Studien zur statuarischen Darstellung der römischen Kaiser* (Berlin, 1968), 104f., especially no. 89f.

On the Augustales and other cult associations: K. Latte, *Römische Religion* (Munich, 1960), 307, with references; P. Kneißl, *Chiron* 10 (1980): 291ff.; Kienast, 209; R. Duthoy, in *ANRW* II 16, 2 (1978): 1254–1309, summarizing earlier studies.

On the *corona civica* and laurel trees above house doors: V. Spinazzola, *Pompeii alla luce degli scavi nuovi*, vol. 1 (Rome, 1953), 134.

On the participation of social groups in public building activity: J. Andreau, *Ktema* 1 (1976): 157–209.

On Pompeiian society: P. Castren, *Ordo populusque Pompeianus* (Rome, 1975).

On the building of Eumachia (fig. 251): L. Richardson, Jr., *Parola del Passato* 33 (1978): 268f. Such multifunctional buildings are characteristic of the Early Imperial period and would reward a more thorough investigation. The individual architectural elements (porticoes, cryptoporticoes, gardens, temples or shrines, entrance halls, exedrae) appear again and again, but combined in very different ways. Cf. G. Dareggi, *BdA*, 1982, 1–36. Even though the orientation of Eumachia's building is so close to the Porticus of Livia in terms of function and ideological content, the former has, architecturally, little in common with its Roman model.

On fig. 252 (vine frieze from the building of Eumachia): V. Spinazzola, *Le Arti decorative in Pompei* (Milan, 1928), pl. 21f.

On the gens Holconia: J. D'Arms, "Pompeii and Rome in the Augustan Age: The Eminence of the Gens Holconia," forthcoming in the Festschrift for F. Jashemski.

On the priestly offices: D. Ladage, *Städtische Priester und Kultämter im lateinischen Westen in der römischen Kaiserzeit* (Cologne, 1971). On the rituals of the imperial cult in the West see now D. Fishwick's book, *The Imperial Cult in the Latin West* (Leiden, 1987).

On the honorary statues among the upper class see Zanker 1983, 251–66.

On fig. 253: see most recently S. Sande, *ActaAArtHist* 5 (1985): 220ff., with further references and, in my view, a wrong identification. Just because we are dealing with a shrine of the imperial cult does not mean that all the statues displayed there were of members of the imperial house. This is clear, for example, from the statues found in the cella of the Temple of Fortuna Augustus in Pompeii.

Cities of Marble: The New Self-Assurance in the West

E. Gabba, "Italia Augusta," in *Mélanges Carcopino* (Paris, 1966), 917–26; idem, in *Hellenismus in Mittelitalien*, ed. P. Zanker (Göttingen, 1976), 315–26. Cf. the references in Kienast, 344ff.

On the theater buildings see G. Béjor, "L'edificio teatrale nell'urbanizzazione augustea," *Athenaeum* 57 (1979): 126–38; M. Fuchs, *Untersuchungen zur Ausstattung römischer Theater* (Mainz, 1987).

On the seating arrangement in the theater see E. Rawson, in *BSR* 55 (1987): 83–114.

On the differences between the Roman and Greek theater see M. Bieber, *The History of the Greek and Roman Theatre*⁴ (Princeton, 1971).

Among the earliest examples of preserved emperor statues from a *scaenae frons* are the portraits from the theater at Volterra, whose patron, A. Caecina A. F. Severus (consul, 2 / 1 B.C.) was closely associated with Augustus; cf. O. Luchi, *Prospettiva* 8 (1977): 37ff.; Fuchs, op. cit., 99.

On fig. 256: W. Herrmann, *Römische Götteraltäre* (Kallmünz, 1961), 91; P. Gros, in *JdI* 102 (1987): 339–63.

On the display of statues in the forum of Pompeii see A. Mau, *RM* 11 (1896): 150–56; H. Döhl and P. Zanker, in *Pompei 79*, ed. F. Zevi (Naples, 1983), 185ff.

On figs. 257–58 (walls and gates): H. Kähler, *JdI* 57 (1942): 1–104; Kienast, 345, 349.

On Saepinum: A. U. Stylow, *Chiron* 7 (1977): 487ff.; *Saepinum: Museo documentario dell' Altitia*, ed. M. Torelli (Campobasso, 1982), 51.

On fig. 259: P. Zanker, *AA*, 1981, 349–61; C. Nicolet, *MEFRA* 79 (1967): 29–76; J. D'Arms, op. cit.

On fig. 260: *Antike Denkmäler*, vol. 3 (Berlin, 1926), pl. 31; M. Rostovzeff, *RM*, 1911, 158.

Illustration Sources

Many friends and colleagues have made available the original photographs reproduced here. I wish to thank them most warmly, as well as to thank the staffs of all the museums and research institutes listed here.

Photographs of coins from the Niggeler Collection and from the auctions of Münzen und Medaillen AG (Basel) were kindly provided by the Fotoarchiv Antiker Münzen at the University of Frankfurt, through the courtesy of M. Radnoti-Alföldi and H. Schubert.

1. Rome, Terme Museum inv. 1049. H: 2.44 m. Photo Hirmer.
2. After ABr no. 360.
3. Munich, Staatliche Münzsammlung. Museum photo.
4. Florence, Museo Archeologico. H: 1.79 m. INR 63.599.
5. Turin, Museo d'Antichità. H: 33 cm. INR 57.438.
6. Copenhagen, Ny Carlsberg Glyptothek inv. 733. H: 26 cm. Museum photo.
7. Paris, Louvre inv. Ma 1220. H: 24.5 cm. From a cast in the Museum für Abgüsse Klassischer Bildwerke, Munich (H. Glöckler).
8. Cagliari, Museo Archeologico. H: 24 cm. INR 66.2042.
9. Niggeler no. 834. Crawford no. 362.1.
10. *a*) Paris, Louvre inv. Ma 975. L: 5.59 cm. H: 80 cm. Photo Marburg. *b*) Munich, Glyptothek 239. L: 5.60 m. H: 78 cm. Museum photo.
11. *a–b*) MuM Auction 38 (1968) no. 203 (Crawford no. 437.2a).
12. Rome, Via Statilia. INR 75.779.
13. Rome, in front of the Porta Maggiore. H: ca. 11 m. INR 76.2442.
14. Rome, Via Appia. H: ca. 25 m. Fototeca Unione.
15. St. Remy. H: ca. 18 m. Fototeca Unione.
16. After L. Canina, *Gli edifici di Roma antica* (Rome, 1846).
17. *a–b*) Munich, Staatliche Münzsammlung (Crawford nos. 487.1 and 2a).
18. After F. Coarelli, *Roma* (Rome, 1974), 242.
19. Naples, Museo Nazionale inv. 6759. H: 75 cm. INR 37.949.
20. J. Paul Getty Museum, Malibu. Photo R. Senff.
21. Rome, Palatine, Casa dei Grifi. *Monumenti della pittura antica Scoperti in Italia* (Rome, 1935–), vol. 3, fascicle 1, pl. C.
22. Pompeii, Villa dei Misteri. INR 57.834.
23. Vatican Museums, Gall. Statue inv. 735. H: 1.47 m. INR 83.1634.
24. Naples, Museo Nazionale inv. 6210. H: 2.04 m. INR 83.2139.
25. *a*) Niggeler no. 1055 (Giard no. 555). *b*) Tübingen, Archäologisches Institut (Crawford no. 497.2a). Photo D. Mannsperger.

26. Present whereabouts unknown (Crawford no. 540.1). Fototeca Unione.
27. *a*) MuM Auction 39 (1968) no. 257 (Crawford no. 458.1). *b*) British Museum inv. RR 4258. Museum photo. *c*) Niggeler, no. 1007 (Giard no. 19).
28. *a–b*) MuM Auction 28 (1964) no. 253 (Crawford no. 535.1). *c*) Niggeler no. 1003 (Crawford no. 534.2).
29. *a*) Vienna, Bundessammlung. After *Festschrift U. Hausmann* (Tübingen, 1982) pl. 74.6 (Crawford no. 497.1). *b*) Private Collection. After *Festschrift U. Hausmann* pl. 74.2 (Crawford no. 490.1) *c*) Private Collection. After *Festschrift U. Hausmann* pl. 73.12 (Crawford no. 518.2).
30. *a*) Rome, Palazzo dei Conservatori, Medagliere. Photo J. Bergemann. *b*) British Museum. Grueber II 463, no. 16, pl. 110,11.
31. *a*) Niggeler no. 1010 (Giard no. 13). *b*) Present whereabouts unknown. After a cast in the Museo della Civiltà Romana, Rome. Photo Musei Capitolini.
32. *a–b*) Niggeler no. 1015 (Giard no. 68).
33. La Alcudia (Mallorca), private collection. H. from chin to part in hair: 24 cm. Photo Deutsches Archäologisches Institut, Madrid (P. Witte).
34. *a–b*) British Museum inv. RR 4255 (Crawford no. 494.2a). Museum photo.
35. Naples, Museo Nazionale inv. 25218. H: 18 mm. After *JdI* 89 (1974): 249.
36. *a*) Niggeler no. 1027 (Giard no. 916). *b*) Niggeler no. 1030 (Giard no. 927). *c*) Niggeler no. 1028 (Giard no. 920).
37. *a–b*) MuM Auction 52 (1975) no. 478 (Crawford no. 498.1).
38. Hannover, Kestner Museum inv. K1191. H: 1.2 cm. Museum photo.
39. Cologne, Römisch-Germanisches Museum inv. 72.153. H: 3.7 cm. Museum photo.
40. Rome, Palatine. After G. Carettoni, *Das Haus des Augustus auf dem Palatin* (Mainz, 1983), 8.
41–42. Casts from denarii in the Bibliothèque Nationale, Paris. Museum photos.
43. *a*) Paris, Bibliothèque Nationale (Giard no. 60). *b–c*) Munich, Staatliche Münzsammlung. Museum photo.
44. Paris, Bibliothèque Nationale (Giard nos. 49 and 43).
45. New York, Metropolitan Museum of Art inv. 19.192.21. H: 9.9 cm. (*CVA, Metropolitan Museum IV B F,* pl. 24). Museum photo.
46. Boston, Museum of Fine Arts inv. 00.311. H: 29 cm. Museum photo.
47. After British Museum Catalog Grueber II 510.
48. Rome, Capitoline Museum. E. La Rocca, *L'età d'oro di Cleopatra* (Rome, 1984), 41 (Crawford 543.1).
49. Naples, Museo Nazionale inv. 6713. *Guida,* Ruesch, 272. 0.76 × 1.34 m. Photo Institut für Klassische Archäologie, Munich.
50. Rome, Villa Albani inv. 1014. H: 74 cm. Helbig, vol. 4, no. 3240. Photo Institut für Klassische Archäologie, Munich.
51. After Gros, *Aurea Templa,* pl. 20.
52. Rome, Museo della Civiltà Romana. Photo Musei Capitolini.
53. *a*) After P. Pensabene, *Tempio di Saturno* (Rome, 1984), pl. 120. *b*) Photo Musei Capitolini.

54. *a*) After H. Bauer, *RM* 76 (1969): pl. 62. *b*) After R. Falconi, *BSR* 30 (1962): pl. 10.2.

55. Rome, Palazzo dei Conservatori, Museo Nuovo inv. 2776. L: 3.36 m. H: 0.85 m.

56. Munich, Antikensammlungen. Photo B. Gossel-Raeck.

57. Fototeca Unione.

58. Drawing by M. Pfanner, after an original by J. Ganzert.

59. Reconstruction drawing by H. von Hesberg.

60. Vatican, Cortile della Pigna inv. 5137. H: ca. 1.20 m. Museum photo.

61. After a schematic drawing by M. Pfanner.

62. *a*) Present whereabouts unknown. Fototeca Unione. *b*) British Museum. H. Mattingly, *Coins of the Roman Empire in the British Museum* (London, 1923–), vol. 1, no. 622, pl. 14.14.

63. Leipzig, Archäologisches Institut. H: 23.5 cm. L: 36 cm. Photo Institut für Klassische Archäologie, Munich.

64. Rome, Palazzo dei Conservatori. Antiquarium Comunale inv. 4372. H: 22 cm. After Anselmino, *Terracotta architettoniche*, pl. XII.52.

65. Bonn, Akademisches Kunstmuseum inv. D161. H: 21.7 cm. Museum photo.

66. Munich, Staatliche Münzsammlungen. E. Brandt et al., *Antike Gemmen in deutschen Sammlungen*, vol. 1, no. 3 (1972), 47, no. 2734, pl. 256. Museum photo.

67. Vienna, Kunsthistorisches Museum. E. Zwierlein-Diehl, *Die antiken Gemmen des Kunsthistorischen Museums in Wien*, vol. 2 (1979), 65, no. 805, pl. 36. Museum photo.

68. Munich, Staatliche Münzsammlungen (Giard no. 362). Photo Hirmer.

69. Boston, Museum of Fine Arts inv. 60316. G. H. Chase, *Catalogue of Arretine Pottery* (Boston, 1916), 49, no. 26.

70. Naples, Museo Nazionale inv. 9302, from Pompeii, Casa dei Dioscuri VI 9, 6–7. HBr pl. 131; *a*. INR 37.1294. *b*. After *Museo Borbonico* VI, pl. 14.

71. Niggeler no. 1078 (Giard no. 1012).

72. Photo Capitoline Museum.

73. Rome, Antiquario Palatino. H: 62 cm. Photo Soprintendenza Archeologica di Roma.

74. Present whereabouts unknown. After C. Vermeule, *Numismatica*, 1960, 5.

75. *a*) After A. Alföldi, *Die zwei Lorbeerbäume des Augustus* (Bonn, 1973) pl. II.8. *b*) Niggeler no. 1062 (Giard no. 1225). *c*) After Alföldi, op. cit., pl. III.3.

76. *a*) MuM Auction 43 (1970) no. 271 (Giard no. 1144). *b*) MuM Auction 44 (1971) no. 26 (Giard no. 912). *c*) Paris, Bibliothèque Nationale (Giard no. 112). Museum photo.

77. Vienna, Kunsthistorisches Museum inv. IX A 26. Diameter: 22 cm. W. Oberleitner, *Geschnittene Stein* (Vienna, 1985), 38. Museum photo.

78. Rome, Palazzo dei Conservatori, Museo Nuovo inv. 855. Helbig, vol. 2, no. 1741. INR 60.1249.

79. Arles, Musée Lapidaire. Diameter: 0.65 m. After Alföldi, op. cit., pl. 41.

80. *a*) Niggeler no. 1061 (Giard no. 1313). *b*) MuM Auction 38 (1968) no. 325 (Giard no. 1130). *c*) Niggeler no. 1069 (Giard no. 1130).
81. Boston, Museum of Fine Arts inv. 27.733. Width: 1.9 cm. M. L. Vollenweider, *Die Steinschneidekunst und ihre Künstler in spätrepublikanischer und augusteischer Zeit* (Baden-Baden, 1966), 51, pl. 49.2. Museum photo.
82. Vienna, Kunsthistorisches Museum inv. IX A 56. H: 6 cm. Oberleitner, op. cit., 35. Museum photo.
83. Vatican, Braccio Nuovo inv. 2290. H: 2.04 m. Helbig, vol. 1, no. 411. Photo Alinari.
84. Naples, Museo Nazionale inv. 4885. H: 5.4 cm. From the Villa dei Papiri in Herculaneum. INR 64.1804.
85. After F. Brown, *Cosa* (Ann Arbor, 1980), fig. 68.
86. Rome, Villa Medici. H: 1.56 m. After a cast. Fototeca Unione.
87. Photo J. Ganzert.
88. Photo J. Ganzert.
89. *a*) MuM Auction 38 (1968) no. 328 (Giard no. 1098). *b*) British Museum. Mattingly, *Coins of the Roman Empire in the British Museum* (London, 1923–), vol. 1, no. 369, pl. 7, 20.
90. Fototeca Unione, after an unknown original.
91. Venice, Museo Archeologico inv. 263. H: 93 cm. (Dütschke V no. 303). Museum photo.
92. After A. Boethius and J. B. Ward Perkins, *Etruscan and Roman Architecture* (London, 1970), 190.
93. Paris, private collection. H: 10 cm. After Fondation E. Piot, *Monuments et Mémoires*, vol. 5 (1899): cf. fig. 185.
94. Reconstruction by E. La Rocca and G. Foglia, *Amazzonomachia*, exhibition catalog (Rome, 1985), 91.
95. INR 71.154.
96. Photo G. Fittschen-Badura.
97. Photo Institut für Klassische Archäologie, Munich.
98. Photo G. Fittschen-Badura.
99. *a–c*) Paris, Louvre inv. 358. Museum photos.
100. *a–b*) Photos G. Fittschen-Badura.
101. Florence, Uffizi inv. 972. H: 1.50 m. INR 75.293.
102. *a–b*) Rome, Museo Capitolino, Stanza dei Filosofi. H: 59 cm. Helbig, vol. 2, no. 1382. Museum photos (B. Malter).
103. *a*) Paris, Bibliothèque Nationale, Giard no. 365. *b–c*) Niggeler no. 1047 (Giard no. 515).
104. Rome, Terme Museum inv. 56230. H: 2.17 m. Giuliano I, 1, no. 170. INR 65.1111.
105. Fondi, Museo Civico. H: 1.77 m. INR 173 VW 81.
106. After *BCH* 78 (1962): 155 (Colin).
107. Antiquarium Comunale on the Caelian Hill. Fototeca Unione.
108. Rome, Palazzo dei Conservatori, Museo Nuovo inv. 855. H: 1.05 m. INR 60.1472.

109. Vatican, formerly Belvedere inv. 1115. H: 95 cm. Photo German Archaeological Institute, Rome.

110. Vatican Museums, Museo Gregoriano Profano inv. 1156 / 7. H: 1.04 m. L: 4.72 m. Photo Institut für Klassische Archäologie, Munich.

111. Rome, Capitoline Museum inv. 1909. H: 90 cm. INR 50.45.

112. Rome, Terme Museum, magazines, from the Mithraeum under San Stefano Rotondo. H: 63 cm. Photo Valdernini.

113. After G. Carettoni et al., *La Pianta marmorea di Roma antica* (Rome, 1960), pl. 18.

114. After *Città e Architettura nella Roma imperiale* (*Analecta Romana*, suppl. 1984), 43 (F. Coarelli).

115. After W. Friedländer and A. Blunt, *The Drawings of Nicholas Poussin*, Catalogue Raisonné, vol. 5 (London, 1974), no. 294.

116. After E. Buchner, *RM* 83 (1976): 353.

117. Fototeca Unione.

118. After E. Rodriguez Almeida, *Forma Urbis Marmorea Aggiornamento generale* (Rome, 1980), drawn and completed by M. Pfanner.

119. INR 73.998 (after a model).

120. After Boethius and Ward Perkins, op. cit., 222.

121. After G. Alföldy, *Römische Sozialgeschichte*³ (1984).

122. Model of Rome, Museo della Civiltà Romana. Photo Musei Capitolini (B. Malter).

123. After an engraving by Rossini, 1824.

124. INR 72.2403.

125. Leiden, Rijksmuseum inv. 41931 / 2.61. D: 4 cm. Museum photo.

126. Rome, Ara Pacis Augustae. 4.60 × 11 × 10 m. INR 66.104.

127. MuM Auction 38 (1968) no. 310 (Giard no. 221).

128. Paris, Louvre inv. MA 1280. Photo G. Fittschen-Badura.

129. After *BdA* 1 (1921): 328.

130. Rome, Palazzo dei Conservatori, Braccio Nuovo inv. 2392. H: 1.65 m. Photo Anderson.

131. Parma, Museo Nazionale inv. 404. H: 88 cm. INR 67.1640.

132. *a–b*) Niggeler no. 1039 (Giard no. 273).

133. Paris, Bibliothèque Nationale (Giard no. 330).

134. Paris, Bibliothèque Nationale (Giard no. 365).

135. INR 32.1744.

136. Photo Capitoline Museum (B. Malter).

137. Cf. fig. 248*a*. INR 62.1794.

138. *a*) Palestrina, Museo Barberiniano. INR 77.1553; *b–c*) Vienna, Kunsthistorisches Museum inv. 604; 605. H: 94 cm. W: 81 cm. After *Antike Plastik* 4 (1965): pls. 54–55.

139. *a–b*) Rome, Palazzo Primoli, via dei Soldati 25. H: 90 cm. W: 1.90 m. INR 74.1008 / 12.

140. Photo G. Fittschen-Badura.

141. Photo G. Fittschen-Badura.

142. Naples, Museo Nazionale inv. 6715. *Guida* Ruesch, 149. H: 87 cm. Photo Alinari.

143. Paris, Louvre. H: ca. 65 cm. After Gusman, *L'art décoratif*, pl. 5.

144. Once Berlin, Staatliche Museen inv. 3779.62. H: 36 cm. D: 35.3 cm. Museum photo.

145. *a*) Niggeler no. 1032 (Giard no. 989). *b*) MuM Auction 38 (1968) no. 333 (Giard no. 1016).

146. *a*) MuM Auction 43 (1970) no. 27 (Giard no. 1228). *b*) Munich, Staatliche Münzsammlung. Museum photo.

147. Impression of a glass paste, probably once Berlin, Staatliche Museen, Antiquarium inv. 2816. H: 2.4 cm. Photo Institut für Klassische Archäologie, Munich (H. Glöckler).

148. Vatican Museums, Braccio Nuovo inv. 2290. H: 2.04 m. *a*) Photo Institut für Klassische Archäologie, Munich. *b*) Photo Alinari.

149. After P. Zanker, *Forum Augustum* (Tübingen, 1968).

150. Cf. above fig. 86. INR 1931.

151. Algiers, Musée Nationale d'Antiquités. Photo Alinari.

152. Brescia, Museo Civico. H: 1.95 m. Photo Instituto Centrale di Restauro.

153. Naples, Museo Nazionale inv. 251. H: 2.10 m. INR 83.2259.

154. Rome, Terme Museum inv. 108522. H: 2.28 m. Cf. Giuliano I 8, 1, 219.

155. *a–b*) Rome, Capitoline Museum inv. 58. H: 3.60 m. *a*) INR 75.2261. *b*) INR 75.2253.

156. *a–b*) Pompeii IX 13, 5. After G. E. Rizzo, *La Pittura ellenistico-romana* (Milan, 1929), pl. 194.

157. Photo Institut für Klassische Archäologie, Munich.

158. Once Berlin, Antiquarium. Dimensions: 37 × 42.5 cm. After H. von Rohden and H. Winnefeld, *Architektonische Tonreliefs*, pl. 127.1.

159. Photo G. Fittschen-Badura.

160. Florence, Uffizi inv. 336. H: 70.7 cm. INR 77.1759.

161. Paris, Louvre inv. 8. 41 × 38 cm. *a*) Photo Marburg. *b*) Photo Giraudon.

162. After *BdA* 35 (1950): 109, fig. 2.

163. Luni, Museo Archeologico (formerly Turin, Museo Archeologico). H: 84 cm. Dütschke 4, 35f. no. 48. INR 30.232.

164. After A. Degrassi, *Inscriptiones Italiae* XII, 3 (Rome, 1947), 4.

165. Photo G. Fittschen-Badura.

166. Model. Rome, Antiquario del Foro di Augusto. Fototeca Unione.

167. *a*) Niggeler no. 1051 (Giard no. 529). *b*) Niggeler no. 1049 (Giard no. 522).

168. *a*) *Münzhandlung Basel* 6 (1936) no. 1516 (Giard no. 548). *b*) *Bank Leu* 265 (1966) no. 44 (Giard no. 537).

169. Photo G. Fittschen-Badura.

170. Photo G. Fittschen-Badura.

171. Niggeler no. 1075 (Giard no. 1457).

172. Bonn, Rheinisches Landesmuseum. W: 8.4 cm. Photo Glyptothek, Munich.

173. Niggeler no. 1076 (Giard no. 1645).

174–75. Corinth, Museum. Photo American excavations.

176. Rome, Capitoline Museum inv. 745. H (chin to part in hair): 26.5 cm. Photo G. Fittschen-Badura.

177. Vatican Museums, Belvedere inv. 1115, fig. 109. INR 75.1289.

178. Cherchel, Musée Archéologique. H: 2.28 m. Photo G. Fittschen-Badura.

179. *a*) MuM Auction 38 (1968) no. 334 (Giard no. 1366). *b*) Niggeler no. 1071 (Giard no. 1432). *c*) Niggeler no. 1073 (Giard no. 1394). *d*) after a cast in the Seminar für Griechische und Römische Geschichte, Frankfurt. *e*) Munich, Staatliche Münzsammlung. Museum photo.

180–81. Paris, private collection, now badly damaged. After Fondation E. Piot, *Monuments et Memoirs*, vol. 5 (1899).

182. Vienna, Kunsthistorisches Museum inv. IX A 79. 19 × 23 cm. Museum photo.

183. *a–b*) London, British Museum inv. GR 1866.8–6.1. H: 22 cm. Museum photos.

184. Vienna, Kunsthistorisches Museum inv. IX A 95. H: 9 cm. Museum photo.

185. Tripoli, Museum. H with plinth: 3.10 m. INR 61.1723.

186. Sorrento, Museo Correale. H: 1.17 m. INR 6518.

187. Rome, Palazzo dei Conservatori, Museo Nuovo inv. 1386. H: 1.56 m. INR 7500.

188. Rome, Antiquario Palatino. H: 17 cm. INR 70.2047.

189. Naples, Museo Nazionale inv. 6008. H: 1.08 m. After a cast in the Akademisches Kunstmuseum, Bonn. Museum photo.

190. Private collection (Mattingly I no. 192 ff.). Photo Hirmer.

191. Rome, Palazzo dei Conservatori, Museo Nuovo inv. 1873. H: 1.47 m. Photo Alinari.

192. Rome, Palazzo dei Conservatori, Mon. Arc. inv. 980. H: 26.5 cm. After H. Stuart-Jones, *The Sculptures of the Museo Capitolino* (Oxford, 1912; reprinted Rome, 1969), pl. 83.

193. Rome, Antiquario Palatino. H: 62 cm. Photo Soprintendenza Archeologica di Roma.

194. Copenhagen, Ny Carlsberg Glyptothek inv. 538. H: 2.12 cm. Museum photo.

195. Venice, Museo Archeologico inv. 11. H: 2.17 m. Photo Institut für Klassische Archäologie, Munich.

196. Copenhagen, Ny Carlsberg Glyptothek inv. 531. H: 2.20 m. Museum photo.

197. Munich, Glyptothek inv. 214. H: 1.65 m. Museum photo.

198. Pergamon, German excavations, 389 610a / Zi 13. W: 4.9 cm. Photo courtesy of G. Hübner.

199. Berlin (West), Antikenmuseum, Staatliche Museen Preussischer Kulterbesitz inv. 196236. W: 9.3 cm. Museum photo (I. Geske).

200. London, British Museum. H: 25 cm. Museum photo.

201. Nîmes, Maison Carrée. Photo Institut für Klassische Archäologie, Munich.

202. Rome, Forum of Augustus, Antiquario. After *Antike Plastik* 13 (1973): pl. 3.

203. Rome, Tabularium. Photo Anderson.

204. Photo G. Fittschen-Badura.

205. Venice, Museo Archeologico inv. 114. H: 72.7 cm. INR 68.5077.

206. Cf. fig. 84. INR 69.657.

207. After *The Athenian Agora III* (Princeton, 1957), pl. 3.

208. Brugg, Vindonissa Museum. W: 7.6 cm. After A. Leibundgut, *Die römischen Tonlampen in der Schweiz* (1977), pl. 23.3.

209. Torre Annunziata, Roman villa. Photo Institut für Klassische Archäologie, Munich.

210. Ionides Collection (formerly at Marlborough). H: 4.5 cm. After J. Boardman, *Engraved Gems: The Ionides Collection* (Evanston, 1968), fig. 19.

211. *a–b*) Rome, Galleria Doria. H: 88 cm. INR 71.1463; 71.1468.

212. Naples, Museo Nazionale inv. 6882. *Guida,* Ruesch, 1789. H: 91 cm. INR 67.2357.

213. Naples, Museo Nazionale. INR 77.1773; 77.1776.

214. Naples, Museo Nazionale inv. 72987. Photo Alinari.

215. Detail of fig. 144. Staatliche Museen zu Berlin.

216. London, British Museum inv. Q870. After T. Hölscher, *Victoria,* pl. 13.1.

217. Heidelberg, Archäologisches Institut der Universität inv. LA 99. Museum photo (K. Guhl).

218. Naples, Museo Nazionale. H: ca. 45 cm. INR 83.1993.

219. Pompeii, Herculaneum Street. In the foreground, tomb of Q. Calventius Quinctus. H of the altar: 2.25 m. INR 77.2128.

220. *a–b*) Perugia, tomb of the Volumnii. Dimensions: 40.5 × 76 × 57 cm. *a*) INR 82.2042. *b*) Photo Institut für Klassische Archäologie, Munich.

221. *a–b*) New York, private collection. Photo courtesy of Metropolitan Museum of Art.

222. Rome, Palatine, House of Augustus. Photo Soprintendenza Archeologica di Roma.

223. Rome, Terme Museum inv. 1118. H: 2.30 m. After J. Charbonneaux, *L'art en siècle d'Auguste* (Lausanne, 1948).

224. Naples, Museo Nazionale inv. 147501. INR 59.1972; 59.1978; 59.1974.

225. Turin, Museo Archeologico. H: 38 cm. Dütschke IV no. 172. INR 74.1589.

226. Munich, Glyptothek inv. 455. 33.5 × 29 cm. Museum photo.

227. Rome, Terme Museum inv. 1074. Photo Anderson.

228. Rome, columbarium in Vigna Codini. Photo Anderson.

229. *a*) Rome, Capitoline Museum inv. 354. H: 41 cm. Museum photo. *b*) Rome, Capitoline Museum inv. 353. H: 48 cm. Museum photo. *c*) Rome, Capitoline Museum inv. 346. H: 40 cm. Museum photo. *d*) Munich, Glyptothek inv. 413 (ABr no. 69). H: 40 cm. Museum photo.

230. Reconstruction after K. Tuchelt, *IstMitt* 25 (1975): fig. 15.

231. London, British Museum. *a*) Pella A.1096, *British Museum Catalogue of Greek Coins,* uncertain 17 (23 B.C.). *b*) Teos A.1319, BMC 67. *c*) Aradus A.1480, BMC 356 (7 B.C.).

232. Corinth, Museum inv. 116 A. H (chin to part in hair): 28 cm. Photo Corinth excavations.

233. Once Samos inv. 46. H: 48.5 cm. Photo H. Weber.

234. Aphrodisias, Caesareum. After K. Erim, *Revue Arch.,* 1982, 164, fig. 3.

235. Aphrodisias, Caesareum. After K. Erim, in *V. Kazi Sonuclari Toplantisi, 525.*
236. MuM Auction 43 (1970) no. 278 (Giard no. 1701).
237. London, British Museum. Museum photo.
238–39. Palestrina, Museo Barberiniano. INR 59.168; 59.172.
240. Palestrina, Museo Barberiniano. INR 57.1546.
241. Sketch by M. Pfanner, after Mazois and La Rocca (provisional and in part hypothetical).
242. Ostia, Forum, drawn by M. Pfanner after G. Calza.
243. Pola, Temple of Roma and Augustus. *a)* Photo T. Schäfer. *b)* Photo Alinari.
244. Turin, Museo Archeologico (Dütschke IV no. 6 ff.). H: 45 cm. INR 30.225.
245. Naples, Museo Nazionale (formerly Antiquario Flegreo). H: 1.13 m. *a)* Photo Soprintendenza Archeologica di Napoli (Caserta). *b)* INR 83.1888.
246. Paris, Louvre inv. 1838. 0.79 × 1.11 m. After a cast. Photo Institut für Klassische Archäologie, Munich.
247. Tunis, Bardo Museum. H: 1.18 m. INR 63.388.
248. After *Forum Italiae* I, 7, 67. Drawn by M. Pfanner.
249. Tripoli, Museum. H: ca. 2.20 m. INR 61.1751.
250. Tripoli, Museum. H: 2.20 m. INR 61.1733.
251. Schematic drawing by M. Pfanner, after LaRocca, *Guida,* 105 (with provisional restorations).
252. *a)* INR 66.638. *b)* After V. Spinazzola, *Le arti figurative* (1928) 22.
253. Naples, Museo Nazionale inv. 6041. H: 1.87 m. INR 76.1157.
254. Fototeca Unione.
255. After de Franciscis, in R. Graefe, *Vela erunt* (Mainz, 1979), pl. 148.1.
256. Arles, Museum (Esp. I 140). H: 85 cm. INR 41.506.
257. Turin, Porta Palatina. After a model in the Museo della Civiltà Romana, Rome. INR 73.944.
258. INR 75.2653.
259. Naples, Museo Nazionale inv. 6233. H: 2.02 m. INR 74.1288.
260. Avezzano, Palazzo Torlonia. 0.62 × 1.23 m. After a cast in the Museo della Civiltà Romana, Rome. INR 79.2757.

Index of Sites and Museums

Algiers, Musée Nationale d'Antiquités, relief with cult statue group, 196–97; fig. 151
Aphrodisias, reliefs from building housing imperial cult, 301; figs. 234, 235
Argos, statue of Hera by Polyclitus, 250
Arles, Musée Lapidaire
    altar from theater, 326; fig. 256
    marble copy of *clipeus virtutis*, 95–96; fig. 79
Athens
    Acropolis
        Athena Parthenos by Phidias, 199–200
        Erechtheum, 256–58, 298
        Parthenon, 298
        Propylaea, 257
        round temple of Roma and Augustus, 298
    Agora, 261; fig. 207
    Altar of Twelve Gods, 160
    Odeum of Agrippa, 261; fig. 207
    Olympieion, 21
    Roman Agora, 261–62
Avezzano, Palazzo Torlonia, city relief, 329; fig. 260

Berlin
    Antikenmuseum, stamp from Arretine bowl, 253; fig. 199
    once Antiquarium
        glass paste with kneeling Parthian, 187; fig. 147
        silver krater from Hildesheim, 183, 272–73; figs. 144, 215
        terra-cotta revetment plaques, 206; fig. 158
Bonn
    Akademisches Kunstmuseum, antefix of dolphins, 84; fig. 65
    Rheinisches Landesmuseum, sword sheath, 218; fig. 172
Boston, Museum of Fine Arts
    Arretine clay bowl, 86, 266–67; fig. 69
    relief with Dionysiac reveler, 60; fig. 46
    sardonyx with Octavian in chariot drawn by hippocamps, 97–98; fig. 82

Brescia, Museo Civico, bronze statue of Victoria, 197; fig. 152
Brugg, Vindonissa Museum, clay lamp with Victoria, 266; fig. 208

Caesarea Maritima
    round temple of Roma and Augustus, 250, 298, 317
    statue of Augustus, 250
Cagliari, Museo Archeologico, portrait of unknown man, 11, 293, 295; fig. 8
Chercel, Musée Archéologique, cuirassed statue, 192, 223; fig. 178
Cologne
    altar for Roma and Augustus, 302
    Römische-Germanisches Museum, glass cameo, 50; fig. 39
Copenhagen
    Ny Carlsberg Glyptotek, portrait of Pompey, 9–10, 293–94; fig. 6
    statue of Livia Augusta, 250, 320; fig. 196
    statue of Tiberius, 225–26, 249; fig. 194
Corinth, Museum
    portrait of Augustus, 300–302; fig. 232
    statues of Gaius and Lucius, 220; figs. 174, 175
Cosa, Capitolium, reconstruction of Italic temples, 105; fig. 85
Crete, Corycian Cave, 262–63

Ephesus
    Parthian monument, 300
    Temple of Augustus, 298

Florence
    Museo Archeologico, so-called Arringatore, 5; fig. 4
    Uffizi
        altar of Lares, 121; fig. 101
        marble relief with Temple of Vesta, 207; fig. 160
Fondi, Museo Civico, statue of *lupercus*, 129; fig. 105
Formia, statue of *togatus,* 163; fig. 129